HARSHA

A POLITICAL STUDY

HARSHA

A POLITICAL STUDY

BY

D. DEVAHUTI

OXFORD
AT THE CLARENDON PRESS
1970

Oxford University Press, Ely House, London W. 1
GLASGOW NEW YORK TORONTO MELBOURNE WELLINGTON
CAPE TOWN SALISBURY IBADAN NAIROBI DAR ES SALAAM LUSAKA ADDIS ABABA
BOMBAY CALCUTTA MADRAS KARACHI LAHORE DACCA
KUALA LUMPUR SINGAPORE HONG KONG TOKYO

PRINTED IN GREAT BRITAIN
AT THE UNIVERSITY PRESS, OXFORD
BY VIVIAN RIDLER
PRINTER TO THE UNIVERSITY

FOR MY PARENTS

SHRI PRITHVI RAJ

AND

SHRIMATI PHOOL VATI

AND FOR

PROFESSOR A. L. BASHAM

PREFACE

THE reign of Harsha of Sthāṇv-īśvara and Kanauj (A.D. 606–47) is a comparatively well-documented period of ancient Indian history. Our most important Chinese source is the Ta Tʻang Hsi Yü Chi of Hsüan-tsang in which the Buddhist pilgrim records his experiences in India. His biography by Hui Li supplements this account. In addition the Chinese official histories and religious works have preserved accounts of the diplomatic exchanges between Tʻai Tsung, the Tʻang emperor and Harsha Śīlāditya. On the Indian side the most informative single work is Bāṇa's incomplete biography of Harsha.

The literary writings in Chinese and Sanskrit first attracted the attention of scholars and translators in the middle of the nineteenth century. S. Julien published his *Histoire de la vie de Hiouen-Thsang et de ses voyages dans l'Inde, depuis l'an 629 jusqu'en 645* in 1853, supplemented by *Mémoires sur les Contrées occidentales* . . . , the translation of the *Ta Tʻang Hsi Yü Chi* of Hsüan-tsang in 1857–8. There followed English translations by S. Beal in 1884 and T. Watters in 1904–5. Beal also translated the *Life* of Hsüan-tsang by Hui Li in 1888. Of the several Chinese notices on Indo-Chinese missions and the adventures of the last envoy Wang Hsüan-tʻsê, only the account of Ma Tuan-lin gained currency through the French and English translations in the nineteenth century. The translations of ten other notices appear for the first time in the present study.

The text of Bāṇa's *Harsha-charita* with the commentary of Śaṅkara was published in the last quarter of the nineteenth century and an annotated text with exhaustive notes by P. V. Kane appeared in 1918. In the meantime Bāṇa's *Kādambarī* had been translated by C. M. Ridding in 1896 and his *Harsha-charita* by E. B. Cowell and F. W. Thomas in 1897.

Other literary and political writings, and epigraphic and numismatic records which throw light on Harsha's times have been discussed in detail in the main body of the present book. The period of the gradual discovery and decipherment of Harsha's inscriptions and coins belongs to the late nineteenth and early twentieth centuries.

All the Sanskrit sources, literary, epigraphic, and numismatic, have been consulted in the original along with translations whenever the latter were available. For Chinese materials I have used not only the existing translations but also fresh renderings of all the important passages from the *Hsi Yü Chi* and the *Life* with the help of the erudite scholar of Chinese language and philosophy, Mr. D. C. Lau of the School of Oriental and African Studies. The last chapter, 'The Indo-Chinese Missions and the Death of Harsha', is based on information derived from the relevant passages in ten hitherto unused Chinese works[1] and the already known account of Ma Tuan-lin. Repetitive for the most part but divergent in certain details the translations of all the passages have been included in the text, not only because they have been made for the first time but also in order that the conclusions based on them may be scrutinized by scholars. These translations, too, I owe to Mr. Lau, who made them as literal as possible.

The first biography of Harsha, *Harṣa Vardhana, empereur et poète* by M. L. Ettinghausen appeared in 1906. In 1922 K. M. Panikkar brought out *Śri Harsha of Kanauj*. R. K. Mookerji's study, *Harsha* was published in 1926. In 1937 R. S. Tripathi wrote the *History of Kanauj* in which he devoted 130 of the total 420 pages to the reign of Harsha. In recent years a notable work that has appeared in Hindi is a cultural study of the Harsha-charita by V. S. Agrawala (1953). Some other biographies of Harsha exist in Indian languages as well as some novels on the personalities of the period. The general histories of India, of course, include a section on Harsha. The latest detailed work of this nature is the *History and Culture of the Indian People* of which the third volume, *The Classical Age* (1954), has a chapter 'Harsha-vardhana and His Time' by R. C. Majumdar, who is also the general editor of the series. There are, moreover, numerous articles on specific aspects of Harsha's career by well-known scholars.

In view of so much published material it is indeed surprising that no full-length study of Harsha has been attempted in recent years. Those that exist are narratives centred on the king. That the present dissertation appears more than four decades after the last exclusive study on Harsha and several years after briefer accounts is a negative virtue. A more positive recommendation for the book, I hope, is its wider approach. I have tried to study the impact on each other of the ruler and his times and to examine the times as part of a continuous political tradition both in its ideological and practical aspects. Polity, moreover, has been viewed in the contemporary socio-economic setting.

[1] Three of these were noticed by Lévi. See Bibliography for Chinese primary and secondary sources.

This, of course, could not have been achieved without the invaluable pioneer work on Harsha, nor without the many studies on ancient Indian polity. To these sources of knowledge I am deeply indebted.

Harsha's personality as portrayed in contemporary and later sources is, indeed, arresting, and the seventh century A.D. in which he flourished is a significant epoch in Indian history. It is the last outstanding instance, in the Hindu-Buddhist era, of centrally maintained political equilibrium in a large empire. The gradual shift towards political devolution was presaged by Harsha's qualified centralization. Economically, although both internal and external trade continued to thrive, a distortion in the socio-economic pattern caused in no small measure by the political background both of the Harshan and pre-Harshan era is indicated by the abnormally high value placed on land as a source of income as well as a symbol of status. A variety of stresses, many of them inherent in the social tradition itself, had started the trend towards constrictions in family and community life. In the arts and literature balance was still maintained between form and content, and although the former would ultimately obscure the latter, the process of degeneration in the artistic sphere was much slower owing to the relatively more personal-, rather than group-motivation in this field of human endeavour.

I have tried to maintain a fastidious regard for detail when fixing the political outlines of a period, as in Chapter II; for the meaning of facts cannot be divined without first establishing them. The historian of ancient India will have to contend with this uninspiring task for a long time yet. At the other extreme may be placed my appraisal of *maṇḍala*, a political system designed for the achievement and maintenance of sovereignty through delicate checks and balances and its application to Harsha's empire. Through this discussion, it is my endeavour to make the reader aware of Indian political, and ultimately cultural, values which should be borne in mind when appraising an ancient Indian institution or when comparing it with ancient or modern non-Indian systems.

Lack of data for this study has sometimes caused frustration. At other times the challenge of this insufficiency and the opportunity to arrive at a pattern with the help of indirect sources of information have proved most rewarding.

Feelings about History, as well as thoughts about it, have inspired historical works, and similar feelings, evoked by similar facts, have also been expressed in imaginative works in the divers genres of literature. There is for example, a lyrical genre, an epic genre, a narrative genre, and a dramatic genre; and the feeling for the poetry in the facts of History has availed itself of all these.[1]

I might add that since the latter are not expressly written for the purpose of recording history, the historian gets more objective history from them. What he needs are keen perception, empathy, and patience to be able to commune with those who have left no direct message for him.

I would like to apologize for an innovation—the use of hyphens to spell long Sanskrit words. It may irritate the technical expert but it will unquestionably provide greater ease of reading on the part of the general, especially non-Indian, reader. The method used is explained in the guide to pronunciation.

Plurals of Sanskrit words have been formed by adding a terminal 's' to them, a technically incorrect but accepted practice. Common usage is generally employed, usually involving the inconsistent use of the stem form and the nominative case. The Pālī terms have sometimes been Sanskritized. Brahman (to denote class or caste) has been preferred to the anglicized Brahmin. Many of my translations are directly from the original Sanskrit texts (and from Chinese texts with the help of Mr. Lau) which are not always in agreement with the existing published translations. All the same references to the latter have been included in the footnotes, along with those to the original texts, for purpose of easy checking.

I have deliberately not translated significant multi-faceted terms like *dharma*; the reader will soon begin to sense their meaning. Sometimes words have been translated afresh to allow for a more comprehensive connotation than they usually carry, e.g. 'authority' in preference to 'punishment' for *daṇḍa*. It is comparable to the narrow term sacrifice for *yajña* which by usage denotes only rite and not the more fundamental meanings of devotion, sacrifice in thought, etc. I have also avoided, as far as possible, translation of technical terms like *sāmanta* and *maṇḍala*. The latter has no counterpart in other societies, the former if translated as feudatory brings to mind the European feudal system of the Middle Ages which was essentially different from the *sāmanta* institution.

The present work has grown out of a doctoral thesis for the University of London prepared under the supervision of Professor A. L. Basham,

[1] A. J. Toynbee, *A Study of History*, x, p. 113.

then at the School of Oriental and African Studies. He also read the draft of this book. For his guidance and encouragement, critical appreciation, and willingness to help, I cannot thank him adequately. Nor can I fully express my gratitude to Mr. D. C. Lau for his generous help without which the value of this work would have been considerably less. Dr. Wang Ling and Mr. Tamotsu Sato of the Australian National University gave me their precious time for further clarification of the Chinese materials used in this book, and the late Mr. Arthur Waley resolved some doubts for me. I would also like to express my thanks to Professor L. Petech for his kind courtesy in providing me with the results of his research on Nepalese Inscriptions.

For information on the subject of Indian cultural influences in Japan in connection with the migration of Harsha's *Nāg-ānanda*, I would like to thank the members of the Institute for the Study of Ancient Arts, and the officials of the Kasuga Shrine, and the Shōsōin Museum at Nara, as well as my sister Mrs. Veena Sachdev, who not only helped me communicate with them but also drew my attention to many subtle points.

To my friend, Miss Mariel Eckermann, my sincere thanks for helping me in multiple ways. In this case, words are, indeed, a poor means of expression.

Dr. J. Raj and Mrs. B. Bykersma have assisted me with the taxing task of index making. Mr. Krishna Mohan Shrimali of St. Stephen's College, Delhi, has kindly checked some difficult references for me. I would like to express my thanks to all these friends. The library staff at the School of Oriental and African Studies, London, and at the Queensland University facilitated my work with their competent and willing help. Finally my appreciative thanks to Misses G. Schmidt and M. Chodzinski for the typing of a difficult manuscript.

CONTENTS

LIST OF PLATES

(AT END)

MAP

GUIDE TO PRONUNCIATION

ACCENT

ACCORDING to post-classical Sanskrit and the most common present-day usage a syllable is long if it contains a long vowel or diphthong, or if its vowel is followed by more than one consonant. The vowels *e* and *o* are originally diphthongs, and so are always long (although no diacritical mark is printed over them). The letter *h*, when it follows another consonant, is generally not considered a consonant in determining the length of a syllable. Thus, for example, *th* is one consonant, not two; and if a short vowel is followed by this and no other consonant, the syllable is short.

VOWELS

Most vowels are pronounced substantially as in German or Italian. Their approximate English equivalents are listed below.

a = *o* in mother or *u* in but
a = *a* in father (never as *a* in fathom)
e = *ey* in prey
i = *i* in pin
ī = *i* in machine
o = *o* in so
u = *u* in full
ū = *u* in rule
ṛi (It is classed as a short retroflex vowel. For a better indication of its approximate modern pronunciation we have used *ṛi* instead of the older form *ṛ*) = *wri* in writ.

DIPHTHONGS

ai = *ai* in aisle
au = *ow* in owl

CONSONANTS

Indian languages have distinct categories of unvoiced, unvoiced aspirate, voiced, voiced aspirate, and nasal consonants under the headings guttural, palatal, retroflex, dental, and labial, but English speakers generally find it hard to imitate or even recognize some of the differences. For example the unvoiced retroflex *t* is distinguished as *ṭ* from the unvoiced dental *t* which is left as *t*. In fact the former is closer to the English *t* sound while the latter is more like the soft Italian *t*. The same applies to the voiced retroflex *ḍ* and the voiced dental *d*, and so forth. For all practical purposes, therefore, it would be advisable to pronounce the consonants essentially as in English, with the following exceptions.

g is always hard as in give.

j is pronounced as in English and not as in German or French.

sh and *ś* may both be pronounced like *sh* in shut; in Sanskrit, however, the former is a retroflex, the latter a palatal sound.

ṇ distinguishes the retroflex nasal from *n* the dental nasal.

ṁ and *ṅ* indicate nasalization of a preceding vowel like the *n* in French Jean.

ñ stands for the palatal nasal.

ch is pronounced as *ch* in church.

chh is a highly aspirated *ch* sound.

ḷ is a special Tamil letter pronounced by placing the tongue on top of the hard palate and then letting it fall loosely forward.

ṭ, *ṭh*, *ḍ*, and *ḍh* are retroflex consonants. Their special sounds may be ignored by the general reader.

ḥ at the end of a word or syllable is a distinct emission of breath; *h* after another consonant is an integral part of that letter and aspirates it in the following manner:

th to be pronounced as in ant-hill, not as in thin; *ph* as in shepherd, not as in phrase.

HYPHENATION

Finally an abundant use of hyphenation has been made in this book to simplify, for the general reader, the pronunciation of the euphonically combined (*saṅdhi*) long Sanskrit words and phrases, e.g. *artha-śāstra* instead of *arthaśāstra*, *kumār-āmātya* instead of *kumārāmātya*, *maha-sāṅdhi-vigrah-ādhikṛita* instead of *mahāsāṅdhivigrahādhikṛita*. The long vowel has been generally carried forward to the succeeding part as in the case of *āmātya* and *ādhikṛita* above. I have, however, refrained from undoing the *saṅdhi* in deference to those who know Sanskrit as the phrases then would not only have looked but also sounded strange to them. At times, with admitted inconsistency, some expressions and titles are not hyphenated, either because they are very well known or because they occur only once or twice in the book.

ABBREVIATIONS

A.B.	*Aitareya Brāhmaṇa*
A.B.O.R.I.	*Annals of the Bhandarkar Oriental Research Institute*
Agrawala, V. S.	*Harsha-charita — Ek Sāṅskṛitik Adhyayan* ('Harsha-charita, a Cultural Study')
Alex.	Plutarch, *Parallel Lives* (*The Life of Alexander*)
Amara.	*Amara-kosha*
Anu.	*Anuśāsana Parva of the Mahā-bhārata*
Ap. Pṛi.	*Aparājita Pṛichchhā*
Artha.	Kauṭilya, *Artha-śāstra*
A.S.I.A.R.	*Archaeological Survey of India, Annual Reports*
A.V.	*Atharva Veda*
Bār. Sūtra	*Bārhaspatya Sūtra*
Baudh. Dh. Sūt.	Baudhāyana, *Dharma-sūtra*
Beal	S. Beal, *Buddhist Records of the Western World* (A translation of Hsüan-tsang's *Hsi Yü Chi*)
Bendall	*Journey in Nepal*, pp. 72 ff. (Four inscriptions referred to as Bendall, no.)
B.M.C.	J. Allan, *Catalogue of the coins of the Gupta dynasties and of Śaśāṅka, King of Gauḍa* (in the British Museum)
Bom. Gaz.	*Bombay Gazetteer*
B.P.L.	G. H. Ojha, *Bhāratīya Prāchīna Lipi-mālā*
Bṛ.	Bṛihaspati, *Smṛiti* or *Dharma-śāstra*
Bṛ. Up.	*Bṛihad-āraṇyaka Upanishad*
B.S.O.A.S.	*Bulletin of the School of Oriental and African Studies*
C.A.G.I.	A. Cunningham, *Ancient Geography of India*
Chatuḥ	Ārya-deva, *Chatuḥ-śatikā*
C.I.I.	*Corpus Inscriptionum Indicarum*
D.H.N.I.	H. C. Ray, *Dynastic History of Northern India*
Dynasties	Louis de La Vallée Poussin, *Dynasties et Histoire de l'Inde depuis Kanishka jusqu'aux invasions musulmanes* (*Histoire du Monde*, tome vi.2)
E.H.I.	V. A. Smith, *Early History of India*
E.I.	*Epigraphia Indica*
Ettinghausen	M. L. Ettinghausen, *Harṣa Vardhana*, etc.
Frag.	J. W. McCrindle (Tr.), *Ancient India as described by Megasthenes* (*fragments of the Indika of*) *and Arrian*
Gaut.	Gautama, *Dharma-sūtra*

G.D.A.M.I.	N. L. Dey, *Geographical Dictionary of Ancient and Medieval India*
Gnoli	R. Gnoli, *Nepalese Inscriptions in Gupta characters*
H.C. text	Bāṇa-bhaṭṭa, *Harsha-charita* (Sanskrit text with Śaṅkara's commentary)
H.C. trans.	*Harsha-charita*, trans. by E. B. Cowell and F. W. Thomas
H.C.I.P.	R. C. Majumdar (Gen. ed.), *History and Culture of the Indian People*
H.M.H.I.	C. V. Vaidya, *History of Medieval Hindu India*
Hist. Dh.	P. V. Kane, *History of Dharma-śāstra*
Hsi Yü Chi	Hsüan-tsang, *Ta-T'ang Hsi Yü Chi*
Hyd. Arch. Ser.	*Hydarabad Archaeological Series*
I.A.	*Indian Antiquary*
I.H.Q.	*Indian Historical Quarterly*
Ind. Cul.	*Indian Culture*
Indraji	Bhagwanlal Indraji and G. Bühler, 'Inscriptions from Nepal', *I.A.* ix (1880), pp. 163 ff. (23 inscriptions referred to as Indraji no.)
I-tsing	J. Takakusu, *A Record of the Buddhist Religion as practised in India and the Malay Archipelago* (A translation of I-tsing's *Nan-hai-chi-kuei-nai-fa-chʽuan*)
J.A.H.R.S.	*Journal of the Andhra Historical Research Society*
J.A.R.S.	*Journal of the Assam Research Society*
J.A.S.	*Journal of the Asiatic Society*, Calcutta (Fourth Series)
J.A.S.B.	*Journal of the Asiatic Society of Bengal*
J.A.S.B. (N.S.)	*Journal of the Asiatic Society of Bengal* (New Series)
J.A.S.B.L.	*Journal of the Asiatic Society of Bengal* (Third Series, Part I, Letters)
J.B.B.R.A.S.	*Journal of the Bombay Branch of the Royal Asiatic Society*
J.B.B.R.A.S. (N.S.)	*Journal of the Bombay Branch of the Royal Asiatic Society* (New Series)
J.B.O.R.S.	*Journal of the Bihar and Orissa Research Society*
J.I.H.	*Journal of Indian History*
Jour. Dept. Lett.	*Journal of the Department of Letters*
Jour. Num. Soc.	*Journal of the Numismatic Society of India*
J.R.A.S.	*Journal of the Royal Asiatic Society of Great Britain and Ireland* (First Series), 1834–63; (New Series), 1865–
Kāmaṅdaka and *Kāmaṅdakīya*	Kāmaṅdaka, *Nīti-sāra*
Kāt.	Kātyāyana, *Smṛiti*, or *Dharma-śastra*
Kathā	Somadeva, *Kathā-sarit-sāgara*

'Les Missions'	S. Lévi, 'Les missions de Wang Hieuen-tsʻe dans l'Inde', *Journal asiatique*, IXᵉ sér., tome xv, 1900, pp. 297 ff. and pp. 401 ff.
Lévi	S. Lévi, *Le Népal* (23 inscriptions referred to as Lévi no.)
'*Life*'	S. Beal, *The Life of Hiuen-tsiang* (A translation of Hui Li's *Ta Tzʻu-ên Ssu San-tsang Fa-shih Chuan*)
Mahā-vagga	*Mahā-vagga* of the *Vinaya*
Mañju-śrī-mūla-kalpa	*Ārya Mañju-śrī-mūla-kalpa*
Manu	Manu, *Smṛiti* or *Dharma-śāstra*
M.A.S.I.	*Memoirs of the Archaeological Survey of India*
Nār. or *Nārada*	Nārada, *Smṛiti* or *Dharma-śāstra*
N.H.I.P.	R. C. Majumdar and A. S. Altekar (eds.), *A New History of the Indian People*, vol. vi (*The Vākāṭaka-Gupta Age*)
N.I.A.	*New Indian Antiquary*
P.H.A.I.	H. C. Raychaudhuri, *Political History of Ancient India*
P.T.O.C.	*Proceedings and Transactions of the All-India Oriental Conference*
Q.J.M.S.	*Quarterly Journal of the Mythic Society*
Records	T. Watters, *On Yuan Chwang's Travels in India* (A translation of Hsüan-tsang's *Hsi Yü Chi*)
R. Des Rotours	*Traité des fonctionnaires (et) Traité de l'armée trad. de la* Nouvelle Histoire des Tʻang
R.V.	*Ṛig. Veda*
Sabhā.	*Sabhā-parva of the Mahā-bhārata*
Śānti.	*Śānti-parva of the Mahā-bhārata*
Ś.B.	*Śatapatha Brāhmaṇa*
S.B.E.	*Sacred Books of the East*
Sinha, B. P.	*The Decline of the Kingdom of Magadha*
Śukra	Śukra, *Nīti-sāra*
Takakusu 52	Takakusu, J. (ed.), *Taishō Issaikyō* series
T.B.	*Taittirīya Brāhmaṇa*
T.S.	*Taittirīya Saṁhitā*
T.U.	*Taittirīya Upanishad*
Vedic Index	A. A. Macdonell and A. B. Keith, *Vedic Index of Names and Subjects*
V.S.	*Vājasaneyī Saṁhitā*
Waley	A. Waley, *The Real Tripitaka* and other pieces
Watters	T. Watters, *On Yuan Chwang's Travels in India* (A translation of Hsüan-tsang's *Hsi Yü Chi*)
Yāj.	Yājña-valkya, *Smṛiti* or *Dharma-śāstra*

I

SOURCES

A STUDY of the political history of Harsha's reign, A.D. 606–47, is of absorbing interest because of the comparative abundance and reliability of source materials. In this context an examination of the political scene of the post-Gupta period is also necessary for an understanding of the political pattern as it emerged in Harsha's day in its various aspects. They are physical, in the rise of various dynasties aspiring for supremacy through territorial expansion, ideological, in the development of socio-political theories and ideology as expressed in the contemporary *smṛitis*, and institutional, as manifested through the methods of organization from the village level to that of inter-state relations.

Need for a survey of the post-Gupta political scene

Epigraphic evidence

A connected story of the events of the sixth century may be reconstructed mainly on the basis of epigraphic material, which when stripped of the conventional ornamental phrases proves a most trustworthy source. For a knowledge of the events and institutions of Harsha's reign we can draw upon the numismatic and inscriptional evidence left not only by Harsha himself but by his predecessors, the Imperial Guptas, and by his contemporaries such as the Later Guptas, the Maukharis, the Maitrakas, the Gurjaras of Broach, the Chālukyas, and the Kings of Nepal, Bengal, Assam, and Orissa. The comparative dependability of such source materials makes up for the sparsity of information yielded by them.

The records were issued mainly to authorize land-tax donations or to commemorate royal victories, but they also contain a good deal of valuable incidental information. The number of relevant inscriptions for our period is very large indeed, but only four of them belong to Harsha. We are also in possession of some Vardhana coins.[1]

[1] The texts and translations of Harsha's inscriptions originally appeared in the *E.I.* iv, vii, and xxi, and in the *C.I.I.* iii. Harsha's coins are discussed in Appendix II, and those of his contemporaries, the Maukharis, in Appendix III. The seals of Śarvavarman Maukhari and Śaśāṅka are included among the illustrations. The most important single inscription bearing on Harsha's political career, that issued by his Chālukya adversary Pula-késin II, may be consulted in the *E.I.* vi.

Most of the relevant records for our period have been reproduced and translated in the various issues of the *Epigraphia Indica*, the *Memoirs of the Archaeological Survey of India*, the journals of the regional archaeological departments, and the third volume of the *Corpus Inscriptionum Indicarum*, all of which are duly listed in the Bibliography and

Architectural evidence

The only architectural evidence for the reign of Harsha may be sought in Nālandā, although it is not yet possible to attribute any specific structures to him.[1]

Texts on polity

Other sources of information are the *smṛitis* and the *artha-śāstras*, texts on law, conduct, and polity. As in earlier days so during the post-Gupta period works of this nature continued to be produced. They reflect traditional and contemporary views on the formulation and execution of policies and laws concerning government and society. Many of their contents need to be corroborated by more easily verifiable evidence so that the factual can be distinguished from the didactic, although the latter too can be appreciated in its own right. Among the more important socio-political texts produced between A.D. 400 and 800 may be listed the *Nīti-sāra*, 'Essence of Statesmanship', by Kāmaṅdaka, the *smṛitis* by Kātyāyana and Devala, and Asahāya's commentary on the *Nārada-smṛiti*. For an understanding of these works, however, it is necessary to acquire a knowledge of the earlier texts such as Kauṭilya's *artha-śāstra*, Yājña-valkya's *smṛiti*, and so forth.[2]

Literary works

Among works of fiction, part of whose value lies in their being the least motivated sources of historical evidence, the *Daśa-kumāra-charita*, 'Adventures of the Ten Princes', by Daṇḍin, written not long before Harsha's time, is perhaps the most important. There are also three plays by Harsha himself, namely the *Ratnāvali*, the *Priya-darśikā*, and the *Nāg-ānanda*. Of these the first two portray courtly romance in conventional style, but the last with its Buddhist theme is more animated and has an air of conviction about it. All three throw considerable light on the social, economic, and religious life of the period as well as on the capabilities of their author.[3] Another literary writing of the period, Bāṇa's *Kādambarī*, is discussed below along with his other important work, the semi-historical biography of Harsha.

Biographies and travel accounts

Two very welcome sources on our period are biographies and travel accounts, but they need very careful examination, for ulterior motives and flights of fancy are more likely to be at play in works of this nature

the footnotes. Some of the above periodicals, as well as others such as the *Journal of the Numismatic Society of India*, the *Journal of the Royal Asiatic Society*, and the *Indian Antiquary*, comment on Indian coin finds. Among books on epigraphic material, the works of G. V. Acharya, J. Allan, C. J. Brown, A. Cunningham, A. S. Gadre, R. Gnoli, E. J. Rapson, C. R. Singhal, D. C. Sircar, and V. A. Smith have been used and listed.

[1] For a history of the Nālandā establishment see below p. 144, n. 3.

[2] For a detailed discussion of contemporary *smṛiti* and *artha-śāstra* literature, see below, pp. 130 ff.

[3] For a discussion of Harsha's literary and artistic achievements and the value of his writings for the historian, see below, pp. 154–7.

than in short records such as inscriptions. We possess two such works, the *Harsha-charita*, or 'The Story of Harsha', by an Indian poet, Bāṇa-bhaṭṭa, and the *Hsi Yü Chi*, or 'The Records of the Western World',[1] by the Chinese Buddhist pilgrim, Hsüan-tsang. The latter work is supported by 'The Life of the Master of the Law',[2] Hsüan-tsang's biography, written by the monk Hui Li on the basis of information obtained from Hsüan-tsang himself. These works are the main bases for reconstructing the story of Harsha's reign, but, being written by authors towards whom Harsha was favourably disposed, their trustworthiness needs to be inquired into.

Hsüan-tsang's testimony

The family, religious, and national background of Hsüan-tsang, the writer of the travel account, the *Hsi Yü Chi*

When examining the impressions gained by the Chinese traveller Hsüan-tsang, who remained in India for approximately thirteen years (*c.* A.D. 630–44), about the administration of Harsha, it is well to remember that he came of a family of administrators, and that, despite the fact that he was a Buddhist monk, he evidently had a keen interest in politics and a background of the Confucian classics and Chinese political thought.

Hsüan-tsang's great-grandfather had served as prefect of Shang-tang in Shansi in north-central China, under the later Wei dynasty (A.D. 386–534). His grandfather had obtained employment in the civil service by his distinguished scholarship, and was appointed President of the Imperial College. Hsüan-tsang's father was well known for his ability and talent but, being a simple and contented man, did not seek prestige or promotion. Anticipating the fall of the Sui dynasty (*c.* A.D. 589–618) he occupied himself with his books and resolutely refused the many offers of provincial and district offices. A Confucianist, he probably took the attitude that one could influence politics even by one's actions as a layman. Hsüan-tsang, born in A.D. 602, was the youngest of the four sons of Hui. His love of books became apparent at a very early age and, being the son of a scholar, he was given his first lessons in Confucianism and in other schools of Chinese thought as soon as he was ready to receive them.

His second brother, a Buddhist disciple, took Hsüan-tsang with him to a Buddhist convent when he was not yet twelve. Before long, at the grand

[1] Henceforth referred to as 'Records'. Our own rendering of Chinese passages from the 'Records' will be referred to in the footnotes as *Hsi Yü Chi* text. References to the English translations of the 'Records' by S. Beal and T. Watters will be given as Beal and Watters respectively.

[2] The complete Chinese title is: *Ta-tzʻu-ên Ssu San-tsang Fa-shih Chuan*, or 'Life of the Master of the Law, Tripiṭaka, of the Great Monastery of Motherly Love'. The work will be henceforth referred to as 'Life'.

ordination of new Buddhist monks held at Lo-yang in Honan, Hsüan-tsang was selected, despite his youth, to be a recluse under royal patronage. His older colleagues were amazed at his zeal and intelligence. Between the impressionable years of 13 and 20, Hsüan-tsang was tossed about from one monastery to another, in the general confusion that ensued from the fall of the Sui dynasty. There was lack of peace and order, the teachings of Confucius and of the Buddha were neglected, and no religious conferences took place at the capital. While people were still suffering from the effects of political changes, natural calamities such as famines afflicted most parts of the country, and riots took place in most cities. In search of peaceful conditions, Hsüan-tsang and his brother went first to Ch'ang-an, the T'ang capital in northern China, then to Han-chung, and finally, like many other Buddhist priests, to Ch'êng-tu in the south-west, a place unaffected by famine. During his stay at Ch'êng-tu, Hsüan-tsang distinguished himself in all fields of Buddhist studies and by his twentieth year was fully ordained as a *bhikshu*.

In A.D. 626 the capital witnessed more political changes in the *coup d'État* carried out by the Prince of Ch'in, later the Emperor T'ai-tsung of T'ang. Hsüan-tsang, however, continued to live and study at Ch'êng-tu, and later at Chao-chou and Ch'ang-an, until he finally made up his mind to go and study Buddhism in the land of its birth. In spite of official hindrance in obtaining a passport and the tremendous hazards that lay in such a long journey, Hsüan-tsang set forth for India in A.D. 629.

Visit to India

He stayed there for nearly thirteen years, travelling, going on pilgrimages, studying, debating, and taking note of everything. Apparently Hsüan-tsang committed many of his observations and impressions to writing. On his return to China he wrote a record of his western travels.

The author's attitudes as reflected in his work

A critical examination of Hsüan-tsang's account reveals that in general it is a trustworthy description of conditions that prevailed in Harsha's time, but that at places it has been affected by the author's preconceived ideas on government and administration, his early scholastic training, the code of behaviour of his country, and, last but not least, his fervour for Buddhism.

The projection of Chinese values

Hsüan-tsang tended to present, on the basis of scanty evidence, an exaggerated picture of conditions as he would have liked them to be. It was natural for the Chinese pilgrim to try to establish the importance of 'filial piety' in Indian society, because it was one of the highest virtues according to the Chinese way of life. It was, no doubt, a sacred duty of sons and daughters in Indian society to revere their parents and elders, and the law punished them if they failed in fulfilling their duty, but the punishment was limited to fines.[1] Hsüan-tsang, however, records that those who violated filial piety had their nose and ears or hands and feet cut off, or were exiled from the country or banished into the wilderness.[2]

Of Buddhist religiousness

The pilgrim was also anxious to see in the land of the Buddha the universal application of the doctrine of non-violence. He therefore writes with obvious satisfaction that Harsha 'forbade the eating of meat in the five Indias [and declared that] the killing of life would be punished without pardon'.[3] We have no confirmatory evidence of this edict, and it seems very unlikely that a practical statesman of Harsha's calibre would have considered its promulgation. An earlier statement of Hsüan-tsang refers to meat-eating by the Hīnayāna Buddhists of A-kʻi-ni (Yenki) and Ku-chih.[4] Harsha could hardly have ignored the need of the Hīnayāna followers of his territories. In fact, in his general description of India, Hsüan-tsang mentions the kinds of meat permissible and forbidden for consumption by the people.[5] Bāṇa's reference to hares that 'ran hither and thither, pursued by furiously running crowds armed with clubs and struck at every place like polo balls'[6] points, not only to the absence of a ban on animal-killing, at least in the early part of Harsha's reign, but also to the cruel way, even if practised during the course of a military march, in which the poor creatures were slain. It is, however, possible that, as his Buddhist fervour increased in his middle age, Harsha forbade or restricted meat-eating in the royal palace, as his predecessor Aśoka had done. Hsüan-tsang, through either misunderstanding or wishful thinking, might well have exaggerated this into a general prohibition.

Hsüan-tsang's religious fervour also finds expression in his miraculous Buddhist stories. Most of them are to be discarded as only partially true, inasmuch as they had some basis in historical happenings that lent themselves to a colourful rendering. The pilgrim reproduced the stories as he heard them, because he unquestioningly believed in anything that exalted his faith. Many episodes purporting to be his personal experiences

[1] The *Kātyāyana Smṛiti* does not mention this crime. Kauṭilya (*Artha.* iii. 20) states 'When between father and son . . . one abandons the other . . . the first amercement [the lightest] shall be levied.' *Manu* (viii. 389), for the same sin, 'unless guilty of a crime causing loss of caste', fixes a fine of 600 *paṇas*, for defaming 100 *paṇas*.

For the serious crimes of murder and adultery in this relationship, punishment was of course much severer, but obviously Hsüan-tsang is not referring to such extreme cases.

[2] Watters i, p. 172.

[3] *Hsi Yü Chi* text, v. 4a; cf. Watters i, p. 344.

[4] Watters i, pp. 53–60. The three pure kinds of flesh permitted were: (i) Unseen, unheard, unsuspected. (ii) Natural death. (iii) Bird-killed.

[5] Beal i, pp. 88–9; Watters i, p. 178.

[6] *H.C.* text, p. 212; trans., p. 209.

are probably the result of self-suggestion in his ardent desire to prove himself a devoted disciple of the Buddha.[1]

Reliability of figures in the *Hsi Yü Chi*

The authenticity of Hsüan-tsang's figures regarding area, distances, or population, as well as certain details about the location of places, may also be sometimes questioned. In many cases the 'Life' and the 'Records' make conflicting statements. Thus the former locates Kapitha (or Sankisa) to the east of P'i-lo-shan-na,[2] the latter to its south-east, although the distance given is the same. Again, while the 'Life' places the capital of Chīna-bhukti at a distance of 50 *li*[3] from the Tamasa-vana monastery, the 'Records' give the figure 500 *li*. While Hsüan-tsang in his 'Records' assigns an area of 7,000 *li* to the Kingdom of Kashmir, other Chinese authorities, e.g. Ma Tuan-lin,[4] give it the more probable area of 4,000 *li*. Evidently some of these mistakes may be mere slips of memory or copyists' errors. Indeed, considering the number of figures that Hsüan-tsang has provided us with in the course of his long narrative, the incidences of such discrepancies are remarkably few. In fact, the modern historian, in his anxiety to avoid credulity, is prone to disavow certain figures which although seemingly unbelievable may be considered at least probable on a closer examination of evidence.[5] The enormous number of 10,000 students for the monastic-cum-educational establishment at Nālandā[6] does not appear impossible if we are prepared to rely on Hsüan-tsang's testimony recording fairly large figures of 1,000 or more brethren for far smaller monasteries. Harsha is said to have invited a thousand learned monks of Nālandā to take part in the philosophical assembly at Kanauj. The Chinese account,[7] as well as archaeological evidence, reveals that some buildings at Nālandā had at least as many as four storeys. Moreover, as H. D. Sankalia points out, 'The Nālandā of medieval times . . . unquestionably extended far beyond the limits of the site so far acquired for excavation.'[8]

From Hsüan-tsang's minute details regarding the places he visited, it would seem that he brought back with him a mass of papers consisting partly of records of his own experiences and partly of impersonal

[1] e.g. Beal i, pp. 93–4; ii, p. 173; 'Life', p. 49.

[2] Watters i, pp. 332–3 restores it as Vilasāṇa or Bhilasana. The 'Life', p. 81, has the rendering P'i-lo-na-na, which agrees with Watters's D. Text of the *Hsi Yü Chi* recognized in Japan and Korea. Cunningham (*C.A.G.I.*, p. 418) identifies the capital of P'i-lo-shan-na with the great mound of ruins called *Atranji-khera* situated on the right or west bank of the Kāli Nadi, four miles to the south of *Karsāna*, and eight miles to the north of *Eyta* on the Grand Trunk Road'.

[3] Approximately six *li* equal a mile.

[4] As quoted by Watters i, p. 261.

[5] The apparently exaggerated figure of 5,000 for Harsha's elephant corps may not be too wide of the mark. See below, pp. 188–90.

[6] 'Life', p. 112.

[7] Ibid., p. 109.

[8] Sankalia, p. 217.

accounts of the various Indian and neighbouring kingdoms.[1] The material that he lost in the Indus flood on his return journey, fifty manuscript copies of the *Sūtras*, and seeds of various kinds, was later replaced. Apart from the fact that Hsüan-tsang had some written material to aid him, his memory of events was also fresh, since he was able to complete his account by the autumn of A.D. 646, within three years of taking leave from Harsha and within two years of leaving India. These circumstances further enhance the reliability of Hsüan-tsang's testimony.

Is Hsüan-tsang partial to Harsha?

The criticism often levelled against Hsüan-tsang[2] that he gives a biased picture of his Indian patron—not only because of the latter's munificence towards him, but also because of Harsha's marked inclination towards Buddhism—rests rather on presumption than on positive evidence. Although Hsüan-tsang is enthusiastic when writing about his co-religionists and lacks zeal when describing Hindu or Hīnayāna kings, he repeatedly gives evidence of his sense of balance.

The pilgrim is not blindly partial to the Buddhist rulers of India nor oblivious to the worthy qualities of her non-Buddhist kings. The Buddhist Kings of Jālandhara,[3] Kośala,[4] and Chih-chi-to (Jājhotī)[5] are praised for their love of virtue, wisdom, and sagacity, but Hindu rulers, notably those of Maheśvara-pura,[5] Pāri-yātra,[6] and Ujjain,[7] are also complimented on their bravery and learning. Promoters of Hīnayāna, such as the rulers of Hiraṇya-parvata[8] and Gurjara,[9] are pronounced wise and benevolent. But the ruler of Valabhī, although a Buddhist and a son-in-law of Harsha, is described by Hsüan-tsang as 'shallow in wisdom and statecraft and hasty in disposition'.[10] The people of Bharukachchha, 'wedded to error and true doctrine alike', having some ten *sanghārāmas* and being adherents of both the Great Vehicle and the *Sthavira* school, are still described as 'cold and indifferent, . . . crooked and perverse',[11] while the people of Mati-pura, who, according to the pilgrim, are also equally divided in their religious beliefs, though the proportion of temples and *sanghārāmas* (50:20) points to a majority of non-Buddhists, are, nevertheless, described as sincere and truthful and fond of learning.[12]

The pilgrim's account of Mahā-rāshṭra[13] is significant in this connection. The great monarch, Pulakeśin II, who was neither a Buddhist nor

1 Waley, pp. 89–90.
2 R. C. Majumdar, *Ancient India*, p. 263; S. K. Banerjee, *I.H.Q.* 27 (1951) 312–20.
3 Beal i, p. 176. 4 Beal ii, p. 209. 5 Ibid., p. 271.
6 Beal, i, p. 179. 7 Beal ii, p. 271.
8 Ibid., p. 187. 9 Ibid., p. 270. 10 Ibid., p. 267.
11 Ibid., p. 259. 12 Beal i, p. 192.
13 Beal ii, pp. 255 ff.; Watters ii, pp. 239 ff.

a patron of the pilgrim, and who was a confirmed enemy of Hsüan-tsang's enthusiastic admirer Harsha, is thus described: 'Pulakeśi is far-sighted in his plans and his beneficent actions are felt over a great distance. His subjects serve him with utmost loyalty. Śīlāditya Mahārāja has conquered the nations from east to west and carried his arms to remote districts, but the people of this country alone have not submitted to him.'[1]

The King of Gauḍa, one of the scant examples of religious persecutors in ancient India, is said to have damaged and destroyed various sacred relics of the Buddhists. Though the Chinese pilgrim brings such facts to our notice and makes known his natural abhorrence of such acts, he cannot justly be accused of slandering Śaśāṅka as some historians have alleged.[2] Hsüan-tsang's denigration of Śaśāṅka is confined to calling him a heretic and attributing his death to a disease which struck him down after he was told that his orders to destroy an image of the Buddha had been carried out. Compared with Hsüan-tsang, Bāṇa is far more vehement in denouncing Śaśāṅka as the murderer of Harsha's elder brother Rājya-vardhana.[3]

Hsüan-tsang wrote in China under the patronage of his own emperor, too far away and too secure to be affected by the reactions his account might produce in India. There is no doubt that Hsüan-tsang had a special regard for Harsha, but he was under no pressure whatsoever to give a favourable account of India or her peoples or rulers. If regard for his Indian patron could have influenced Hsüan-tsang's attitudes so could his deep-rooted respect for the tenets of the religions he had studied which taught him to be honest and truthful. Hsüan-tsang's sole aim was to study and promote Buddhism, not to humour princes and rulers or seek favours from them. More than once he risked their annoyance by delaying or refusing to meet their requests that he should visit them and stay with them for as long as they wished. At Turfan Hsüan-tsang went without food for three days to convince the king of his determination to go to India and to get reversed the king's order forcibly stopping him from proceeding further. In India he refused Harsha's first invitation in order to complete the work in hand, complying only with his second request for a meeting. Hsüan-tsang was constrained to visit Kāma-rūpa (Assam) because the second summons of King Kumāra was accompanied with the threat that he would deliberately harm the cause of Buddhism if the pilgrim did not oblige.

[1] *Hsi Yü Chi* text, xi. 12b; cf. Beal ii, p. 256; Watters ii. p. 239.
[2] R. C. Majumdar, *History of Bengal*, i, pp. 62, 71–6. [3] *H.C.* trans., pp. 179–80.

Hsüan-tsang's love for his country, the Chinese emperor's generous patronage, and the monk's obvious keenness to keep his patron pleased might be expected, if anything, to check his enthusiasm for Harsha, the more so because the two emperors were in diplomatic contact with each other, and it would have been impolite on Hsüan-tsang's part to eulogize the foreign ruler more than his own.

The testimony of Hsüan-tsang's biography, the 'Life'

The 'Life', written by two of Hsüan-tsang's disciples, Hui-li and Yen-ts'ung, is complementary to the 'Records', and throws light on various aspects of Indian life in the seventh century. While focusing on topics of Buddhist interest, it makes incidental note of certain facts about Harsha's career which would otherwise have remained unknown to us. The 'Life' generally corroborates the information given by the 'Records', but not unoften it states new facts or clarifies those mentioned in the latter work.

Chapters 1–5 of the book were written by the monk Hui-li and were completed between the end of A.D. 648 and the summer of 649. Chapters 6–10, dealing with Hsüan-tsang's career after his return to China, are by the monk Yen-ts'ung, who continued and perhaps to some extent edited the work of Hui-li. The latter died in *c.* A.D. 670, or a little later, and all ten chapters were published by Yen-ts'ung in A.D. 688.[1]

The material of the 'Records' had been put together by Hsüan-tsang's helpers under his own supervision. As Hui-li was on the board of amanuenses for the 'Records' and was in close contact with Hsüan-tsang while writing the biography, the 'Life', although a second-hand account, which also underwent some editing, may yet be considered as only slightly inferior to the 'Records' as a reliable source for Harsha's reign.

The scrutiny of Hsüan-tsang's attitudes and background and an examination of the two works for which he provided material, while guarding us against some weaknesses of our sources, also testify to the value and the general dependability of their evidence.

The other Chinese sources which provide nearly all the information on the Indo-Chinese missions and the death of Harsha are quoted in detail in Chapter VII and listed in the Bibliography.

Bāṇa's testimony

The testimony of Harsha's biography by Bāṇa

Bāṇa, the court poet of Harsha, has been accused by some scholars of writing a biased and therefore dubious account of the life of his patron in the latter's biography entitled *Harsha-charita*. For several reasons,

[1] Waley, p. 280.

however, we believe that, behind the obvious exaggeration and panegyrics, typical of the courtly literature of the time, there is to be found a realistic picture of contemporary life and many facts about Harsha's character and achievements in Bāṇa's *Harsha-charita*.

Bāṇa's family background, childhood, and early youth

Bāṇa-bhaṭṭa was the son of a learned brahman. His mother died when he was very young and his father when he was fourteen. Although lovingly brought up by his father, most of Bāṇa's time during these years was naturally spent in the teacher's home where it was customary for pupils to stay. His early youth after his father's death was spent in sowing wild oats. His life as a wanderer, and his love of mixing with people of all types, gave Bāṇa, in addition to a dubious reputation, a boldness of character and a sympathetic understanding of human nature.

The scope of Bāṇa's contacts and experience

While on the one hand he had dear friends in a bard, a goldsmith, a drummer, a scribe, a maid-servant, and two half-brothers of low caste,[1] on the other he had, especially as he grew older, ample opportunity to mix with high-class Brahmans, learned scholars, royal courtiers, and even the King himself. His first-hand knowledge of the life of the people of all social strata, as well as his easy access to royal quarters, qualified Bāṇa for giving an authentic and realistic account of events, unless of course he chose to do otherwise in order to please his benefactor. Though most of the contents of the *Harsha-charita* refer to the earlier part of its hero's career, when Bāṇa had not made Harsha's personal acquaintance, yet the kind of episodes described in the work, such as the beginning of a campaign, a royal birth, a royal wedding, etc., must have been witnessed by Bāṇa during Harsha's reign and supplied him with the necessary details regarding such events. As for the description of Harsha's accession, his treaty with the King of Kāma-rūpa, or his search for his bereaved sister, Bāṇa no doubt depended on hearsay, but it is evident that, because of his inquisitive nature, to which weakness Bāṇa confesses more than once, and lively disposition, as well as his versatility in mixing with different kinds of people, Bāṇa collected all the available information on these colourful topics. There is little doubt that he picked up much court gossip, but the general tenor of his work suggests that most of his important statements are based on authentic information.

Bāṇa, the sensitive, subtle, and spirited writer

Bāṇa has made use of his material very cleverly in the *Harsha-charita*. He has the courage to refer to facts which were not flattering to Harsha's reputation, though also practical wisdom so to weave them into the web of his words that they would not cause offence to his patron. The *Harsha-charita* affords numerous examples of Bāṇa's skill in achieving

[1] *H.C.* text, p. 42; trans., p. 33.

this effect. The brief period of uncertainty that followed the death of Rājyavardhana, who fell fighting for the defence of Kanauj, was, we surmise, used by Harsha for canvassing the ministers of that kingdom in favour of his own succession to the throne of Kanauj. Bāṇa expresses it in this manner: 'He [Harsha] was embraced by the goddess of The Royal Prosperity [Lakshmī], who . . . forced him, however reluctant, to mount the throne . . . .'[1] The discourse between the envoy of the King of Kāma-rūpa and Harsha, as worded by Bāṇa, gives one the impression that the author was well aware of the importance of Kāma-rūpa's friendship for Harsha, especially at the beginning of the latter's reign, a fact also established through other sources of information on Harsha's period. The story of this alliance has so been presented as neither to harm facts nor to hurt Harsha's pride.[2]

As for Bāṇa's exuberant descriptions, keeping in mind the florid style of his period, it is not very difficult to separate fact from flattery in the *Harsha-charita*. Our knowledge of Harsha's personal appearance, for example, may be considered to be practically nil, though Bāṇa devotes several pages to it.[3] By reading other Sanskrit poets, we learn that the features of their heroes and heroines were described to the minutest detail in completely formal and standardized phrases. The information given about royal attire should, however, be considered authentic, as also the description of the dress and appearance of the forester, Nirghāta.

Some of Bāṇa's descriptions, such as those of the king's household, the royal camp, and the forest dwelling in the Vindhayas, despite the artificial style of those days, are so vivid and, indeed, so complete that they wholly transport us to his times. Bāṇa's sense of humour and his lively and vigorous style spare neither the common servant nor the royal master in the course of his narrative. This fundamental realism is nowhere better shown than in the passage containing the ejaculations of his soldiers and retainers on the occasion of Harsha's marching forth on his *dig-vijaya*. 'Quick, slave, with a knife cut a mouthful of fodder from this bean field: who can tell the fate of his crop when we are gone?', or 'Only let this one expedition be gone and done with . . . . Let it go to the bottom of hell . . . . Good luck to this servitude of ours . . . . Goodbye to this camp, the pinnacle of all unpleasantness.' Also 'The king is Dharma incarnate' and, 'Where's the king? What right has he to be king!'[4]

Bāṇa's novel *Kādambarī* gives further evidence of his lack of inhibition

[1] Ibid., p. 70; trans., p. 57.
[2] Ibib., p. 214–25; trans., pp. 211–23.
[3] Ibib., pp. 69–77; trans., pp. 56–64.
[4] Ibid., pp. 211, 212; trans., pp. 207, 208, 209.

and his strong-mindedness. While enjoying royal munificence he ridicules the foolish king who is easily taken in by the flattery of his roguish courtiers. A brahman by birth he finds nothing disapprobatory in transforming the goddess Lakshmī into an untouchable.

Thus we see that, despite Bāṇa's position at Harsha's court, his works display a refreshing, almost saucy, boldness. It seems safe to conclude that, ignoring certain topics on which Bāṇa lavished his poetical skill and eulogies too generously, we can, by and large, depend on his works as an important source of information on conditions in Harsha's time.

II

KINGDOMS OF NORTHERN INDIA IN THE LATTER HALF OF THE SIXTH CENTURY A.D.

The decline of the Guptas

THE second quarter of the sixth century witnessed the downfall of the great Gupta empire. It also saw the filling of the vacuum which they left, not by another paramount sovereign power, but by several lesser dynasties, which, taking advantage of the unsettled conditions, declared their independence of Gupta suzerainty.

The Hūṇa attacks

From the time of Skanda Gupta onwards, the Hūṇa invaders of Central Asia continually disturbed the peace of the Guptas. Skanda Gupta had successfully repulsed their attack in *c.* A.D. 455.[1] The Eran inscription of A.D. 510[2] records the brave fighting of Bhānu Gupta, probably against the Hūṇa chief Tora-māṇa. The latter's son Mihira-kula had a chequered career in India, on some occasions scoring brilliant victories, on others suffering humiliation and defeat. Hsüan-tsang records his discomfiture at the hands of Bālāditya,[3] generally identified with Nara-siṁha Gupta. Yaśo-dharman, too, in his Mandsor inscription dated A.D. 533, claims that 'respect was paid to his feet by even that [famous] king Mihira-kula whose head had never [previously] been brought to the humility of obeisance to any other save Sthāṇu'.[4] The repeated Hūṇa incursions and the meteoric appearance of Yaśo-dharman shook the Gupta empire to its very foundations. The tendency to family rifts, which started with the accession of Skanda Gupta and continued to increase in later reigns, added to the confusion.

The tail-end of the line

Vishṇu Gupta Chandrāditya was probably last in the line of the great Gupta emperors and is known to us from his Nālandā seal[5] as well as

[1] *C.I.I.* iii, nos. 13 and 14.
[2] Ibid., no. 20.
[3] Beal i, p. 168; Watters i, p. 288.
[4] *C.I.I.* iii, no. 33. Sthāṇu is an epithet of Śiva. Sthāṇv-īśvara, the original home of the Vardhanas, to be described later, gets its name from Sthāṇu, to whom the main temple in the city was dedicated.
[5] *E.I.* xxvi. 235 ff.

from his gold coinage of rather low gold content.[1] The fifth Dāmodarpur copperplate dated A.D. 543–4,[2] which accords the titles *Pṛithvī-pati Parama-daivata Parama-bhaṭṭāraka* and *Mahārāj-ādhirāja* to a Gupta emperor whose name is lost, is almost certainly a record of Vishṇu Gupta's period. The Valabhī grant of A.D. 545[3] contains one of the last references to the nominal suzerainty of the Imperial Guptas in an outlying province of their empire. An inscription recently discovered at the village of Sumaṇḍala in Khallikoṭe, Orissa,[4] records that King Pṛithivīvigraha was ruling over Kaliṅga, in the domain of the Guptas, in the year 250 (= A.D. 569–70). On the basis of this R. C. Majumdar believes that 'some Gupta emperors continued to rule for another quarter of a century'[5] (i.e. from *c.* A.D. 550 to 570). Rather it appears that the Kaliṅga royal house was an old feudatory family that had owed allegiance to the Guptas in the heyday of their power and continued to record the fact and to date in the Gupta era as a matter of convention. For it is not likely that, while the Later Guptas and the Maukharis, who had been subject to the Imperial Guptas, were still fighting each other for supremacy, the Imperial line would become obscure and pass its last years in ignominy. Rather than humble their overlords, the Maukharis, and especially the Later Guptas with the same cognomen, would almost certainly have identified their cause with that of an old-established dynasty which, though feeble, was still regarded with a special awe. It appears therefore that some old Gupta feudatories in the comparatively remote region of Orissa who did not entertain very high ambitions for themselves continued to use the conventional formula even some twenty years after it had lost its meaning. A land-grant dated A.D. 551–2 of Kumār-āmātya Mahārāja Nandana found at Gayā,[6] in the heart of Magadha, makes no reference to Gupta suzerainty. About this, R. C. Majumdar remarks: 'As there is no reference to any Gupta ruler in this record, we may conclude that by A.D. 550 the Guptas had ceased to exercise effective authority over the greater part of Magadha.'[7] That Gupta suzerainty ceased to be recognized in Magadha only shortly before the date of the Gayā inscription is evident from the use of only humble titles by Nandana, for if a long time had elapsed between the fall of the Guptas and the appearance of Nandana the latter would have assumed more

[1] Rapson, *Catalogue of Indian Coins*, p. 26. B. P. Sinha, *Decline of the Kingdom of Magadha*, p. 425, quotes Allan's report on Gupta gold coins. The gold content of Vishṇu Gupta's coins is stated to be 43 per cent; that of his predecessor Skanda Gupta was 78 per cent.

[2] *E.I.* xvii. 193.

[3] *E.I.* xv. 114–15 and xvii. 193.

[4] *I.H.Q.* xxvi. 75.

[5] *H.C.I.P.* iii, p. 44.

[6] *E.I.* x. 49 ff.

[7] *H.C.I.P.* iii, p. 44.

pretentious titles. The Jaina work *Hari-vaṁśa* records that Gupta rule lasted 231 years. Reckoning from A.D. 320, the beginning of the Gupta era, it brings down Gupta rule to the middle of the sixth century A.D. Fleet expresses the opinion that the number given by the *Hari-vaṁśa* is not far from accurate.[1] New powers, many of which had once been feudatories of the Guptas, were now beginning to clash with each other in an attempt to gain supremacy. These were the Later Guptas in Magadha, the Maukharis in the eastern districts of modern Uttar Pradesh, the Vardhanas in western U.P. and eastern Panjab, the Varmans in Kāmarūpa, the Maitrakas in Valabhī, the Kaḷachuris in Mālava, and the Chālukyas in Vātāpi (Bādāmi).

The Later Guptas

Working backwards from A.D. 554, the date of the Harāhā inscription of Īśāna-varman Maukhari,[2] who was a contemporary of Kumāra-gupta, the fourth king of the Later Gupta dynasty, and allotting an average of about twenty years' rule to each monarch in that unstable period, we arrive at the date *c.* A.D. 500 for the first Later Gupta king, Kṛishṇa-gupta. His line is recorded in the Aphsaḍ inscription of his descendant Āditya-sena.[3] The first Maukhari king, Hari-varman, was in a direct line the third predecessor of Īśāna-varman, as Kṛishṇa-gupta was of Kumāra-gupta. Thus Hari-varman's rise may be assigned to the same period as that of Kṛishṇa-gupta, at the end of the fifth or the beginning of the sixth century.

The founders

Kṛishṇa-gupta

Both the Later Guptas and the Maukharis doubtless served as feudatories under the Imperial Guptas. The Aphsaḍ inscription attributes to Kṛishṇa-gupta, the founder of the dynasty, the simple titles of *nṛipa* and *śrī*, and states that he was of good descent (*sadvaṁśah*). The third king, Jīvita-gupta, is called *Kshitīśa Chūḍā-maṇi*, or 'the best among kings'. *Kśiti-pāla*, synonymous with *Kshitīśa*, occurs among the various terms which Bāṇa employs to describe Harsha's feudatories.[4] None of the Later Gupta inscriptions claim any family relationship with the Imperial Gupta dynasty. The name-ending 'gupta', and the provenance of the Later Gupta inscriptions, therefore should not mislead us into believing that the Later Guptas belonged to the main Gupta line, which came into prominence in the fourth century A.D. As stated by R. C. Majumdar, 'they may be regarded as the residuary legatees of the Gupta empire'.[5]

Unconnected with the Imperial Guptas

[1] *I.A.* xv. 142.
[2] *E.I.* xiv. 110 ff.
[3] *C.I.I.* iii, no. 42.
[4] See below, p. 159.
[5] *N.H.I.P.* vi, p. 209.

Fleet, writing at the end of the last century, designated the dynasty of Kṛishṇa-gupta as the Later Guptas of Magadha.[1]

Their early home

In the last sixty years there has been endless controversy among scholars as to the home of the Later Guptas. Hoernle regarded them as a branch of the Imperial Gupta family ruling in eastern Mālava.[2] Among his main supporters is H. C. Raychaudhuri, who holds that Mālava was the chief centre of the Later Guptas until the rise of Harsha, and that they shifted their headquarters to Magadha under Āditya-sena when the dynasty gained strength after Harsha's death.[3] Against this Mālava theory we advance the Magadha theory, according to which the Later Guptas might initially have been connected with Mālava, inasmuch as the first or the second king of the line may have been a feudatory or a governor of Bhānu-gupta of the eastern Imperial branch. This original association with Mālava might, among other factors, have persuaded Mahā-sena-gupta to settle there when he was practically driven out of the Gangetic plain. We hold, however, that at a fairly early stage in their career, the Later Guptas had established a stronghold in Magadha. The slow disintegration of the Gupta empire aroused the ambitions of many potential feudatories, and a footing in Magadha was most important for achieving effective success against any other claimants to the throne of the Guptas. In fact the name-ending 'gupta' may have been chosen and cherished by the Later Guptas in an attempt to bring the family closer, in the eyes of the people, to the well-established Imperial Gupta dynasty. The arguments in favour of both the Mālava and the Magadha theories are discussed at length below.

Translocation between Mālava and Magadha

The Mālava theory

The main defence of the former is that Mādhava-gupta of the *Harsha-charita*, who is the same as Mādhava-gupta of the Aphsaḍ inscription, is described by Bāṇa as the son of the King of Mālava.[4] It is also asserted that, as the Deo-Barnark inscription of Jīvita-gupta II, of the post-Harsha period, mentions the names of two Maukhari kings, Śarva-varman and Avanti-varman, immediately after that of Bālāditya-deva, as donees of Vāruṇikā, a village in the Shahabad district of Bihar, the possibility of the rule of any other line except those of the Imperial Guptas and Maukharis in that region is excluded. Moreover, Hsüan-tsang, who visited Magadha in the seventh century A.D., records the names of two kings, Pūrṇa-varman and Śaśāṅka, in connection with Magadha, but not that of Mādhava-gupta, to whom he otherwise refers.[5]

[1] *C.I.I.* iii, Introd., p. 14.
[2] *J.R.A.S.* (1903) 551 ff.
[3] *P.H.A.I.*, 4th ed., pp. 492–3.
[4] *H.C.* text, p. 138; trans., p. 119.
[5] An enthusiastic biographer of the Maukharis, E. A. Pires (*The Maukharis*, pp. 14–16), claims, without adequate testimony, that the Maukharis inherited Magadha

The Magadha theory

None of these arguments disprove the theory that the Later Guptas, until the early years of the reign of Mahā-sena-gupta (*c.* A.D. 562?),[1] were the rulers of Magadha. Nor can the Mālava theory satisfactorily explain the victory of Mahā-sena-gupta over a King of Kāma-rūpa in a battle which was probably fought on the banks of the river Lauhitya (Brahma-putra). Raychaudhuri claims that Mahā-sena-gupta could have achieved it in the same way as did Yaśo-dharman of Mālava. Moreover, he says, '(When) Kumāra-gupta had pushed to Prayāga . . . (and) Dāmodara-gupta . . . had broken up the . . . array of . . . elephants belonging to the Maukhari . . . (and) the Gauḍa expansion had already been stopped for a time by the victories of Īśāna varman . . . what was there to prevent the son of Dāmodara-gupta . . . from pushing on to the Lauhitya?'[2]

It seems to us, however, that the Aphsaḍ inscription does not give such a bright picture of the fortunes of the Later Guptas as is depicted by some scholars. Maukhari power appears to have been in ascendancy—indeed, from the time of Kumāra-gupta onwards—for, though the Aphsaḍ inscription attributes to him a victory over Īśāna-varman Maukhari, it also states that (Kumāra-gupta) 'cherishing heroism and adherence to truth [*śaurya-satyavrata*] . . . went to Prayāga; [and there] honourably decorated with flowers, plunged [*magnaḥ*] into a fire [kindled] with dry cow-dung cakes, as if [simply plunging to bathe] in water'. Most historians take this verse to indicate that Kumāra-gupta's territory extended to Prayāga, and Fleet, in a footnote on the verse, states that it does not necessarily mean that Kumāra placed himself on the funeral pyre while still alive. Instances, however, are not wanting in ancient Indian history of kings vowing to abandon all the comforts of life, or even to embrace death, if a cherished objective is not reached. Harsha made a comparatively simple promise when he said that he would not lift food with his right hand until his brother's enemies were punished.[3] Kumāra-gupta, it appears, made the grim vow of giving up life if he did not succeed in achieving his object, which may have been to kill his Maukhari adversary or to seize a certain portion of his territory. The Aphsaḍ inscription probably exaggerates his victory over Īśāna-varman. Whatever the degree of Kumāra-gupta's success, he seems to have felt that he had failed in realizing his object and should therefore part with life in fulfilment

from the Imperial Guptas, perhaps because he also believes, again on the basis of a very doubtful assumption, that 'the Maukharis actually dominated Magadha before Chandra Gupta I usurped the throne from them. Pires's argument for the latter is that the Magadha-kula of the *Kaumudi-mahotsava* is synonymous with the Kota family of the Allahabad inscription of Samudra Gupta. Also see below, pp. 66–7, 86–7, 160.

[1] B. P. Sinha, *Decline of the Kingdom of Magadha*, p. 175.

[2] *J.B.O.R.S.* xv. 651 ff.

[3] Beal i, p. 213.

of his sacred vow. The general belief that attainment of heaven was ensured for those who died at the holy city of Prayāga may have guided Kumāra-gupta's choice of site. Prayāga may have formed part of Kumāra-gupta's domains, but he could have fulfilled this wish irrespective of whether the city fell within his own territory or that of his adversary because of Prayāga's very special status as a place of pilgrimage.

Kumāra-gupta's son, Dāmodara-gupta, continued the struggle with his Maukhari rivals. He is said to have fought a fierce battle against the Maukhari king, on whom he probably inflicted great losses, but at the cost of his own life.[1]

Raychaudhuri's assertion that there was nothing to prevent the son of Dāmodara-gupta from pushing on to the Lauhitya from his kingdom of Mālava, which already extended up to Prayāga, seems unjustified if we accept that the Later Guptas were passing through such difficult times. Moreover, the Later Guptas, if they were ruling in Mālava as suggested by Raychaudhuri, would be little concerned with the subjugation of the distant Kāma-rūpa (Assam), especially if the territory of a formidable enemy, the Maukharis, lay between the two kingdoms. We believe that Mahā-sena-gupta achieved success against Susthita-varman mainly because his kingdom lay close to Kāma-rūpa, and to the east of that of the Maukharis, so that he did not have to pass through the territory of one enemy before reaching that of the other.

Hsüan-tsang does not mention the name of Mādhava-gupta in connection with Magadha, probably because he is recording only the religious activities of the 'pious and heretical' kings of that region. The argument deduced from the Deo-Barnark inscription is far from conclusive because the mention of Śarva-varman and Avanti-varman after Bālāditya-rāja proves simply that Magadha was under Maukhari rule from the time of Śarva-varman onwards. Bāṇa's statement that Mādhava-gupta and Kumāra-gupta were sons of the King of Mālava only suggests that Mahā-sena-gupta was ruling over Mālava at the time he sent his sons to Prabhākara-vardhana's court.

The Aphsaḍ inscription throws further light on the abode of the Later Guptas. It eulogizes Jīvita-gupta, the third member of the Later Gupta dynasty, in the following terms: he was 'the very terrible scorching fever of fear, [who] left not [his] haughty foes even though they stood on sea-side shores . . . or even though they stood on that mountain [Himālaya]

[1] K. C. Chattopadhyaya, *D.R. Bhandarkar Comm. Vol.*, pp. 181 ff., argues that the passage in the Aphsaḍ inscription does not convey that the King died, but that he lost consciousness and later woke up. However, Fleet's translation indicates that Dāmodara-gupta died in battle. This view is generally accepted.

which is cold'. The reference seems to be to the people of Gauḍa, who were chastised by the Later Gupta king, probably in the name of the Imperial Guptas. The fourth Maukhari king, Īśāna-varman, also conducted a campaign against a people on the sea-coast whom he definitely states to be Gauḍas, and forced them to take shelter in the marshes of that region. Thus the clash of Jīvita-gupta with a ruler of Bengal suggests that his centre of power must have been close to that region.

The Aphsaḍ inscription also informs us that the next Later Gupta king, Kumāra-gupta, chastised the Maukhari king, Īśāna-varman. The plantain trees, masses of water, and rocks are once again alluded to in similes, which suggests that this battle too was fought in the neighbourhood of Gauḍa. The probability that the Later Guptas' centre of power was in this region is thus further strengthened.

While Gauḍa, the butt of Later Gupta and Maukhari attacks, comprised south-east Bengal, the ultimate aim of the aggressors was probably to gain control of north-west Bengal as well, which appears at this time to have been ruled by Dharm-āditya, the second member of a new dynasty founded by Gopa-chandra.[1] Both the Later Guptas and the Maukharis were intent upon uprooting this new power, for a hold over the important province of Bengal would have conclusively tipped the scales in favour of her possessor.

Dāmodara-gupta

Kumāra-gupta's son, Dāmodara-gupta, also fought the Maukharis, who may have been led either by Īśāna-varman or by one of his sons. This was probably a fierce battle, because both families were getting impatient to achieve a final victory. Dāmodara-gupta lost his life in the encounter, but the result of the battle does not seem to have been decisive.

Mahā-sena-gupta

Dāmodara-gupta was succeeded by Mahā-sena-gupta, who appears to have achieved noteworthy success at the beginning of his career. Probably to secure an initial advantage over the Maukharis, Mahā-sena-gupta associated himself with the rising Pushpa-bhūti dynasty by giving in marriage his sister, Mahā-sena-guptā, to Āditya-vardhana,[2] the grandfather of Harsha. The Maukharis must have felt uneasy, flanked on both sides by rivals allied to each other, a typical example of the policy of *maṇḍala*.

[1] *I.A.* xxxix. 193–216 and *E.I.* xviii. 74 ff. Six copperplate grants have preserved the names of three kings of this dynasty, viz.: Gopa-chandra, Dharm-āditya, and Samāchāra-deva. They all assumed the title *mahārāj-ādhirāja*, and their period may be fixed between A.D. 525 and 575.

[2] The similarity in names is the basis for this presumption. As the practice of naming sisters and brothers in this manner was common in those days, it is a fairly safe conclusion.

Noteworthy success attended Mahā-sena-gupta's next campaign against Kāma-rūpa. It was probably a spell of anarchy or weak rule in Bengal[1] in *c.* A.D. 575 which encouraged the ambitious king to engage in this war. The Aphsaḍ inscription records his victory in unambiguous terms. In contrast to the statements about his predecessors, who are said merely to have 'churned that formidable milk ocean, which was the army of the glorious Īśāna-varman' or 'broken up the proudly stepping array of mighty elephants belonging to the Maukhari', Mahā-sena-gupta is specifically stated to have acquired great fame 'marked with the honour of victory in war over Śrī Susthitavarman'.[2]

Attacks on Magadha and the exit of Mahā-sena-gupta

After this reputed success, however, Mahā-sena-gupta fell on evil days. It seems that one invader after another sought to conquer Magadha, and, with his natural enemies, the Maukharis, to take advantage of any adverse situation, the Later Gupta King was virtually obliged to flee to Mālava. The Chālukya king Kīrti-varman, who ruled from A.D. 567 to 597 and extended his territory in the south, is also stated to have subdued Aṅga, Vaṅga, Kaliṅga, and Magadha.[3] The conventional claim is no doubt an exaggeration, but his sweeping raids on territories adjacent to those of Mahā-sena-gupta must have served to raise the morale of the Maukharis and undermine that of the Later Guptas. Moreover, the chronicles of Tibet record that her powerful king Srong-bstan-sgam-po, who ruled between A.D. 581 and 600, led a victorious campaign into Central India,[4] which may be taken to mean Bihar or U.P. This raid may have further weakened the position of Mahā-sena-gupta, and his Maukhari adversary, Śarva-varman, finding a suitable opportunity to assert his power, may have won a victory over the Later Gupta. Though such a battle is not alluded to in any of the Maukhari inscriptions available to us, the Deo-Barnark inscription of Jīvita-gupta II, in referring to Śarva-varman and Avanti-varman as donors of the village of Vāruṇikā in Magadha, confirms the fact of Maukhari rule there from the reign of Śarva-varman onwards.[5]

It is probable that in Bengal Jaya-nāga came to power at this time. He appears to have been the predecessor of Śaśāṅka,[6] and his Vappa-ghosha-vāṭa grant[7] and coins may be ascribed approximately to this period.

[1] See below, p. 34.

[2] *C.I.I.* iii, no. 42. Because of the name-ending, Susthita-varman should not be mistaken for a Maukhari king. It was a common appellation for many *kshatriya* families.

[3] *I.A.* xix. 7 ff. The Mahā-kūṭa pillar inscription of Maṅgaleśa.

[4] S. Lévi, *Le Népal*, pp. 147 ff.

[5] Until the Later Gupta Āditya-sena replaced the Maukharis after the death of Harsha.

[6] See below, pp. 35–6.

[7] *E.I.* xviii. 60 ff.

The extent of Mahā-sena-gupta's Mālava

Thus pressed from all sides Mahā-sena-gupta retired to Mālava, but evidence shows that there too his power was questioned, now by a Kaḷachuri king. The Abhoṇā plates of Śaṅkara-gaṇa,[1] dated A.D. 595–6 (the year 347 of the Kaḷachuri era), are stated to have been issued from the victorious camp of Ujjain. Mahā-sena-gupta, whose headquarters must have been at Ujjain, since it was the capital city of Mālava, was now probably pushed eastwards in the direction of Vidiśā, where he spent the rest of his days until his death in *c.* A.D. 601.[2] In A.D. 608–9 the Kaḷachuris occupied Vidiśā also, as is evident from their Vadner grant dated 608.[3] In *c.* A.D. 616–17 the Maitrakas gained control of Ujjain.[4]

There has been much speculation as to what comprised the Mālava of Mahā-sena-gupta. On the basis of the commentator's note in Vātsyāyana's *Kāma-sūtra*,[5] dated at around the fifth century A.D., that Mālava without a prefix should be taken to denote Eastern Mālava, R. S. Tripathi[6] and D. C. Sircar[7] identify Bāṇa's Mālava with the modern district of Bhilsa. H. C. Raychaudhuri discusses the term *Sapta-Mālava*[8] and puts forward the suggestion that Mahā-sena-gupta probably held *Pūrva-Mālava* or east Mālava, parts of U.P., and at times Magadha as well.[9] B. C. Law holds a similar view.[10]

Bāṇa's testimony

It would be safe to assume that all the notices of Mālava by Bāṇa refer to the same region. The different contexts in which Mālava appears in the *Harsha-charita* and the *Kādambarī* afford some clues to its situation. The Lāṭas, Mālavas, and Gurjaras are mentioned together,[11] which suggests that geographically they were close to each other. As noticed by B. P. Sinha,[12] Bāṇa, in his description of Ujjayinī, refers to the lovely Mālavīs (the women of Mālava) who adorned that beautiful city.[13] The Mālava of the *Kādambarī* and the *Harsha-charita* being the same, Mahā-sena-gupta was the ruler of Ujjain among other cities. That Ujjain was

[1] The son of Kṛishṇa-rāja of the Sankheda grant of Santilla (*E.I.* ix. 296) and father of Buddha-rāja.

[2] Harsha became the King of Sthāṇv-īśvara in A.D. 606. Working backwards from this date and allowing five years for the various events that crowded the years before his accession (Rājya-śrī's wedding, Rājya-vardhana's campaign against the Hūṇas, Prabhākara-vardhana's illness and death, Rājya's return and war against Mālava), we get A.D. 601 as the date of the presentation of Kumāra-gupta and Mādhava-gupta at the court of Sthāṇv-īśvara. The same presumably was the date of the death of the princes' father Mahā-sena-gupta.

[3] *E.I.* xii. 30 ff.

[4] *P.T.O.C.* (Seventh), pp. 659 ff.

[5] *Adhikaraṇa*, iii.

[6] *History of Kanauj*, p. 46.

[7] *J.A.S.B.L.* xi (1945) 69 ff.

[8] *P.H.A.I.* (4th edn.), p. 492, n. 4.

[9] Op. cit., p. 512.

[10] *Tribes in Ancient India*, p. 64.

[11] *H.C.* text, p. 120; trans., p. 101.

[12] *Decline of the Kingdom of Magadha*, pp. 180–1.

[13] *Kādambarī*, trans., pp. 211 and 214.

the chief city of an extensive kingdom is shown by the account of Hsüan-tsang, according to whom the distance between Ujjain and the next Kingdom, Chih-chi-to, or Jājhotī, in Bundelkhand,[1] was above 1,000 *li*, i.e. about 167 miles.[2] The fact that the actual distance between the two cities is about double Hsüan-tsang's figure leads us to believe that the pilgrim probably reached his figure of 1,000 *li* by calculating the distance between the boundary of the province whose main city was Ujjain, i.e. Mālava, and Jājhotī. B. P. Sinha concludes from this that the eastern boundary of Mahā-sena-gupta's Mālava may have touched modern Eran, from where Jājhotī is approximately 167 miles.[3] The important city, Vidiśā, would also thus be included in Mahā-sena-gupta's Mālava. Ujjain, a Mālava town according to Bāṇa, fell into the hands of Kaḷachuris in A.D. 595–6, but Mahā-sena-gupta, who lived until *c.* A.D. 601, and whose sons went to the court of Sthāṇv-īśvara in that year, was still called the King of Mālava by Bāṇa in the *Harsha-charita*. We therefore reach the obvious conclusion that Mahā-sena-gupta continued to stay in one of the eastern cities of his kingdom, which was probably Vidiśā. As we have seen, Vidiśā was not occupied by the Kaḷachuris until A.D. 608–9, the date of their Vadner grant.

Hsüan-tsang's testimony

The Chinese pilgrim's account gives the description of a certain Mo-la-po ruled by a Valabhī king. Vincent Smith discussed the question of its location at great length and reached the conclusion that Mo-la-po was bounded on the north by the Gurjara kingdom of Bhinmal, on the north-west by Vad-nagar (A-nan-to-po-lo), on the east by the kingdom of Avanti, on the west by Valabhī, and on the south by the mouth of the

[1] Cunningham, *C.A.G.I.*, pp. 550 ff. Watters ii, p. 251 identifies it with Chitor on the basis of the distance recorded by Hsüan-tsang. But Chitor is situated to the north-west of the city of Ujjain, whereas the direction taken by the pilgrim from Ujjain to Chih-chi-to is stated to be north-east, both in the 'Records' (Beal ii, p. 271) and the 'Life' (p. 150). Moreover, the pilgrim describes the country 'as especially celebrated for the fertility of its soil'. He tells us that the land was regularly cultivated and yielded abundant crops, among which were wheat and pulses. Fruit and flowers grew in abundance, and the climate was temperate. This description definitely fits Bundelkhand better than it does Rajasthan. H. C. Ray (*D.H.N.I.*, vol. ii, pp. 669–70) brings to our notice a fragmentary inscription of the Chandellas (*E.I.* i. 221) which records that Jejā (Jaya-śakti) gave his name to Jejā-bhukti. As Jaya-śakti's date cannot be earlier than about the beginning of the ninth century, Cunningham's identification must be given up. We must not, however, forget that inscriptions always make grandiose claims for their kings, connecting their names with celebrated dynasties or celebrated towns. Jejā-bhukti, Jejākā-bhukti, or Jejā-bhuktikā may have existed for a long time before Jaya-śakti, whose advent added to the importance of that place. Also, as Cunningham observes (*C.A.G.I.*, pp. 552–3), there may be some connection between the facts that a brahman king ruled Chih-chi-to in Hsüan-tsang's day (Beal ii, p. 271), and that the Jajhotiya brahmans inhabit this region today, along with Chandella Rajputs.

[2] Beal ii, p. 271; also see Watters ii, p. 251.

[3] *Decline of the Kingdom of Magadha*, p. 186

Māhī river.[1] Despite the fact that Hsüan-tsang attributes to Mo-la-po a greater area than allowed by Smith, the latter's findings seem to be convincing. As observed by B. P. Sinha, the pilgrim when recording the area of Mo-la-po might have included in it the area of her vassal states as well.[2] Most scholars now associate the Mo-la-po of Hsüan-tsang with the Mālavaka-āhāra of the Valabhī inscriptions.[3] In this connection, the significance of two small notes inserted by Hsüan-tsang at the beginning of the descriptions of Mo-la-po and Fa-la-pi has been generally missed by scholars. The Chinese pilgrim observes that another name for Mo-la-po was South-lo, or South-lo-lo, and for Fa-la-pi (Valabhī) North-lo. King Śīlāditya of the Mo-la-po of Hsüan-tsang has been identified with the Valabhī king of that name who was the elder brother of Khara-graha I. On the basis of the former's Bhadreniyaka grant,[4] in which the two brothers are compared with Indra and Upendra, and in which, contrary to common practice, Śīlāditya's own son does not appear as *dūtaka*, it is rightly surmised that a clash occurred between the two brothers, and Śīlāditya had to concede a considerable portion of his domains to his brother Khara-graha.[5] The Valabhī kingdom was divided into north and south, Śīlāditya retaining Mo-la-po with its dependencies, and Khara-graha occupying the northern portions of the kingdom. These two divisions are apparently referred to as South-lo-lo and North-lo by Hsüan-tsang. Beal gives Lara as the Sanskrit equivalent of lo-lo, while Watters suggests Lāṭa, which seems to be a more probable identification.

Mādhava-gupta

Bāṇa's *Mālava-Rājaputra*, Kumāra-gupta, is not mentioned in the genealogical list of the Later Guptas, probably because he predeceased his younger brother Mādhava-gupta without having played a significant role in the annals of his family. Mādhava-gupta, however, is given his appropriate place in the Aphsaḍ inscription of Āditya-sena. This may be because Harsha invested him with the government of Magadha in the latter part of his reign.[6] The description in the Aphsaḍ inscription of Mādhava-gupta's career tries to offer an honourable explanation as to why he left Mālava to join the court of Sthāṇv-īśvara. It is said of him: 'When the slaughter of [his] foes had been achieved . . . [war?] was

[1] *Early History of India*, pp. 343–4.

[2] *The Decline of the Kingdom of Magadha*, p. 183.

[3] *C.A.G.I.*, p. 561; B. C. Law, *Tribes in Ancient India*, pp. 64–5.

[4] *E.I.* xxi. 116 ff.

[5] See J. Fleet, *C.I.I.* iii, no. 39.

[6] Neither Bāna nor Hsüan-tsang refers to it, but the fact that Mādhava-gupta's son Āditya-sena established his sovereignty over Magadha immediately after Harsha's death suggests the possibility that Mādhava-gupta was in some manner connected with Magadha during Harsha's reign. Also see below, pp. 66–7, 86–7.

averted by him; people did obeisance . . . "(*My*) mighty enemies have been slain by me in battle; there remains nothing more for me to do"—thus he, the hero, determined in his mind; (and then) with the desire to associate himself with the glorious Harshadeva . . .'[1]

Thus for nearly half a century the Later Guptas were eclipsed by Harsha's rise to power, until Āditya-sena revived the fortunes of his house in *c.* A.D. 650, by re-establishing his hold over Magadha.

The Maukharis

Origin of the name

The Maukharis were a very ancient tribe whose branches were spread over different parts of the country. Vāmana and Kaiyaṭa, the famous expositors of Pāṇini's system of grammar, writing in the medieval period,[2] explain the formation of certain words by citing the example *Maukharya.* They take the term to be a patronymic. Hirananda Sastri, however, thinks that an ancestor of the tribe was honoured by the adjective *Mukhara*, meaning leader, and his descendants came to be known Maukharis after him.[3] According to Bāṇa, too, *Mukhara* was the progenitor of Graha-varman's line.

Various records of them from the earliest times

The first inscriptional evidence of the existence of the Maukharis is a clay seal with the Prakrit legend *Mokhaliṇam* written in Mauryan Brahmi characters. The seal was secured by Cunningham at Gayā and proves that a Maukhari clan lived there as early as the third and fourth centuries B.C.[4] Three short inscriptions of the Maukharis discovered in the Kotah State by A. S. Altekar[5] yield the date 294 of the *kṛita* era which stands for the Mālava *saṁvat* and establishes that the Maukharis were well known in the middle of the third century A.D. Three more inscriptions of the Maukharis, of a line of three kings, Yajña-varman, Śārdūla-varman, and Ananta-varman, have been found in the Barābar and Nāgārjuni hill caves near Gayā.[6] According to Indraji, Bühler, Kielhorn, and N. G. Majumdar, they should be placed in the period after the Guptas and before Harsha. An enthusiastic biographer of the Maukharis, E. A. Pires, has, on the basis of some very obscure references in a literary work, the *Kaumudi Mahotsova,* tried to establish that before Magadha came under the Imperial Guptas it was ruled by the Maukharis. By a

[1] *C.I.I.* iii, no. 42.

[2] Keith, *History of Sanskrit Literature*, p. 429: 'Kaiyaṭa's commentary on the *Mahābhāṣya* . . . may belong to the twelfth century but . . . tradition places [it] earlier . . .' Vāmana composed his work before I-tsing visited India (A.D. 671–95).

[3] *E.I.* xiv. 111.

[4] *C.I.I.* iii, Introd., p. 14.

[5] *E.I.* xxiii. 42 ff.; xxiv. 251 ff.

[6] *C.I.I.* iii, nos. 48–50.

consensus of opinion the whole argument is quite unconvincing.[1] Yet another Maukhari name happens to be mentioned in Bāṇa's *Harsha-charita*, that of one Kshātra-varman,[2] but it is not possible to establish an identification. Pires has attempted to show that he was the same as the Maukhari king defeated by the early Kadamba ruler Mayūra-śarman of the Chandravallī inscription,[3] though the record in question does not contain any reference to Kshātra-varman. The inscription merely contains the word *Mokari*, with which it abruptly ends. This record does, however, prove, as remarked by B. A. Saletore,[4] that a Maukhari family lived in Karṇāṭaka in the neighbourhood of Puṇaṭa, the latter place name occurring immediately before Mokari in the Chandravallī inscription.

Another branch of the Maukharis, which rose to power in our period, is known from several seals and inscriptions. We obtain the following genealogy from the royal seals: The post-Gupta Maukharis

1. Mahārāja Hari-varman = Jaya-svāminī
2. Mahārāja Āditya-varman = Harsha-guptā
3. Mahārāja Īśvara-varman = Upa-guptā
4. Mahārāj-ādhirāja Īśāna-varman = Lakshmī-vatī
5. Mahārāj-ādhirāja Śarva-varman = Indra-bhaṭṭārikā
6. Mahārāj-ādhirāja Avanti-varman
7. Mahārāj-ādhirāja Graha-varman = Rājya-śrī[5]

Two more Maukhari names apparently belonging to the dynasty are on record. The Harāhā inscription of Īśāna-varman[6] mentions Sūrya-varman Maukhari, as another son of Īśāna-varman, and a Nālandā seal[7] discloses a clearly inscribed *Su*, followed probably by *va* or *cha*, as the first letter of the name of the son and successor of Avanti-varman.

The first three kings of the line are given the simple title *mahārāja*. Like their contemporaries, the Later Guptas, the Maukharis doubtless served as feudatories of the Imperial Guptas. The similarity between the names of the second Maukhari queen and the second Later Gupta

[1] Neither the date nor the historicity of the *Kaumudi Mahotsava* can be established with any certainty. It is indeed far-fetched to identify the Chaṇḍa-sena of the play with Chandra-Gupta I and its two other characters named Sundara-varman and Kalyāṇa-varman as Maukharis. Equally improbable is the identification of the Magadha-kula or Magadha dynasty of the play with the Kota family of the Allahabad pillar inscription of Samudra Gupta. The question is discussed at length by Jagan Nath, *Eastern and Indian Studies*, volume presented to F. W. Thomas, 1939, pp. 115 ff.

[2] *H.C.* text, p. 199; trans., p. 194.

[3] *Archaeological Survey of Mysore Annual Report* (1929), pp. 50 ff.

[4] *Indian and Iranian Studies*, volume presented to Sir E. Denison Ross, 1939, pp. 307 ff.

[5] See below, pp. 67–8.

[6] *E.I.* xiv. 110 ff.

[7] *E.I.* xxiv. 284–5.

king suggests that they were brother and sister, and that the two rising families, at this early stage of their history, were friendly enough to form a matrimonial alliance. The third king Īśvara-varman's Jaunpur inscription[1] refers to his conflict with the Āndhras, but this battle does not seem to have borne any significant result in favour of the Maukhari, as he did not introduce any change in his title. His son Īśāna-varman's career, however, was long and eventful. The Harāhā inscription records that Īśāna-varman defeated 'the Lord of the Āndhras' and the Śūlikas, and also 'caused the Gauḍas to remain within their proper realm'. The chastisement of the Gauḍas may have been Īśāna-varman's first military achievement, and it was probably this battle which brought him into conflict with the Later Gupta king Kumāra-gupta, whose domains were adjacent to Gauḍa and whose immediate predecessor had also attempted to subjugate this kingdom. Īśāna-varman was defeated by Kumāra-gupta, but he does not appear to have suffered any serious losses.[2] As is evident from his Harāhā inscription, he added considerably to the family's prestige if not to its possessions, and earned for himself the higher ranking title *mahārāj-ādhirāja*. The 'Lord of the Āndhras' defeated by Īśāna-varman, was probably King Mādhava-varman I of the Vishṇukuṇḍin dynasty.[3] The identity of the Śūlikas is more difficult to establish. They have been variously identified with the Mūlakas,[4] the Choḷas,[5] the neighbours of the Āndhras,[6] and the inhabitants of the south-east coast along Kaliṅga, Vidarbha, and Chedi.[7] H. C. Raychaudhuri's identification of the Śūlikas with the Chālūkyas seems to be the most probable.[8] *Śūlika* may be another dialectic variant of Chālukya, since in the Mahākūṭa pillar inscription their name appears as Chālikya, and in the Gujarat records we find the forms Solaki and Solaṅki.[9] Battles against these distant powers are, however, not likely to have added to the territory of the Maukharis.

Īśāna-varman

Sūrya-varman

Īśāna-varman's son Sūrya-varman, known to us from the Harāhā inscription, does not seem to have come to the throne and may have predeceased his father. His name is not mentioned in the Asirgarh[10] or Nālandā seals[11] of the family, which place Śarva-varman after Īśāna-varman. One Sūrya-varman is described in the Sirpur Stone inscription,[12] by his daughter's son Mahā-śiva-gupta, as 'born in the unblemished

[1] *C.I.I.* iii, no. 51.
[2] See above, pp. 17–18.
[3] *P.H.A.I.* (4th edn.), p. 509.
[4] T. G. Aravamuthan, *The Kaveri, the Maukharis and the Sangam Age*, p. 97.
[5] H. Heras, *J.A.H.R.S.* i. 130–3.
[6] S. K. Sastri, *J.A.H.R.S.* ii. 180.
[7] Hirananda Sastri, *E.I.* xiv. 110 ff.
[8] *P.H.A.I.*, p. 509.
[9] *Bom. Gaz.* i, pt. i, p. 156.
[10] *C.I.I.* iii, no. 47.
[11] *E.I.* xxi. 73 ff. and xxiv. 283 ff.
[12] *E.I.* xi. 184 ff.

family of the Varmans, great on account of their supremacy over Magadha'. The editor of the inscription ascribes the characters to the eighth or ninth century A.D., but a careful re-examination reveals their close similarity to those of the seventh-century records.[1] The Sūrya-varman of the Sirpur inscription may well be the same as the royal prince of the Harāhā inscription. The Māllār plates[2] of Mahā-siva-gupta were inscribed at the request of his maternal uncle, Bhāskara-varman, who apparently was the son of Sūrya-varman. His claim to the Maukhari throne seems to have been overridden by that of his cousin Avanti-varman, the son of Śarva-varman.

Śarva-varman

Īśāna-varman was succeeded by his son, mahārāj-ādhirāja Śrī Śarva-varman. He was the contemporary of the Later Gupta king, Mahā-sena-gupta. It appears that Mahā-sena-gupta's flight to Mālava, after the Tibetan and Chālukya raids on Magadha, cleared the way for Śarva-varman, who was thus neatly rid of a rival. Śarva-varman annexed Magadha to his hereditary kingdom, the capital of which was Kanauj, and firmly established Maukhari supremacy in the *Madhya-deśa.* The Deo-Barnark inscription and the Nālandā seal of Śarva-varman refer to him with full imperial titles. He also issued coins.

A seal of Śarva-varman has been found at Nimāḍ in Asirgarh, but it seems most unlikely that his authority extended as far as modern Burhanpur. The wars against the Āndhras and Śūlikas seem to have been defensive battles,[3] which did not increase the territory of the Maukharis. Moreover, Sūrya-varman, believed by us to be the elder brother of Śarva-varman, was connected with the royal house of Mahā-kośala.[4] If his and his son's claim to the throne of Kanauj was transgressed by Śarva-varman and his son Avanti-varman the relations between the two parties could not have been very friendly. Any addition to territory in the Nimāḍ district by the Maukharis of Kanauj therefore would have meant passing through the hilly region that lay between the two hostile kingdoms of Mahā-kośala and Mālava. Śarva-varman would not be inclined to take such a risk. Moreover Fleet informs us[5] that the seal was found at Asirgarh, which formerly belonged to Mahārāja Sindhia, in a box containing his property. This raises further doubts as to whether the seal was originally found at Asirgarh or was picked up by

[1] Cf. Fleet, *C.I.I.* iii, pp. 235 and 245; Pravara-sena's inscription was first assigned to the eighth century A.D. A correction was made later and the record was stated to belong to the fifth century A.D.

[2] *E.I.* xxiii. 113 ff.

[3] For the Āndhra king Mādhava-varman I of the Vishṇu-kuṇḍin dynasty himself appears to have taken the offensive. As noticed by Jouveau-Dubreuil, *Ancient History of the Deccan*, p. 92, he 'crossed the river Godāvarī with the desire to conquer the Eastern region'.

[4] *E.I.* xi. 184 ff.

[5] *C.I.I.* iii, p. 219.

the Mahārāja at some other place and added to his possessions. Fleet also states that the published accounts do not make it clear whether the original seal was found or only the impression of it. That seals are easily portable should also be taken into account. Śarva-varman's kingdom may have stretched to the northern fringes of the Vindhyas, whence this seal may have travelled to Nimāḍ. His territory may even have extended to Bundelkhand, for the Barāhā copperplate of Bhoja-deva dated A.D. 835–6[1] records that a Parameśvara Śarva-varmmadeva granted some land in the Udumbara *vishaya* of Kālinjara-maṇḍala. The proposed identifications of the Śarvva-varmma-deva of this inscription with Māra-Śarva[2] and *Mahārāja* Śarvva respectively by Hiranand Sastri[3] and Bhandarkar[4] do not appear convincing. We agree with B. P. Sinha, who has discussed the problem in detail,[5] that the Parameśvara Śarva-varmmadeva of the Barāhā inscription is the same as the Maukhari king of that name and title in the Deo-Barnark inscription.

Yet another inscription found outside U.P. mentions the name 'Śarva-varman'. The Nirmaṇḍ record of *Mahārāja* Samudra-sena, inscribed in seventh-century characters, states that he renewed some grants which had previously been made by '*Mahārāja* Śarvavarman'.[6] Nirmaṇḍ is north of Sthāṇv-īśvara, in the Kangra district of the Panjab. If the Maukhari adversary of Dāmodara-gupta who is credited with having given battle to the Hūṇas[7] is the same as Śarva-varman, the extension, even if briefly, of Maukhari influence in the Panjab and the identification of the Śarva-varman of the Nirmaṇḍ inscription with the Maukhari king of that name appear feasible. In fact no other power but the Maukharis, and among them Śarva-varman, appears to fit in with the circumstances. The Vardhanas were not very strong at this stage, and Āditya-vardhana could not have chastised the Hūṇas with his limited resources. The task of curbing this menace was therefore left to the Maukharis, whose power was in ascendancy at this time. Āditya-vardhana, as a lesser king, may have willingly allowed Śarva-varman to pass through his territory to repel the Hūṇas, who were in fact a greater danger to his own small kingdom than to the Maukharis of the Gangetic *doab*. He may even have assisted Śarva-varman in the task. The Maukharis, on their part, do not seem to have used the occasion to humiliate the Vardhanas, because none

[1] *E.I.* xix. 15 ff.
[2] *E.I.* vi. 250.
[3] *E.I.* xix. 15 ff.
[4] *E.I.* xviii. 235 ff.
[5] *Decline of the Kingdom of Magadha*, pp. 199–200.
[6] *C.I.I.* iii, no. 80.
[7] The *Harsha-charita*, too, testifies to the disturbing activities of the Hūṇas at this time.

of their inscriptions which narrate the other achievements of Śarva-varman allude even to a nominal lordship over the Vardhanas. Perhaps the matrimonial alliance with the Later Guptas had placed the Vardhanas in a bargaining position with the Maukharis, who did not wish to lose their goodwill. Moreover, it was prudent to maintain friendship with the frontier kingdom which could act as a buffer between the Hūṇas and themselves.

Avanti-varman

Śarva-varman was succeeded on the throne by his son Avanti-varman. Their relationship has now been definitely established on the basis of the Nālandā seal of the latter.[1] Avanti-varman inherited the extensive domain of his father and enjoyed full imperial titles.[2] His coins are more numerous than those of his predecessors.[3] The readings of the dates on all the Maukhari coins are, however, very doubtful, and it will not be safe to depend on them for fixing the chronology of the Maukharis.

Avanti-varman appears to have been an unambitious ruler and had an uneventful reign, but a peaceful career did not in any way lessen the prestige of his royal house, at least in his lifetime. References to the family of Graha-varman (Avanti-varman's son) in the *Harsha-charita* show that the Maukharis were held in high esteem even by Prabhākara-vardhana, who had considerably increased his power and enhanced the status of his dynasty during the peaceful reign of his contemporary, Avanti-varman. In Bāṇa's words, Prabhākara-vardhana, suggesting Graha-varman as a suitable match for their daughter, said to his queen, 'Now at the head of all royal houses stand the Mukharas, worshipped like Śiva's foot-print, by all the world'.[4] In the *Kādambarī*, Bāṇa represents his *guru* Bhatsu or Bharva as being 'honoured by crowned Maukharis'.[5] Avanti-varman may have died in *c.* A.D. 600.

The probable dates of Īśāna-, Śarva-, and Avanti-varman

R. C. Majumdar[6] fixes the following dates for the reigns of Īśāna-varman, Śarva-varman, and Avanti-varman on the basis of Dikshit's reading of the coins:

Īśāna-varman	*c.* A.D. 550–76
Śarva-varman	*c.* A.D. 576–80
Avanti-varman	*c.* A.D. 580–600.

As we have noted earlier, the dates on all the Maukhari coins are very indistinct. Dikshit's interpretation of the figures allots very little time

[1] *E.I.* xxiv. 283 ff.
[2] Ibid. and *C.I.I.* iii, no. 46.
[3] *J.R.A.S.* (1906), pt. ii, p. 843.
[4] *H.C.* text, p. 141; trans., p. 122.
[5] *Kādambari*, trans., p. 1.
[6] *H.C.I.P.* iii, p. 70.

to the busy and eventful reign of Śarva-varman. For reasons summarized below we would rather suggest the following probable dates:

Īśāna-varman	*c.* A.D. 550 to 560–5
Śarva-varman	*c.* A.D. 560–5 to 585
Avanti-varman	*c.* A.D. 585 to 600.

Īśāna-varman's Harāhā inscription[1] is dated A.D. 554. His victories referred to in this record probably took place before he was defeated by Kumāra-gupta, because the Aphsaḍ inscription of the Later Guptas describes him as the 'glorious Īśāna-varman, a very moon among kings'.[2] That the battle between these two kings took place after A.D. 554 is also suggested by the absence of even a remote allusion to this event in the Maukhari record.

Śarva-varman, who definitely extended the Maukhari dominion, perhaps in three directions,[3] must have enjoyed a long reign. His several coins, his Asirgarh seal, and references to him in the records of other kings all point to an eventful and long career. Twenty to twenty-five years therefore appears to be the reasonable duration of his reign.

Avanti-varman, who might have succeeded to the throne in his middle age and who was the contemporary of Prabhākara-vardhana and Mahāsena-gupta, may be allowed a comparatively short reign of approximately fifteen years. We believe that his rule ended in *c.* A.D. 600, since, as recorded by Bāṇa, his eldest son Graha-varman himself sought the hand of Rājya-śrī in marriage around A.D. 603–4.[4] Avanti-varman, had he been alive, would certainly have figured prominently in Bāṇa's long description of the wedding.

Graha-varman and his brother Suva

His son Graha-varman succeeded Avanti-varman, at least to the throne of Kanauj. Until the time of his death, Magadha as well as Kanauj seems to have been ruled by one and the same Maukhari king, Avanti-varman, whose seal has been found at Nālandā, but some changes seem to have taken place on his death. Another Maukhari seal also found at Nālandā gives the title and name 'Para . . . rājā [dhi] rāja Śrī Suva [or Suca]' for a son of 'Paramamāheśvara [Mahārā] jādhirāja Avantivarman Maukhari'.[5] Since Graha-varman is described as the eldest son of Avanti-varman in other available records, Suva (or Sucha) must have been one of his younger sons. After Avanti-varman's death the throne of Kanauj passed on to the rightful heir, for, as Bāṇa tells us, it was at

[1] *E.I.* xiv. 110 ff.
[2] *C.I.I.* iii, no. 42.
[3] See above, pp. 27–8.
[4] See below, p. 68.
[5] *E.I.* xxiv. 283 ff.

Kanauj that Graha-varman met his untimely death, leaving his widow as a captive in the enemies' hands.

The changes that took place on Avanti-varman's death do not appear to have come about by a friendly settlement between the brothers, Graha-varman and 'Suva'. It seems to us that the latter was a rebel, for had that not been the case 'Suva', who may be the Suvrata of the *Ārya Mañju-śrī-mūla-kalpa*,[1] would have had his inscription so phrased as to include the name of his elder brother. It is probable that 'Suva' had been appointed the governor of Magadha by his father, on whose death he declared his independence. The division of the ancestral domains at this juncture was fatal for the Maukharis, because the new dynasties that had fed themselves on the remains of the Imperial Guptas had by now achieved strength and stability in their respective territories in different parts of north India and the time was once again ripe for a strong and capable man to establish his paramountcy.

'Suva' seems to have predeceased his brother Graha-varman, since the Nālandā seal is the only record we have of him. Apparently he had a very brief career. It seems that his kingdom of Magadha never again formed part of the Maukhari territories. A seal-matrix of Mahā-sāmanta Śaśāṅka, discovered cut in the rock of the hill-fort of Rohtas-garh,[2] testifies to his hold over Magadha even before he assumed independent status in Gauḍa. That he had attained that status before A.D. 605–6, the date of Prabhākara-vardhana's death, is evident from Bāṇa's account.

As we shall see later, in western India the King of Mālava, probably a scion of the Later Gupta dynasty, was nurturing the ambition to revive his family fortunes.

The Mālava and Gauḍa axis against Kanauj

Soon after the marriage of Rājya-śrī to Graha-varman, the old king Prabhākara-vardhana sent his son Rājya-vardhana, accompanied by Harsha, to chastise the Hūṇas. It was probably at this time that the Kings of Mālava and Gauḍa formed an alliance, their aim being to attack in turn the kingdoms of Kanauj and Sthāṇv-īśvara, which lay sandwiched between their own, with their combined forces.[3] Apparently their ambition was to share the hegemony of northern India. Prabhākara-vardhana's illness and death provided the opportune moment for striking the blow, and we learn from the *Harsha-charita* that, while the two brothers, Rājya-vardhana and Harsha, each argued about abandoning the throne in favour of the other, the news was brought that 'his majesty Graha-varman was by the wicked lord of Mālwa cut off from the living along

[1] Mañju-śrī-mūla-kalpa, trans., pp. 57 ff.

[2] *C.I.I.* iii, no. 78.

[3] *H.C.* text, pp. 183 and 186; trans., pp. 173 and 178.

with his noble deeds. Rājya-śrī also ... has been confined like a brigand's wife with a pair of iron fetters ... and cast into prison at Kānyakubja'. 'There is, moreover a report', added the messenger, 'that the villain, ... purposes to invade and seize this country as well.'[1] Thus the short career of the last of the independent Maukharis ended in tragedy.[2]

The defeat of Kanauj and the involvement of the Vardhanas

Rājya-vardhana at once set out to punish the King of Mālava. His troops, it is said, routed the enemy 'with ridiculous ease',[3] but his own career was cut short by death at the hands of Śaśāṅka, the ally of the King of Mālava. Śaśāṅka had the makings of a paramount king, but Harsha and his counsellors handled the situation in a masterly manner. Harsha's possession of Kanauj and the alliance with Kāma-rūpa obliged Śaśāṅka to confine himself to the territories he had already occupied before Harsha came on the scene.

Bengal and Śaśāṅka

Vaṅga, Sama-taṭa and Gauḍa

The kingdom of Gopa-chandra, Dharm-āditya, and Samāchāra-deva,[4] which loosely comprised south-east Bengal, may be called Vaṅga, though the old name Sama-taṭa for eastern Bengal was also in use in our period, as may be seen from Hsüan-tsang's records.[5] North-west Bengal came to be designated Gauḍa around this time[6] and gained importance with the rise of Śaśāṅka. The Gauḍa people, however, appear also to have inhabited south Bengal, which may in fact have been the centre from which they spread outwards. Both the Later Gupta and the Maukhari inscriptions issued earlier in the century allude to the close proximity of the Gauḍas to the sea.

Śaśāṅka not related to the Gupta families

Śaśāṅka of Gauḍa started his career in Magadha as a *mahā-sāmanta* or feudatory chief, as his seal-matrix cut in a rock of the hill-fort of Rohtasgarh in south-west Bihar refers to him by this title.[7] Some scholars, on the grounds of certain similarities between the coins of the Imperial Guptas and those of Śaśāṅka, as well as on the basis that the variant Narendra-gupta is used for Śaśāṅka in one manuscript of the *Harsha-charita*,[8] have tried to establish his relationship either with the Imperial

[1] *H.C.* text, p. 183; trans., p. 173.

[2] Hsüan-tsang (Beal ii, pp. 118 and 174) refers to a king Pūrṇa-varman of Magadha. Pūrṇa-varman may have been a scion of the Maukhari line. It appears that he was a feudatory of Harsha, who may have bestowed on him the governorship of Magadha which had at one time formed part of the Maukhari domains.

[3] *H.C.* text, p. 186; trans., p. 178.

[4] Known through the Faridpur copperplates: *I.A.* xxxix. 193 ff.; for numismatic record see *B.M.C.*, p. cvi ff.

[5] Beal ii, p. 199; Watters ii, pp. 187 ff.

[6] The first clear epigraphic mention of the Gauḍas is made in the Harāhā inscription of Īśāna-varman (*E.I.* xiv. 110 ff.).

[7] *C.I.I.* iii, no. 78.

[8] Bühler, *E.I.* i. 70.

Gupta or with the Later Gupta dynasty.[1] Both contentions are inadequately supported. Śaśāṅka's coins, in fact, as suggested by J. Allan, are more closely related to those of 'Jaya' or Jaya-nāga, another King of Gauḍa.[2] As for the common name-ending 'Gupta', it is an argument of little value without other corroborative evidence.

Mahā-sāmanta Śaśāṅka's overlord

The question of the identification of the overlord of whom Śaśāṅka was the *mahā-sāmanta* also bristles with difficulties. Scholars have put forward divergent views. According to K. L. Barua[3] and R. C. Majumdar,[4] Śaśāṅka began his career as a feudatory of Mahā-sena-gupta. We believe however that, harassed by numerous enemies, Mahā-sena-gupta was forced to abandon Magadha some time in the period *c.* A.D. 586–90. Thence the region came under the suzerainty of Avanti-varman Maukhari. A seal of his son 'Suva' has been found at Nālandā in Magadha. As it ascribes full imperial titles to 'Suva' it must have been issued after Avanti-varman's death in *c.* A.D. 600. Until then 'Suva' may have been acting as the governor of Magadha, appointed by his father. As the beginning of Śaśāṅka's career may be reasonably placed around A.D. 600, he must have been a feudatory of the Maukharis, not of the Later Guptas.

Nor could Śaśāṅka have been a feudatory chief of Jaya-nāga as suggested by B. P. Sinha.[5] There were no doubt many connecting links between the two: both were associated with Karṇa-suvarṇa, as Hsüan-tsang informs us with regard to the former, and the Vappa-ghosha-vāṭa grant testifies in the case of the latter. Their coins too bear certain similarities. We believe that Śaśāṅka succeeded to Jaya-nāga's possessions in Bengal. But there is no reliable evidence[6] of Jaya-nāga's hold over Magadha at this time at the cost of the more powerful and older-established Maukharis. Śaśāṅka is therefore not likely to have been a feudatory of Jaya-nāga.

According to B. C. Sen, 'Śaśāṅka began his career as a *Mahāsāmanta* in Magadha . . . probably held under Avantivarman. . . . in this capacity (he) may have exercised some sort of control over the Varmans of Gayā.' After the defeat of Avantivarman by the Cālukyas, he made himself 'master of Magadha', '. . . (and) swooped down upon Puṇḍravardhana

[1] R. D. Banerji, *History of Orissa*, i, p. 129, 'he belonged to the Gupta dynasty of Magadha'; and Vidyavinoda, *Kāmarūpa Śāsanāvali*, Introd., p. 85, 'he was the son of Mahāsenagupta'.

[2] *B.M.C.*, p. cv.

[3] *Early History of Kamarupa*, pp. 58–9.

[4] *History of Bengal*, p. 56.

[5] *Decline of the Kingdom of Magadha*, pp. 222 ff.

[6] The discovery of a solitary coin-mould of 'Jaya' at Nālandā (*A.S.I.A.R.* (1935–6, p. 52) is very flimsy evidence to prove Jaya's hold over Magadha. No argument may be safely built on the basis of such easily portable remains unless supported by other corroborative evidence.

immediately after the death of Mahāsenagupta.'[1] D. C. Ganguly expresses the view that Śaśāṅka was a high feudatory of Magadha under the Maukhari kings Avantivarman and Grahavarman, and later on he conquered Magadha and invaded Gauḍa, and therefore he was a native of Magadha and a successful conqueror of Gauḍa.[2]

We agree with these scholars inasmuch as they place Śaśāṅka's feudal career in the reign of Avanti-varman Maukhari, and ascribe to him first the conquest of Magadha and then that of Gauḍa, but, as our earlier account of the Later Guptas and the Maukharis would indicate, we totally differ from them with regard to the circumstances under which Śaśāṅka's power began and spread. Nor do we share Ganguli's view that Śaśāṅka was a native of Magadha. In contemporary sources, the *Harsha-charita* and the 'Records', as well as in the *Mañju-śrī-mūla-kalpa*, he is invariably described as a Gauḍa or the King of Gauḍa. Had his connections with Magadha been of any significance, and certainly if they had lasted until the end of his career as held by some scholars,[3] the fact would have been mentioned in Śaśāṅka's own records or in other accounts of the period, for Magadha was historically the seat of paramount kings and the symbol of supremacy. Harsha, for instance, though more famous as the King of Kanauj, is mentioned as the King of Magadha in the Chinese official records.

Śaśāṅka—a Gauḍa or a Māgadha

Śaśāṅka's predecessors in Vaṅga and Gauḍa

It will be well to discuss here briefly the chronology of the Bengal rulers from Gopa-chandra to Śaśāṅka. This may be ascertained mainly on the basis of the numismatic and epigraphic evidence left by them. By a general consensus of opinion Gopa-chandra's rise to power may be placed in *c.* A.D. 525, when the Imperial Guptas were on the decline. Next in line was probably Dharm-āditya, who was followed by Samāchāra-deva. The latter's rule lasted until *c.* A.D. 575. That 'Jaya' and Śaśāṅka, apparently unrelated to each other or to the aforementioned three Bengal kings, were nevertheless the next two Gauḍa rulers in that order, may be ascertained by a comparative examination of the coins of Samāchāra-deva, also known as Narendr-āditya, and of 'Jaya' and Śaśāṅka.

The coinage of Samāchāra-deva

An archer-type coin, probably of Samāchāra-deva, has a bull standard on the obverse and is described as follows: Archer type, weight 148·2 grains, obverse, the King standing on left, holding bow in left hand and arrow in the right. Bull (Nandī) on left, beneath left arm 'Shaha (?) cha', no trace of marginal legend; reverse, Goddess (Lakṣmī), nimbate,

[1] *Some Historical Aspects of the Inscriptions of Bengal*, p. 261.
[2] *I.H.Q.* xii. 456 ff.
[3] See below, p. 42.

seated facing on lotus, holding lotus in left hand and fillet in outstretched right hand, with the legend, apparantly, *Śrī Narendra.*[1]

The coins of 'Jaya'

With this we may compare the coins, found in Bengal, of 'Jaya', who may be identified with the Mahārāj-ādhirāja Jaya-nāga of the Vappa-ghosha-vāṭa grant issued from Karṇa-suvarṇa. 'Jaya's' coins are described thus: 'Archer type, on the obverse, King, nimbate, standing left, holding bow in left hand and arrow in the right. *Cakra* standard on left. Beneath left arm (*Jaya*). No trace of marginal legend. On the reverse—Goddess (Lakṣmī), nimbate, seated facing on lotus, holding lotus in left and fillet in outstretched right hand; above, on left, an elephant sprinkling her [and the legend] (*Śrī-Prakāṇḍayasāh*?).'[2] The design of an elephant, or possibly two elephants, sprinkling water on the goddess Lakshmī is also faintly visible on the seal of the Vappa-ghosha-vāṭa grant of Jaya-nāga.

Śaśāṅka's coins

Śaśāṅka's coins are described as follows: 'Obverse, Śiva, nimbate, reclining to left on bull (Nandī) to left, with left hand uplifted, holding uncertain object; moon (*śaśāṅka*) above on left. On right (*Sri-sa*), below (*jaya*); reverse Goddess (Lakṣmī), nimbate, seated facing on lotus, holding lotus in left hand which rests on knee, and with outstretched right hand empty; above, on either side elephant sprinkling water over her (*abhiṣeka*). No symbol. On right *Śrī śaśāṅkaḥ*.'[3]

The only difference between the coins of Samāchāra-deva Narendrāditya and 'Jaya' Prakāṇḍa-yaśaḥ is that the former has the sign of the Nandī on his coins, while the latter has a Chakra standard. The coins of Samāchāra-deva are believed to be earlier than those of 'Jaya'.

The reverses of the coins of Jaya and Śaśāṅka are very similar, but on the obverse Śaśāṅka's coins are invariably characterized by the signs of the bull and the moon, the symbols used also by Bāṇa whenever he metaphorically refers to Śaśāṅka in the *Harsha-charita.*[4]

The order of succession of Jaya and Śaśāṅka

Allan reached the conclusion that the coins which have 'Narendrāditya' on the reverse were earlier than those of Śaśāṅka.[5] We believe that coins with 'Jaya' and 'Prakāṇḍa-yaśaḥ' inscribed on them too predate those with the legend *śrī-śa* (apparently for Śaśāṅka) with *jaya* beneath it. How else indeed is *jaya* on Śaśāṅka's coins to be interpreted, especially in view of the fact that similarities between their currencies strongly suggest some connection between Jaya-nāga and Śaśāṅka, as

[1] See V. A. Smith, *Catalogue of Coins at the Indian Museum, Calcutta*, i, pp. 120 and 122, illustration Pl. XVI, nos. 11 and 13. Also see N. K. Bhattasali in the *J.A.S.B.* (N.S.) xxxvii, Num. suppl. 239, who identifies them as the coins of Samāchāra-deva.

[2] *B.M.C.*, p. 150.

[3] Op. cit., p. 147.

[4] e.g. *H.C.* text, pp. 178, 258; trans., pp. 168, 260.

[5] *B.M.C.*, Introd., sections 67–9, Pl. XXIV.

held by Allan?[1] It seems to us that, having acquired Jaya's legacy rather through a show of strength than by succession, Śaśāṅka reinforced his claims by recounting on his early coins any friendly connection he might have had with his predecessor. However, as some scholars[2] contend that Jaya-nāga followed Śaśāṅka, the question perhaps needs a more detailed examination. The basis of their contention is the order of certain verses in the *Mañju-śrī-mūla-kalpa*. The earlier contain the description of Śaśāṅka's career, the later refers to the rule of one Nāga-rāja over Gauḍa.[3] The order in which they are mentioned may reasonably be taken to indicate the sequence of the reigns of Śaśāṅka and Nāga-rāja. But it is erroneous to equate Nāga-rāja of the second verse with Jaya-nāga. As noted by the commentator K. P. Jayaswal the section should be taken to refer to the rule of the Nāgas under the Bhāra-śivas.[4] In fact the *Mañju-śrī-mūla-kalpa*, in its typical style disguising real characters by the use of synonyms, corroborates numismatic evidence a few verses later, by stating: 'Jaya the serpent (Jayanāga) conquered the people of the South-East. Kesarī (Lion) and another named Soma (Śaśāṅka) became kings. (This) led to the division of the Gauḍa nation . . .'[5] Clearly the veiled allusions are to the historical Jaya-nāga Śaśāṅka. Bhattasali also advanced the argument that as Jaya's coins are more debased than those of Śaśāṅka, their average weights being respectively 136 grains and 145·8 grains, and as debasement of coins generally indicates a later date, Jaya must have followed Śaśāṅka. Needless to say, this criterion applies to a dynasty on the decline and not in the reverse case.

It seems reasonable to assume that Harsha, whose power progressively increased during his period of rule, would not allow another Gauḍa to assume power, let alone rule in strength for any length of time, once Śaśāṅka was out of the way. Jaya-nāga we know had a fairly long reign, during which he was able to issue coins and inscriptions. The *Mañju-śrī-mūla-kalpa* appears to portray the state of affairs correctly when it describes Gauḍa as weak and divided after Śaśāṅka. There is strong epigraphic evidence to show that, after Śaśāṅka, Harsha's overlordship was acknowledged by the lesser kings of north and central Orissa. Probably Harsha had waited for the fulfilment of his ambition to annex parts of Orissa until the redoubtable Śaśāṅka was dead.

[1] *B.M.C.* p. cv.

[2] R. C. Majumdar, *History of Bengal*, i, p. 79; R. N. Saletore, *Life in the Gupta Age*, p. 71; N. K. Bhattasali, *J.A.S.B.* (N.S.) xii, Num. suppl., 6 ff.

[3] *Mañju-śrī-mūla-kalpa*, Ch. 53, sections 33–7, verses 715–50. In translation as *An Imperial History of India*, pp. 53–5.

[4] Op. cit., trans. and commentary, pp. 47 and 52.

[5] Op. cit., p. 66.

The career of Jaya-nāga

Jaya-nāga's chronological position having been established, we may briefly relate the facts about his sparsely documented career. He may have begun it by conquering south-east Bengal or south and east Bengal as stated in the *Mañju-śrī-mūla-kalpa*. South-east Bengal was the home of the Gauḍas, at least earlier in the century, as we have noted before. It is through his conquest of south Bengal that Jaya-nāga succeeded to the kingdom of Samāchāra-deva. His eastern adversaries may have been the kings whose gold coins have been found scattered in that region. Two whose names can be read with certainty are Pṛithu-vīra and Sudhany-āditya.[1] His Vappa-ghosha-vāṭa grant, which styles him as *mahārāj-ādhirāja*, establishes, from its provenance, Jaya-nāga's hold over Karṇa-suvarṇa.

The Gauḍa victor of the Doobi plates

There is also evidence to suggest that Jaya-nāga extended his influence into Kāma-rūpa. The Doobi plates record the heroism of two young Kāma-rūpa princes, Su-pratishṭhita-varman and Bhāskara-varman, in a battle against the Gauḍas, who attacked their country soon after the death of their father Susthita-varman.[2] According to P. D. Chaudhuri, who first published the record, the text of the fifth plate implies that the brothers succeeded in repulsing the Gauḍa army, but since then D. C. Sircar has rightly interpreted it to mean that 'Supratishṭhita and Bhāskara, in spite of their resistance, were captured by the enemy and carried to Gauḍa. Later, because of their fine qualities, the brothers were restored to their kingdom.'[3]

R. C. Majumdar[4] and P. C. Chaudhuri[5] hold the view that the Gauḍa army of the Doobi inscription was led by Mahā-sena-gupta, '(who) was regarded as king of Gauḍa rather than that of Mālava'. According to B. P. Sinha the reference is to an invasion of Kāma-rūpa by Śaśāṅka '(who) would naturally have tried to emulate his distinguished predecessor Mahāsenagupta in attempting to make his weight felt in Kāmarūpa'.[6] We demonstrate below by a process of elimination that the Gauḍa exploit of the Doobi grant should be attributed to Jaya-nāga, who ruled Bengal in the period between the reigns of the two above-mentioned kings.

Earlier we have shown that Mahā-sena-gupta was preoccupied with external enemies during the latter part of his rule over Magadha. He is not likely to have engaged in offensive campaigns at that time. In any

[1] *B.M.C.*, no. 620, and *Numismatic Chronicle* (1934), p. 235. Also see S. K. Chakrabortty, *Transactions of the International Numismatic Congress* (1936), p. 405.

[2] *J.A.R.S.* xii, nos. 1–2, 16 ff.

[3] *I.H.Q.* xxvi. 241 ff.

[4] *H.C.I.P.* iii, pp. 76 and 92.

[5] Ph.D. thesis, London University, 1953, pp. 266 ff.

[6] *The Decline of the Kingdom of Magadha*, p. 243.

case had he been responsible for this achievement it would certainly have been related in the Aphsaḍ inscription, which commemorates in glowing terms his victory over Susthita-varman. Moreover the Doobi plates specify the invaders as Gauḍas. Majumdar's reasoning that Mahā-sena-gupta must have been regarded as a Gauḍa because Śaśāṅka, the inheritor of his territories in Magadha and Bengal, was also described as a Gauḍa is indeed weak. A King of both Magadha and Gauḍa would doubtless emphasize, and be better known, for his possession of the former, and those vanquished by him would sooner acknowledge defeat at the hands of a Magadhan potentate than by a Gauḍa.[1]

B. P. Sinha's view that it was Śaśāṅka who invaded Kāma-rūpa also appears untenable. The raid referred to in the Doobi grant took place much earlier than Śaśāṅka's hold over Bengal, which we may safely presume, was necessary for invading Assam. The text of the fifth plate shows that the battle took place soon after the death of Susthita-varman which we place between A.D. 590 and 595. We have earlier tried to show that Mahā-sena-gupta's rule in Magadha was over by that date. The province came under Maukhari supremacy and Śaśāṅka governed the modern Rohtasgarh district as a feudatory of the latter. His independent career did not begin until after the death of his overlord 'Suva' some time after A.D. 600, when Śaśāṅka overran Magadha, taking possession of Gauḍa after Jaya-nāga's death. His invasion of Kāma-rūpa thus could not have taken place before *c.* A.D. 604–5, while the battle recorded in the Doobi inscription must have occurred just before the beginning of the seventh century when Jaya-nāga was in power in Bengal.

Moreover, if Śaśāṅka had won an early victory over Bhāskara-varman, the event would almost certainly have been alluded to by Bāṇa. The *Mañju-śrī-mūla-kalpa* also, although it speaks of Śaśāṅka's extension of power as far as Banaras, contains no mention of any incursions by him into Kāma-rūpa.

Jaya-nāga satisfactorily fulfils the requirements implicated in the Doobi record. Master of the Gauḍas towards the end of the sixth century, he quickly seized the opportunity to extend his power after the death of the King of Kāma-rūpa. Luck favoured him and he succeeded in capturing the heirs to the throne. They were, however, soon reinstated in their possessions, most probably because with his limited resources Jaya-nāga could do no more than maintain a very loose hold over a kingdom of Kāma-rūpa's size and importance.

[1] Note references to the Maukharis, 'great because of their supremacy over Magadha', Sirpur Stone inscription (*E.I.* xi. 184 ff.).

The emergence of Śaśāṅka as an independent ruler

Jaya-nāga does not appear to have survived this event very long. His death may have occurred in *c.* A.D. 602–3, because by the date of Harsha's accession to the throne, A.D. 606, Śaśāṅka was already well established in Gauḍa. The *Mañju-śrī-mūla-kalpa* describes his career before that of Rājya-vardhana, the elder brother of Harsha who died before being formally proclaimed King. Actually within these few years, following his Maukhari overlord's death, Śaśāṅka appears to have launched himself on an independent career, sacking in the wake of his exploits in Magadha the Buddhist monasteries in that province. Alternatively, his anti-Buddhist deeds could be ascribed to a slightly later date, when he was heading for an invasion of Kanauj to join his Mālava ally; at any rate they had been committed prior to Harsha's accession, for, according to the divine counsel of the Bodhi-sattva Avalokiteśvara, Harsha was to accept the throne, in order to put right the wrong done by Śaśāṅka to the Law of the Buddha. Hsüan-tsang makes several references to Buddhist persecution by Śaśāṅka, thus recording one of the rare examples of religious intolerance in ancient India.

We resume the account of Śaśāṅka's rise to power. Having overrun the greater part of Magadha, taking in his sweep Banaras, Kuśi-nagara, Gayā, and Pāṭali-putra,[1] Śaśāṅka turned towards Gauḍa, which appears to have been an easy prize on account of Jaya-nāga's timely removal from the scene. Śaśāṅka was now definitely a power to be reckoned with. Bāṇa in his typical metaphorical style refers to this imminent danger in his description of the night approaching, while the two brothers Rājya-vardhana and Harsha were still mourning the death of their father. 'In the firmament', writes Bāṇa, alluding to the Śaiva adversary whose name was a synonym of moon, and in the process creating one of his remarkable word images, 'the rising clear-flecked moon shone like the pointed hump of Śiva's tame bull, when blotted with mud scattered by his broad horns.'[2] The *Mañju-śrī-mūla-kalpa* too declares Rājya-vardhana to be 'as powerful as Soma [Śaśāṅka]'.[3] Recorded in a Buddhist work the comparison may safely be taken to indicate that the former was the weaker of the two, for Śaśāṅka's bias against Buddhism was well known.

It seemed as if the Vardhana house was faced with a dismal future after the death of Prabhākara-vardhana. Their father dead, the princes

[1] *Mañju-śrī-mūla-kalpa*, verse 715; and Beal ii, pp. 42, 91, and 118.
[2] *H.C.* text, p. 178; trans., p. 168.
[3] *Mañju-śrī-mūla-kalpa*, verse 720. To create the effect of prophecy Śaśāṅka is called Soma, both names being synonyms of the moon; Rājya-vardhana is referred to as Ra, and Harsha as Ha.

Rājya-vardhana and Harsha were grief-stricken and unable to decide on the succession. Taking advantage of the calamitous situation for both Sthāṇv-īśvara and Kanauj, for the young king of the latter state had suffered a blow through the death of his best supporter, Prabhākara-vardhana, the two ambitious kings of Mālava and Gauḍa formed an alliance with a view to annexing Kanauj. In the encounter with the King of Mālava, Graha-varman was killed and his wife taken prisoner. Casting aside all other considerations, Rājya-vardhana immediately set out to avenge his brother-in-law's death, but he too lost his life at the hands of Śaśāṅka. Had it not been for the youthful Harsha's courage and presence of mind, the unexpected alliance between Sthāṇv-īśvara and Kāma-rūpa, and the sound strategy of the elder statesmen of both Sthāṇv-īśvara and Kanauj. Śaśāṅka and the King of Mālava would have dominated northern India. However, the combined forces of the two important kingdoms, led by a common ruler and his loyal lieutenants, completely altered the situation. Bāṇa's narrative concludes with an account of Harsha's army on the march, the metaphors in the closing paragraph strongly suggesting a violent battle ending in victory for Harsha.[1] The poetical rhetoric is supported by the *Mañju-śrī-mūla-kalpa*, which says, 'Harsha defeated Soma, who was forbidden to move out of *his country*',[2] meaning apparently Gauḍa, of which he is elsewhere stated to be the king.

The above evidence, as well as a close examination of Hsüan-tsang's testimony on the subject, disproves the contention of some writers that Śaśāṅka held Magadha until his death, which they place shortly before A.D. 637, when Hsüan-tsang visited the province.[3]

Śaśāṅka's hostility towards Buddhism

Five references to Śaśāṅka in Hsüan-tsang's work connect him with acts of oppression against Buddhism.[4] They all give the impression that Śaśāṅka's activities had taken place several years before the time of the pilgrim's visit, and it is indeed surprising that scholars have interpreted them to convey that Śaśāṅka was active in Magadha until not long before A.D. 637, when Hsüan-tsang was visiting the sacred Buddhist sites in Magadha.[5]

[1] *H.C.* text, pp. 257–8; trans., pp. 259–60.

[2] *Mañju-śrī-mūla-kalpa*, verse 725.

[3] R. C. Majumdar, *H.C.I.P.* iii, p. 80; Mookerji, *Harsha*, pp. 63 and 73.

[4] Beal i, p. 212; ii, pp. 42, 91, 118, and 121; Watters i, p. 343; ii. pp. 43, 92, 115–16, and 192.

[5] *C.A.G.I.* (1924), p. 646; R. C. Majumdar (*H.C.I.P.* iii, p. 107) writes: 'Śaśāṅka must have died before, probably not long before A.D. 637, when Hiuen-Tsang refers to it as a recent event', and again, 'According to the M.M.K. Harsha marched against Puṇḍra, . . . defeated him . . . and then returned . . . and, as Hiuen-Tsang testifies, Śaśāṅka regained possession of Magadha.'

The story in the 'Records' of the supernatural counsel by the Bodhisattva Avalokiteśvara to Harsha before his accession clearly shows that Śaśāṅka had committed some anti-Buddhist activities before A.D. 606.[1]

The second relevant passage speaks of the oppression of the Buddhists of Kuśī-nagara by Śaśāṅka. It may be translated as: 'Subsequently Śaśāṅka-rāja destroyed the law of the Buddha. The monks were without comrades, and years and months quickly passed.'[2]

The third reference to Śaśāṅka is preceded by a long description of Aśoka's acts of piety performed in Magadha. The pilgrim writes:

> When Aśoka had ascended the throne . . . he paid the stone constant worship in person. Afterwards the kings of various kingdoms all wanted to carry it off to their own country but . . . they could not move it at all.
>
> Lately Śaśāṅka-rāja, when he was overthrowing the law of the Buddha . . ., chiselled the stone to remove the [sacred] marks and flung it into the Ganges but it came back to its old place.[3]

The Chinese character for 'lately' does not convey any specific time-limit. Śaśāṅka was certainly very recent compared to Aśoka, and the pilgrim may well have used the term 'lately' for events that had taken place perhaps thirty years before his visit.

The next reference to Śaśāṅka is again preceded by a narration of Aśoka's pious acts:

> Aśoka bathed the roots of the *Bodhi* Tree . . . and got a stone wall built around it. . . . In late times Śaśāṅka-rāja . . . slandered the religion of the Buddha . . ., destroyed the convents, and cut down the *Bodhi* Tree . . . .
>
> Some months afterwards Pūrṇavarman, the King of Magadha . . . reverently bathed the roots of the tree and it revived again . . . .[4]

Hsüan-tsang then proceeds to narrate how the nearby *vihāra* with its excellent image of the Buddha came to be built, and records that 'Śaśāṅka, having cut down the *Bodhi* Tree, wished to destroy this image. But having seen its loving features his mind had no rest or determination, and he turned homewards . . .'[5]

The pilgrim then relates that Śaśāṅka ordered one of his officers to have the image removed and replaced by one of Śiva. The officer merely erected a wall to hide the Buddha's statue, but when he reported that the King's orders had been executed Śaśāṅka was divinely punished and contracted a disease which resulted in his death.

[1] Beal i, p. 212.

[2] *Hsi Yü Chi* text, vi. 21b.

[3] Op. cit. viii. 5a.

[4] Op. cit. viii. 19a. Pūrṇa-varman had probably been appointed the governor of Magadha by Harsha: see below, pp. 86–7.

[5] Op. cit. viii. 21a.

Did Śaśāṅka regain Magadha

From the above references R. C. Majumdar concludes that 'Śaśāṅka regained possession of Magadha'[1] after he had been defeated and confined to Gauḍa by Harsha, as recorded in the *Mañju-śrī-mūla-kalpa*. But none of Hsüan-tsang's statements suggest that Śaśāṅka regained Magadha. On the contrary, it is to be noticed that the pilgrim records Śaśāṅka's departure from Magadha after destroying the Buddhist relics. The story of Śaśāṅka's death immediately after the desecration of the Buddha-image is most suspect, because it is just such an episode as Hsüan-tsang would introduce in order to create effect. A very similar story is told about the anti-Buddhist king, Pushya-mitra Śuṅga, in the northern Buddhist sources.[2] The account of Pushya-mitra's sudden destruction with all his army, after his promulgation at Sākalā of a law promising 100 dīnaras for the head of every Buddhist monk slain by his subjects, is manifestly false, and it is reasonable to assume that Hsüan-tsang's story of Śaśāṅka is likewise untrue. The legend of Pushya-mitra was almost certainly known to Hsüan-tsang, for it exists in more than one Chinese version, and we suspect that he had Pushya-mitra's fate in mind when he wrote of a similar curse on Śaśāṅka. According to the *Mañju-śrī-mūla-kalpa*, Śaśāṅka died of a disease of the mouth which caused high fever, and then death.[3] It is thus probable that the Gauḍa king did die after a serious illness, which Hsüan-tsang, because of his religious bias, attributes to his impious acts, but there is no real evidence that Śaśāṅka died immediately after overrunning Magadha. In fact it seems that it was after this exploit that he occupied Gauḍa, from where he led his armies against Kanauj. Ultimately this venture failed because Harsha succeeded in avenging the defeat and death of his brother-in-law, the King of Kanauj. Through his military strength Harsha was able to contain Śaśāṅka in Gauḍa, but from that centre the latter ruled successfully for several years after these events, according to the *Mañju-śrī-mūla-kalpa*, 'owing to his good deeds as a Buddhist in the previous birth'. In fact there is evidence to prove that he even extended the frontiers of his kingdom in the south-west towards Orissa some time between A.D. 606 and 620.

The greater part of Bengal was already under Śaśāṅka before he came into conflict with Harsha. The *Mañju-śrī-mūla-kalpa* connects Śaśāṅka with Puṇḍra-vardhana in north Bengal.[4] According to Hsüan-tsang, his capital was Karṇa-suvarṇa,[5] which is to be located in west Bengal.

[1] *H.C.I.P.* iii, p. 107.
[2] J. Przyluski, *La Légende de l'empereur Açoka*, pp. 301 ff.
[3] *Mañju-śrī-mūla-kalpa*, trans., p. 50.
[4] Op. cit., text, verse 723.
[5] Beal i, p. 210.

Śaśāṅka no doubt was also in possession of south Bengal, as he later expanded his kingdom as far as the Ganjam district of Orissa. His suzerainty over east Bengal is doubtful, even though one of his Rāja-līlā type of coins has been found at Muhammadpur, near Jessore.[1] Coins are an easily portable commodity. Thus the kingdom to which Śaśāṅka was 'confined' by Harsha covered a wide expanse of territory. Failure in his westward exploits and the loss of the important province of Magadha did not damp the spirits of the ambitious Śaśāṅka, who decided to divert his prowess in other directions. Since his north-eastern neighbour, King Bhāska-ravarman, had already strengthened his position by an alliance with Harsha, Śaśāṅka directed his attention to the more vulnerable kingdom of Orissa.

Śaśāṅka's control over parts of Orissa

North and central Orissa were under the sovereignty of the Mānas, at least from A.D. 579 to 602–3,[2] the dates of the Soro plate A[3] and the Patiakella grant[4] of Mahārāja Śambhū-yaśas and Mahārāja Śiva-rāja respectively. The kingdom of Kongoda to the south of Uḍra was ruled by the Śail-odbhava dynasty, which for some time at least seems to have acknowledged the suzerainty of the Mānas. The great-grandson of the founder of this dynasty was Mādhava-rāja II, who ascended the throne some time before A.D. 619. His Ganjam plate dated in that year (G.E. 300) was issued 'while the Mahārāj-ādhirāja, the glorious Śaśāṅka-rāja, was ruling.'[5] It seems that the whole region of north and central Orissa, as far as the Ganjam district in the south, was subjugated by Śaśāṅka, probably after his westward expansion had been checked by Harsha in A.D. 606–7.

Two copperplates issued during Śaśāṅka's reign have been found at Midnapur[6] and testify to Gauḍa mastery over Daṇḍa-bhukti and Utkala. Midnapur copperplate no. 2 is dated year 8, which we take to be the regnal year of *mahā-pratīhāra* Śubha-kīrti's suzerain Śrī Śaśāṅka.[7] Presuming *c.* A.D. 603 as the year of the beginning of Śaśāṅka's independent career, the dating of the Midnapur plate no. 2 would indicate that he had conquered Daṇḍa-bhukti in northern Orissa by *c.* A.D. 611. Midnapur copperplate no. 1 is dated year 13 (or G.E. 303?).[8]

[1] *B.M.C.*, p. cxxvii. [2] *J.A.S.B.L.* xi. 4 ff. [3] *E.I.* xxiii. 197 ff.
[4] *E.I.* ix. 285 ff. [5] *E.I.* vi. 143 ff.
[6] *J.A.S.B.L.*, Series 3, xi. 1 ff.
[7] Ibid., 'Year 8, 12th day of Pauṣa . . . "while the illustrious Śaśāṅka is protecting the earth; while this Daṇḍabhukti is being ruled by Mahāpratīhāra Śubhakīrti".'
[8] Ibid.: R. C. Majumdar reads the date as 19 or 309 (G.E.) but B. P. Sinha (*Decline of the Kingdom of Magadha*, pp. 236–8) adduces good reasons to show that the second numeral of the date may be read as 3, on a comparison with other grants where a similar sign, most probably denoting 'la' has been read as 3 by various scholars (G. Bühler, *E.I.*

Thus Śaśāṅka was the master of both Daṇḍa-bhukti and Utkala by A.D. 616.[1]

Four more copper records of that period have been discovered at Soro in the Balasore district of Orissa[2] which, when compared with each other and with the Midnapur plate no. 1, establish that Śaśāṅka was in occupation of Uttara Tośālī, i.e. the modern Balasore and Midnapur districts, by A.D. 608, or three years before the date furnished by the Midnapur plate no. 2.

The Balasore copperplate inscription[3] dated year 5, the fourth day of *Mārgga*, records that the *mahā-pratīhāra mahārāja sāmanta śrī* Bhānuḥ, for the enhancement of the religious merit of Śrī *parama-bhaṭṭāraka-pāda*, donates land to the *mahā-mahattaras* Priya-mitra-svāmin, Chāṭu-mitra-svāmin, Dhruva-mitra-svāmin, and Āruha-mitra-svāmin.

The Soro plate D dated year 5, the seventeenth day of Phālguna, was issued by the *mahā-pratīhāra mahārāja* Bhānu-datta to Priya-mitra-svāmin, Vaṭa-mitra-svāmin, Dhruva-mitra-svāmin, and Āruṅga-mitra-svāmin.

The Soro plate B dated year 15, the thirteenth day of Vaiśākha, was issued by the *mahā-bal-ādhikṛita*, *aṅtaraṅga*, and *mahā-sāṅdhi-vigrahika* Soma-datta to Dhruva-mitra-svāmin and Āruṅga-mitra-svāmin, etc.

The Soro plate C dated year 15, the twenty-fourth day of Māgha, was issued by Soma-datta to Dhruva-mitra-svāmin and Āruṅga-mitra-svāmin.

The identification of the Soma-datta of the Soro plates B and C with the Soma-datta of the Midnapur copperplate no. 1 is no doubt correct. Thus we may presume that the unnamed sovereign in the former plates was also Śaśāṅka, whose suzerainty was acknowledged in Uttara Tośālī in A.D. 618.

The Bhānuḥ and Bhānu-datta of the Balasore copperplate inscription and the Soro plate D are also doubtless the same person. The *parama-bhaṭṭāraka*, for the enhancement of whose religious merit land was granted by *mahārāja sāmanta* Bhānuḥ in the year 5, must be Śaśāṅka, who held sway over northern Orissa by A.D. 608.

According to R. C. Majumdar,[4] Bhānu-datta succeeded Soma-datta

iii. 131 ff.; D. C. Sircar, *J.A.H.R.S.* vii. 229 ff.; G. H. Ojha, *B.P.L.*, Table 71, etc.). We think that the date is very likely 13, denoting the regnal year of Śaśāṅka and not 303 (G.E.), because three other plates discovered at Soro in Balasore, testifying Śaśāṅka's suzerainty in that region, are also dated in the regnal years of the suzerain.

[1] Ibid.: 'While the illustrious Śaśāṅka is protecting the earth, while Daṇḍabhukti along with Utkala is being ruled by the illustrious feudatory Mahārāja Somadatta'.

[2] *I.H.Q.* xi. 611 ff., and *E.I.* xxiii. 197 ff.

[3] *I.H.Q.* xi. 611 ff.

[4] *H.C.I.P.* iii, p. 94.

as the governor of Utkala, but we believe that the order should be reversed, because Soma-datta's plates are dated in the year 15, while those of Bhānu-datta are dated in the year 5. The fact that the names of the first two donees of Bhānu-datta's plates have been dropped in Soma-datta's plates also points to the same conclusion.

Earlier we referred to the Ganjam plate of Mādhava-rāja II of the Śail-odbhava dynasty, which is dated year 300 of the Gupta era, and records the suzerainty of *mahārāj-ādhirāja Śaśāṅka-rāja* over the victorious Koṅgoda.[1] This date, A.D. 619–20, is the last known date of Śaśāṅka.

The end of Śaśāṅka and further extension of Harsha's empire

The *Mañju-śrī-mūla-kalpa* also records that Śaśāṅka's rule lasted seventeen years and some weeks. Our postulate, based on various dynastic data that Śaśāṅka started his independent career in *c.* A.D. 603, is seriously strengthened by this statement considered in conjunction with the epigraphic evidence discussed above. Mādhava-rāja II seems to have assumed independent status soon after issuing the Ganjam inscription, because his Puri plates[2] dated year 13 (A.D. 623)[3] show that he had celebrated an *Aśva-medha* before his thirteenth regnal year. Unlike the former record, the latter mentions no suzerain. Thus, the dates of Śaśāṅka's independent rule may be reasonably fixed as from A.D. 603 to 620.

According to the *Mañju-śrī-mūla-kalpa,* 'After the death of Soma, the Gauḍa political system... was reduced to mutual distrust, raised weapons and mutual jealousy—one (king) for a week; another for a month; then a republican constitution, such will be the daily (condition) of the country on this bank of the Ganges. . . . Thereafter Soma's son Mānava will last for eight months. . . .'[4]

It may be inferred from this account that Harsha did not rush to occupy Gauḍa immediately after the death of Śaśāṅka, probably because he was engaged in another part of the empire. The confusion that ensued was probably anticipated, and Harsha seems to have felt confident that neither his ally Bhāskara-varman of Kāma-rūpa nor the lesser ruler of Orissa would try to annex Gauḍa. We do not know exactly when Harsha brought Bengal under his control, but it would be safe to assume that he was in possession of it before, probably long before A.D. 643, when he attacked Koṅgoda in Orissa. It is even possible that Mānava was installed King of Gauḍa by Harsha, in accordance with prevalent political practice.

1 *E.I.* vi. 143 ff.
2 *E.I.* xxiv. 151–3, date doubtfully read as 23.
3 D. C. Sircar has finally deciphered the date as 13: *I.H.Q.* xxvii. 166–7.
4 *Mañju-śrī-mūla-kalpa*, trans. and commentary, p. 51.

On Mānava's death or deposition by Harsha, the province may have been ruled by a direct representative from the centre. Some scholars, on the basis of a land-grant of Bhāskara-varman, issued from the victorious camp of Karṇa-suvarṇa, surmise that he came into possession of the Bengal 'east of the Bhāgīrathī or north of the Padmā river'[1] after Śaśāṅka's death, and that Harsha's hold was confined to the south of the Padmā. But there is no real basis for this contention. We shall deal with this question in detail in the chapter on Harsha's conquests.[2] Śaśāṅka's death opened a new field for expansion in the east for Harsha.

The Maitrakas of Valabhī

The decline of the Guptas and the early Maitrakas, Bhaṭārka and Dhara-sena I

In the reign of Skanda Gupta (*c.* A.D. 454–67)[3] Saurāshṭra was governed by Parṇa-datta, who had been appointed the warden of the important coastal province by the Emperor.[4] There was a short interregnum complicated by family factions after Skanda Gupta's death, which seems to have loosened the imperial grip on the distant province. We know that the Maitraka chief Bhaṭārka established his line of hereditary kings in the reign of Budha Gupta (*c.* A.D. 477–500).[5] However, both the founder and his son Dhara-sena I claimed for themselves only the comparatively humble title of *senā-pati*.

After the death of Budha Gupta there were further dynastic troubles. Disputes over succession led to the partition of the empire; the Hūṇas attacked and conquered an extensive part of northern India; the Vākāṭaka King Hari-sheṇa (*c.* A.D. 475–500) claimed victories over Lāṭa and Avanti,[6] while Yaśo-dharman, who rose to power in Mālava, according to the Mandsor inscription carried his arms as far as the eastern extremity of the Gupta empire.[7] The very fact, however, of so many new powers contending for supremacy at the same time led to the weakening of their strength. Hari-sheṇa proved to be the last great Vākāṭaka king, since no record of any of his successors is known to exist. The Hūṇas were repulsed by both Yaśo-dharman and the Imperial Gupta emperor, Nara-siṁha Gupta, while the former disappeared abruptly from the political stage. Thus Budha Gupta's brother, Nara-siṁha Gupta, succeeded in re-establishing the authority of his dynasty.

Droṇa-siṁha and the question of his overlord

It seems that, taking advantage of these disturbances, the third member of the Maitraka dynasty, Dhara-sena I's brother Droṇa-siṁha,

1 R. C. Majumdar, *H.C.I.P.* iii, p. 107. 2 See below, pp. 82–3, 87–8, 91.
3 A. L. Basham, *B.S.O.A.S.* xvii, pt. 2 (1955), 367.
4 *C.I.I.* iii, no. 14.
5 R. C. Majumdar: see *H.C.I.P.* iii, p. 61 n. 2.
6 *Hyd. Arch. Ser.* (1941), no. 14, 11. 7 *C.I.I.* iii, pp. 142 ff.

decided to assume the status *mahārāja*. The death of Bhānu Gupta, probably in the Eran battle, may have encouraged Droṇa-siṁha to declare his intention of placing the dynasty on a completely independent footing. The Imperial Gupta emperor, Nara-siṁha Gupta, was prudent enough to accept his new status as an accomplished fact, and he may well be 'the sole lord of the circumference of the territory of the whole world who in person installed Droṇa-siṁha in royalty by performing the *abhiṣeka* ceremony'.[1] Fleet[2] identified 'the sole lord' of the Maliya copperplate of Dhara-sena II with Yaśo-dharman, but the discovery of Droṇa-siṁha's grant dated A.D. 502 proves that his coronation had taken place in or before that year, hence Yaśo-dharman, who rose to power later, could not be the suzerain in question. K. J. Virji[3] argues that the paramount ruler referred to in the Valabhī grants, who bestowed the title of *mahārāja* on Droṇa-siṁha, was not an Imperial Gupta ruler, but the Vākāṭaka king Hari-sheṇa, because, as well as the latter's claim to have conquered Lāṭa and Avanti, a daughter of a King of Ujjayinī is said to have married Dhruva-sena-I of Valabhī-pura,[4] and this king was 'undoubtedly the Vākāṭaka monarch'. But support is lacking for this contention. On the basis of Valabhī inscriptions, Droṇa-siṁha's reign should be placed between *c.* A.D. 500 and 520, whereas Hari-sheṇa's career came to an end in *c.* A.D. 500. Virji quotes Jayaswal's dating, A.D. 490–520, for Hari-sheṇa's reign,[5] but as this is purely conjectural, she extends the latter limit by a few years, quoting Jouveau-Dubreuil's view that Hari-sheṇa ruled from A.D. 500 to 530.[6] More recently, however, V. V. Mirashi, on the basis of the Ajantā inscription of the Vākāṭakas, has established that Hari-sheṇa ruled from *c.* A.D. 475 to 500.[7] It is therefore most unlikely that he was Droṇa-siṁha's overlord.

Almost certainly the paramount sovereign referred to in the Maitraka inscription was an Imperial Gupta monarch. Association with no other dynasty could have been so proudly recorded by Droṇa-siṁha's descendants some ninety years after his death. Moreover, all the Valabhī records are dated in the Gupta era. There are also noteworthy similarities between Droṇa-siṁha's grant and the Gupta records.[8] Cunningham

[1] *C.I.I.* iii, no. 38: the Maliya copperplate inscription of Mahārāja Dharasena II, dated A.D. 571–2.

[2] *I.A.* xv. 187.

[3] *Ancient History of Saurashtra*, p. 29.

[4] See Darśana-sāra, quoted by C. L. J. Shah, *Jainism in Northern India*, p. 68.

[5] K. P. Jayaswal, *History of India* (Nāga-Vākāṭaka Imperial Period), pp. 79 and 103.

[6] Jouveau-Dubreuil, *Ancient History of the Deccan*, p. 76.

[7] *Hyd. Arch. Ser.* (1941), no. 14.

[8] See A. M. T. Jackson in his examination of Droṇa-siṁha's grant in *J.B.B.R.A.S.* xx (1902) 1 ff.

suggested that Budha Gupta was the overlord referred to in Dhara-sena II's inscription, but, since the former's last known date is A.D. 494–5, we consider the Imperial Gupta emperor Nara-siṁha Gupta as a more likely possibility. Troubled times heralded his reign and lasted well until the middle of it. He may therefore have willingly recognized the independent status of an erstwhile feudatory to secure the alliance of a dynasty on the rise.

Dhruva-sena I

Mahārāja Droṇa-siṁha was succeeded by his brother *mahā-sāmanta, mahārāja* Dhruva-sena I, who in his grant dated A.D. 525[1] records that he acquired the throne by the strength of his own arms, which seems not to refer to a disputed succession to the throne but to a re-affirmation of Maitraka authority after the fall of Yaśo-dharman, whose Mandsor inscription is dated A.D. 533.[2] Dhruva-sena also bore the titles of *mahā-pratīhāra, mahā-daṇḍa-nāyaka*, and *mahā-kārtika*,[3] and 'meditated at the feet of a paramount lord', who, again, must have been an Imperial Gupta; a scion of the family was still ruling in Bengal in A.D. 543–4. However, the power of the Maitrakas increased under the rule of Dhruva-sena, because we find a Gārulaka[4] king, Varāha-dāsa II of Girnar, acknowledging the suzerainty of Dhruva-sena (not of Guha-sena or Dhara-sena II, as stated by R. C. Majumdar)[5] in a copperplate dated A.D. 549.[6] Dhruva-sena's earliest known grant is dated A.D. 525,[7] therefore he ruled for at least twenty-five years.

Dhruva-sena I was probably succeeded by his ageing younger brother, Dhara-paṭṭa, who apparently died after a short reign, since the latter's son Guha-sena is known to have issued a grant in A.D. 559,[8] only ten years after the last known date of his uncle Dhruva-sena I. The succession of Dhara-paṭṭa to the throne of Valabhī, however, cannot be established with complete certainty, because, although he is styled *mahārāja* in the records of his grandson, Dhara-sena II,[9] his name is not to be found in the grants of his son, Guha-sena.[10]

[1] *E.I.* xi. 106 ff. [2] *C.I.I.* iii, no. 35.

[3] *E.I.* xi. 106 ff., and *J.R.A.S.* (1895) 382 ff.

[4] For greater details see *Bom. Gaz.* viii. 590; *E.I.* xi. 17; and *Journal of the University of Bombay*, iii. 79.

[5] *H.C.I.P.* iii, p. 63. Also see Niharranjan Ray, *I.H.Q.* iv. 463.

[6] A. S. Gadre, 'The Five Vaḷā Copperplate Grants', *Journal of the University of Bombay*, iii. 79 ff. [7] *E.I.* xi. 106 ff.; *I.A.* xxxix. 129.

[8] *I.A.* vii. 67 ff. [9] *I.A.* xv. 187 ff.

[10] *I.A.* iv. 174, v. 207, vii. 67. Virji (*Ancient History of Saurashtra*, p. 36) notices that the first plate of one of the three grants of Guha-sena, which might have contained Dhara-paṭṭa's name, is missing. On the other hand both the plates of the third grant dated A.D. 567 are well preserved, yet Dhara-paṭṭa's name does not appear in them. As the beginning of the description of Guha-sena after that of Dhruva-sena I is very abrupt Virji suspects a mistake on the part of the scribe, but there is little reason to

Guha-sena

Guha-sena's first known record is dated A.D. 559,[1] while that of his successor belongs to 571;[2] he may, therefore, have ruled for about ten years. The fact that Guha-sena dispensed with the title *mahā-sāmanta* and used only *mahārāja* shows that Maitraka power increased further during his time. His wealth, prowess, and good government are repeatedly referred to in his records, and the objects of his grants testify to his devotion to both Śiva and Buddha.

Dhara-sena II

Guha-sena was succeeded by his son Dhara-sena II, whose various grants range between A.D. 571 and 589. The earliest known date of his successor, however, is A.D. 605;[3] Dhara-sena therefore may have ruled for a long period of approximately thirty years. No vital change in the fortunes of the Maitrakas seems to have occurred in the reign of Dhara-sena II. His first two grants, dated A.D. 571,[4] ascribe to him the simple title *sāmanta*. His record dated A.D. 573[5] attributes to him the title *mahā-rāja*, while in his grants of the years 588 and 589,[6] although he is given the ordinary titles *mahā-sāmanta* and *mahā-rāja* in the text, in the royal signature he is described as *maha-dhirāja*.

The Gārulaka king, Siṁh-āditya, son of Varāha-dāsa II and the great-grandson of the founder of the dynasty, *mahā-rāja* Sūra,[7] was a contemporary of Dhara-sena II, and his copperplate grant dated A.D. 574 has been found, along with the Maitraka grants, at Palitāṇā. No reference to any Maitraka *mahā-rāja* is made in Siṁha-āditya's grant, such as in that of his predecessor Varāha-dāsa, but the facts that the grants of both the dynasties are found at the same place and that Dhara-sena II assumed the title *mahā-dhirāja* indicate that the Gārulakas continued to be loyal to the Maitrakas.

Śīlāditya I Dharm-āditya; devolution of power to brother and son

After the death of Dhara-sena II, in *c.* A.D. 590, his son Śīlāditya I Dharmāditya came to the throne. He was no doubt the same as the devout Buddhist king Śīlāditya of Mo-la-po of Hsüan-tsang's description. Śīlāditya's reign lasted approximately twenty-five years, because the last known grant of his predecessor is dated A.D. 589,[8] while the first known record of his brother and successor Khara-graha I was issued in A.D. 616.[9] His authority over Valabhī seems to have been shared by Khara-graha I towards the end of the reign. Support for this conjecture

doubt his accuracy. The fact that Dhara-sena II applies the title *mahārāja* to Dhara-paṭṭa is at present the only possible argument in favour of the latter's succession to the throne of Valabhī.

[1] *I.A.* vii. 67.
[2] *I.A.* xv. 187.
[3] *E.I.* xi. 115; *I.A.* i. 45.
[4] *I.A.* xv. 187; *J.B.B.R.A.S.* (N.S.) iv. 38.
[5] *E.I.* xxi. 179.
[6] *I.A.* vi. 11.
[7] *E.I.* xi. 17.
[8] *I.A.* vi. 11.
[9] *P.T.O.C.* (Seventh), pp. 659 ff.

may be found in the inscriptions of the period and possibly in Hsüan-tsang's account. The Alīnā copperplates of Śīlāditya V mention that Śīlāditya I (Dharmāditya), 'excessively full of respect (*for him*) [i.e. for Khara-graha], (*behaved*) as if he were (*the god Indra*) the elder (*brother*) of Upendra'.[1] The simile is significant, for, according to legend, Upendra won the contest against his elder brother Indra[2] and henceforth received due deference from the latter. Khara-graha's importance increased, it seems, sometime after A.D. 609, the date of the seventh grant of Śīlāditya, in which the former is for the first time mentioned as *dūtaka*.[3] As is clear from all the copperplate records issued from the time of Dhruva-sena III onwards, Śīlāditya I had a son named Ḍera-bhaṭṭa, described therein as the master of the countries lying between the Sahya and the Vindhyas, which he apparently conquered during his father's lifetime. Dera-bhaṭṭa's son, named after his grandfather Śīlāditya, is also said to have been 'the lord of the earth, the bulky breasts of which are the Vindhya mountains'. This addition to Valabhī territory may have been made when the civil war between Maṅgaleśa and Pula-keśin was weakening the Chālukyas, whose Aihoḷe inscription refers to the earlier gloomy period when 'the whole world was enveloped by the darkness of enemies'.[4]

An explanation of the south Lo and north Lo of Hsüan-tsang

A note to the text of the *Hsi Yü Chi*, perhaps by a commentator, describes Mo-la-po as South Lo, as against Fa-La-pi, which is designated North Lo.[5] This distinction may have been made to signify that, though parts of the same greater kingdom, the two regions had at certain times been governed by members of a collateral line of the main ruling family. Thus it is possible that Śīlāditya ruled with full authority until *c.* A.D. 610, when his brother Khara-graha asserted himself and declared independent control over certain parts of the hereditary kingdom. This also explains why members of Śīlāditya I's line did not rule from Valabhī until thirty-five years after his death. Śīlāditya I was a contemporary of Harsha for about nine years.

Vardhana, Maitraka, and Chālukya stakes in Mālava

Vardhana and Maitraka interests clashed over Mālava. The memory of his father's exploits in Lāṭa and Mālava, against the Kaḷachuris and Deva-gupta respectively,[6] must have aroused in Harsha ambitions to repeat the campaign and finally annex Mālava. Deva-gupta's deadly

[1] *C.I.I.* iii, no. 39, pp. 181–2.
[2] *Vishṇu Purāṇa* v. 30; Fleet, *C.I.I.* iii, no. 39, p. 182.
[3] G. V. Acharya, *The Historical Inscriptions from Gujarat*, no. 51.
[4] *I.A.* viii. 237; *E.I.* vi. 1 ff.
[5] Watters ii, pp. 243 and 246; Beal ii, pp. 260, n. 56 and 266, fn. 71; *Hsi Yü Chi* text, xi. 14a and 17a.
[6] See below, pp. 63–4.

campaign against his brother-in-law, the Maukhari king Graha-varman, must have turned ambition into political necessity if Harsha was to vindicate his honour. But in the meantime the Maitrakas, taking advantage of the political confusion, caused, on the one hand, by the Kanauj campaign involving both Deva-gupta and the Vardhanas, and, on the other, by civil wars among the Chālukyas, temporarily occupied Ujjain in *c.* A.D. 610. Khara-graha I's Virdi grant of A.D. 616 was issued from Ujjayinī.[1] The fall of the Kaḷachuri dynasty, which had previously held Ujjain, may also be placed at *c.* A.D. 610. The Sarasavāni plates, dated A.D. 609–10, of the Kaḷachuri king Buddha-rāja are the last known record of the dynasty.[2]

This much-coveted city remained with the Maitrakas until the Chālukya king Pula-keśin II defeated the Lāṭas, the Mālavas, and the Gurjaras, when Ujjain too must have come under his control. The Chālukya exploits must be placed before A.D. 623, the date of the Kheṭaka record of Dhara-sena III, in which the Maitraka ruler is given simply a religious epithet, *Parama-māheśvara*.[3] This region, which touched the south-western boundary of Harsha's empire, later caused conflict between the Vardhana and the Chālukya monarchs. The topic is discussed in detail in the chapter on the extent of Harsha's empire.

Khara-graha I

Śīlāditya of Valabhī was succeeded by his brother Khara-graha I in *c.* A.D. 615. He had enjoyed high status in the reign of his brother. It does not seem that Maitraka power suffered any diminution in his reign. Of Khara-graha's two available grants, one was issued from the famous camp of Ujjayinī[4] and the other from Valabhī.[5] Harsha's suspicion of the Maitrakas must have continued during Khara-graha's reign, though he did not yet openly show it. Khara-graha's reign was short, for the only known inscription of his successor, Dhara-sena III, is dated A.D. 623.[6]

Dhara-sena III and the diminution of Maitraka power on account of Pula-keśin

Dhara-sena III was the son of Khara-graha I. His reign too was brief, because the next Maitraka ruler, Dhruva-sena II Bālāditya, issued his first copperplate grant in A.D. 629.[7] Bālāditya's reign, which coincided with the great military achievements of Pula-keśin II, witnessed a serious diminution in the territory and prestige of the Maitrakas. The Aihoḷe inscription of Pula-keśin records that, 'subdued by His splendour, the Lāṭas, Māḷavas and Gurjaras became as it were teachers of how feudatories, subdued by force, ought to behave'.[8] Dhara-sena III seems to have made Kheṭaka, the modern Kaira, in the south of his kingdom, the

[1] *P.T.O.C.* (Seventh), p. 659.
[2] *E.I.* vi. 297.
[3] *E.I.* xxi. 181 ff.
[4] *P.T.O.C.* (Seventh), p. 659.
[5] A. S. Gadre, *Important Inscriptions from the Baroda State*, i, pp. 7 ff.
[6] *E.I.* i. 86.
[7] *I.A.* vi. 12 ff.
[8] *E.I.* vi. 10.

base of operations, because his only known record was issued from that city.[1] Dhara-sena claims no regal titles in this inscription, dated A.D. 623, which may have been the fateful year in which Pula-keśin's forces invaded the 'north-western' countries. The Maitrakas were deprived of their possessions in the Mālava region, and their power was so adversely affected that neither Dhara-sena nor his successor, Dhruva-sena, bore any regal titles, the former owing to Pula-keśin's conquests, and the latter on account of Harsha's successful attack on Valabhī.

A record, dated A.D. 643, of the Chālukya Rāja Vijaya-rāja,[2] issued from Vijaya-pura but found at Kheṭaka, from where Dhara-sena III also issued his inscription, records the grant of two villages in the modern Surat and Broach districts and testifies to the appointment of a Chālukya viceroy by Pula-keśin to govern his newly acquired provinces in the north-west of his empire. Vijaya-rāja records his genealogy as beginning from Jaya-siṁha-rāja, whose son was his own father, Vallabha Raṇa-vikrānta Rāja-buddha-varman, probably the first viceroy appointed by Pula-keśin.

Dhruva-sena II, Bālāditya, the son-in-law and subordinate ally of Harsha

Dhara-sena III was succeeded on the throne of Valabhī by his younger brother, Dhruva-sena II, Bālāditya. The latter's first and last known grants bear the dates A.D. 629[3] and A.D. 640;[4] he was thus a contemporary of Harsha for the whole duration of his reign. Dhruva-sena II is no doubt the same as Tʻu-lu-pʻo-po-tʻa of the 'Records', during whose reign the Chinese pilgrim visited Valabhī. Hsüan-tsang records that Dhruva-bhaṭṭa was the nephew of Śīlāditya Dharmāditya, and the son-in-law of Harsha Śīlāditya.[5] Throughout the period of his rule Dhruva-sena II enjoyed the subordinate friendship of Harsha. Hsüan-tsang informs us that the King of Valabhī attended the quinquennial assembly convoked by Harsha in A.D. 643, and guarded the 'arena of charity' on the west of the confluence at Prayāga. From his grants Dhruva-sena, like his predecessors, appears to have been of a tolerant disposition and bestowed favour on both Hindu and Buddhist institutions. In his inscriptions he styles himself *parama-māheśvara*, i.e. a devotee of Śiva. Dhruva-sena II is also to be identified with the Valabhī king of the Gurjara records, who on being defeated by the great lord, the illustrious Harsha-deva, took shelter at the court of Dadda.[6] The latter was probably Dadda II, whose first and last known records are dated respectively A.D. 629 and 641.[7]

[1] *E.I.* xxi. 181 ff.; *J.B.B.R.A.S.* (N.S.) iii. 185.
[2] *I.A.* vii. 241 ff.
[3] *I.A.* vi. 12 ff.
[4] *E.I.* viii. 196.
[5] Beal ii, p. 267; Watters ii, p. 247.
[6] *I.A.* xiii. 77–9: this episode is first mentioned in the Gurjara King Jaya-bhaṭa III's record dated A.D. 736.
[7] *E.I.* xxiv. 179.

Harsha's Valabhī campaign

Harsha's western campaign may be placed between A.D. 630 and 634, the dates respectively of the Lohner grant and the Aihoḷe inscription of Pula-keśin II.[1] The former does not allude to any conflict between Harsha and Pula-keśin, but the latter records the military achievements of the Chālukya in detail. He is said to have worsted in battle the Lāṭas, Mālavas, and Gurjaras, as well as Harsha. The war between Harsha and Pula-keśin, however, was started by the former, who first invaded the territory of the Maitrakas and then that of the Chālukyas. Harsha's attack on Valabhī seems to have been guided by two motives: to secure a strategic position for his southern campaign and to add to his economic prosperity by controlling a coastal trade centre.

Dhruva-sena's temporary asylum at the Gurjara court of Dadda II

Dhruva-sena II's flight to the Gurjara country may have taken place in A.D. 632, the date of his third grant,[2] which was to be followed by four more records, but only after a gap of six years. The question has often been raised as to how the ruler of a small feudatory state was in a position to protect the powerful Valabhī king against an even more powerful enemy, Harsha. The explanation lies in the fact that the Maitrakas had been considerably weakened by the sweeping raids of the Chālukyas, while the Gurjaras, though they had lost their independence, had been greatly strengthened by entering the Chālukya fold. In actual fact, therefore, the King of Valabhī was under the protection of the Chālukya monarch through his feudatory Dadda II, which incidentally was an additional provocation for Harsha later to attack Pula-keśin. It appears that the Maitraka king's stay in the Gurjara kingdom was brief, that he did not receive any tangible help from the Chālukyas, and that at least preliminary negotiations between him and Harsha were conducted from the court of the Gurjaras. Dadda II, in his own inscriptions, does not boast of having given shelter to a king in distress, because his own power issued from his overlord. Nor does Pula-keśin's Aihoḷe inscription record the event, presumably because Harsha had by that time succeeded in winning over Dhruva-sena to his side. The fact is mentioned for the first time in A.D. 736, in the record of Jaya-bhaṭa III, when the Gurjaras were in a position to claim easy praise.

Harsha's generous and politic terms to Dhruva-sena II through matrimony and offer of territory in Mālava

The matrimonial alliance with the Maitraka king was an act of great political astuteness on Harsha's part. The security resulting from such a connection weaned Dhruva-sena away from Pula-keśin's circle of influence. Dhruva-sena now probably had an assurance of independence greater than that he could have expected from the Chālukyas. Throughout

[1] *H.C.I.P.* iii, p. 235; *E.I.* vi. 1 ff.; also see A. S. Altekar in *A.B.O.R.I.* xiii. 300 ff.

[2] *J.B.B.R.A.S.* (N.S.) i. 53.

his reign Harsha possessed the friendship and loyalty of the Maitrakas and was assured of the safety of the western extremity of his empire. In the course of his western campaign Harsha, we believe, captured certain parts of Mālava, which he apparently made over to Dhruva-sena II. The latter's grants dated A.D. 639 and 640, discovered at Nogāvā, ten miles north of Ratlam, were issued respectively from Nava-grāma (Nogāvā) and Chandra-putraka in Mālavaka.[1] They establish the fact that the Maitrakas regained possession of the area which had been lost to them as a result of the Chālukya invasion. To suppose that Dhruva-sena reoccupied the Mālava territories independently would be to expect a deed which at this stage lay beyond his strength. Harsha, on the other hand, during the course of his march to Valabhī, must have overrun parts of Mālava, which after the death of Deva-gupta had fallen into the hands of Pula-keśin. It was a shrewd decision to offer Mālava to Dhruva-sena II. Harsha thus created an area of suspicion between the Maitrakas and the Chālukyas, fulfilled Dhruva-sena's aspiration to recover the territory he had lost, and won for himself a friendship all the more valuable for its timing. Pula-keśin might, indeed, have started military preparations at this stage to face Harsha's offensive.

The date and place of the issue of the Nogāvā grants has led some historians to think that Harsha's attack on Valabhī took place after A.D. 640, during the reign of Dhara-sena IV, the successor of Dhruva-sena II.[2] It is argued that, had the latter been involved in a conflict with Harsha, Hsüan-tsang would have made a reference to the event. But there is no real basis for doubting Dhruva-sena II to be the Valabhī king of the Gurjara grant. Hsüan-tsang may not be expected to record an unpleasant episode concerning two pro-Buddhist monarchs, who were closely related and one of whom was a patron of the Chinese pilgrim. Moreover, the last known date of the Gurjara Dadda II, with whom Dhruva-sena II sought asylum, is A.D. 641. Our identification of the refugee at Dadda II's court with Dhruva-sena II rather than with his son Dhara-sena IV is further supported by the dates of some of the records of these three kings. The last known land grants of Dhruva-sena II and Dadda II are dated respectively 640 and 641, while Dhara-sena IV's first grant with the grand title *chakra-vartī* is dated 645–6.[3] Probably

[1] *E.I.* viii. 190 ff.; *A.S.I.A.R.* (1902–3) 232 ff.

[2] B. Indraji, *Bom. Gaz.* i. pt. 1, 116; K. C. Chattopadhyaya, *Proceedings of the Indian History Congress, Third Session*, pp. 596–600; R. C. Majumdar, *H.C.I.P.* iii. 110 and 147; 'Dharasena IV, who ascended the throne of Valabhī about A.D. 644, assumed imperial titles and called himself a *Chakravartī*. Whether this led to hostility between him and Harsha-vardhana, which forced him to take refuge with King Dadda II of Nāndīpurī, we do not definitely know.'

[3] *I.A.* i. 45.

he ascended the throne in 644 as his father Dhruva-sena II represented Valabhī in Harsha's quinquennial assembly in 643. Holder of the title *chakra-vartī* in 645–6 and possessor of the old Gurjara stronghold of Broach from where he issued two more grants in 649,[1] Dhara-sena IV could not be the king who sought political asylum with the Gurjaras. It is apparent that he increased the prestige of his dynasty soon after acquiring the throne. His strength issued from the facts that the Chālukya power had declined, leaving their governors in southern Gujarat open to attack, and his overlord Harsha's end was near. The identity of the Valabhī king of the Gurjara grant is therefore definitely to be established as Dhruva-sena II, and not as Dhara-sena IV.[2]

Dhara-sena IV and the restoration of Maitraka to power

The twelfth ruler of the Maitraka dynasty was Dhara-sena IV, the son and successor of Dhruva-sena II, Bālāditya. The first and last known dates of his grants are, respectively, A.D. 645–6[3] and A.D. 649.[4] He assumed, for the first time in the history of the Maitrakas, full imperial titles such as *parama-bhaṭṭāraka*, *mahārāj-ādhirāja*, *parameśvara*, and *chakra-vartī*. He was Harsha's contemporary for a very brief period, and no doubt assumed these titles not long before Harsha's death, when the latter's hold on the outlying provinces of his loosely knit empire may have weakened. Dhara-sena's reign also coincides with the feeble period of the Chālukyas, whose power rapidly declined after the death of Pulakeśin in *c.* A.D. 642, to be revived again after more than twelve years by his son and successor, Vikram-āditya I. K. P. Jayaswal's suggestion that Dhara-sena IV assumed imperial titles by virtue of being a grandson of Harsha is rather far-fetched, since the marriage between Dhruva-sena II and Harsha's daughter seems to have taken place in *c.* A.D. 632. Dhara-sena would have been too young for the achievements with which he is credited if he had been the child of this marriage. He must have been the son of an older queen of Dhruva-sena. Dhara-sena IV died in A.D. 650.

[1] *I.A.* xv. 335.

[2] Cf. C. V. Vaidya, *H.M.H.I.* i, pp. 242–3; Niharranjan Ray, *I.H.Q.* iv. 464; A. S. Altekar, *A.B.O.R.I.* xiii. 304; H. D. Sankalia, *Archaeology of Gujarat*, p. 17; R. C. Parikh, *Kāvyānuśāsana*, Historical Introduction, p. lxiv.

[3] *I.A.* I. 45.

[4] *I.A.* xv. 339.

III

THE VARDHANAS

Sthāṇv-īśvara

THE region of Sthāṇv-īśvara in eastern Panjab was the cradle of the dynasty of the greatest seventh-century monarch of northern India. A graphic account of this kingdom is to be found in Bāṇa's *Harsha-charita*, supplemented and corroborated by Hsüan-tsang's description of Sa-t'a-ni-ssŭ-fa-lo in the 'Records', though the latter appears to ignore the fact that it was the paternal kingdom of Harsha.

Situation

The Chinese pilgrim informs us that Sthāṇv-īśvara was situated north-west of Mathurā, at a distance of over 500 *li* (approximately 83 miles). It was more than 7,000 *li* 'in circuit', and its capital was 20 *li* or so. The capital was surrounded for 200 *li* by a district called Dharma-kshetra, 'the place of religious merit',[1] the famous battlefield of the ancient Mahā-bhārata war. According to Bāṇa, Sthāṇv-īśvara was a *jana-pada-viśesha* in the *jana-pada* of Śrī-kaṇṭha.[2] References in the *Harsha-charita* make it clear that Sthāṇv-īśvara, the capital, was situated on the banks of the River Sarasvatī.[3] Comparing the Indian and the Chinese descriptions, the kingdom of the Vardhanas may be said to have extended from the River Satluj in the west to the upper reaches of the Ganga in the east, with its capital at Sthāṇv-īśvara. Bāṇa, furthermore, tells us that the region of Śrī-kaṇṭha was so called after a *Nāga* of that name.[4]

Flora and fauna

The *Harsha-charita* also contains a description of the flora and fauna of the region. Bāṇa remarks on the fertility of the soil, which produced

[1] Beal i, p. 184; Watters i, p. 314.

[2] *H.C.* text, p. 96; trans., p. 81. Monier Williams's *Sanskrit–English Dictionary* gives the following among the meanings of *jana-pada*: a community, nation, the people (as opposed to sovereign); an empire, an inhabited country, etc.; *jana-pada-viśesha* is not given as one word.

In line with some of the 'republican' governments of the day described as *gaṇa* or *jana-pada*, e.g. that of the Yaudheyas, Śrī-kaṇṭha may have enjoyed *jana-pada* status in earlier days. But, as is apparent from the *Harsha-charita*, *jana-pada* had lost its former meaning long before Baṇa's time. Harsha's remote ancestor Pushpa-bhūti emerges as a minor king of the *jana-pada* of Śrī-kaṇṭha. Later in the narrative too, Bāṇa uses the word to denote simply 'region'. Cowell and Thomas translate it as 'national' in that context (see *H.C.* text, p. 198; trans., p. 192).

Sthāṇv-īśvara appears to have been the most important district, 'the special *jana-pada*', the capital city of Śrī-kaṇṭha.

[3] *H.C.* text, pp. 102, 203, etc.; trans., pp. 86, 198, etc.

[4] Op. cit., p. 112; trans., p. 94; also see below, p. 58.

wheat, rice, sugar-cane, beans, and herbs in abundance. Rice is, at present, grown on the lower slopes of the Himalayas, while sugar-cane is cultivated in the eastern parts of the region; we may assume that these crops were also raised in Harsha's day. Bāṇa also enumerates plantains, pomegranates, citrons, grapes, dates, and saffron among the products of the region, though he somewhat exaggerates the adaptability of the climate of Śrī-kaṇṭha by adding coconut to his list of fruits.[1] Cows, buffaloes, sheep, horses, camels, and monkeys, as well as parrots and sparrows, are mentioned among the fauna of the land.[2]

Economic life

Hsüan-tsang's brief description of Sthāṇv-īśvara agrees with that of Bāṇa inasmuch as the former records that the soil of the region was rich and fertile, the crops abundant, and the climate warm. Hsüan-tsang, however, notes that few of the inhabitants of the region were given to farming; the majority were traders. He further remarks that rarities from other lands were collected in Sthāṇv-īśvara and that 'rich families vied with each other in extravagance'. 'The manners and customs of the people', he observes 'were illiberal.'[3] Bāṇa's omission of this aspect of the region's economic life may be explained by the fact that trade acquired greater importance in this part of Harsha's empire after his western campaign, when the trade routes of the Arabian Sea became accessible to traders in the interior. The removal of the Hūṇa menace too must have acted favourably on the north-western inland trade with Afghanistan and Persia.

Religion

On the subject of the religious beliefs of the inhabitants of Sthāṇv-īśvara, Hsüan-tsang comments, no doubt with regret, that non-Buddhists were very numerous and that there were in the capital only three Buddhist monasteries, with over 700 professed Buddhists, all Hīnayān-ists, as against over 100 Hindu temples.[3] The Brahman Bāṇa, of course, expresses his great admiration for the land 'where the laws of caste usage are forever unconfused, . . . (where) disasters were cut away, as if excised by numerous axes chiselling stone for temples'.[4]

Puṣpabhūti, the progenitor of the Vardhana dynasty

Bāṇa thereafter introduces us to the political history of Sthāṇv-īśvara. 'In that country', he writes, 'there arose a monarch named Puṣpabhūti . . .'. He, 'like a third added to the Sun and Moon, shalt be the founder of a mighty line of kings. . . . Wherein shall arise an emperor named

[1] Coconut may be grown on a small scale as far inland as the Satluj-Yamunā Doāb, but it is far-fetched to imagine that it was a common fruit which grew in abundance in that region.

[2] *H.C.* text, pp. 94–5; trans., pp. 79–80; cf. *C.A.G.I.*, pp. 377 ff.

[3] Watters i, p. 314.

[4] *H.C.* text, pp. 94 and 96; trans., pp. 79 and 81.

Harṣa, . . . world-conquering like a second Māndhātṛi. . . .'[1] Puṣpabhūti apparently made some territorial acquisitions, for he is described as being 'honoured by citizens, dependents, councillors and neighbouring sovereigns, whom his arm's might had conquered and made tributary'.[2] Bāṇa refers to him as *Śūra Śūrasenākramaṇe*,[3] 'a hero in invading Śūra-sena', which lay in the region of Mathurā.

Puṣpabhūti, the Nāgas, and the Early Guptas

The date and the identity of the progenitor of the Vardhana dynasty is not easy to establish. Certain references by Bāṇa, however, lead us to believe that Puṣpabhūti was probably a contemporary of the early Imperial Guptas. The Nāgas, whose coins have been found at Mathurā,[4] held sway over the Śūra-sena region in the early decades of the fourth century. The region of Śrī-kanṭha, which lay in the neighbourhood of Nāga domains, is said to have got its name from a Nāga, Śrī-kanṭha, who, according to Bāṇa, was defeated by Puṣpabhūti in a duel.[5] This may be a garbled recollection of a war between the founder of the Vardhana line and a Nāga king of Mathurā, when the former made a bid for power over Nāga territory. But Puṣpabhūti or his successor cannot have been allowed to retain his newly-won independence for long, because with the advent of the mighty Samudra Gupta all the kingdoms east of the Chenab came under Gupta sway.[6] Puṣpabhūti's Sthāṇv-īśvara, which had previously been under the Nāgas, was subjugated by Samudra Gupta as well as the main Nāga domains, to the east of it, and the Yaudheya territory to its west. That Puṣpabhūti was a remote and semi-legendary figure at the time of Bāṇa is evident from the account of his royal career, which is chiefly devoted to the description of the performance of a Śaiva sacrifice.[7] The clash between the Nāga king, who is made to appear a supernatural being, and Puṣpabhūti is said to have occurred in connection with this religious rite. Nor, indeed, does Harsha mention Puṣpabhūti in any of his inscriptions.

1 *H.C.* text, pp. 98 and 115; trans., pp. 83 and 97. The above description also indicates that the Vardhanas did not claim connections with the divinely descended families of the Sun and the Moon. *Śūrasenākramaṇe* involves a pun, and the phrase may be taken to mean: a hero 'in attacking an army of heroes'. It would seem, however, that Bāṇa intended to imply that Puṣpabhūti attacked the land of the Sūra-sena people.

2 Op. cit., p. 100; trans., p. 85.

3 Op. cit., p. 100; trans., p. 84 and p. 84 fn. 9: *ākramaṇe*, translated as 'vanquishing' and 'conquering', is better rendered as 'invading'.

4 F. E. Pargiter, *Dynasties of the Kali Age*, p. 53; *Jour. Num. Soc.* v. 21 ff.; A. S. Altekar, *N.H.I.P.*, pp. 36–7; B. C. Law, *Historical Geography of India*, p. 109: 'The Mathurā-Nāga Statuette Inscription amply proves the prevalence of serpent-worship in Mathurā.'

5 *H.C.* text, pp. 112–13; trans., pp. 94–5.

6 *C.I.I.* iii, no. 1.

7 *H.C.* text, pp. 109 ff.; trans., pp. 91 ff.

The early Vardhanas

The advent of Harsha's father, Prabhākara-vardhana, is recorded by Bāṇa in the following words: 'From this Puṣpabhūti there issued a line of kings.... In which line were born kings.... thronging the regions with their armies . . . strong to support the world.... The line so proceeding, there was born in course of time a king of kings named Prabhākara-vardhana....'[1] The third ancestor of Prabhākara, Nara-vardhana, whose place in the Vardhana genealogy is known to us from Harsha's records, must have lived at the beginning of the fifth century A.D. So that the progress of Puṣpabhūti's dynasty, founded when the Early Guptas were gaining power in the Gangetic Doab, cannot be followed for almost a century and a half—indeed, throughout the period of Gupta dominance—until it was revived by kings with the name-ending -vardhana. No doubt Bāṇa omits the account of their vicissitudes during the Gupta period because the Vardhanas at that stage were a family of little if any importance. The invasion of the Hūṇas and the rise of Yaśo-dharman in Mālava must have had repercussions on the fortunes of the Vardhanas, though nothing is known about it from available records. The Hūṇas, however, seem to have been considered a danger by all Indian kings, because they were not only resisted by the Imperial Guptas and the Yaśo-dharman, but also by the lesser Maukharis and Prabhākara-vardhana.

The names of Prabhākara-vardhana's three ancestors and their queens, as recorded in Harsha's Baṅskhera[2] and Madhu-ban inscriptions,[3] are as follows:

Mahārāja Nara-vardhana m. Vajriṇī-devī
Mahārāja Rājya-vardhana I m. Apsaro-devī
Mahārāja Āditya-vardhana m. Mahā-sena-guptā-devī.

Working back from the date of Harsha's accession in A.D. 606,[4] and assigning an average rule of twenty-five years to each king, we may ascribe Nara-vardhana's reign to some period between *c.* A.D. 505 to 530, perhaps towards the latter half of this range. He bore the simple title of *mahārāja*. His son, Rājya-vardhana I, may have ruled from A.D. 530 to 555, while the latter's son, Āditya-vardhana, whose queen, Mahā-sena-guptā, was in all probability a sister of the Later Gupta king, Mahā-sena-gupta, may have wielded power from *c.* A.D. 555 to 580. This also agrees with our dating of the reign of Mahā-sena-gupta, who may have succeeded to the throne between the years 570 and 575, and who, in

[1] *H.C.* text, pp. 119–20; trans., pp. 100–1.
[2] *E.I.* iv. 208.
[3] *E.I.* i. 67.
[4] See below, Appendix I.

order to strengthen himself against the Maukharis, may have secured an alliance with the Vardhanas by marrying off his sister to Āditya-vardhana.

Prabhākara-vardhana

Āditya-vardhana's son Prabhākara-vardhana, also known as Pratāpa-śīla, was the first ruler of the dynasty to assume the imperial title *parama-bhaṭṭāraka mahārāj-ādhirāja*. The Bañskhera inscription describes him as one 'whose fame crossed the four oceans and who subjugated other kings by means of his valour or love'. Bāṇa also credits Prabhākara-vardhana with several victories. He described him as 'a lion to the Hūṇa deer, a burning fever to the king of Sindhu, a troubler of the sleep of the Gurjara king, a bilious fever to that scent-elephant, the lord of Gandhāra, destroyer of the skill of the Lāṭas, an axe to the creeper which is the goddess of fortune [or sovereignty] of Mālava.'[1] These rulers seem to have incurred little if any loss of territory at the hands of Prabhākara-vardhana, but Bāṇa's rhetoric does indicate that the King of Sthāṇv-īśvara was an ambitious ruler who attacked his neighbours on the slightest pretext. War was to him 'a favour. A foe the discovery of a treasure.' There is no doubt that ultimately Prabhākara-vardhana succeeded in winning for himself a distinguished status among contemporary rulers. Through his campaigns he is said to have 'levelled on every side, hills and hollows, clumps and forests, trees and grass, thickets and anthills, mountains and caves'. According to the ancient treatises on law these served as landmarks showing boundaries between districts and regions.[2]

Prabhākara-vardhana's likely campaigns—the Hūṇas

We attempt a historical reconstruction of events alluded to in Bāṇa's rhetoric. The Hūṇas, though no longer a major danger in the time of Prabhākara-vardhana, were still active enough, and continually raided their neighbours. They may have had a principality on the banks of the Satluj, where it flows in the hilly tracts of the Gangri region. The prince Rājya-vardhana, when deputed by his father to attack the Hūṇas, is said to have 'entered the region which blazes with Kailāśa's lustre'.[3] Mount Kailāśa is a spur of the Gangri range, which lies at its foot in the south-west.[4] The success of the crown prince against the Hūṇas[5] seems to have been the basis of Bāṇa's phrase *Hūṇa-hariṇa-kesarī*, 'a lion to the Hūṇa deer', for Prabhākara-vardhana.[6] The fact that their raids did not recur in Harsha's reign also supports the view that Rājya-vardhana attained success in his campaign against the Hūṇas. These observations may

[1] *H.C.* text, p. 120; also see trans., p. 101.
[2] *Yāj.* ii. 151; *Manu* viii. 246–7.
[3] *H.C.* text, p. 150; trans., p. 132.
[4] *G.D.A.M.I.*, p. 82.
[5] *H.C.* text, p. 176; trans., p. 165: 'arrow-wounds received in battle while conquering the Hūṇas'.
[6] Op. cit., p. 120; trans., p. 101.

provide a tentative answer to the questions[1] whether any conflict took place between Rājya-vardhana and the Hūṇas, and if so what was the result of the campaign; it also answers the query whether Bāṇa in his pithy phrases alludes to the prince's own expedition, or to a previous one led by his father.

Sindh

Prabhākara-vardhana is also said to have come into conflict with the King of Sindhu. The area indicated by the term 'Sindhu' has varied from period to period. On the basis of Hsüan-tsang's account, it may be said that the whole region from just below the great confluence of the Satluj and the Indus down to the sea was politically subject to Sindh.[2] Hsüan-tsang describes 'Sin-tu' proper as approximately 1,167 miles 'in circuit', with its capital at 'P'i-shan-p'o-pu-lo',[3] which Cunningham[4] attempts to identify with Abhijānava-pura or Alor. Bāṇa is probably referring to this kingdom of Sindhu, which lay not very far south-west of Sthāṇv-īśvara, and was one of the three kingdoms of Ṭakka, Sindhu, and Gurjara which touched the boundary of the Vardhana kingdom in the west. Harsha too is said to have 'won fame by pounding a King of Sindh'.[5] The King of Sindhu against whom Prabhākara-vardhana fought must have been a member of the Rāi dynasty, probably Rāi Sihras II, the son of Rāi Sāhasī.[6]

[1] Raised by R. C. Majumdar, *H.C.I.P.* iii, p. 98.

[2] Beal ii, pp. 276, 279, and 280; Watters ii, pp. 256–61. The kingdoms of A-tien-po-chih-lo, Pi-to-shih-lo, and A-fan-t'u are said to have been subject to Sin-tu; also see Watters's map.

[3] Watters ii, pp. 252–4.

[4] *C.A.G.I.*, pp. 286–7, 296–7. According to various Persian works, including the thirteenth-century *Chach-nāmā*, also known as *Tārikh-i-Hind wa Sind* and *Fathnama*, the capital city of Sindh was 'ar-Rūr' (present Rohri?).

[5] *H.C.* text, p. 91; trans., p. 76.

[6] Tuhfat ul-Kirām (A.H. 1181, A.D. 1784). Extracts translated by Lt. Postans in *J.A.S.B.* xiv (1845), pt. i, 78–9. According to *Chach-nāmā* (extracts trans. by H. M. Elliot, i, pp. 131–211) and *Ta'rīkh-i-Ma'sūmī*, also known as *Tarikh-i-Sind* (extracts trans. by H. M. Elliot, i, pp. 212–52), the three princes of the Rāi dynasty who immediately preceded Chach were Rāi Dīwāji, Rāi Sihras, and Rāi Sāhasī, but the *Tuhfat-ul-Kirām* mentions two more—Rāi Sihras II and Rāi Sāhasī II. It also says that the Rāis ruled for a period of 137 years from A.D. 485 to 622, which gives a fair average of 27 years rule to each king. But Chach, the successor of the Rāis, was a brahman, whereas Hsüan-tsang, who visited Sindh in *c.* A.D. 640, describes the ruler of Sindh as a *śūdra*. It is therefore possible that the rule of the Rāis may have continued until *c.* A.D. 640. The caste of the Rāis cannot be decided with full certainty. Chach is said to have defeated and killed a king named Mahrat, who was a relation of Sāhasī, and who is variously described as a chief of Jaipur, Jodhpur, or Chitor. According to H. C. Ray (*D.H.N.I.* i, p. 5 n. 1 and p. 6) he was quite likely of the Mori or the Maurya tribe, which claimed to belong to the Paramāra branch of the Rājputs. One tradition, however, connected with the ancestry of Chandragupta Maurya regards the Mauryas to be of *śūdra* origin (*P.H.A.I.*, pp. 266–7). Is it possible that Hsüan-tsang, on the basis of the latter tradition, described the Rāi king as belonging to the *śūdra* caste? Another possibility is that the Rāis were not of Maurya but of Ṭāk origin. Several writers state that the Ṭāks were one of the three aboriginal, and therefore non-Aryan,

The Gurjaras

The Gurjaras, with whom Prabhākara-vardhana had to contend, may be located in Rājasthān. The question of their origin is controversial. According to K. M. Munshi[1] they were the inhabitants of a large, homogeneous country named Gurjara-deśa, whose isolated fragments still retain the old name in one form or another, such as Gujarāt, Gujar-khān, or Gujarān-vālā. Most scholars, however, are of the view that the term 'Gurjara' primarily denoted a people, and that the name has been retained by the modern Gujars. It is also believed by many historians that the Gurjaras were of foreign origin. According to Vincent Smith, the most important element in the Hūṇa group of tribes, after the Hūṇas themselves, was that of the Gurjaras.[2] The sudden rise of the Gurjaras in the sixth century A.D., and the attempt on the part of their royal dynasties to fabricate a mythical origin, lends support to this view. The problem, however, has been repeatedly discussed by scholars.[3] We agree with R. C. Majumdar that 'this question must be left open till more definite evidence is available'.[4]

The earliest Gurjara kingdom of Māṇḍavya-pura (modern Mandor, five miles north of Jodhpur) was founded by Hari-chandra in *c.* A.D. 550. The Jodhpur inscription of Pratīhāra Bauka[5] records that Hari-chandra had four sons, of whom the third, Rajjila, had a son named Nara-bhaṭa and a grandson named Nāga-bhaṭa. R. C. Majumdar fixes their period of rule between *c.* A.D. 550 and 640.[6] Prabhākara-vardhana may have made incursions into Gurjara territory towards the end of Rajjila's reign or soon after the latter's death in *c.* A.D. 590.

Gandhāra

Gandhāra, another of Prabhākara-vardhana's enemies, was situated on the western bank of the Indus, and is to be identified with Kan-t'o-lo of the 'Records'.[7] Hsüan-tsang states that the country, with its capital at Purusha-pura (Peshawar), was subject to Kapiśa. The northern part of the region (i.e. modern West Panjab and part of North West Frontier Province) that lay between Gandhāra and Sthāṇv-īśvara was subject to Kashmir at the time of Hsüan-tsang's visit in *c.* A.D. 631.[8] But the

races of Sindh. The question of their origin has been dealt with at length by Cunningham (*A.S.I.A.R.* ii, pp. 8 ff.). Hsüan-tsang may have classed the Rāis among *śūdras* because of their non-Aryan Ṭāk origin. Mahrat may have been an ancestor of Rawat Chāṭa Ṭāk, who played an important part in the wars of Pṛithvī-rāja, according to Chānd Bardāi.

[1] *The Glory that was Gurjaradeśa*, pt. iii, pp. 1 ff.

[2] *Early History of India* (4th edn.), p. 427.

[3] *I.H.Q.* x. 337, 613; xi. 167; xiii. 137; *Ind Cul.* i. 510; iv. 113; *J.B.O.R.S.* xxiv. 221.

[4] *H.C.I.P.* iii, p. 65.

[5] *E.I.* xviii. 87 ff. Cf. also *Jour. Dept. Lett.* x. 1 ff.

[6] *H.C.I.P.* iii, p. 65.

[7] Beal i, pp. 97 ff.; Watters i, pp. 198 ff.

[8] The principalities of Taksha-śilā (Watters i, p. 240), Siṁha-pura (loc. cit., p. 248), Wu-la-shih (Uras) (loc. cit., p. 256), Pan-nu-ts'o (Punach) (loc. cit., p. 283), and Rāja-pura (loc. cit., p. 284) are said to have been subject to Kashmir.

political set-up of the Panjab may have been quite different at the time of Prabhākara-vardhana. Kashmir's power increased only after the accession of Durlabha-vardhana of the Kārkoṭa dynasty in *c.* A.D. 601. The principalities which formed part of Kashmir in Hsüan-tsang's day were previously in Kapiśa's orbit of influence, and may have been treated as extensions of her province of Gandhāra.[1] Another Panjab kingdom, Cheh-ka, or Ṭakka, stretching between the Beas and the Sindh, with its principalities extending south-westwards, is mentioned by Hsüan-tsang, but does not figure by that name anywhere in connection with Prabhākara-vardhana's campaigns, presumably because the territory concerned was within Gandhāra. Bāṇa's statement regarding the discomfiture of Gandhāra appears therefore to be based on any raids that Prabhākara-vardhana may have conducted north-west of Sthāṇv-īśvara. An upper hand in such a campaign, along with his victories over Sindhu, would make it seem that Prabhākara-vardhana made his weight felt practically over the whole of north-west India.

The Lāṭas

According to Bāṇa again, Prabhākara-vardhana was 'the destroyer of the skill of the Lāṭas' and 'an axe to the creeper, the royal fortune of the Mālavas'. Lāṭa, the strip of land between the rivers Māhi and the lower Tāptī, at this time may have formed a part of the domains of the Kaḷachuris, who held power during the latter half of the sixth century. The Mauryas of the Koṅkaṇ, who used the Kaḷachuri era beginning A.D. 248–9, probably acknowledged their supremacy. The second Kaḷachuri king, Śaṅkara-gaṇa, issued a charter from his residence, at the victorious camp of Ujjayinī in A.D. 595.[2] He is credited with reinstating many kings who had lost their thrones. The Kaḷachuri victory over Ujjain was won at the expense of the Later Gupta king Mahā-sena-gupta,[3] who seems to have obtained some help from Prabhākara-vardhana, whom we believe to have been his nephew, when attempting to defend his domains. Perhaps the despatch of a few military contingents by the Vardhana king against the power that ruled over Lāṭa appears to have been exaggerated by Bāṇa to glorify his patron's father.

Mālava

Deva-gupta of Mālava, known to us from Harsha's inscriptions and to be identified with the 'wicked lord of Mālava' who killed Graha-varman,[4] may have been one of the 'kings who were reinstated in their thrones' by the Kaḷachuri king Śaṅkara-gaṇa. We have suggested earlier

[1] For the political history of Afghanistan and Panjab at this time see *D.H.N.I.* i, pp. 59–63.

[2] The Abhoṇā plates: *E.I.* ix. 296.

[3] See above, p. 21.

[4] *H.C.* text, p. 183; trans., p. 173; also see above, p. 31.

that Mahā-sena-gupta, after being expelled from Magadha, chose to live in Mālava because of his possible earlier connections with that region.[1] A collateral branch of Mahā-sena-gupta's line may have existed in Mālava for a long period, and Deva-gupta may have been a member of that line. He may have sided with Śaṅkara-gaṇa against Mahā-sena-gupta and the former may have rewarded him with subordinate kingship over Mālava. Though Mahā-sena-gupta was an old man and too weak to re-establish his authority over Mālava, Prabhākara-vardhana, with the ambition to increase his own power, seems to have championed the cause of his uncle. A war against Deva-gupta, though devoid of decisive results, seems to have formed the basis of Bāṇa's statement. Mahā-sena-gupta, at this time of great stress, decided to send his two young sons to the court of Sthāṇv-īśvara. The event is alluded to both in the *Harsha-charita*[2] and in the Aphsaḍ inscription of Āditya-sena.[3]

The Royal Family

As for his faith, Prabhākara-vardhana is said to have been a devotee of the Sun.[4] He had many wives,[5] among whom Yaśo-vatī[6] was the chief queen.[7] She does not seem to have belonged to an important dynasty. Had that been the case Bāṇa would certainly have made note of it.[8] However, she enjoyed an extraordinarily high status. It may be inferred from Bāṇa's account that children from no other wife would do, and the King prayed for progeny by Yaśo-vatī for many years before the gods fulfilled his wish. 'Solemnly at dawn, at midday, and at eve he muttered a prayer [to the Sun] for offspring.'[9] Later they had three children.

The eldest prince, Rājya-vardhana, may have been born towards the

[1] See above, p. 16.

[2] *H.C.* text, p. 138; trans., p. 119.

[3] *C.I.I.* iii, no. 42.

[4] See Harsha's inscriptions, *E.I.* i. 72; iv. 211; *C.I.I.* iii, p. 232; *A.S.I.A.R.* (1917–18), p. 44; *H.C.* text, p. 123; trans., p. 104: 'The king was by natural proclivity a devotee of the sun. Day by day at sunrise he bathed, arrayed himself in white silk, wrapt his head in a white cloth, and kneeling eastwards upon the ground . . . .' The latter part of the description seems to betray foreign, probably Persian, influence.

[5] This is mentioned several times in the *Harsha-charita*: text, pp. 126, 133, 167, etc.; trans., pp. 107, 114, 151, 154, etc.

[6] Yaśo-matī, according to the Sonpat Seal inscription: *C.I.I.* iii, no. 52.

[7] *H.C.* text, p. 123, and Harsha's inscriptions. It is interesting to note that it was Yaśo-vatī alone who performed *satī*, in fact just before her husband's death, an uncommon act.

[8] According to A. F. R. Hoernle [*J.R.A.S.* (1903) 556] Yaśo-vatī was the daughter of King Yaśo-dharman of Mālava. R. K. Mookerji (*Harsha*, pp. 61, 64, etc.) agrees with this view, which is mainly based on similarity of names and on the fact that Yaśo-vatī is said to have been born in a family rendered glorious by Dharma (*H.C.* text, p. 167) and born of a brave father (ibid.). This view is clearly defective because Yaśo-dharman of Mālava probably disappeared from the political scene soon after A.D. 533, the date of his inscription, whereas Yaśo-vatī's parents, on the basis of an indirect reference in the *Harsha-charita* (text, p. 166; trans., p. 152), outlived her and her husband.

[9] *H.C.* text, p. 123; trans., p. 104.

end of A.D. 586, as he is stated to have been nearing his sixth year[1] when Harsha, who was born in A.D. 590, on June 4, according to C. V. Vaidya,[2] 'could just manage five or six paces with the support of his nurse's finger'.[3] Rājya-vardhana's birth was celebrated with great rejoicing at the capital.

The event of Harsha's birth, however, is naturally given greater importance by his biographer, and includes such details as were always noted for the purposes of horoscopy. It is stated that Harsha, conceived in the month of Śrāvaṇa, was born in the month of Jyeshṭha, on the twelfth day of the dark fortnight, the moon being in the Kṛittikā constellation, just after the twilight time.[4] A Maga[5] astrologer told the King that the child was born at a conjuncture of the planets which was fittest for the birth of a universal emperor. According to the *Harsha-charita* all the planets were in their exaltation at the time of Harsha's birth, but the accuracy of this statement is questionable.[6]

Great festivities followed Harsha's birth.[7] Some interesting facts are revealed in Bāṇa's account of the celebration. Prisoners were freed; shops were given up to general pillage.[8] The royal treasury probably made good the loss incurred by shopkeepers on such occasions. Wives of feudatory kings brought endless presents, consisting mostly of flowers, nuts, and perfumes. 'The whole population of the capital set a-dancing.'

The youngest child, the princess Rājya-śrī, was born in A.D. 592.[9] The name of another scion of the Vardhana family is mentioned by Bāṇa. One Kṛishṇa is said to have been a brother of Harsha.[10] He was probably a cousin of Harsha, or his stepbrother, born of one of the subordinate wives of Prabhākara-vardhana.[11]

The Princes' royal companions: Bhaṇḍi

About the time that Rājya-śrī was born (*c.* A.D. 592), and the princes Rājya-vardhana and Harsha were respectively about 6 and 2 years old, Yaśo-vatī's brother is said to have presented his son Bhaṇḍi, aged 8, to

[1] According to Indian custom the child when approximately 4¾ years of age would be described as nearing his sixth year, i.e. about to enter into his sixth year after completing five.

[2] *J.B.B.R.A.S.* xxiv. 252–4.

[3] *H.C.* text, p. 134; trans., p. 115.

[4] *H.C.* text, p. 128.

[5] For the Bhojakas or Magas, worshippers of the sun, see Wilson's *Vishṇu Purāṇa* (Hall's edn.) v, p. 382; P. V. Kane, *Notes on the Harsha-charita* (henceforth *H.C.*), Ch. IV, p. 23.

[6] C. V. Vaidya, *J.B.B.R.A.S.* xxiv. 252 ff.; P. V. Kane, *Notes on the H.C.*, Ch. IV, p. 24.

[7] *H.C.* text, pp. 110 ff.; trans., pp. 110 ff.

[8] See *H.C.* trans., p. 111 n. 2.

[9] It is said that the princess was conceived when Harsha 'could just manage five or six paces with the support of his nurse's fingers', i.e. when he was just over a year old. *H.C.* text, p. 134; trans., p. 115.

[10] *H.C.* text, p. 52; trans., p. 40: cf. P. V. Kane, *Notes on the H.C.*, Ch. II, p. 107.

[11] It is common practice in India to refer to cousins or stepbrothers as brothers.

serve on the Vardhana princes.[1] This may have been done to earn the goodwill of the Vardhana monarch, under whose care the child would also have better opportunities for a good general education including military training. 'To this additional son', writes Bāṇa, 'the king's regard was equally attached.'[2] The three princes received intensive training in archery, swordsmanship, and other allied skills. Bhaṇḍi attained an important position in the royal household and served the family capably and loyally.[3]

and the Mālava princes

In *c.* A.D. 601, when Rājya-vardhana and Harsha were approximately 15 and 11 years of age, two Mālava princes, Kumāra-gupta and Mādhava-gupta, were introduced to the royal household to serve on the Vardhana princes. They are to be identified with Mahā-sena-gupta's sons, the younger of whom is mentioned in the Aphsaḍ inscription of Āditya-sena as one 'who desired to associate himself with the glorious Harṣadeva'.[4] The name of the elder brother, Kumāra-gupta, is not included in the genealogical lists in the Later Gupta inscriptions, probably because he predeceased his younger brother, Mādhava-gupta, by several years. At the time of presentation Kumāra-gupta is stated to have been about 18 years of age, 'neither very tall nor very short', while the younger prince, who may have been approximately 16 'for height and dignity resembled a moving realgar mountain'.[5] Their status was lower than that of Bhaṇḍi.[6] Because of his trustworthiness and ability, however, Bhaṇḍi, it seems, was never spared from his duties at the centre when Harsha came to occupy the throne. The Mālava princes too probably spent the greater part of their lives at Harsha's court, although the younger brother, Mādhava-gupta, appears to have been entrusted with the governorship of Magadha towards the end of his career.

On Bāṇa's testimony Harsha seems to have been particularly attached to Mādhava-gupta, who accompanied him on his first military campaign and was with him during the search for his sister in the Vindhya forest. The King's 'favourite, the son of the king of Mālava',[7] seated behind him in the court when Bāṇa was first admitted into Harsha's presence,

[1] *H.C.* text, p. 135; trans., p. 116.
[2] *H.C.* trans., p. 117.
[3] Bhaṇḍi accompanied the princes on their campaign against the Hūṇas and stayed with Harsha, who spent some time hunting on the skirts of the Himalayas (see *H.C.* trans., p. 135). He accompanied Rājya-vardhana on the expedition against the King of Mālava (op. cit., p. 175). On Harsha's orders he continued the march to Kanauj to rescue it from the King of Gauḍa (op. cit., p. 224). Finally we know from Hsüan-tsang (Beal i, p. 210) that Bhaṇḍi (Po-ni) advised the statesmen of Kanauj to declare Harsha as their king.
[4] *C.I.I.* iii, no. 42.
[5] *H.C.* text, pp. 138–9; trans., pp. 120–1.
[6] Cf. *H.C.* text, pp. 135 and 138–40; trans., pp. 115–17 and 120–1.
[7] *H.C.* text, p. 79; trans., p. 66.

may well have been Mādhava-gupta if he was not Kumāra-gupta. It seems reasonable to suppose that, after the death of Pūrṇa-varman of Magadha, Harsha bestowed the governorship of that province on Mādhava-gupta, whose son Āditya-sena was therefore able to re-establish the authority of the Later Guptas in Magadha after Harsha's death.[1]

The elder Mālava prince, Kumāra-gupta, apparently had a very short and uneventful career and as mentioned earlier seems to have died very young.

A romantic episode portraying Harsha's gallantry in saving the life of a royal personage from the wiles of an elephant is punningly referred to in the *Harsha-charita*.[2] The commentator identifies the rescued king with one Kumāra[3] who we think was the same as the elder Mālava prince, Kumāra-gupta.[4]

The Vardhana–Maukhari matrimonial alliance

While the five young companions, their ages ranging between 11 or 12 and 18, advanced towards maturity, practising themselves in the arts of war, the young princess Rājya-śrī 'gradually grew up in daily increasing familiarity with friends expert in song, dance, etc. and with all accomplishments. In a comparatively limited period she came to maturity.'[5] A period of eighteen months to two years may by now have elapsed after the presentation of the Mālava princes. Rājya-śrī could not have been much more than 11 when her nuptials were planned. 'Not too tightly

[1] 'Life', p. 154 refers to Pūrṇa-varman's death, while the Aphsaḍ (Gayā) inscription (*C.I.I.* iii, no. 42), the earliest of Āditya-sena, proves the re-emergence of the Later Guptas in Magadha. R. S. Tripathi, *History of Kanauj*, p. 100, and B. P. Sinha, *Decline of the Kingdom of Magadha*, p. 263, place Pūrṇa-varman and Harsha in the same category as rulers of Magadha, the latter succeeding the former. We believe that this is an erroneous evaluation of their respective positions in the political system of the period. It should be remembered that Hsüan-tsang, whose account is the basis of our information, indiscriminately styles all rulers, petty or big, subject or independent, as kings. Harsha's sphere of influence undoubtedly extended to Magadha and well beyond at the time of Hsüan-tsang's visit. Pūrṇa-varman may well have been a scion of the Maukhari family, and with his usual political sagacity Harsha may have patronized him as the 'king' of Magadha. A continuance of the same policy would guide the choice of Mādhava-gupta for the same role. After Śaśāṅka's chastisement early in his reign, Harsha ruled as the paramount ruler of practically the whole of northern India, including Magadha.

[2] *H.C.* text, p. 91; trans., p. 76.

[3] Ibid., commentary below text.

[4] An identification of the elephant too is offered by the commentator. It is stated to be Darpa-śāta, Harsha's favourite war elephant. This, however, is not acceptable, for elsewhere (*H.C.*, text, p. 64; trans., p. 51) Bāṇa testifies to having seen the animal in Harsha's stables, presumably not long before narrating the episode in question. The commentator Śaṅkara composed his work sometime between the ninth and twelfth centuries A.D. (P. V. Kane, *Notes on the H.C.*, Introd., pp. xli–xlii). By this time Darpa-śāta's name must have passed into legend, for he was not treated like an ordinary beast even in Harsha's day, as is evident from Bāṇa's detailed description (*H.C.* text, pp. 64–5; trans., pp. 51–6). The commentator therefore seems to have been tempted to suggest this identification.

[5] *H.C.* text, p. 140; trans., p. 121.

embraced by womanhood'[1] is how she is described at the time of her wedding. She was to be given in marriage to the Maukhari king Graha-varman, who among others had sent his envoy to ask for the princess's hand. The prospect of an alliance with an important ruling family may have been one of the reasons why Prabhākara-vardhana married off his daughter at an early age. Bāṇa attributes to him the following words: 'the Mukharas stand at the head of all royal houses . . . worshipped like Śiva's footprint by all the world'.[2] Graha-varman is said to have been the eldest son of Avanti-varman, and succeeded his father on the throne of Kanauj.[3] Bāṇa's detailed description of the marriage preparations throws a flood of light on the social customs and everyday life of that period. A few references of political interest also occur in this section. We are told that the feudatory kings and their queens assisted in several ways in the manifold tasks entailed in getting ready for the great occasion.[4] The wedding may have taken place around A.D. 603–4, when Rājya-śrī was nearly 12 years of age.

Prince Rājya-vardhana despatched against the Hūṇas

A family responsibility over and an important ally secured, the King attended to more pressing matters. We are told that Rājya-vardhana's campaign against the Hūṇas was organized after Rājya-śrī's marriage. Described as of an age which 'now fitted him for wearing armour',[5] Rājya-vardhana may have been about 18 when he set out on his mission. As noted earlier, the prince's success against the enemy is testified not only by Bāṇa's observations to this effect but also by the fact that Harsha's reign was free from the Hūṇa menace.

Prabhākara-vardhana's illness and death-bed bequest in favour of Harsha

While the princes were away, Prabhākara-vardhana became seriously ill. Harsha, summoned by emissaries from the hunt he was enjoying at the foot of the Himalayas, much closer to the capital than his brother's field of action, arrived just in time to receive his father's last instructions. It appears that Rājya-vardhana returned only after completing his task, and probably received the sad news somewhere on the way. He arrived at the capital several weeks after Prabhākara-vardhana's death, when 'The horror of the days of impurity had passed . . . . Grief was becoming

[1] *H.C.* text, p. 146; trans., p. 128.

[2] *H.C.* text, p. 141; also see trans., p. 122.

[3] This supports the view that Avanti-varman had more than one son.

[4] *H.C.* trans., p. 124: 'Even kings girt up their loins, and busied themselves in carrying out decorative work set as tasks by their sovereign.'

[5] *H.C.* text, p. 150; trans., p. 132. Describing the appearance of a dishevelled Rājya-vardhana returning from the campaign after his father's death, Bāṇa writes 'his beard showed but a faint growth' (*H.C.* text, p. 176; trans., p. 166). If taken to denote the prince's youth and not an unshaven beard, and the former seems to be Bāṇa's intention from the choice of his words, then it is an understatement and a part of the poet's rhetoric, since Rājya-vardhana was 19 years old in 605.

a moral theme . . .'.[1] The King's illness must have been sudden and brief. Of his three children only Harsha managed to be by his bedside.

From the time of the fatal illness of Prabhākara-vardhana, Bāṇa begins to prepare his readers for Harsha's succession in preference to Rājya-vardhana. The theme is pursued subtly, but with such tenacity[2] that it is surprising that writers on the subject have not so far drawn attention to it. Did Harsha in some way connive at gaining the throne? The question is of minor importance, but we must examine our testimony closely as the doubt has never been raised before.

According to Harsha's inscriptions, Hsüan-tsang's account, and the *Mañju-śrī-mūla-kalpa*, Rājya-vardhana succeeded Prabhākara-vardhana, but the fact remains unsupported by Bāṇa's biography of Harsha. As Bāṇa records the events in such great detail, one wonders why, if Rājya-vardhana inherited the throne, he does not state so explicitly; rather by implication he indicates the contrary.

Mention of Rājya-vardhana as the heir apparent is conspicuous by its absence in the last two speeches of the ailing King. Surprisingly, no regret is expressed at his absence, no inquiries made after him of Harsha, who had been the last to see his brother, no advice given to the younger son to serve the elder loyally on the latter's accession to the throne. The King is in fact shown as bequeathing his title to Harsha, at least verbally: 'Upon you my happiness, my sovereignty, my succession, and my life are set, and as mine, so those of all my people. . . . You bear marks declaring the sovereignty of the four oceans, . . . you, . . . through the merits of a whole people are born for the protection of all the earth . . .'.[3] And, again, 'To declare this earth yours is almost a vain repetition . . . . Succeed to this world, is a command too mean for an intending conqueror of both worlds. . .'. 'Support the burden of royalty. . . Protect the people . . .'.[4]

The impression created by the above words is confirmed by later descriptions. Harsha's fears regarding his brother's aversion to the throne, expressed in the following words by Bāṇa, are most unnatural: 'Pray heaven my brother, when he learns of our father's death, . . . may not . . . assume two robes of bark! or seek a hermitage as a royal sage! . . . Never may indifference due to the transitoriness of things lead him to slight the advances of sovereign glory! . . . Once arrived here may he not, when pressed by the kings, display a contrary mind!'[5]

[1] *H.C.* text, p. 175; trans., pp. 164–5.
[2] See *H.C.* trans., pp. 154–76. [3] *H.C.* text, p. 158; trans., pp. 142–3.
[4] *H.C.* text, pp. 168–9; trans., pp. 155–6.
[5] *H.C.* text, pp. 173–4; trans., pp. 162–3.

The account proceeds logically and Harsha's fears prove true. On return, 'all the kings being admitted' to their presence, Rājya-vardhana thus addressed himself to Harsha: 'It is some native cowardice . . . which has rendered me subject to the flame of filial grief . . . . My mind seeks to avoid . . . glory . . . . I desire . . . a hermitage . . . . Therefore do you receive from my hands the cares of sovereignty . . . . I have abandoned the sword.'[1]

It is unaccountable why Harsha did not openly protest against his brother's unusual decision if he was really grieved by it. It seems significant that Bāṇa depicts Harsha as suffering great mental torture only in silence, which in the circumstances might actually be taken for a tacit acceptance of the offer.

The Mālava–Gauḍa–Kanauj conflict. Sthāṇv-Īśvara enters the war

The report of an unexpected disaster resolved the apparent dilemma. A courier arrived with the news that as soon as Prabhākara-vardhana's death was rumoured the King of Mālava had attacked and killed Graha-varman Maukhari and imprisoned in Kānya-kubja his young wife, the Vardhana princess. Moreover, taking advantage of Sthāṇv-Īśvara's adverse circumstances, he proposed to invade that kingdom as well.[2] The desperate Rājya-vardhana immediately abandoned the decision to retire, and declared his resolve to avenge family honour. 'This task, my noble brother,' he said to Harsha, 'is my royal house, this my kin, my court, my land, my people . . . . this and no other is my assumption of the bark dress . . . . Let all the kings and elephants stay with you. Only Bhaṇḍi here must follow me with some ten thousand horse.'[3]

Bāṇa's account of Rājya-vardhana's reaction to the humiliating news is, in his usual style, full of suggestive similes which presage the prince's death,[4] but the exultation over a truly *kshatriya*-like act is not accompanied, as might be expected of a poet of Bāṇa's skill, by an expression through metaphorical allusion of grief at the event which was to follow. Moreover, Harsha, who had listened in silence to his elder brother's earlier declarations regarding his giving up the succession, is shown protesting aloud on this occasion at not being allowed to join the campaign. Rājya-vardhana thereupon consoled him by saying, 'for the province of your prowess you have already the earth . . . . forgive this one unshared morsel of wrath.'[5]

[1] *H.C.* text, pp. 179–80; trans., pp. 169–70.
[2] *H.C.* text, p. 183; trans., p. 173.
[3] *H.C.* text, p. 184; trans., pp. 174–5.
[4] *H.C.* text, pp. 183–4; trans., p. 174: 'On his [Rājya-vardhana's] broad brow a deadly frown broke forth, darkening like Yama's sister . . . . On his cheeks appeared an angry flush, as if Sovereignty, delighted by his taking up arms, were celebrating an ovation by scattered vermilion powder.'
[5] *H.C.* text, p. 185; trans., p. 176.

It is hard to escape the conclusion that the unusual twists in the story, from the time of Prabhākara-vardhana's illness to the time of Rājya-vardhana's death, however cleverly manipulated, were rendered inevitable because of some episode uncomplimentary to the author's hero. In spite of the speech attributed to Prabhākara-vardhana virtually bidding Harsha to succeed him, it is difficult to see why the King would want to suppress the rightful claim of his eldest son to the throne. That he entrusted Rājya-vardhana with the responsible task of tackling the Hūṇas is a proof of his faith in the ability of the elder prince.

Why did not Harsha make known to Rājya-vardhana, and to all witnesses present, his great mental anguish at being offered the throne which should fittingly have been occupied by his brother? Why did he not reject the proposal even once, in an effort to persuade Rājya-vardhana to act in the traditional way? On the other hand, why did he choose to speak out and protest at being left behind when his brother wished to set out for Kanauj with Bhaṇḍi and ten thousand cavalry to take revenge on the King of Mālava? Did Harsha depend on the support of the key man Bhaṇḍi,[1] whom he had been able to win over to his side after the King's death and before the return of his brother to the capital? Was it the pressure of such a situation that forced Rājya-vardhana to offer the throne to Harsha, perhaps with a view to seizing power for himself later? Did Rājya-vardhana reckon that the sudden Kanauj episode provided him with an opportunity to change the situation in his own favour? Was the decision to conduct the campaign on his own, and to take Bhaṇḍi and a body of picked soldiers with him, guided by such a motive? Success against the King of Mālava and control over Kanauj would have placed Rājya-vardhana in a very strong position indeed. It is not possible to answer these questions, but the fact that Bāṇa's narrative gives rise to them proves that a complex situation existed even if it remains obscure. In any case the problem was easily and summarily solved by Rājya-vardhana's early death in the Kanauj campaign. Harsha became the rightful successor to the throne. Requirements, both of graciousness and of filial piety, were fulfilled on his part by revering the memory of his deceased elder brother in family records, royal grants, and inscriptions. The suspicion, if warranted, attached to the circumstances in which he became king was both covered up and forgotten by several aiding factors, for instance many events crowded in a very short

[1] His importance for the Vardhanas as a courtier cannot be minimized. After Rājya-vardhana's death and the sack of Kanauj it was he, if we accept the identification of Hsüan-tsang's Po-ni with Bhaṇḍi, who through his clever canvassing secured for Harsha the additional and more important kingdom of Kanauj: see Beal i, pp. 210–11.

period, culminating in the speedy removal from the scene of the rival successor, in the most natural circumstances. For Hsüan-tsang, or the much later author of the *Mañju-śrī-mūla-kalpa*, no undignified situation may even have existed, so regular Harsha's succession seemed after the death of Rājya-vardhana, who would automatically be considered the intervening monarch between his father and younger brother. Hsüan-tsang, however, was aware of some prevailing story about Harsha's initial diffidence in ascending the throne. He relates it in connection with Kanauj, most probably because he associated the Vardhanas with the city that was Harsha-vardhana's capital at the time of his visit.[1]

Rājya-vardhana's death

As befitted a *kshatriya* by vocation (by birth a *vaiśya*),[2] Rājya-vardhana died in a military campaign, but not, as might have been expected, on the battlefield. To Harsha, waiting in the capital, news was brought by a discomfited cavalry officer that, although Rājya-vardhana had succeeded in routing the Mālava forces, he 'had been allured to confidence by false civilities on the part of the King of Gauḍa and then weaponless, confiding, and alone, despatched in his own quarters.'[3]

The King of Gauḍa of this statement is to be identified with Śaśāṅka, Deva-gupta's ally in the grand design to annex first Kanauj and then Sthāṇv-īśvara. The battle between Rājya-vardhana and Deva-gupta was in all likelihood fought at Kanauj. The latter must have been killed in the conflict, for he is heard of no more. In the meantime Śaśāṅka, instead of an open fight, appears to have tried unscrupulous means of getting rid of the enemy as testified by the *Harsha-charita* and other contemporary sources.

Harsha in his inscriptions states that his brother 'in consequence of his adherence to his promise gave up his life in the mansion of his foe'.[4] According to Hsüan-tsang, Śaśāṅka and his ministers asked Rājya-vardhana 'to a conference and murdered him'.[5] The same author later states that, 'owing to the fault of his ministers, he [Rājya-vardhana] was

[1] Beal i, pp. 211–12; Watters i, pp. 343 ff. It is possible that Harsha expressed hesitation at occupying the throne of Kanauj, not because of his lack of confidence but rather because common custom demanded that succession should pass on to a Maukhari. The presence of Pūrṇa-varnam may have presented just such a hurdle. In the circumstances, modesty on his part, rather than assertion, appears to have won Harsha the support of the Kanauj ministers and courtiers.

[2] The Chinese text simply states that Harsha was of *fei-she* (*vaiśya*) extraction. The explanation given in the notes (Beal i, p. 209 n. 12, 'Life', p. 83 n. 1, cf. Watters i, pp. 344–5) that he was a Bais Rajput stems from Cunningham (*C.A.G.I.*, pp. 432–3). There is nothing in the original which warrants this explanation. Also see below, p. 109.

[3] *H.C.* text, p. 186; trans., p. 178. Later in the narrative Bāṇa makes another reference to Śaśāṅka's villainy by warning Harsha through his army commandant against the dangers of being too trustful. *H.C.* text, p. 198; trans., p. 192.

[4] *E.I.* i. 72–4.

[5] Beal i, p. 210.

led to subject his person to the hand of his enemy'.[1] Hsüan-tsang's biographer records that Śaśāṅka, 'hating the superior military talents of the king [Rājya-vardhana], made a plot and murdered him'. The commentator to the *Harsha-charita*, though by no means wholly reliable, for he was writing long after the event took place, gives us some details about the cryptic story. He explains that 'Śaśāṅka enticed Rājya-vardhana through a spy by the offer of his daughter's hand, and while the unlucky king with his retinue was participating in a dinner in his enemy's camp, he was killed by the Gauḍa king in disguise'.[2]

However discreditable Śaśāṅka's conduct may have been, Rājya-vardhana's response, whether caused by trust or foolishness, resulted in the defeat of the Vardhana army. The details of the humiliating episode are therefore omitted by Harsha in his inscriptions and by Bāṇa in his biography of Harsha. The same example is followed by Hsüan-tsang and others, causing thus a different wording in each case to describe the same event.

Much has been made of this discrepancy by some authors,[3] in spite of the fact that all sources agree that Rājya-vardhana's death took place in suspicious circumstances. While all informants may be expected to be sympathetic to Rājya-vardhana there is nothing particularly unusual or abhorrent, by standards accepted then as now, in plotting an enemy's death in war. Śaśāṅka appears to have been a practical, hard-headed man and may have felt that Rājya-vardhana, being the brother-in-law of the murdered king, should be removed from the scene surreptitiously rather than in open combat, for almost certainly the Kanauj forces would have rallied round the Vardhana on the battlefield. In view of this situation the almost legalistic case made out by Śaśāṅka's defenders to prove his innocence remains weak if the validity or necessity of giving the matter such treatment is admitted.

Śaśāṅka's exit

Śaśāṅka succeeded in getting rid of an important foe but his position remained insecure. Not only had his ally the King of Mālava been destroyed by the Vardhana forces but perhaps also the Kanauj courtiers and army were now more hostile towards him than ever before. Rājya-vardhana, moreover, was survived by a younger brother who would naturally make an all-out effort to avenge his many losses. Nor was Śaśāṅka's rear flank safe. His neighbour Bhāskara-varman, the King of

[1] Op. cit., p. 211; The phrase 'owing to the fault of his ministers' may also be interpreted as 'owing to a lack of virtue on the part of the ministers' (*Hsi Yü Chi* text v. 3a).

[2] *H.C.I.P.* iii, p. 122.

[3] R. P. Chanda, *Gauḍa-rāja-mālā*, pp. 8 ff.; R. C. Majumdar, *H.C.I.P.* iii, pp. 121 ff.

Kāma-rūpa (Assam), fearing Śaśāṅka's increasing power, had probably already dispatched an envoy to seek a treaty with the Vardhanas, for Harsha was met by him on the first stage of his march from Sthāṅv-īśvara to Kanauj. Afraid perhaps of an attack on Gauḍa by Bhāskara-varman now that circumstances had turned against him, Śaśāṅka gave up his prize of Kanauj and hurried back to his capital.

Harsha enters the war

On hearing the news of his brother's defeat and death, Harsha promptly resolved to organize a *dig-vijaya* or 'conquest of the four quarters'. This bold undertaking was generally reserved for more powerful monarchs, but, as political terminology had become rather hyperbolic by Harsha's time, Bāṇa employs the term *dig-vijaya* to describe Harsha's north-Indian campaign. By the time Bāṇa wrote his incomplete biography Harsha had probably conquered the 'five Indias' referred to by Hsüan-tsang. His achievements were therefore impressive enough to admit of grandiose treatment, especially by a poet.

Harsha was particularly fortunate in having the solid support and encouragement of his lieutenants to back his schemes. An elder states-man of Sthāṇv-īśvara, Siṁha-nāda, who was also the commander of the armed forces, strongly advised Harsha to embark on an extensive mili-tary campaign. 'Think not . . . of the Gauda king alone,' he counselled, 'so deal that for the future no other follow his example.' Accordingly Harsha instructed his minister of war and peace to issue the usual proclamation challenging all kings either to fight or to submit. The commandant of the elephant corps, apparently the most important wing of the army, was ordered to lead the preparations for a speedy massing of the forces.

The ambitious venture proved a success, firstly through a correct assessment of the actual and potential military and political strength of the parties involved, and secondly through a lucky combination of cir-cumstances. Rājya-vardhana's death in mysterious conditions prepared for Harsha a sympathetic climate at Kanauj, while it affected Śaśāṅka's reputation adversely. But, even more important is the fact that Śaśāṅka's neighbour, the King of Kāma-rūpa, sought on his own initiative a sub-ordinate alliance with Harsha, perfectly timed to give the latter both the psychological and the strategic advantage over Śaśāṅka.

Sthāṇv-īśvara–Kāma-rūpa alliance

The seventh chapter of the *Harsha-charita* describes the eastward march of the Vardhana army and Harsha's interview with the envoy from Kāma-rūpa. Bāṇa entitles the chapter 'The Gift of the Umbrella' after the present offered by King Bhāskara-varman of Kāma-rūpa to Harsha. An umbrella shading the king was the symbol of royal authority according to Indian custom. This umbrella was especially valuable as it was an heirloom and was also something of a marvel since it had the property of emitting coolness, apart from sheltering a person from the sun. The fact that he surrendered it clearly shows that Bhāskara-varman was greatly afraid of Śaśāṅka and most anxious to secure Harsha's support even at the cost of compromising his own status. For Harsha too the alliance was equally important at this stage. His pleasure and gratification at the offer show up as clearly in Bāṇa's description of his audience with the Kāma-rūpa envoy, as, indeed, does Bhāskara-varman's anguish at having to accept an inferior status in the relationship. Responding to the latter's overture for friendship, Harsha is reputed to have told the emissary: 'How could the mind of one like me possibly even in a dream show aversion . . ., when such a great and noble spirit . . . bestows his love . . . upon me?'[1] The envoy, though he expressed his master's profuse gratitude at the acceptance of his request, went on to describe in great detail the misfortunes of those in need of favour. The overspill of sentiment on this subject reflects no doubt Bāṇa's own love of freedom. The envoy's speech includes such remarks as 'Even your majesty's generous words give a pain to my noble master' or 'This dreadful name of servant, like a torrent of mud, lays everything low.' Again, sorrowful in the helplessness of having to bow his haughty head, 'Better for a manly man is a moment of manliness; at the price of bowing the wise deem not even the joy of a world-sovereignty worth a bow. Therefore let your majesty, approving of our love, bethink himself that the king of Assam died only a few days ago.'[2]

The desired meeting between Bhāskara-varman and Harsha may have taken place at the successful termination of the latter's eastern campaign, pushing Śaśāṅka to his native Gauḍa. It seems that Harsha, in the tradition of paramount sovereigns, used this opportunity formally to instal Bhāskara-varman on the throne of Kāma-rūpa. Such ceremonies were significant.[3] Acknowledgement of his suzerainty by an important, lesser king added to the prestige of the overlord, while the former felt protected

[1] *H.C.* text, p. 221; trans., pp. 218–19.

[2] *H.C.* text, pp. 221, 224, 225; trans., pp. 219, 222, 223. The whole speech of the envoy, full of flattering and deflating effects at the same time, is a most skilful example of the poet's punning, such as would arouse any diplomat's envy. In case Harsha might be annoyed at not being offered whole-hearted submission, the first sentence in the examples cited above may be equally correctly translated as 'Nothing but eagerness to see one another will hereafter pain the two kings', and the last as 'Therefore let your majesty, approving of our love, consider the King of Assam arrived within a few days'.

[3] The Maitraka King Droṇa-Siṁha's anointing by a Gupta overlord is proudly related in the Valabhī grants: see *C.I.I.* iii, no. 38.

against any likely threat from an ambitious neighbour. In all likelihood Bāṇa's reference[1] to the anointing of one Kumāra among Harsha's achievements recounts an installation ceremony customary in early Indian political practice.

In spite of some scholars' opinion to the contrary[2] there is no reason to doubt that the King of Kāma-rūpa acknowledged the superiority of Harsha. As Harsha's power and prestige grew with the years, the relationship between him and Kumāra or Bhāskara-varman became confirmed as one of a paramount sovereign receiving homage from an internally independent yet subordinate member of the loose hegemony of states that were under his direct or indirect influence. An incident related by Hsüan-tsang, to be placed towards the end of Harsha's reign, illustrates the point well. When Hsüan-tsang was a guest of the King of Kāma-rūpa, Harsha, returning from a military campaign in nearby Orissa, despatched a messenger asking Bhāskara-varman to send the Chinese pilgrim to his camp. 'He can take my head, but he cannot take the Master of the Law yet', replied the King of Kāma-rūpa. Harsha, enraged at the insolence, retorted peremptorily: 'Send the head, that I may have it immediately . . . .'[3] Bhāskara-varman realized his folly and at once set out for Kajangala (Ka-shêng-ki-lo), near Rāj-mahal, where Harsha was encamped, with the much-sought-after Buddhist scholar. On arrival, however, he was received without incident. Harsha apparently had the quality of discretion in full measure.

Bhaṇḍi's return The meeting between Harsha and the envoy from Kāma-rūpa took place at the very outset of Harsha's eastward march, in fact at the first encampment on the outskirts of his capital. He continued on his course

[1] *H.C.* text, p. 91; trans., p. 76. Cowell and Thomas take *Kumāra* to be a common noun and translate it as 'young prince', but we think that Harsha's achievement would not have been considered worthy of mention if Kumāra in this case did not stand for the King of Kāma-rūpa. Not that the passage in question does not use common nouns of this nature, such as *kshiti-bhṛit* and *bhūbhṛit*, which apparently do not refer to any specific kings. But our assumption regarding Kumāra in this passage is based on a number of other references in the *Harsha-charita* which clearly show that Kumāra was the King of Assam (*Prāgjyotisheśvareṇa Kumāreṇa*: *H.C.* text, p. 214). Cowell and Thomas make an obvious mistake in this case by rendering the phrase as 'heir apparent of Assam' (p. 211), omitting the translation of the word *Īśvara* altogether. Elsewhere, however, when *Prāgjyotisheśvara* does not occur with Kumāra (text p. 220), they have translated it as 'the sovereign of Assam' (p. 218). Hsüan-tsang mostly uses the name Kumāra for the King of Kāma-rūpa and states that it was his title (Beal ii, p. 196). The *Hsin T'ang Shu*, in the context in which it gives the name of 'the king of eastern India' has Shih-chiu-ma (Srī Kumāra) (see below, p. 215) is obviously referring to the King of Kāma-rūpa. Bāṇa addresses him by different names, e.g. Kumāra, Bhāskara-varman, and Bhāskara-dyuti (*H.C.* text, pp. 214 and 217).

[2] R. C. Majumdar, *H.C.I.P.* iii, p. 113; R. S. Tripathi, *History of Kanauj*, p. 104.

[3] 'Life', p. 172.

by 'ceaseless marches'. Probably half-way between Sthāṇv-īśvara and Kanauj he was met by Bhaṇḍi, who had arrived 'with the Mālava king's whole force, conquered by the might of Rājya-vardhana'.[1] The spoils of war included captive soldiers and women, elephants and horses, jewels and ornaments, and other royal insignia such as lion-thrones, chowries, and umbrellas. Bhaṇḍi is said to have narrated the unfortunate story in full, concluding thus: '. . . after his majesty Rājya-vardhana was taken to paradise and Kānya-kubja was seized by the man named Gupta, Queen Rājya-śrī burst from her confinement, and with her train entered the Vindhya forest.'[2] Relating Rājya-śrī's plight once again on a later occasion Bāṇa records that 'she was sent away from Kānya-kubja, from her confinement there during the Gauḍa trouble, through the action of a noble named Gupta'.[3] The mention of two characters, both bearing the name Gupta, to whom are attributed acts of contradictory purport, creates some confusion. In fact the person responsible for casting Rājya-śrī into prison in the first place may also be safely assumed to be a man named Gupta, Deva-gupta of Mālava.[4] However, the Gupta who is said to have seized Kanauj after Rājya-verdhana's death must be identified with Śaśāṅka, who is also known as Narendra-gupta in one manuscript of the *Harsha-charita.*[5] It is, however, difficult to identify the 'noble named Gupta'. Even if action on the part of the 'Gupta' be deemed accidental and not intentional the use of the epithet 'noble' (*kula-putra*, 'gentleman') precludes the possibility of his being Śaśāṅka, who would be styled king. The 'Gupta' of this statement may have been a member of the Kanauj household but he could equally well have been a kind-hearted man of Śaśāṅka's camp who viewed the young Queen's imprisonment as an act of unnecessary cruelty.

Search for Rājya-śrī and her recovery

Harsha decided to go in search of his sister instead of leading the army, a task which he entrusted to Bhaṇḍi, perhaps on the latter's advice. This course may have been dictated by considerations both humane and political. The former are obvious. The latter too would be better served if Bhaṇḍi could prepare the psychological climate at Kanauj for acceptance there of Harsha's leadership. Moreover the presence beside him of the late king's queen would definitely enhance Harsha's chances of succession to the Maukhari domains.

The Vindhya region extended well up to the outskirts of the Gangetic Doab kingdoms, and Harsha, travelling on horseback, arrived there in

[1] *H.C.* text, p. 225; also see trans., p. 223.
[2] Ibid., p. 226; also see trans., p. 224.
[3] Ibid., p. 249; also see trans., pp. 250–1.
[4] Ibid., p. 183; also see trans., p. 173.
[5] G. Bühler, *E.I.* i. 70.

'comparatively few days'. There some non-Aryan Śabara tributary chiefs of the forest took him to the hermitage of a Buddhist monk, Divākara-mitra,[1] one of whose disciples led Harsha to his sister, who, unable to bear her grief, was about to end her life by entering fire. Harsha's timely arrival prevented the unhappy event; instead Rājya-śrī sought his permission to become a Buddhist nun, seeing little meaning in return to ordinary life without 'a husband or a son'. Divākara-mitra thereupon interceded on behalf of Harsha, who wished to take his sister back with him, and advised Rājya-śrī to obey her brother while she was thus overpowered by grief. Harsha was clear in his mind about what he wished to do. He wanted to complete his *dig-vijaya* campaign, to carry out in 'righteous vengeance' the vow 'to destroy the insolent enemies who had slain my brother'.[2] He wanted to enter upon the normal tasks of administration, 'to console my subjects in their sorrow for my father's death'.[3] And while he was engaged in these normal kingly occupations he wanted Rājya-śrī to be with him. 'I desire that she should remain at my side and be comforted with . . . your Buddhist doctrines.' Indeed the 'Life', describing a scene over thirty years later, represents Rājya-śrī as sitting behind the King, presumably in an open court, when Hsüan-tsang gave a discourse on Buddhism while Harsha was residing at Kajangala.[4] Since the King was encamped there temporarily on his way back from his campaign in Orissa, it also proves that Rājya-śrī accompanied her brother on such occasions. The *Fang-chih*, in fact, represents Harsha as 'administering the government in conjunction with his widowed sister'.[5] No Indian source refers to the practice of joint government of this type, so if the *Fang-chih* has recorded a fact it has indeed preserved an important piece of information. If Harsha was swayed not only by emotional reasons for keeping his sister from entering the Buddhist Order but also by considerations of expediency, he showed extraordinary political foresight. The presence beside him of the Maukhari Queen, especially towards the beginning of his reign, would have

[1] Though Buddhist, the monk–teacher had disciples, it seems, of all existing beliefs. Bāṇa's description of the establishment throws much light on the religious and educational practices of the time. We are told that 'various Buddhists . . ., Jainas in white robes, . . . followers of Vishṇu [Bhāgavatas], . . . of Kapila, . . . of Chārvāka, . . ., of Kaṇāda, . . . and of the Upanishads, . . . all [were] diligently following their own tenets, pondering, urging objections, raising doubts, resolving them, giving etymologies, disputing, studying, and explaining . . .'. Bāṇa, however, indulges in his poetic excesses by depicting the birds and the animals of the hermitage, too, as engaged in tasks of piety and learning. See *H.C.* text, pp. 236–7; also see trans., p. 236.

[2] *H.C.* text, p. 256; trans., pp. 257–8.

[3] Ibid., p. 256; trans., p. 258.

[4] 'Life', p. 176.

[5] See Watters i, p. 345.

rendered Harsha's acquisition of the Maukhari kingdom proper and beyond reproach. Later the practice of their joint appearance became a habit. Indeed, the company of this woman of 'great intelligence', as she is described by the author of the 'Life',[1] may have been of positive advantage to the King.

Harsha's cautious accession to Kanauj

Bāṇa's account of Harsha comes to a close with his recovery of Rājya-śrī and the return of the search party 'to his camp stationed along the bank of the Ganges'.[2] It seems reasonable to assume that on arrival at Kanauj, which had already been vacated by Śaśāṅka, the question of appointing a new successor to the Maukhari throne was given first priority. While Bāṇa's incidental remark about Harsha being seized by the 'Goddess of the Royal Prosperity', however reluctant he was to mount the throne,[3] may, if recording a fact, be referred to the situation in Sthāṇv-īśvara after Rājya-vardhana's return, Hsüan-tsang's detailed account of the difficulties of succession seems to describe Harsha's predicament at Kanauj.[4] Po-ni, to be identified with Bhaṇḍi,[5] appears from Hsüan-tsang's account to have emphasized Harsha's affection for his family when proposing him as king. With no strong male claimant for the throne, the brother of the widowed Queen of Kanauj would be expected to benefit if this virtue was highlighted.

[1] p. 176.

[2] *H.C.* text, p. 257; trans., p. 258.

[3] *H.C.* text, p. 70; trans., p. 57.

[4] Our interpretation is not free from difficulties. While certain facts fit in better in the context of Sthāṇv-īśvara, others seem plausible only in connection with Kanauj. Thus Prabhākara-vardhana and Rājya-vardhana, who are recounted by Hsüan-tsang as Harsha's immediate predecessors on the throne of Kanauj as far as the pilgrim is concerned, were Kings of Sthāṇv-īśvara. At Kanauj Harsha succeeded Graha-varman Maukhari. On the other hand Bhaṇḍi is depicted as exhorting the assembled ministers to accept Harsha as the new king, a procedure that would be quite unnecessary at Sthāṇv-īśvara. Again, Harsha is said to have sought miraculous guidance from a Bodhi-sattva statue situated in the vicinity, on the banks of the Ganga, which presupposes that the scene of action was Kanauj and not Sthāṇv-īśvara.

In any case, since Hsüan-tsang associates the Vardhana family with Kanauj and not at all with Sthāṇv-īśvara, although the latter place appears in his itinerary, he may be expected to ascribe to Kanauj all happenings irrespective of whether they took place there or at Sthāṇv-īśvara. We have to make our own judgement, in the light of other evidence, when determining the place of action, which was almost certainly Kanauj in this case.

[5] Unlike most scholars, who identify Bhaṇḍi of the *Harsha-charita* with Po-ni of the Chinese works, R. S. Tripathi (*History of Kanauj*, p. 75 n. 1) suggests that they were two different persons, Bhaṇḍi a courtier of Sthāṇv-īśvara, Po-ni of Kanauj, and that there is no other basis for their identification except similarity in the sound of their names. We do not agree with Tripathi's view. Po-ni's action at Kanauj fits in exactly with what might be expected of Bhaṇḍi. Since Hsüan-tsang associates the Vardhanas only with Kanauj, he may be expected to speak of Bhaṇḍi only in connection with that place.

The affair of Harsha's succession to the throne of Kanauj is recorded by Hsüan-tsang in the following words:[1]

The great minister Po-ni whose office/wisdom, and reputation were high and of much weight, addressing the assembled ministers/officials[2] said, 'The destiny of the nation is to be fixed today. The old king's son [Rājya-vardhana] is dead; the brother of the prince [Harsha-vardhana], however, is humane and affectionate, and his disposition, heaven conferred, is filial and respectful. Because he is strongly attached to his family, the people will trust in him. I propose that he assume royal authority. Let each one give his opinion on this matter, whatever he thinks.' There was no dissension and they all admired his virtue.

On this the ministers and officials[3] all exhorted him to take authority saying: 'Let the royal prince attend! The accumulated merit and the conspicuous virtue of the former king were so illustrious as to cause his kingdom to be most happily governed. When he was followed by Rājya-vardhana we thought he would end his years [as king]; but, owing to the badness of his ministers, he was led to subject his person to the hand of his enemy, and the kingdom has suffered great affliction; but it is because he lacked good ministers. The opinion of the people, as shown in their songs, proves their real submission to your eminent qualities. Reign, then, with glory over the land; conquer the enemies of your family; wash out the insult laid on your kingdom and glorify the deeds of your illustrious father. Great will your merit be in such a case. We pray you reject not our prayer.'

The prince replied: 'The importance of succession to the throne has always been a difficult matter throughout the ages. Setting up a ruler on the throne—this should be done with great circumspection. I am indeed of little virtue and my father and brother have orphaned me. Would my being the king be of any use! Although public opinion thinks me fit for the throne, how dare I forget my insufficiency. Now, on the banks of the Ganga there is a statue of the Avalokiteśvara Bodhi-sattva which has witnessed many spiritual wonders. I will go and request a response.'

Forthwith, coming to the spot where the figure of the Bodhi-sattva was, he remained before it fasting and praying. The Bodhi-sattva was moved by his sincerity and appeared in bodily form and enquired, 'What do you seek that you are so earnest in your supplications?' The prince answered, 'I have suffered under a load of affliction. My kindly father indeed is dead and to add

[1] At the risk of incorporating unnecessary details for the historian we give above a revised literal translation of the whole section concerned (*Hsi Yü Chi* text, v. 3a) because it differs at places from the versions of Beal (i, pp. 211 ff.) and Watters (i, pp. 343 ff.). Although the differences appear to be minor they can sometimes considerably alter the emphasis and thus the interpretation.

[2] The Chinese character *liao-shu* may be taken to mean ministers, statesmen, or subordinate colleagues, but is perhaps best translated as officials. *Shu* here indicates plural.

[3] The term *fu ch'en chih shih* may also be translated as 'officials who aid the king and those who are in charge of affairs'; *Hsi Yü Chi* text, v. 3a.

to this cruel punishment my good brother has been murdered. I am aware that I am lacking in virtue, nevertheless the people would exalt me to royal dignity, to glorify my illustrious father. Yet, I am indeed but ignorant and foolish. In my trouble I ask for holy direction.'

The Bodhi-sattva replied, 'In your former existence you lived in this forest as an *Araṇya-bhikshu* [forest monk] and by your earnest diligence and unremitting attention you inherited a power of religious merit which resulted in your birth as a prince. The Law of the Buddha having been destroyed by the king of Karṇa-suvarṇa, you, when you become king, should revive it. If you be compassionate to the distressed and cherish them, then before long you shall rule over the five Indias. If you would establish your authority, attend to my instruction, and by my secret power you shall receive additional enlightenment, so that not one of your neighbours shall be able to triumph over you. Ascend not the lion-throne [kingly throne], and call not yourself *mahārāja*.'

Having received these instructions, he departed and assumed the royal office. He called himself Kumāra [prince]; his title was Śīlāditya.

The foregoing citation makes it clear that the Kanauj ministers readily agreed to Bhaṇḍi's proposal and exhorted Harsha to assume authority, but he modestly made excuses. On being pressed he sought the guidance of the Bodhi-sattva Avalokiteśvara, who oracularly advised him to accept power in order to undo the harm that Śaśāṅka had done to Buddhism, but not to use such royal insignia as a lion-throne or an imperial title. Thereupon Harsha took office under the name Kumāra [prince] Śilāditya. He must have assumed full royal dignity as soon as he felt strong and secure enough to do so, perhaps at the conclusion of his first extensive military campaign. His inscriptions, of course, belonging to the latter part of his reign, describe him as *mahārāj-ādhirāja*.

Mastery over Kanauj must have greatly increased both Harsha's power and prestige, and considerably facilitated his task of further expansion. Although he consolidated the greater part of northern India under his rule during the early part of his career, his attempts at further extension of his boundaries continued until almost the end of his reign. While much of the territory was directly administered by Harsha, considerably large and strong kingdoms were loosely under his hegemony, acknowledging him as the paramount sovereign.

IV

THE EXTENT OF HARSHA'S EMPIRE

Dig-vijaya

THERE were Indian kings who, by choice or lack of it, were content to concentrate on the administration of the territory bequeathed to them, but generally speaking, however large an inherited empire, the newly enthroned monarch would wish to extend his domain to the furthest natural limits of the country. While the majority of kings ruled over only a part of the geographical entity that was India, there were some who extended their political control beyond the natural frontiers, into central Asia and, in the singular case of the Choḷas, by naval attack to Śrī Vijaya (Malaya and Indonesia).

Harsha's motives for *dig-vijaya*

As for Harsha, if he was to acquire the status of *mahārāj-ādhirāja*, 'king of kings', large-scale conquest was necessary, for at the time of his accession in A.D. 606 he was the master of only a small kingdom in east Panjab, held perhaps in respectful awe by some of the neighbouring kings his father is said to have defeated. Harsha was directed to launch an extensive military campaign not only by ambition or through the counsel and encouragement of his military advisers but also by the very valid motive of redeeming his family honour by avenging the losses inflicted on both the Vardhanas and the Maukharis.

The eastward march and Śaśāṅka's discomfiture

Strengthened by his hold over Kanauj, which was henceforth to be his capital, and with his army reinforced, Harsha Śīlāditya started his eastward march, traversing the region that lay between Kanauj and Gauḍa. The concluding passage of the *Harsha-charita* metaphorically describing the scene of sunset alludes to bloody wars and the discomfiture of Śaśāṅka.[1] According to the *Ārya Mañju-śrī-mūla-kalpa*, also, Harsha 'defeated Soma [Śaśāṅka] [who] . . . was forbidden to move out

[1] *H.C.* text, p. 258; trans., p. 260. 'Then the evening appeared, . . . the ocean had its waves dyed in the evening glow as if it were once more crimson with the blood of the demons . . . . At the close of the evening-tide, the moon was brought to the King as a respectful offering by the Night, as if it were the impersonated Glory of his Race bringing him a cup from the pearl Mountain, to slake his boundless thirst for fame,—or the . . . glory of the Kingdom bringing him the stamp of primeval King on the silver patent of his sovereignty, to encourage him in his resolve to bring back the golden Kṛita age,—or the Goddess of the Future conducting a messenger from the White Dvīpa to animate him to the conquest of all the seven Dvīpas.'

of his country, [being ordered] to remain therein [thenceforth]. He [Harsha] returned, having been honoured in that kingdom of the Mlechchha.'[1] It seems that, continuing his march from Kanauj and winning the allegiance of the petty rulers through whose territories he passed, Harsha ultimately reached Gauḍa and inflicted a defeat on Śaśāṅka. That Harsha's aim was not achieved by a mere show of force, and that the two armies met each other in the battlefield, is also borne out by the Buddhist work, which, because of its distaste for killing, feels the necessity of justifying Harsha's act: 'Adopting the duty of *Kṣātra*, with the sense of personal injury and indignation, he, though kind, prone to religion, and learned, kills many and becomes an oppressor of living creatures, for the reason of being engaged in the duty of chastisement.'[2]

Hsüan-tsang's statements regarding Harsha's early conquests are in line with those of Bāṇa and the *Mañju-śrī-mūla-kalpa*. According to the Chinese pilgrim, 'as soon as Śīlāditya became ruler he got together a great army, and set out to avenge his brother's murder and to reduce the neighbouring countries to subjection. Proceeding eastwards he invaded the states which had refused allegiance and waged incessant warfare until in six years he had subjugated [or repulsed] the five Indias.'[3]

The 'five Indias' of Hsüan-tsang and of the indigenous literature

Before discussing his eastern conquests, which, because of the situation of Gauḍa, formed the first part of Harsha's *dig-vijaya* campaign, it will be well to examine briefly the implication of the term 'five Indias' used by Hsüan-tsang. It is used with a significantly geographical connotation at least three times in the 'Records': in the general description of India and in the accounts of Kanauj and Mahā-rāshṭra. But Hsüan-tsang causes confusion by using the term inconsistently. In the first case he applies it to the whole subcontinent, in the second and third to the territory under Harsha's rule which was the northern half of the subcontinent only. In the general description of India, he writes, 'The countries embraced under this term of India [In-tu] are generally spoken of as the five Indies .... on three sides it is bordered by the great sea; on the north it is backed by the Snowy Mountains.'[4]

As noted by Watters,[5] not only Hsüan-tsang but other Chinese travellers too observed that India had five main divisions, north, east, west, central, and south.[6] Apparently they followed the notion then

[1] *Mañju-śrī-mūla-kalpa*, verses 725–6. [2] Op. cit. 723–4.

[3] *Hsi Yü Chi* text v. 4a. The reading *ch'en* means subjugated or subdued; the variant *chü* means fought, repulsed, or resisted. Beal (i, p. 213) writes 'subdued'; Watters (i, p. 343) writes 'fought' but he also discusses the variant reading.

[4] Beal i, p. 70. [5] i, p. 140.

[6] 'I-tsing calls India in general the West (Si-fang), the Five *Countries* of India (Wu-t'ien), Āryadeśa (A-li-ya-t'i-sha), Madhyadeśa (Mo-t'i-t'i-sha), Brahmarāshṭra

prevalent in India. Amongst the indigenous sources[1] the Purāṇas, in the *Bhuvanakosha* section, divide the country into *madhya-deśa, udīchya, prāchya, dakshiṇā-patha*, and *aparānta*, sometimes adding to the list the Himalayan and Vindhyan regions also. The *Kāvya-mīmāṁsā* of Rāja-śekhara (tenth century A.D.) refers to *pūrva-deśa, dakshiṇā-patha, paśchād-deśa*, and *uttarā-patha*. A Tantric work of the seventeenth century, the *Śakti-saṅgama*, also divides India into five sections, but from a Tantric viewpoint. Hsüan-tsang's use of the term 'five Indias' to denote the whole country is thus entirely explicable. His application of the same term to Harsha's domains, however, is harder to justify unless interpreted figuratively or explained by a copyist's error.

In his account of Harsha's exploits as the King of Kanauj, Hsüan-tsang states that after six years of warfare the King subjugated the 'five Indies',[2] and in describing the conflict between Harsha and Pula-keśin of Mahā-rāshṭra he mentions that the former gathered troops from the 'five Indies'[3] but was unable to conquer the enemy. One Chinese text has the variant 'five Gauḍas' for 'five Indias'.[4] This reading fits the context perfectly. There is both literary and epigraphic evidence to show that Gauḍa was used to denote *uttarā-patha*, the north, just as Draviḍa was used as a generic term for *dakshiṇā-patha*, the south, the Vindhyas dividing the two regions. The *Śabda-kalpa-druma* quotes stanzas from the *Skanda Purāṇa* giving the five divisions of the south- and north-Indian brahmans, grouped respectively as *pañcha-Draviḍa* and *pañcha-Gauḍa*. The names listed under the latter term are Sārasvata (eastern Panjab), Kānya-kubja, Gauḍa, Mithilā, and Utkala. A *pañcha-Gauḍīya* community is mentioned in an inscription of A.D. 926,[5] while a late tradition making an exaggerated claim for King Bhoja of Mālava of the eleventh century A.D. states that he was the master of both Gauḍa and *dakshiṇā-patha*, the former term signifying the whole of northern India.[6] Apparently the overlord of the *uttarā-patha* or the *dakshiṇā-patha* was a sort of partial *chakra-vartī*. Leaving aside the obviously hyperbolic claims of

(Po-lo-mên-kuo), or Jambūdvīpa (Chan-pu-chou).' I-tsing's *A Record of the Buddhist Religion*, translated by Takakusu, p. lii. In Fa-hien's *Record of Buddhist Kingdoms* (translated by J. Legge, p. 42) we find reference to the Middle Kingdom or Madhya-deśa.

[1] The following information is derived from D. C. Sircar's *Geography of Ancient and Medieval India*, p. 73.

[2] Beal i, p. 213.

[3] Ibid. ii, p. 257.

[4] See Gauri Shankar Chatterji, *Harsha Vardhana* (in Hindi), p. 104. I have not succeeded in locating the text and am therefore unable to give the reference to the original.

[5] *E.I.* xxxii. 48; also *Rāja-taraṅgiṇī*, iv, v. 468.

[6] 'Bhoja rājena bhoktavyaḥ sa-gauḍo dakshiṇā-pathaḥ': *Bhoja-prabandha* (sixteenth century), Calcutta edn., p. 3; cf. *D.H.N.I.* ii, p. 858.

petty kings in their family inscriptions, we sometimes find the conquerors of the north or the south conventionally described as *chakra-vartī* and their territories as extending to the four extremities of the Indian subcontinent. The same monarchs are then more realistically represented as masters of land north or south of the Vindhyas, as the case may be.[1]

Although the ideal of suzerainty over the whole country was always there, difficulties in the way of attaining it made monarchs prize overlordship over just the north or the south as well. The Sāta-vāhanas were proud to declare that their chargers drank the water of the three seas.[2] The Chālukyas of Bādāmi claimed lordship over land lying within the three seas.[3] Pula-keśin styles Harsha as the 'master of the whole of *uttarā-patha*' in his record, apparently to emphasize the fact that even a king of that stature could not defeat him.

The fact that Hsüan-tsang claims for Harsha mastery over the five Gauḍas[4] long before he conquered Utkala, one of the regions listed under that term, may be explained by an understandable lack of historical precision on the part of an author whose prime concern was Buddhism. Moreover, Harsha was the master of most of northern India when he attacked Pula-keśin, and he had successfully completed his final campaign in Orissa before the pilgrim left India. Hsüan-tsang's claim for Harsha is not false but early by a good many years.

If on the other hand we accept 'five Indias' as the correct reading for the two references in question, the term may be understood to have been used figuratively, depicting Harsha as a *chakra-vartī*. As is evident from the definition of 'five Indias', Hsüan-tsang was too well aware of what it implied to have credited Harsha with actual dominion over the whole subcontinent.

The cities occupied between Kanauj and Bengal

Hsüan-tsang does not name the districts that Harsha conquered during his eastern campaign undertaken to avenge his brother's death at the hands of Śaśāṅka. They were presumably the same that the pilgrim

[1] King Deva-pāla of the ninth century A.D. is described as the king of the entire subcontinent in the *Gauḍa-lekha-mālā*, p. 38. Page 72 of the same work limits his southern boundary to the Vindhyas.

[2] Nasik inscription of Queen Balasirī: *E.I.* viii. 60–5. See also *H.C.* text, p. 251; trans., p. 252. Bāna describes a Sātavāhana king as lord of the three seas.

[3] *E.I.* xix. 64 ff. Although India has sea only on three sides, the *kshetra*, or field of the *chakra-vartī*, is traditionally stated to be bounded by the four seas, the northern sea being explained as the Central Asian 'sea of sand', 'sky', or the mythical sea of the Purāṇas' concept of the earth's geography. Mostly the Himalayas are considered to be the northern limit. *Dakshiṇā-patha*, the land south of the Vindhyas, is generally described as encircled by the three seas, the Bay of Bengal, the Indian Ocean, and the Arabian Sea.

[4] Going, that is, by the reading *pañcha-Gauda* in his accounts of Kanauj and Mahā-rāshṭra.

himself visited in his journey from Kanauj to Bengal. He lists them in the following order: Ayodhyā, Haya-mukha, Prayāga, Kośāmbi, Viśoka, Śrāvastī, Kapila-vastu, Rāma-grāma, Kuśī-nagara, Vārāṇasī, Chan-chu,[1] Vaiśālī, Vṛijji, Magadha, Īraṇa-parvata, Champā, and Kajaṅgala. Hsüan-tsang is silent about the political status of these 'countries' except in a few instances. In every case authority appears to have issued ultimately from Harsha, directly when the ruler is not specified and indirectly when it is.

Kapila-vastu

Regarding the then dilapidated Kapila-vastu, Hsüan-tsang says that it had no supreme ruler, each of its towns appointing its own chief.[2] Apparently the ancient 'republic', especially in view of its sanctity as the Buddha's birthplace, was allowed by Harsha to retain its old tradition of autonomy and of distribution of authority.

Magadha

Magadha is stated to be under the rule of Pūrṇa-varman 'the last descendant of Aśoka'. But Pūrṇa-varman is more likely to have been a Maukhari than a Maurya, and the problem of his identification is solved if we take note of the fact that the pilgrim has made these observations while giving an account of the vicissitudes of the celebrated *Bodhi* tree. 'In late times Śaśāṅka-rāja... slandered the religion of the Buddha..., destroyed the convents, and cut down the *Bodhi* tree .... Some months afterwards Pūrṇa-varman, the king of Magadha, the last of the race of Aśoka-rāja..., reverently bathed the roots of the tree, and it revived again....'[3] Pūrṇa-varman may have been considered the last of the race of Aśoka in the sense that he was the last to have restored the *Bodhi* tree, 'which had often been injured by cutting'[4] and which had been also worshipped and restored to life by Aśoka-rāja.[5] There is also a possibility that Hsüan-tsang was told that Pūrṇa-varman was a Maukhari but that he understood it as Maurya. This could easily happen in a Prākṛit *Mohariya* for *Maukharika*, with the diminutive *ka* widely used in popular speech in those days.

It appears that Harsha, after occupying Kanauj, pacified Pūrṇa-varman, a scion of the Maukhari family, by appointing him governor of the important province of Magadha. It is also possible that Pūrṇa-varman, who was probably a descendant of the Maukhari 'Suva', known from his Nālandā seal, gained control of that province after Śaśāṅka's withdrawal from Kanauj and subsequently from Magadha; but, as Śaśāṅka's retreat was caused by Harsha's rise to power, Pūrṇa-varman

[1] Means 'fighting lord' or 'lord of battle', identified with Ghazipur by A. Cunningham (*C.A.G.I.*, p. 502).
[2] Beal ii, p. 14; Watters ii, p. 1.
[3] *Hsi Yü Chi* text, viii. 19a: cf. Beal ii, p. 118.
[4] Beal ii, p. 116.
[5] Ibid., p. 117.

must have become subordinate to the latter. Harsha, whose general policy seems to have been to reinstate vanquished rulers in any case, would not depose or disturb one whose claim he himself may have transgressed a little by inheriting the Maukhari kingdom of Kanauj. That Magadha came under Harsha not towards the end of his reign, when he is specifically styled as the King of Magadha by the Chinese envoys,[1] but rather towards its beginning is supported by the following facts. To give battle to Śaśāṅka in Puṇḍra-vardhana[2] Harsha must have passed with his army through Magadha, acquiring control over that region. To hold court at Kajaṅgala too he would have had to cross Magadha.[3] We are also told that he built a bronze *vihāra* at Nālandā in Magadha.[4] The first event certainly and the last two probably took place during the lifetime of Pūrṇa-varman. He may have died before A.D. 637, as Hsüan-tsang, who visited Nālandā in that year, refers to an image of the Buddha as 'the work of Pūrṇa-varman-rāja of old days'.[5]

Other cities of U.P. and Bihar

Apart from the cases of Kapila-vastu and Magadha no other district lying between Kanauj and Puṇḍra-vardhana is stated to have had a local 'ruler'. We may presume that they were administered by officers of the central government at Kanauj. Evidence is available of Harsha's control over these 'kingdoms'. According to R. Burn[6] the coins of Śīlāditya found at Bhiṭaura (Fyzabad district) are to be attributed to Harsha, which confirms his suzerainty over the region of Ayodhyā. That Prayāga formed a part of the Vardhana empire is shown by the fact that Hsüan-tsang attended there the sixth quinquennial religious assembly of Harsha's reign.[7] Śrāvastī's inclusion in his domains is proved by Harsha's Madhu-ban inscription, which records grant of land in that city.[8] 'The king of the neighbouring state' who 'deposed the ruler of Īraṇa-parvata and gave the capital to Buddhist brethren, erecting in the city two monasteries',[9] may well have been Harsha. 'In his progress to east India' Harsha stopped at Kajaṅgala, building there a temporary residence where 'he dealt with the affairs of his different states'.[10]

Puṇḍra-vardhana

Beyond Kajaṅgala lay Puṇḍra-vardhana, the site of the battle between Harsha and Śaśāṅka according to the *Mañju-śrī-mūla-kalpa*. This historic encounter, which finally established Harsha as the supreme ruler of northern India, may be dated *c.* A.D. 606–7. Repulsed in the clash,

[1] See below, pp. 211, 213–14.
[2] *Mañju-śrī-mūla-kalpa*, verse 723.
[3] Beal ii, p. 193.
[4] Watters ii, p. 171; 'Life', p. 119. Also see Beal ii, p. 174 n. 102.
[5] 'Life', p. 119; also Beal ii, p. 174, 'formerly made by Purṇavarma-rāja'.
[6] *J.R.A.S.* (1906), 843–50, also see below, Appendix II.
[7] 'Life', p. 184.
[8] *E.I.* i. 72.
[9] Watters ii, p. 178.
[10] *Hsi Yü Chi* text, x. 4b: cf. Watters ii, p. 183; Beal ii, p. 193.

Śaśāṅka still retained a sizeable kingdom in Bengal. Flanked by two hostile rulers, Harsha on the west and Bhāskara-varman in the east, his expansionist designs found a limited scope in the south-east towards Orissa. But on his death in *c.* A.D. 620 his weak and divided kingdom lay open to annexation by Harsha.

The eastward march from Kanauj culminating in the battle of Puṇḍra-vardhana may be said to constitute the first stage of Harsha's *dig-vijaya* campaign. Not only did it achieve the containment of Śaśāṅka but it secured for Harsha the allegiance of the various petty rulers whose territories he traversed in the process. It may be presumed that, oppressed by Śaśāṅka's excesses and impressed by Harsha's strength, the lesser rulers of the east willingly allowed the latter to march through their territories on his mission of chastisement. On his return journey Harsha might have formalized their subordination to him through friendly alliances. Thus the mantle of authority over the eastern Gangetic valley had in a very short space of time shifted from the Maukharis to Śaśāṅka, and then to Harsha.

The probable westward march of consolidation

We presume that, his honour redeemed, Harsha retraced his steps from Puṇḍra-vardhana to Kanauj. The next logical step, in order to complete his mastery over the 'five Gauḍas', would be to consolidate his hold over the region west of Kanauj. The territory between the Satluj and the Ganga already formed part of Harsha's paternal kingdom of Sthāṇv-īśvara, but the prestige of the Vardhanas had suffered some decline, owing to the activities of Deva-gupta and Śaśāṅka. Though Rājya-vardhana quickly avenged the death of his Maukhari kinsman by inflicting a decisive defeat on the King of Mālava, and Harsha too succeeded in establishing his superiority over Śaśāṅka, a march of inspection was probably necessary to reassert his authority over the subordinate *sāmantas*,[1] to suppress hostile elements, and to extend his arms to neighbouring regions hitherto not under his supremacy.

Cities between Kanauj and Chīna-bhukti in the Panjab

Hsüan-tsang names and describes the following 'kingdoms' lying to the west of Kanauj: Kapitha (modern Sankisa),[2] Pi-lo-shan-na (modern Atrañji-khera),[3] Ahichchhatrā (the eastern Rohilkhand),[4] Goviśāna (near Kāśipur),[5] Brahma-pura (in the hills to the north-east of Haradvār),[6] Mati-pura (modern Madawar),[7] Śrughna (modern Sugh),[8] Sthāṇv-

[1] See below, pp. 159 ff. [2] *C.A.G.I.*, p. 423.
[3] Ibid, p. 417. [4] Ibid., p. 412. [5] Ibid., p. 409.
[6] Ibid., p. 407. R. S. Tripathi (*History of Kanauj*, p. 88) has dealt with Suvarṇa-gotra as well as Brahma-pura, though the latter was the kingdom visited by Hsüan-tsang. Suvarṇa-gotra's location and customs are mentioned by him merely as a point of interest.
[7] *C.A.G.I.*, p. 399. [8] Ibid., p. 395.

īśvara, Mathurā, Pāri-yātra (north of Jaipur),[1] Śatadru (modern Sirhind),[2] Kulūta (Kullū),[3] Jālandhara, and Chīna-bhukti (in eastern Panjab),[4] and Ṭakka (mostly in western Panjab).[5] Districts beyond these are specifically stated to be the dependencies of other northern kingdoms. Harsha, we presume, led a march of inspection and consolidation through the districts mentioned by the Chinese pilgrim, the names of many of which survive to this day.

Mati-pura Of these Mati-pura, identified by A. Cunningham with Madawar or Mandawar, a large town in western Rohilkhand near Bijnor,[6] is said to have been ruled by a Śūdra 'king' who did not believe in Buddhism, and worshipped the *devas*, i.e. the Hindu deities.[7] **Mathurā** Mathurā is said to have been governed by a Buddhist 'king' who, with his ministers, applied himself to religious duties with zeal.[8] The 'kings' of Mati-pura and Mathurā, because of the close proximity of their 'kingdoms' to Sthāṇvīśvara and Kanauj, must have been the feudatories of Harsha.

Pāri-yātra The north-Rājasthan kingdom of Pāri-yātra was ruled by a *vaiśya*.[9] Described as 'brave, impetuous, and warlike' this king may have owed only nominal allegiance to Harsha. Pāri-yātra is also singled out in the *Harsha-charita* as one of the countries which Harsha, at the very beginning of his reign, is advised to conquer.[10] The district may not have been attacked by Harsha in the earlier years of his reign, but must have come under his influence, although not under his direct administration, when he overran the west-central region leading to Valabhi.

Jālandhara Jālandhara, writes Hsüan-tsang, was 'formerly' ruled by a Buddhist convert who was rewarded by the King of Mid India with the important office of the 'sole inspector of the affairs of religion (*the three gems*) throughout the five Indies'.[11] The 'former king' of Jālandhara may be identified with Wu-ti, Udita,[12] or Buddhi[13] of Jālandhara, who, according to the 'Life',[14] was charged by a King of Mid India, to be identified with Harsha, to escort Hsüan-tsang to the borders of India. We think that by his phrase 'former king' the pilgrim here intends us to understand that Wu-ti, at the time of his visit a royal official for the affairs of religion for the 'five Indias', had at one time been the independent King of Jālandhara.

Brahma-pura The hilly district of Brahma-pura, although said to have been ruled

[1] Ibid., p. 387. [2] Ibid., p. 165. [3] Ibid., p. 162.
[4] Ibid., p. 230. [5] Beal i, pp. 165–73; Watters i, pp. 286–91.
[6] *C.A.G.I.*, p. 399. [7] Beal i, p. 190.
[8] Ibid., p. 181. [9] Ibid., p. 179.
[10] *H.C.* text p. 214; trans., p. 210; also see below, p. 178 n. 5.
[11] Beal i, p. 176. [12] As restored by Watters i, p. 297.
[13] As restored by R. S. Tripathi, *History of Kanauj*, p. 87. [14] pp. 189–90.

traditionally by women, must during Harsha's reign have owed allegiance to him, because of its close proximity to Sthāṇv-īśvara.

As for the remaining ten kingdoms, which include Sthāṇv-īśvara, their political status is not mentioned by Hsüan-tsang. Most of them were doubtless under Harsha's direct administration, others, such as the distant Kulūta and Ṭakka, were probably under local rulers but may be presumed to have acknowledged Harsha's supremacy.

The limits of Harsha's direct and indirect control in the west

Hsüan-tsang's account depicts Ṭakka as a kingdom of very large size stretching from the river Beas (P'i-po-che, Vipāsā) to the river Indus (Sin-tu, Sindhu). Its situation between Sthāṇv-īśvara and Kashmir strongly suggests that it was under Harsha's dominating influence, as Kashmir itself had suffered humiliation at Harsha's hands through his superior military strength. An interesting feature of Hsüan-tsang's scheme of dividing his several chapters into various books further supports our view. The pilgrim deals with eight small states of the north-west in his Book III, and starts a new book with his description of Ṭakka. According to Watters, Ṭakka 'designated a country which was not in India', by which he apparently means in Harsha's empire, 'but was one of the foreign states . . ., [therefore it] should have been included in the pilgrim's general survey at the end of the last *chuan*.'[1] We believe the very fact that this is not the case points to Ṭakka's close relations with Harsha.

At the termination of his westward march of consolidation and inspection Harsha may well have regarded his *dig-vijaya* (conquest of the four quarters) complete, at least until such time when power and ambition prompted him to attempt a comparatively more literal execution of the concept. Hsüan-tsang's statement regarding the incessant warfare waged by Śīlāditya for six years to bring the 'five Indias' under allegiance[2] has reference to campaigns approximating to those described above. By A.D. 612 Harsha had bound together countries from Puṇḍra-vardhana (north-western Bengal) in the east to roughly the river Beas in the west. Having firmly established his hold as the supreme political power of northern India, we may assume that Harsha applied himself for the next few years to the task of co-ordinating and strengthening his administrative machinery to meet the needs of his heterogenous empire. As well as devoting himself to tasks of public welfare about which we read in the *Harsha-charita* and the 'Records', Harsha must have kept a vigilant eye on the politics of the frontier provinces, such as Kāmā-rūpa and Ṭakka. As later events prove, he also kept a close watch

[1] Watters i p. 291. [2] Ibid., p. 343; cf. Beal i, p. 213.

on developments in countries still outside his domains, such as Śaśāṅka's Bengal, Sindh, and Saurāshṭra.

Sindh

Bāṇa has punningly referred to Harsha's victory over the King of Sindh.[1] As the kingdom of Sindh extended well up to the point of the confluence of the Panjab rivers not far from the boundaries of Harsha's empire it may not have been difficult for him to conduct a campaign against it. According to the Chinese histories 'there were great troubles in the kingdom [of India] in the years A.D. 618 to 627. The king Śīlāditya made war and fought such battles as had never been before.'[2] It appears to us that the occupation of Sindh and Bengal by Harsha took place around this time. The former event may have taken place in the earlier part of the period mentioned by the Chinese historians. In the east Śaśāṅka's death took place in *c.* A.D. 620,[3] and chaotic conditions prevailed in Gauḍa for nearly one year.[4] In Orissa the Śail-odbhavas declared independence. Probably delayed by the Sindh campaign on the western front of his empire, Harsha arrived at the other extreme in Gauḍa about a year after Śaśāṅka's death and annexed the rich and important Bengal districts of Sama-taṭa, Tāmra-lipti, and Karṇa-suvarṇa, in addition to Puṇḍra-vardhana, which he already had. Hsüan-tsang is silent about the political status of all these 'countries' at the time of his visit. This silence negatively supports other circumstantial evidence in favour of Harsha's suzerainty over the region during the latter half of his reign. The Baṅskhera inscription of Harsha dated the year 22 (A.D. 628–9)[5] was issued from the victorious camp of Vardhamāna-koṭi, to be identified with modern Bardhan-koti in the Dinajpur district of Bengal.[6] D. C. Ganguly,[7] R. C. Majumdar,[8] and K. L. Barua[9] express the opinion that Gauḍa was occupied by Bhāskara-varman, because he passed through it unobstructed with his full retinue to meet Harsha at Kajaṅgala. The argument is almost too weak to deserve attention, for, in view of the fact that he was on a friendly mission to Harsha at the time, it would have been most surprising if his passage had been resisted by Harsha's troops.

Extension of control in the east after Śaśāṅka's death

Orissa does not seem to have been conquered by Harsha at this stage, because Hsüan-tsang refers to his attack on Koṅgoda in *c.* A.D. 640, when the Chinese pilgrim was enjoying the hospitality of the King of Kāma-rūpa.[10] The records of the Śail-odbhava King Mādhava-rāja II

[1] *H.C.* text pp. 90–1; trans., p. 76.
[2] See below, Ch. VII.
[3] See above, pp. 42 and 45.
[4] *Mañju-śrī-mūla-kalpa*, verses 746–8.
[5] *E.I.* iv. 211.
[6] *G.D.A.M.I.*, p. 25.
[7] *I.H.Q.* xv. 122 ff.
[8] R. C. Majumdar, *History of Bengal*, i, pp. 77–8; *J.B.O.R.S.* ix. 311 ff.
[9] *Early History of Kāmarūpa*, pp. 65–6.
[10] 'Life', p. 172.

confirm the view that Harsha did not conquer Orissa in the decade A.D. 620–30. The Purī plates of Mādhava-rāja, probably dated A.D. 623,[1] show that he celebrated an *Aśva-medha* before his thirteenth regnal year. The undated Khurda grant of Mādhava-rāja claims for him sovereignty over the whole of Kaliṅga, and was issued from the victorious camp of Koṅgoḍa. Mādhava-rāja's power, however, was short-lived, for more than one reference in the Chinese records testifies to Harsha's occupation of a major part of Orissa.[2]

Valabhī

The addition to his empire of the territory and manpower probably of Sindh, and more certainly of Gauḍa which increased his strength considerably, seems to have prompted Harsha to prosecute his plans of further conquests. The subjugation of Valabhī would create a bulwark against the rising power of the Chālukyas, an attack on whom was probably Harsha's ultimate aim. The annexation of Bengal, we believe, took place about A.D. 623. Some years later the opportunity was ripe for an attack on Valabhī. Her Maitraka ruler, Dhara-sena III, died in *c.* A.D. 629[3], and was succeeded by his younger brother Dhruva-sena II Bālāditya, T'u-lu-p'o-po-t'a of Hsüan-tsang's account. Harsha's Valabhī campaign was probably conducted in *c.* A.D. 630, and he fully succeeded in detaching the Maitraka king from Pula-keśin's circle of influence. For the rest of his days Dhruva-sena remained a close ally of Harsha. The event has been dealt with in detail in our account of the former's reign.[4] This achievement led Harsha to the next logical military manœuvre, a planned invasion of the Chālukya Pula-keśin II's territory.

Clash with the Chālukyas

Pula-keśin II inherited the Chālukya kingdom of Bādāmi in *c.* A.D. 610, after securing victory in a civil war against his uncle Maṅgaleśa, who wanted to bestow sovereignty on his own son. The civil war brought in its wake confusion and anarchy, but Pula-keśin was soon able to master the situation and effectively to establish his power in the home provinces. Thereafter he set out to conquer new territories, and we learn from his Aihoḷe inscription[5] that in the south he succeeded in reducing the kingdoms of the Kadambas, the Gaṅgas, the Āḷūpas, and the Mauryas, while further north he subdued the Lāṭas, the Mālavas, and the Gurjaras. These latter exploits brought into conflict the interests of the two leading monarchs of India. The Vardhana's discomfiture at the hands of the Chālukya is mentioned after the latter's Gujarat campaign, and no doubt indicates the order in which his campaigns were carried out. We learn

[1] D. C. Sircar, *I.H.Q.* xxvii. 167–9. [2] 'Life', pp. 153, 159, 172.
[3] The date of the first grant of Dhruva-sena II: *I.A.* vi. 13 ff.
[4] See above, pp. 52–5. [5] *E.I.* vi. 9–10.

from the Aihoḷe inscription that 'envious because his troops of mighty elephants were slain in war, Harsha, whose lotuses, which were his feet, were covered with the rays of jewels of the chiefs that were nourished by his immeasurable power . . . was caused by him [Pula-keśin] to have his [Harsha's] joy melted away by fear.' This event is again referred to in the Nirpan,[1] Karnul,[2] and Togarchedu[3] grants of Pula-keśin's successors. According to these grants their illustrious ancestor acquired the title *parameśvara* after defeating Harsha, 'the warlike lord of "the whole region of the north" ' (*Sakal-ottarā-patheśvara*).[4] But Pula-keśin's own record, the Hyderabad grant of A.D. 612, informs us that he acquired this title 'by defeating hostile kings who had applied themselves [or, a hostile king who had applied himself] to the contest of a hundred battles'. These hostile kings may well have been Āppāyika and Govinda, known to us from the Aihoḷe inscription, who threatened to attack Pula-keśin's home province soon after his succession in A.D. 610. The Chālukya monarch emerged victorious in this battle and celebrated his success by adopting the new *biruda* registered in his record dated A.D. 612. We believe that Pula-keśin's successors, wishing to attach additional importance to his success against Harsha, misrepresented the facts of Pula-keśin's adoption of his new title. Some scholars, identifying Harsha with the 'hostile king' of the Hyderabad grant and, accepting the statement of Pula-keśin's successors regarding the title *parameśvara*, have dated the Harsha–Pula-keśin war in A.D. 612 or 613. But we discard this view in favour of that which fixes *c.* A.D. 633 as the date of the battle. It is not likely that Pula-keśin could have defeated Harsha's strong army within two years of accession to a throne the gaining of which had been no easy task. Harsha too, as we know from Hsüan-tsang, was busy extending and consolidating his empire, comprising 'the five Indias', during the first six years of his reign from 606 to 612. The Maitrakas's political success in the decade 610–20 and the fact that Harsha's Valabhī campaign apparently took place in *c.* A.D. 630 show that the great battle must have occurred after the latter date and before that of the Aihoḷe *praśasti*. Moreover, the Lohner grant of Pula-keśin executed in A.D. 630 makes no allusion to Harsha's discomfiture at the hands of the Chālukya monarch, and by its negative evidence further strengthens our conclusion.

Pula-keśin's conquest of the Lāṭas, the Mālavas, and the Gurjaras took place in *c.* A.D. 623,[5] while Harsha's western campaign against the

[1] *I.A.* ix. 124–5. [2] Ibid. xi. 66. [3] Ibid. vi. 85 ff.
[4] *Uttarā-path-ādhipati* in the Nirpan grant. [5] See above, pp. 51–2.

Maitrakas was organized in *c.* A.D. 630. Having alienated Dhruva-sena from the Chālukya's *maṇḍala*, Harsha seems to have taken the offensive against Pula-keśin II. As Harsha was the aggressor, the battle may have taken place on Pula-keśin's territory. We have already made the point that Harsha conquered parts of Chālukya-held Mālava in the course of his march against the King of Valabhī. Pula-keśin, therefore, may well have encountered Harsha's armies on the bank of the Narmadā, but, as Vincent Smith says, 'The king of the Deccan guarded the passes on the Narmadā so effectually that Harsha was constrained to retire discomfited, and to accept that river as his frontier.'[1]

The Chinese pilgrim has also left a record of the famous battle. Writing about Mahā-rāshṭra, which he visited in *c.* A.D. 640, Hsüan-tsang states: 'At the present time Śīlāditya Mahārāja has conquered the east and the west, so that both far and near owe allegiance to him, but the people of this country alone have not submitted to him. He has gathered troops from the five Indias . . . to subdue these people, but he has not yet conquered their troops.'[2] The pilgrim also informs us that Pula-keśin possessed an excellent elephant-corps, and that the beasts were made drunk before being launched into the battlefield. We gather from Bāṇa that the elephant-corps was the strongest division of Harsha's army as well. The Aihoḷe inscription too refers to Harsha's mighty elephants, and the Narmadā battle may well have been one of the most memorable from the point of view of the display of tactics in elephant warfare. The Vardhana army was repulsed and Pula-keśin was successful in preserving his territorial integrity. Harsha's attempt to penetrate the south, though it proved abortive, is indicative of his efforts to realize the ideal of pan-Indian sovereignty. The pattern of his polity was looser than that of the Mauryas and also than that of the more decentralized Guptas, but his aim was the same. Pula-keśin's vast resources and military strength, the hazards of fighting on enemy soil in unfamiliar surroundings, the formidable Chālukya boundary of hilly forests and a wide river—none of these factors could deter Harsha from undertaking a venture which ultimately met with failure, fixing his boundary at the Narmadā.

The four central Indian kingdoms: Bundelkhand Gwalior, Ujjain, and Gurjara

Hsüan-tsang records the names and political particulars of some four

[1] *E.H.I.*, p. 353. R. C. Majumdar, *H.C.I.P.* iii, pp. 105–6, expresses his disagreement with Smith's view, and suggests that the 'battle was fought much further to the north'. This view depends on his theory that the Lāṭas, Mālavas, and Gurjaras were permanently subordinated to Pulā-keśin. We have given above (p. 54) our reasons for believing that this was not the case as far as the Mālavas were concerned.

[2] *Hsi Yü Chi* text, xi. 12b: cf. Beal ii, pp. 256–7; Watters ii, p. 239.

kingdoms that were bounded by the Sarasvatī, the Ganga, and the Narmadā, roughly between the longitudes 70° and 80°. Chih-chi-to, Mo-hi-ssu-fa-lo-pu-lo, Wu-shê-yen-na, and Ku-che-lo are all stated to have had their own 'kings'. Situated close to, or sometimes hemmed in by, territory directly or indirectly under Harsha's control or influence, in what relation did these kings stand with the Vardhana monarch? Chih-chi-to, identified with Jejaka-bhukti (Bundelkhand), is said to have been ruled by a brahman king. The district was so close to Harsha's capital that its 'king' must have owed allegiance to the Vardhana overlord. The same may be said of the brahman 'king' of Mo-hi-ssu-fa-lo-pu-lo or Maheśvara-pura near modern Gwalior. Wu-shê-yen-na or Ujjayini was a city of historic standing. In spite of the fact that it had changed hands several times in less than half a century, or perhaps because of it, its native dynasty appears to have been left in control of its own government. We have earlier deduced that in the course of his western advance Harsha conquered Ujjain and then let it form a part of the Maitraka sphere, respecting the latter's geographical and partly historical claims over that city. Two of Dhruva-sena II's grants dated A.D. 639 and 640 were issued from places within a few miles of Ujjain. However, by allowing Ujjain to be ruled by her own 'king', Harsha would be placing a mild check on the Maitrakas. In any case, since the latter recognized Harsha's position as the paramount sovereign of northern India, all within the Maitraka sphere of influence may be expected to have acknowledged Harsha's supremacy too. The Ku-che-lo of Hsüan-tsang is to be equated with Gurjara. Its capital, P'i-lo-mo-lo, may be identified with Bhinmal.[1] This Gurjara, not to be confused with the more southerly kingdom of Dadda II, lay between Pāri-yātra and Sindh and had once borne the brunt of Prabhākara-vardhana's arms. According to Hsüan-tsang it was under the rule of a 20-years-old *kshatriya* king. A young member of the indigenous line may well be exptected to be the kind of ruler Harsha would like to see on the throne of a kingdom economically unattractive yet welcome as a member of his *maṇḍala*.

Some writers hold that having been checked on the Narmadā frontier in the west Harsha penetrated the Deccan via the eastern route some years later. We do not concur with this view, and shall examine the topic more fully after completing the survey of Harsha's remaining conquests.

Incursion into Kashmir

His Kashmir exploit seems to have been Harsha's next venture after

[1] It was the ancient seat of the Gurjaras; see *N.H.I.P.* vi, p. 400; Beal ii, p. 270 n. 81; Watters ii, p. 250; and *C.A.G.I.*, p. 357. The modern Balmer, lat. 25° 48′ N., long. 71° 16′ E., is suggested to be the site of the ancient Bhinmal. Watters (ii, p. 250) remarks that the Chinese original probably stands for a word like Bhilmala.

his western enterprises. From the account of Hsüan-tsang, who stayed there for two years from A.D. 631 to 633, Kashmir appears to have been an important kingdom with various dependencies. Kalhaṇa's *Rāja-taraṅgiṇī* provides us with the name of the ruler, Durlabha-vardhana. When in Kashmir, the Chinese pilgrim visited a famous *stūpa*, to pay homage to 'a tooth of the Buddha in length about an inch and a half, of a yellowish white colour', which 'on religious days' emitted a bright light.[1] It was, no doubt, the same celebrated relic which was carried away by Harsha a few years later.[2]

In the 'Life', following the account of the Kanauj assembly held at the end of A.D. 642, we are told that 'to the west of the king's travelling palace there was a *sanghārāma* under the patronage of the king. In this building there was a tooth of the Buddha about an inch and a half long and of yellowish white colour. It ever emits sparkling light.'[3] A little later in the text it is recorded that

> in recent times Śīlāditya-rāja, hearing that Kaśmir possessed a tooth of Buddha, coming in person to the chief frontier, asked permission to see and worship it. The congregation, from a feeling of sordid avarice, were unwilling to consent to this request, and so took the relic and concealed it. But the king fearing the exalted character of Śīlāditya . . . found it (the relic) . . . presented it to the king. Śīlāditya seeing it was overpowered with reverence, and exercising force, carried it off to pay it religious offerings. This is the tooth spoken of.[4]

Though Harsha seems to have declared that he merely wished to see and worship the relic, he apparently went to Kashmir with the intention of acquiring it by whatever means necessary. It is clear that the King of Kashmir was frightened rather by Harsha's strength than by his exalted character.

That the ruler of an important kingdom with various dependencies could be cowed into submission by Harsha merely by 'relying on his superior strength in arms' is a positive proof of the latter's power and prestige.

The event may have taken place within two or three years of Hsüan-tsang's departure from Kashmir in 623, because already by A.D. 640 Harsha had conquered Odra or northern Orissa.[5] Harsha's Orissa

[1] Beal i, p. 158.
[2] Watters (i, p. 279) expresses the same view.
[3] 'Life', p. 181.
[4] Ibid., p. 183.
[5] Ibid., p. 154, informs us that Hsüan-tsang's teacher and friend Jaya-sena, with whom the pilgrim stayed for two years at a retreat near Nālandā, had been offered the revenue of eighty large towns in Orissa by Harsha, a gift that the saintly monk declined.

campaign, which lasted until A.D. 642,[1] thus must have started around 637. His visit to Kashmir and the forcible acquisition of the Buddhist relic should therefore be placed in *c.* A.D. 635.[2] Having achieved his aim in a war of nerves Harsha came back from Kashmir, and it does not seem that he had any further political connections with that 'land of the snowy mountains'. There is no indication that Durlabha-vardhana ever visited Harsha's empire, or that a treaty was ever concluded between the two. It was no doubt wise frontier policy on Harsha's part to keep his important neighbours overawed. Thus Kashmir, though not a part of Harsha's *maṇḍala*, had tasted of his power and would not venture to incur Vardhana hostility.

Orissa

Harsha's desire to acquire new territories seems to have been insatiable. Orissa was the next to draw his attention. It was probably the death of the Śail-odbhava king Mādhava-rāja II which prompted Harsha to undertake the campaign. The undated Khurda grant of Mādhava-rāja II,[3] issued from the victorious camp of Koṅgoḍa and claiming for its donor the sovereignty of the whole of Kaliṅga, may be placed between Mādhava-rāja's Puri plates dated A.D. 623 and Pula-keśin's conquest of Kaliṅga in *c.* A.D. 635, because Kośala and Kaliṅga are placed in the Aihoḷe *praśasti* after the discomfiture of Harsha at the hands of the Chālukya. Mādhava-rāja may have survived his defeat by a few years.

The Khurda copperplate, on the basis of its characters, which resemble those of Āditya-sena's Aphsaḍ grant, is ascribed to the latter half of the seventh century A.D.[4] But we think that without violating palaeographic evidence the record may be placed in the fourth decade of the seventh century on the basis of historical evidence. It is not likely that Mādhava-rāja, who was a contemporary of both Śaśāṅka and Harsha, outlived the latter by several years, regained Kaliṅga from the Chālukyas, and left behind a religious inscription recording his mastery over the whole of Kaliṅga. As far as we know, the Eastern Chālukyas continued to exercise their suzerainty in this region in the latter half of the seventh century.

Harsha's victories in Orissa extended to the northern and central areas of that large province. Hsüan-tsang names them as Wu-tʻu, i.e.

[1] 'Life', p. 172, 'Thus passed a month and more, when Śīlāditya-rāja, returning from his attack on Kongyodha, heard that the Master of the Law was residing with Kumāra.' Hsüan-tsang was with Kumāra in 642. (See *C.A.G.I.*, Appendix A, p. 648.)

[2] Niharranjan Ray (*I.H.Q.* (1927) 769 ff.) has tried to corroborate Hsüan-tsang's evidence by drawing attention to the mention of one Harsha in the *Rāja- taraṅgiṇī* of Kalhaṇa. R. C. Majumdar (*I.H.Q.* (1929) 233 ff.) has refuted this assumption on the basis of Kalhaṇa's faulty chronology. On a careful examination of the relevant verses we find that the identification established by Ray is quite unsatisfactory.

[3] R. D. Banerji, *History of Orissa*, i, pp. 122 and 130.

[4] Ganga Mohan Lashkar, *J.A.S.B.* (1904) 282–6.

Oḍra, and Kung-yü-tʻo or Koṅgoḍa.[1] Ka-leng-ka or Kaliṅga, ruled by the Chālukyas, remained untouched by Harsha. Oḍra in the north comprised the modern districts of Midnapur, Balasore, and Cuttuck. Chhatarpur and Ganjam formed part of Koṅgoḍa, to the west of which lay the kingdom of Mahā-kośala, which had recently suffered the brunt of Pula-keśin's arms. We are told that Oḍra and Koṅgoḍa were respectively about 7,000 *li* and 1,000 *li* in circuit, while Kaliṅga is stated to be about 5,000 *li*. Harsha thus was master of the greater part of this south-eastern province with important outlets to the sea.

The 'Life' makes four references to Harsha's conquest of Orissa. As mentioned earlier, we are told that Harsha made an offer of the revenue of eighty large towns of Orissa to the Buddhist monk Jaya-sena.[2] After the conquest of Koṅgoḍa his return via Oḍra is mentioned twice,[3] and he is said to have had a discussion with the priests of the Lesser Vehicle in Oḍra.[4] We believe that Harsha organized a piecemeal conquest of Orissa, not only because he is more than once mentioned as returning via Oḍra but also because he could not otherwise have made his liberal offer of a land-grant in Orissa to Jaya-sena, which he presumably did in person before A.D. 640. We infer that, having conquered Oḍra in A.D. 637–8, Harsha came to Prayāga for his fifth quinquennial assembly,[5] and Jaya-sena, who may have been present on that occasion, was made the offer which he declined because of his strict religious scruples.[6]

Did Harsha enter the deep south?

Koṅgoḍa thus was the southernmost province of Harsha's empire. In the opinion of some scholars,[7] however, Harsha also carried his victorious arms to the far south. The main basis for their assertion is an inscription composed in old Kannaḍa, found near the village of Gaddemane in the Shimoga district of Mysore. It is a *vīragal* set up to commemorate the death of a soldier and on palaeographic grounds may be assigned to the seventh century A.D. The legend is as follows: 'Be it well. While Śila-āditya,[8] the light of the quarters, the most powerful and a thorn in the way of the bravest, ascended the throne of his empire, Peṭṭaṇi Satyāṅka, a brave soldier capable of destroying enemies in the battlefield, pierced

[1] Beal ii, pp. 204 and 206; Watters ii, pp. 193–8.

[2] 'Life', p. 154.

[3] Ibid. pp. 159 and 172.

[4] Ibid. p. 159.

[5] The sixth was celebrated in the presence of Hsüan-tsang in A.D. 643; 'Life', p. 184.

[6] R. D. Banerji, *History of Orissa*, i, pp. 129–30, gives unconvincing reasons to prove that the references in the 'Life' are of no consequence in establishing the fact of Harsha's suzerainty over Orissa.

[7] R. Shamasastry, *Annual Report of the Mysore Archaeological Department*, 1923, p. 83; S. Srikanta Sastri, *J.R.A.S.* (1926), 487; Niharranjan Ray, *I.H.Q.* (1927), 788; Adrish Chandra Banerji, *J.A.H.R.S.* vi (1931–2), pp. 147–58.

[8] Mis-spelling.

through the thick of the battle with the brave Beḍara Rāya, so as to cause frightfulness to Mahendra, and reached the abode of *Svarga* . . .'[1] Those who believe that Harsha penetrated the south identify Śīlāditya of this record with Harsha, and Mahendra with his Pallava contemporary Mahendra-varman I.

In support of their view these scholars further cite a Sanskrit verse composed by Mayūra, a relative of Bāṇa, and a protégé of Harsha.[2] Making the familiar comparison of the earth with the Emperor's consort, Mayūra wrote a passage which punningly alludes to the seizure of different parts of the earth by Harsha. Besides Aṅga and Madhyá-deśa, which we know to have been parts of his domains, mention is made of Kuṅtala, Kāñchī, and the land of the Choḷas as Harsha's possessions. It is claimed that as Mayūra was a contemporary of Harsha there should be some basis even for a piece of rhetoric. Why should Mayūra have referred to these particular parts of the country in praise of his patron? The reason for the poet's choice is no doubt to be found in the fact that the names mentioned were those of the representatives of the three greatest contemporary powers of the south,[3] and had Harsha been able to conquer them he would have become the emperor of the entire Indian subcontinent. The verse, therefore, seems to have been written in a wishful anticipation of Harsha's all-embracing conquests, much in the same way as the subordinate kings in Harsha's army are said by Bāṇa to have uttered the following remarks when their overlord set out for *dig-vijaya*: 'The Deckhan is easily won at the price of valour. Mount Malaya is hard by the Dardura rock . . . and Mahendra joins Malaya.'[4] M. L. Ettinghausen, therefore, seems to offer the correct explanation when he says that the

[1] S. Srikanta Sastri (*J.R.A.S.* (1926) 487), R. S. Tripathi (*Hist. of Kanauj*, p. 122), and R. C. Majumdar (*H.C.I.P.* iii, p. 106 n. 1) take some liberties in interpreting the text. Sastri translates the relevant line as 'when Harsha came conquering', though no word in the text may be taken to convey that Śilāditya travelled any great distance to reach the scene of war. Tripathi and Majumdar, though they do not believe in Harsha's raid on the southern kingdoms, write that the passage mentions that 'when Śīlāditya invaded the south'. The passage in fact does not impart that meaning at all. Our translation is that of Shamasastry (*Annual Report of the Mysore Archaeological Department*, 1923, p. 83). We have had it checked by a competent Kanarese scholar, Dr. Padmarajiah, who supports this reading against Srikanta Sastri's interpretation.

[2] G. P. Quackenbos, *The Sanskrit Poems of Mayūra*, pp. 20–1; Vallabha-deva's *Subhāshitāvalī*, pp. 28–9; C. H. Tawney's translation of the *Prabandha-chintāmaṇi*, pp. 25–6.

[3] Kuṅtala was under the Chālukyas, the Choḷas were the allies of the Chālukyas, while Kāñchī was the stronghold of the Pallavas.

[4] *H.C.* text, p. 214; trans., p. 211. Dakshiṇā-patha (Deckhan of the translation) indicates the region south of the Narmadā; the Malaya-giri (Mount Malaya) ranges are to be located in the southern part of the Western Ghats, south of the Kāverī; the Dardura rock is in the Nilgiri hills; and Mahendra extends from Orissa to Madurā. The passage thus covers the whole of southern India.

verse was written before a campaign, probably that with Pula-keśin, forecasting what Harsha intended to do.[1] Mayūra's evidence thus proves too weak to substantiate the theory of Harsha's invasion of the deep south.

The identification of Śīlāditya and Mahendra of the Gaddemane *vīragal* respectively with Harsha and the Pallava Mahendra-varman I is likewise unsatisfactory and may not be used as a reliable piece of evidence to propound the above-mentioned theory. In our view the *vīragal* commemorates a battle between the Chālukya Śrayāśraya Śīlāditya, who ruled during the last three decades of the seventh century, and the Pallava Mahendra-varman II.

We critically examine below the various identifications offered of the heroes of the Mysore record, giving finally the reasons for our own conclusion.

The site of the Gaddemane inscription and the mention of the Beḍas, who were members of an ancient pre-Dravidian tribe of Karṇāṭaka,[2] clearly show that the battle between Śīlāditya and Mahendra took place in the heart of the Deccan. In view of the political history of this region before and during Harsha's reign, and keeping in mind the facts of his own career, it becomes obvious that Harsha could not have attacked this part of the country either before or after his clash with Pula-keśin.

The Kadambas of the Karṇāṭaka region had already been subjugated by Pula-keśin's father, Kīrti-varman, who ruled from A.D. 566 to 597. As the reign of the latter's brother and successor, Maṅgaleśa, ended in a civil war, Pula-keśin, the next to occupy the Chālukya throne in *c.* A.D. 610, felt the need to reassert his hold over the Kadambas and other neighbouring kingdoms, such as those of the Gaṅgas, the Āḷūpas, and the Mauryas, all of whom are enumerated in his Aihoḷe inscription. The Gaṅgas belonged to southern Mysore, which is also the site of the Gaddemane inscription. As the names of all these dynasties head the list of enemies reduced by Pula-keśin, it is clear that the Chālukya hold had become established on the central kingdoms of the south, including that of Mysore, by *c.* A.D. 620.[3] These victories were followed by further successes against the Lāṭas, the Mālavas, and the Gurjaras. Thereafter in *c.* A.D. 633 occurred the clash with Harsha, bringing further laurels to Pula-keśin.

According to the Gaddemane inscription, Peṭṭaṇi Satyāṅka and Beḍara

[1] *Harṣa Vardhana: empereur et poète*, p. 47.

[2] R. S. Mugali, *The Heritage of Karṇāṭaka*, p. 30: The region between the Narmadā and the Tuṅga-bhadrā is known as Karṇāṭaka.

[3] Pula-keśin's Gujarat campaign is dated A.D. 623: see above, pp. 51–2.

Rāya, who were presumably Śīlāditya's generals, defeated Mahendra's forces 'while Śīlāditya . . . ascended the throne'. Harsha, who ascended the throne in 606, and the initial period of whose reign was beset with formidable difficulties, spent the first six years of his reign in overrunning the 'five Indias'. He could not have invaded the region, which was for most of this time under the effective control of the Chālukyas. As for the possibility that Harsha may have invaded the Deccan and secured victories over Kuṅtala, Kāñchī, the Kadambas, and the Choḷas after his clash with Pula-keśin, southern Indian political history again yields facts which go against the theory.

The episode narrated in the Gaddemane inscription could not, of course, occur after A.D. 633, if we identify Mahendra of the record with Mahendra-varman I, for his rule lasted only until A.D. 630. Kuṅtala, Kāñchī, and Choḷa, mentioned by Mayūra, when not under Chālukya influence, were dominated by another rising power of the peninsula, the Pallavas. The Pallavas, in fact, were responsible for bringing to a close, in A.D. 642, the erstwhile successful career of the Chālukya Pula-keśin II. Until A.D. 654 they dominated the scene in the Deccan. In these circumstances it does not seem possible that Harsha could have ventured to attack, much less succeed against, the Pallavas in their very capital at Kāñchī. Mayūra's rhetoric thus was caused by nothing more than his loyal desire to see his patron rule over the whole of India and is very similar to the passage ascribed to Harsha's flattering feudatories in the *Harsha-charita*. Nor is the Gaddemane inscription a relic of Harsha's glory. More satisfactory identifications of the Śīlāditya and Mahendra of this record can be found among the seventh-century rulers of the two leading dynasties of the Deccan, the Chālukyas and the Pallavas.

B. A. Saletore[1] and G. H. Moraes[2] identify the Śīlāditya of the *vīragal* with the Valabhī prince Ḍera-bhaṭa, who is described in the inscriptions of his dynasty as 'the lord of the earth, whose two breasts are the Sahya and Vindhya mountains'.[3] They argue that Ḍera-bhaṭa, whose territory stretched beyond the Karṇāṭaka, could have easily fought an enemy in Mysore, where the inscription is found. Śīlāditya's adversary Mahendra is identified with the Pallava Noḷamba king Mahendra by Saletore and with the Pallava Mahendra-varman II by Moraes. But we believe that Ḍera-bhaṭa died before the accession either of the Noḷamba king Mahendra, who, as noted by Saletore himself, is placed by L. Rice in the ninth

[1] *Q.J.M.S.* 22. 169–84 and 302–17.

[2] *Kadamba-kula*, pp. 64–7.

[3] *C.I.I.* iii, no. 39: according to N. L. Dey, *The Geographical Dictionary*, p. 171, 'The northern part of the Western Ghats, north of the R. Kāverī'.

century,[1] or of the Pallava Mahendra-varman II, who ruled from A.D. 668 to 670. The two scholars have also made the groundless assertion that Ḍera-bhaṭa was also called Śīlāditya. Both Ḍera-bhaṭa's father and son enjoy this *biruda* in the Valabhī inscriptions, but he himself is never mentioned as Śīlāditya. That Ḍera-bhaṭa's death took place long before the accession of the Pallava king of Kāñchī, or the Noḷamba Pallava, is suggested by the fact that his son, Śīlāditya, of whom the inscriptions say that '(he) was the lord of the earth, the bulky breasts of which are the Vindhya mountains'[2] was dropped as the *dūtaka* from the inscriptions of Dhruva-sena II (A.D. 627–41) after A.D. 638, probably because he died in that year. Thus, if Ḍera-bhaṭa's son Śīlāditya was dead by A.D. 638 (K. J. Virji concurs with this dating),[3] he himself must have died, or at any rate stopped taking active part in the affairs of the state, before that date. Saletore's and Moraes's identifications therefore, when taken as a whole, do not hold, though, as we shall see, the latter's identification of Mahendra with Mahendra-varman II is correct when considered separately.

According to Virji the Śīlāditya of the Gaddemane *vīragal* 'can be no other than the Valabhī prince [Śīlāditya, the son of Ḍera-bhaṭa] who is described as ruling over the lands near the Vindhyas'.[4] She also observes that 'this Śīlāditya . . . was a contemporary of Dhara-sena IV, and may have ruled conjointly with him'. But in an account of Dhara-sena IV's reign given earlier in the book[5] she draws our notice to the facts that as Śīlāditya's (Ḍera-bhaṭa's son) name disappears from Dhruva-sena II's grants from A.D. 638 onwards and is replaced by that of the former's younger brother, Khara-graha II, and not by that of the latter's son and successor, Dhara-sena IV, 'it may be inferred that Śīlāditya must have expired before Dhruva-sena II, and when Dhara-sena IV was not old enough to shoulder the responsibility of this important office [that of a *dūtaka*]'.[6] These observations are contradictory to her earlier statement that: 'This Śīlāditya . . . may have ruled conjointly with him', i.e. with Dhara-sena IV. Even if Śīlāditya were alive during Dhara-sena IV's reign, we do not think that the latter, who assumed the highest titles in his family,[7] would have shared power with a member of the collateral family. We therefore do not concur with Virji, who says by implication[8] that the

[1] *Q.J.M.S.* 22. 305.
[2] *C.I.I.* iii, p. 185.
[3] *Ancient History of Saurashtra*, p. 80.
[4] Op. cit., Appendix D, p. 134.
[5] Op. cit., pp. 77 ff.
[6] Op. cit., p. 80.
[7] *I.A.* i. 14; vii. 73 ff; xv. 339 ff.
[8] *Ancient History of Saurashtra*, p. 135.

Valabhī prince Śīlāditya had an empire, while the Chālukya prince Śrayāśraya Śīlāditya 'was a mere officer of the Chālukyas'. The two Śīlādityas seem to have enjoyed almost similar status in their respective the kingdoms of the Vindhya region and Gujarat, under the patronage of ruling emperors, who were related to them. In any case, we think that, as Śīlāditya's name as *dūtaka* disappears from Dhruva-sena II's grants after A.D. 638 and is replaced by that of his younger brother Khara-graha II, he probably died in that year. This is also Virji's view, which we accept as correct, as against her contradictory remark that Śīlāditya may have ruled conjointly with Dhruva-sena II's son, Dhara-sena IV. Thus Śīlāditya, the son of Ḍera-bhaṭa, whom Virji identifies with the Śīlāditya of the Gaddemane inscription, died long before the reign of the Pallava Mahendra-varman II, who she thinks was the same as the Mahendra of the *vīragal*. When arguing the case for the identification of Śīlāditya of the *vīragal* with the Valabhī Śīlāditya, it is also forgotten that, unlike his father, Śīlāditya is only stated to have been the lord of the land near the Vindhya region, which terminates before Karṇāṭaka begins. It should also be remembered that the achievements with which Ḍera-bhaṭa and Śīlāditya are credited in the records of their successors may be highly exaggerated, for their campaigns might have been no more than raids conducted in the short period of confusion before Pula-keśin could master the situation. Even the Valabhī inscriptions betray that the occupation of territory in the Karṇāṭaka region by the Maitrakas was short-lived, because, while Ḍera-bhaṭa is said to have been lord of both the Vindhya and the Sahya regions, Śīlāditya is credited with authority over the former region only.

The Maitrakas seem to have had a special weakness for the *biruda* Śīlāditya, so much so that both the ruling branch and the collateral family used this title for princes of the same generation. Thus, a bunch of seven Maitraka Śīlādityas, along with the Śīlādityas of other contemporary dynasties, has muddled the wits of many an unwary historian. As we have mentioned earlier, Saletore and Moraes wrongly credited Ḍera-bhaṭa with the title Śīlāditya, and therefore erred in their identification of the Śīlāditya of the Gaddemane inscription. In his recent writings R. C. Majumdar[1] has made a comment on the shortcoming of this identification, but the fact that he has included this observation in an account of Śīlāditya III's reign (A.D. 622–84) shows that he himself has made the mistake of thinking that the two above-mentioned scholars implied that Ḍera-bhaṭa was the same person as Śīlāditya III. Majumdar

[1] *H.C.I.P.* iii, pp. 148–9.

has not noticed that Ḍera-bhaṭa is never referred to by this title in the Valabhī inscriptions. The king styled as Śīlāditya III by Majumdar is named Śīlāditya II by Virji, who makes a distinction between the ruling kings and the princes of the collateral branch that held the same *biruda*. We shall adopt the latter system, which seems to be more accurate.

The Maitraka Śīlāditya II (*c.* A.D. 658–85), though a contemporary of Mahendra-varman II (A.D. 668–70), who is now believed to be the same as the Mahendra of the *vīragal* by most scholars, may not be identified with the Śīlāditya of the same document in the light of the following evidence.

The Nasik plates issued in A.D. 666 by Dharāśraya Jaya-siṁha-varman, the brother of the ruling Chālukya emperor Vikramāditya, record that he defeated the whole army of one Vajjaḍa in the country between the Māhī and the Narmadā. Several Rāshṭra-kūṭa inscriptions of a slightly later period apparently take great pride in recording that the Chālukyas who had defeated Harsha and Vajraṭa were now overpowered by the Rāshṭra-kūṭas. Thus Vajraṭa, who is no doubt the same as Vajjaḍa, must have been a powerful ruler. The territory under Vajraṭa's rule, 'the country between the Māhī and the Narmadā', and the date of the battle strongly suggest that Vajraṭa was probably the personal name of Śīlāditya II. The Maitrakas, however, retained their hold on the territory north of the Narmadā, as is shown by their various grants issued from Kheṭaka and Bharu-kachchha, etc.[1] By A.D. 705[2] the control of the Bharu-kachchha *vishaya* passed into the hands of the Gurjaras, the feudatories of the Chālukyas.

In the time of Vikramāditya I, the Chālukyas had to contend with two strong enemies, the Maitrakas in the north and the Pallavas in the south. Vikramāditya succeeded against both with the help of his brother, Dharāśraya Jaya-siṁha-varman, and the latter's son, Śrayāśraya Śīl-āditya. Jaya-siṁha's success by A.D. 666 against Vajraṭa, who was most probably Śīlāditya II, precludes the possibility of the latter's clash with the Pallava Mahendra-varman II, who ruled between A.D. 668 and 670. Even if it be conceded that the Maitraka Śīlāditya got as far as Mysore in Mahendra-varman's time, why should both of them have fought with each other to the advantage of their common enemy, the Chālukyas?

We concur with R. C. Majumdar[3] that the Śīlāditya of the Gaddemane record was the same as the Chālukya prince Śrayāśraya Śīlāditya, who

[1] Acharya, nos. 82 and 84, dated respectively A.D. 669 and 676.
[2] Navasārī grant of Jaya-bhaṭṭa III: *I.A.* xiii. 70 ff.
[3] *I.H.Q.* v. 235; *H.C.I.P.* iii, p. 106 n. 1.

was a contemporary of two Chālukya emperors, Vikramāditya and Vinayāditya. Two grants of this prince from Nausari and Surat, dated respectively A.D. 671 and 692, eulogize Vikramāditya, who, it is recorded, was responsible for the increase in the power of the prince's father, Dharāśraya Jaya-siṁha-varman. In turn, Jaya-siṁha-varman is said to have 'overcome the Pallava family by his unchecked prowess' and 'obtained unsullied fame by victories in numerous battles'. As both Jaya-siṁha-varman and his son, Śrayāśraya Śīlāditya, despite their successes and their hold over a considerable territory in Gujarat, as is proved by the names of villages granted by the latter in his Nausari and Surat grants, never assumed imperial titles, it is clear that they enjoyed power only as viceroys under the patronage of the rulers of the main line. In return for their governorship of Gujarat they assisted their overlords in campaigns against the Maitrakas and the Pallavas.

The Gaddemane inscription is almost certainly a reminder of one of the successful expeditions undertaken by Śrayāśraya Śīlāditya on behalf of Vikram-āditya, against the Pallavas. The dates of the grants of Jaya-siṁha-varman and his son, Mahendra-varman II, and the wording of the *vīragal* all taken together lead to the conclusion that the Śīlāditya of the Gaddemane record was no other than the Chālukya prince of that name. Jaya-siṁha's Nasik plates[1] are dated A.D. 666, while the first known record of his son, Śrayāśraya Śīlāditya, was issued in 671, which proves that the latter succeeded his father between these two dates. The two years' rule of the Pallava king, Mahendra-varman II, also falls within this period. According to the Gaddemane record, Mahendra's defeat took place 'while Śrī Śīlāditya . . . ascended the throne of his kingdom', which event, as the dates of the two grants show, took place not long after A.D. 666. Mahendra's reign started in A.D. 668. The use of the simple *Śrī* for Śrayāśraya Śīlāditya, who only held the title *yuva-rāja*, is also quite appropriate, though it is incongruous for a king of Harsha's or even of the Maitraka king's stature. The Gaddemane *vīragal* may therefore safely be ignored as evidence for determining the extent of Harsha's empire.

Did Harsha conquer Nepal? Was his era of 606 used by Aṁśu-varman?

Another achievement with which Harsha is credited, erroneously we believe, is the extension of his suzerainty over Nepal. The arguments rest mainly on the assertion that Aṁśu-varman, who ruled in Nepal in the seventh century A.D., used the Harsha era of 606 to date his inscriptions. Some supporting evidence for this conjecture is available but it

[1] Khare, *Sources of the Medieval History of the Deccan*, i, pp. 8 ff.: cf. Mirashi, *I.H.Q.* xx. 353 ff.

is of an inconclusive nature, and in view of the untenability of the main hypothesis is rendered useless.

The two sets of Nepal inscriptions

Of the many problems that exist in the way of identifying the era used by Aṁśu-varman, one is posed by the inscriptions of his contemporaries, wherein a different system of dating is used owing to the dyarchical method of government in Nepal. The main ruling dynasty at Māna-gṛiha provided the nominal overlords, while Aṁśu-varman although only of *mahā-sāmanta* status enjoyed the real power. The two sets of inscriptions may be classified as follows: (1) those belonging to Aṁśu-varman and his successors, with dates ranging from 30 to 194, and (2) from Māna-deva to Śiva-deva, with dates ranging from 386 to 535.[1]

Some opinions on the eras used by them

The digit 5 as the first of the three digit dates of the latter group (from 515 to 535) appears now to be finally deciphered as such, as is evident from R. Gnoli's latest reading of the Nepalese inscriptions. Previously scholars like S. Lévi,[2] H. C. Ray,[3] and N. P. Chakravarti had also read the digit as 5. However, another school of opinion, represented by J. F. Fleet,[4] R. G. Basak,[5] K. P. Jayaswal,[6] and others, read the digit as 3 and attributed this set of inscriptions to the Gupta era.

The dates in group 1 were attributed to the Harsha era by B. Indraji,[7] J. F. Fleet, and R. G. Basak. Vincent Smith concurred with this view.[8] Other authors have advanced yet other views regarding the eras used in the two sets of inscriptions. Indraji and Basak proposed the Vikrama era and R. C. Majumdar[9] the Śaka era for group 2; Lévi suggested a Lichchhavi era for it and a Tibetan era for group 1. His views were accepted by P. Landon[10] and H. C. Ray. K. G. Sankar,[11] D. N. Mookerjee,[12] and D. R. Regmi[13] have offered different suggestions from those mentioned above.

[1] R. Gnoli, *Nepalese Inscriptions in Gupta Characters*, pt. i. It is the first of the three volumes to be published in the series *Materials for the History and Culture of Nepal*, and contains the Sanskrit texts of eighty-nine inscriptions, the entire number so far known. Fifty-one of them are published for the first time.

[2] *Le Népal*, iii, pp. 49–51; for his dates for group I see ii, pp. 153–4 and iii, pp. 70 ff.

[3] *D.H.N.I.* i, pp. 185–234.

[4] *C.I.I.* iii, Appendix IV, pp. 177–91.

[5] *History of North-Eastern India*, pp. 239–302.

[6] 'Chronology and History of Nepal, 600 B.C.–A.D. 880', *J.B.O.R.S.* xxii 157–264.

[7] B. Indraji and G. Bühler, 'Some considerations on the history of Nepal', *I.A.* xiii. 411–28.

[8] *E.H.I.*, p. 354.

[9] 'The chronology of the early kings of Nepal', in *B.C. Law Comm. Vol.* i, pp. 626–41; and in *J.A.S.* i (1959), 47 ff. (published in 1961).

[10] *Nepal*, i, pp. 27–8.

[11] 'The early chronology of Nepal', *I.H.Q.* xi (1935), 304–12.

[12] 'The date of the so-called Harsha era', *N.I.A.* iii (1940–1), 244–54.

[13] *Ancient Nepal*, pp. 92–103 and 125–31.

Aṁśu-varman era for group 1 and Śaka era for group 2

While we await the detailed studies of L. Petech and G. Tucci in the second and third volumes of the Nepal series of which R. Gnoli's is the first, we accept the views of R. C. Majumdar and L. Petech that the Māna-deva Śiva-deva series, beginning with 386 (A.D. 464) and ending with 535 (A.D. 613), is dated in the Śaka era and the latter's view that the records of Aṁśu-varman and his successors, beginning with the year 30 (A.D. 606) and ending with 194 (A.D. 770), are dated in the Māna-deva (or Aṁśu-varman) era of 576.[1]

A chronological list regarding Nepal in Indian and Tibetan sources

Petech's clear exposition is the result of a competent handling of the Indian and Tibetan sources which have preserved a chronological list regarding Nepal deriving from a common tradition. The Indian work is an astronomical text in Sanskrit called the *Sumati-tantra*, which lists, among others, the dynasty of Śaka-rāja for 498 years and, in a note by a later scribe, of Māna-deva for 304 years. This makes us arrive at the date 576 (498+78) for a Māna-deva era, used in the first set of inscriptions belonging to Aṁśu-varman and his successors.

The era used by Aṁśu-varman commenced in 576

The Tibetan tradition is preserved in the work of Sa-skya Paṇ-cʻen known through two quotations. After detecting an error in the Tibetan interpretation it is quite easy to see that the source has preserved the tradition of 498 years for the Śaka-rāja dynasty. It further records that Go-cʻa([Aṁśu]-varman)'s era lasted for 242 years until the accession of Krʻi-gtsug-lde-brtsan Ral-pa-can. As the latter is known to have succeeded in 817, once again we arrive at the date 576 (817—242, counting in the Chinese fashion) but for an era used for the first time by Aṁśu-varman. The name of Māna-deva is not mentioned at all. It is clear, however, that both the Indian and the Chinese sources are referring to the same era. The era of 576 may therefore be named after Aṁśu-varman or Māna-deva. Apparently the former started it but dated it from the accession of the first puppet king he had installed. 576 therefore also signifies Aṁśu-varman's own rise to power.

The Śaka era for Māna-deva Śiva-deva inscriptions

The indication provided by the Indian text and the Tibetan sources that the Māna-deva Śiva-deva series should be attributed to the Śaka era tallies with what the inscriptions suggest. For one notices that the *dūtaka* who issued inscription no. XL (Gnoli) of 535 (A.D. 613) also issued no. XXXVII (Gnoli) of the year 32 (A.D. 608) and no. XXXIX (Gnoli) of the year 34 (A.D. 610). It is, therefore, clear that the Śaka and Aṁśuvarman eras were being used side by side.

The system of reckoning used in Nepal—Bhāradvāja

In any attempt to verify the dates of the Nepalese inscriptions it

[1] 'The chronology of the early inscriptions of Nepal', *East and West* (N.S.), 12, no. 4, pp. 227–32; also see L. Petech, *Mediaeval History of Nepal*.

should be recognized that the Bhāradvāja system of reckoning and not the Sūrya Siddhānta was used in Nepal. This precludes the theory that, on the basis of the Pausha intercalation of the year 34 on one of the inscriptions, Aṁśu-varman's era may be dated from A.D. 595. However, some data still defy the Bhāradvāja reckoning.

Aṁśu-varman's career

On the basis of the above information it may be concluded that, as kingmaker, Aṁśu-varman placed Māna-deva on the throne in 576. Māna-deva's successors were Guṇa-kāma-deva and Śiva-deva. The latter was deposed (or died) in 606. Aṁśu-varman's first inscription is dated 30[1] (576+30 = 606). He preferred to start an era associated with the name of the prince who was nominally his overlord but in reality a protégé who had been dead for some time. His other inscriptions are dated 32 (608),[2] 34 (610),[3] 39 (615),[4] and 45 (621).[5] Those belonging to the first three dates (five of them) style him as *śrī mahā-sāmanta*, those belonging to the latter two as *śrī*. On the other hand his coins of the same period bestow on him full imperial titles, as does his successor Jishṇu-gupta. According to a later Tibetan tradition Sroṅ-btsan-sgam-po (610/20–649) married a daughter of Aṁśu-varman (596–621) but it seems more likely that the bride was the daughter of a Nepalese king named De-ba-lha as recorded in another Tibetan source. The Gopāla Vaṁśāvali mentions one Devala-deva about this period.

The successors of Aṁśu-varman and Śiva-deva Narendra-deva

In 637, when Hsüan-tsang was at Vaiśālī, Aṁśu-varman was already dead and Nepal was being ruled by a Lichcchavi king.[6] He was Udaya-deva. Two more kings succeeded him before his son Narendra-deva was installed on the throne. He was a protégé of the Tibetans who put him there, probably in 641. The Chinese texts record that at the time of Wang Hsüan-tsê's visit to India Na-ling-ti-po or Shih-li Na-lien-to-lo was ruling Nepal. Narendra-deva's inscriptions dated 69 (A.D. 645) and 82 (A.D. 658) corroborate the identification.

The supporting arguments in favour of the untenable hypothesis

The above exposition refutes the theory of Harsha's sovereignty over Nepal based on the view that his era of 606 was used by Aṁśu-varman and his successors. Before closing the discussion, however, we shall briefly deal with the minor supporting arguments advanced in favour of the main hypothesis that the Harsha era was prevalent in Nepal.

Āditya-sena of Magadha and Jaya-deva of Nepal

An inscription of Jaya-deva II[7] of Nepal dated 153 records that his mother Vatsa-devī was the daughter of a Maukhari chief Bhoga-varman

[1] Lévi, no. 13; Gnoli, no. 35. [2] Lévi, nos. 14, 15; Gnoli, nos. 36, 37.
[3] Bendall, no. 2; Indraji, no. 6; Gnoli, nos. 38, 39.
[4] Indraji, no. 7; Gnoli, no. 41. [5] Indraji, no. 8; Gnoli, no. 48.
[6] *Hsi Yü Chi* text, vii. 19a; cf. Beal ii, p. 81; Watters ii, p. 84.
[7] Indraji, no. 15.

and the daughter's daughter of the Later Gupta king Āditya-sena of Magadha. As the date 66 of Āditya-sena's inscription[1] is attributable to the Harsha era, and as the difference of eighty-seven years between the dates of Āditya-sena and Jaya-deva is estimated to be close to the average duration of three Indian generations (seventy-eight years according to Indraji and Bühler, who base it on Indian life-insurance-company records), the date of Jaya-deva's inscription too is ascribed to the Harsha era.[2] Āditya-sena's time, locale, and other circumstances make it almost certain that he used the Harsha era, but the same cannot be said of his great-grandson Jaya-deva. It is not advisable to depend on the modern figures for life-expectancy, which has changed considerably in India even within the last twenty years. Moreover the relationship of the two kings was based, in both generations, on the mother's side. Their respective kingdoms too were many miles apart. The chances of the use of the same era by both are therefore very slender indeed.

The Bais Rajput theory

It has been further pointed out that the Bais Rajputs of Nepal referred to in the *Vaṁśāvalīs* or the Nepalese chronicles may have been Harsha's kinsmen whom he left behind after his conquest of that country. The force of this argument rests on Cunningham's explanation of Hsüan-tsang's statement that Harsha belonged to the *Fei-she* or the *vaiśya* class.[3] The Chinese text does not suggest it in any way. Cunningham contends that, being a celebrated ruler, Harsha must have belonged to the *kshatriya* class; probably he was a Bais Rajput, in which case he would be a *kshatriya* but the 'Bais' led Hsüan-tsang into believing that he was a *vaiśya*. This is indeed weak reasoning as the pilgrim mentions several non-*kshatriya* kings in his account. He can hardly be expected to make a mistake in the case of Harsha, whose class must obviously have been well known in his day.

The Vikram-āditya tradition

Yet another reference in the Nepalese Chronicles is taken to allude to Harsha's hold over Nepal. There the legend is preserved that one Vikram-āditya conquered the country just before the reign of Aṁśu-varman. It is argued that this title, reminiscent of great conquests, could have been applied only to Harsha at that time. But the Chronicles are quite unreliable for purposes of chronology. They associate, for instance, the reign of Aṁśu-varman with 101 B.C., which we definitely know to be inaccurate. This reference, therefore, cannot be considered seriously.

'Tribute from the snowy mountains'

A statement by Bāṇa, crediting Harsha with the extraction of 'tribute

[1] *C.I.I.* iii, no. 42.
[2] *I.A.* xiii. 421.
[3] *C.A.G.I.*, pp. 432–3; also see G. Bühler, *E.I.* i. 68, no. 4; and F. Hoernle, *J.R.A.S.* (1903), 557.

from an inaccessible land of snowy mountains',[1] has also been cited in support of his suzerainty over Nepal. R. K. Mookerji, in fact, quotes it to prove his hold over both Nepal[2] and Kashmir.[3] Harsha's empire included several districts situated at the foot of the Himalayas, and some, indeed, such as the area crossed by Rājya-vardhana to reach the kingdom of the Hūṇas, were well within the Himalayan region. We think, however, that Bāṇa's remark alludes to Harsha's expedition to Kashmir, whose king was forced, because of Harsha's superior military strength, to part with a cherished relic of the Buddha.[4]

Relations between India and Nepal

Because such an issue has been made of the single question of Nepal's political status with regard to Harsha it tends to be forgotten that it is necessary to make a general assessment of India and Nepal's relations in Harsha's time. It should be pointed out that, in view of Vardhana prestige and power, the regular use of the Nepal route by Chinese and Indian secular and religious missions, and the close historical and cultural connections between India and Nepal, the relations between the two are likely to have been as intimate as may be expected under the circumstances.

[1] *H.C.* text, p. 91; trans., p. 76.
[2] *Harsha*, p. 30.
[3] Ibid., p. 40.
[4] 'Life', p. 183.

V

THE PRINCIPLES OF POLITY

Harsha's political heritage

HARSHA did not inherit an empire with a uniform system of administration; by his own exertion he brought together several kingdoms under a loose hegemony. Although inheritors of the Gupta tradition of government, these territories had, with the passage of time and changed conditions, acquired a new political orientation. The machinery of Harsha's administration, therefore, like his scheme of conquest, must have been planned with conscious and systematic effort on the part of the King and his ministers notwithstanding that it generously drew upon earlier patterns. In the matter of political principles too, although it adapted them to the existing situation, seventh-century kingship was indebted to earlier tradition.

From the rank of a King of Sthāṇv-īśvara, Harsha rose to the status of *sakal-ottarā-patha-nātha*, 'the lord of the entire north'. Conferred upon him by one of his adversaries this title is justifiable by reason of the fact that Harsha gradually bestowed political and administrative unity, though not uniformity, upon this vast area, through his long and unbroken career that lasted for more than four decades.

Legal texts of the period

For factual contemporary evidence on Harsha's administration our two most important sources are the familiar *Hsi Yü Chi* and the *Harshacharita*. In addition, for an understanding of the general principles of political theory and organization, we may refer to Kāmaṅdaka's *nīti-sāra*, 'Essence of Statesmanship', Asahāya's commentary on the Nārada *smṛiti*, and the *smṛitis* by Kātyāyana and Devala. Ranging between A.D. 400 and 800,[1] these works do not strictly belong to the period of our study, but they are close enough to Harsha's reign to give us some idea of the political and administrative trend of the times. Unlike earlier writings, however, the literature of these centuries lacks not only vigour and boldness, but even originality. It is a period not of innovators and creative writers but of commentators. This makes it necessary to have a closer look at the period before A.D. 400, which with its fundamental concepts inspired later thought and practice.

[1] *Hist. Dh.* i, Synopsis of contents, pp. xxxi–xxxiv. Also see below, p. 130 n. 1.

Other sources

Other and more direct sources of information on his administration are the coins and copperplates of Harsha and his contemporaries, and the Later Gupta inscriptions of the post-Harsha period. Last, but not least, we are helped by our clearer knowledge of the Gupta governmental machinery which continued to influence later administrative structures. For a general idea of the seventh-century set-up, therefore, we may safely depend on this last source if we make allowance for the modifications that occurred during the century or so of political reshuffle after the decline of the Guptas.

Need for political background

Before attempting to draw a picture of the administration as at work in Harsha's time it will be well to note the undercurrents in political thought and the fundamental bases of ancient Indian polity which motivated the actions of seventh-century monarchs. Familiarity with them becomes all the more necessary as modern historians have the tendency to judge the ancient state by medieval or modern norms and values and not unoften by mixed Indian and non-Indian standards—a tendency, that is, to evaluate a people outside their cultural, geographical, and temporal context. We trace below the evolution of political thought from the earliest beginning to the Gupta period, as the best of India's creative thinking, which continued to inspire writers even long after Harsha's time, found expression in the millennium or more before A.D. 500.

Some characteristic features of Indian polity

The basic concepts of Hindu philosophy, which were the fundamental supports of ancient political and, indeed, all other thought and action, were developed over a long period by many unnamed philosophers. Political ideas that had percolated through these concepts are found scattered all over the Vedic literature, in the epics, and in the Purāṇas, the most sizeable discourse on them being preserved in the *Mahābhārata*. The political scholars and writers, or *smṛiti-kāras*, interpreted political thought and applied it to an administrative structure backed by law. To take an example, the basic concept of *dharma*, the Principle, was a fundamental support of *rāja-dharma*, the principles of the state, which were applied to the administrative structure regarding public matters such as war and defence, taxation, etc., or private matters such as marriage, debt, etc. Justice was based on laws deriving their power generally from the following founts of authority, in the descending order of precedence: *dharma* (moral law), *vyavahāra* (judicial proof), *charitra* (popular usage), and *rāja-śāsana* (king's edict). Laws changed slowly, but sometimes radically from age to age to correspond with political, economic, and social changes and the resulting shift in values and concepts. New *smṛitis* therefore continually flooded the literary scene.

On the whole the king did not exercise legislative powers. His main functions were executive, although he and his ministers and advisers carefully studied the law. Judges in court applied the law to a particular set of circumstances and pronounced the verdict. The government officers then saw to its execution.

The state as governed in practice was the model of the political thinker. Indeed, his thought and advice would not have meant anything to the reader had it been otherwise. Yet with the passage of time many redundant practices would have been included in the *smṛitis*' description of the actual, and many out-of-date theories in their enunciation of the ideal. Political theory was already such an old subject in Harsha's time that we should make a special point of checking the *smṛiti* material against the positively contemporary evidence.

The fundamenta concepts

The beginnings of the fundamental concepts which guided every member of Indian society, and which evolved as time went on, can be traced to the Vedas. We shall deal with those which have direct bearing on political theory, and after a brief account of their development shall note their application to the state in the seventh century.

Dharma

The concept of *dharma* has a very important place in Hindu thought. In this context it has a much wider meaning than 'religion', the modern term by which it is often translated. It is an outlook on and a way of life, which, if adhered to, would help one to live life here at its fullest and best with ensuing results hereafter. The word *dharma* is derived from the root *dhṛi*, which means to sustain or uphold. *Dharma* was natural law for inanimate objects and natural phenomena, an ethical and social standard of behaviour for people, and, as far as the political scientist is concerned, a code of kingly duties for the king.

***Dharma* and *Ṛita* in the Vedas**

In the *Ṛig Veda*, no moral sense was attached to *dharma(n)*, which signified upholder or supporter.[1] But the evolution of the concept began early. Soon it came to signify ordinances or laws.[2] In the *Yajur Veda*, *dharma* means 'firm', 'imperturbable'.[3] But generally during the Vedic period moral content was reserved for another word, *ṛita*, the violation of which demanded of the sinner penitence and prayer to the god Varuṇa. *Ṛita* stood for order, for a regulating principle that ran through the whole realm of creation, god's and man's.[4] Gradually the moral sense of *ṛita* was incorporated in *dharma* and the former fell out of use except

[1] *R.V.* i. 187. 1; x. 92. 2.
[2] A.V. xi. 7. 17; xii. 5. 7; xviii. 3. 1; *T.S.* iii. 5. 2, 2; *V.S.* xv. 6; xx. 9; xxx. 6, etc.
[3] *V.S.* x. 29.
[4] *R.V.* i. 65. 2 and 5; iv. 3. 9–12; iv. 10. 2; ix. 7. 1; *V.S.* xxxii. 12.

in the negative form *anṛita*. The connotation of *dharma* on the other hand continued to expand.

Dharma and *Kshatra* in the Brāhmaṇas and the Upanishads

The Brāhmaṇas and the Upanishads use the word *dharma* in a significant context. According to the *Bṛihad-āraṇyaka Upanishad*, Brahman created the most excellent *kshatra* (strength, power) in the form of gods, then the demigods, then the four classes (castes), and finally the most excellent *dharma*. *Dharma* is the *kshatra* of a *kshatra* (i.e. of a *kshatriya*), therefore there is nothing higher than *dharma*. With the help of *dharma* even the weak rule over the strong, because *dharma* is the truth. Truth and *dharma* are interchangeable.[1] The *Śata-patha Brāhmaṇa* also equates *dharma* with truth.[2]

Truth and *Dharma*

The concept of truth too was undergoing change at this time side by side with that of *dharma*. In the Vedas and the Brāhmaṇas, truth was conceived mainly as a metaphysical concept, the truth of being or of the objective existence of things. The culmination of this concept was realized in the Upanishads and Vedānta, wherein *brahman*, or the absolute, is truth. The notion of truth had also been acquiring a moral content along with the metaphysical, so that speaking truth was considered moral, lying immoral. Starting with the *Ṛig Veda* and developing through the Brāhmaṇas, this moral aspect of truth continued to mature in the Upanishads, Vedānta, and Buddhism. The identification of such a concept of truth with *dharma* in the *Bṛihad-āraṇyaka Upanishad*, therefore, signified the moral content of the concept of *dharma* also. The metaphysical was invested with the moral.

Dharma over *Kshatra*

This stage in the development of the meaning of *dharma* also decides once and for all the ascendancy of *dharma*, moral strength, over *kshatra*, physical strength. The latter term occurs in the Vedas and the Brāhmaṇas, and the problem is posed: where do *brahma* and *kshatra* stand in relation to each other.[3] In the Vedas *brahma*(*n*) denotes hymn, prayer, sacred word, formulation of truth, substratum, etc., ideas that developed

[1] In the beginning [of creation] there was *Brahman*, one only. That being one, was not strong enough. It created . . . the most excellent *Kshatra* viz: those *Kshatras* [powers] among the *Devas* [i.e. various gods]. Therefore there is nothing beyond the *Kshatra*. At the *Rājasūya* sacrifice the Brahman sits below the *Kshatriya*. But *Brahman* is nevertheless the birth-place of the *Kshatra* . . . *Brahman* was [still] not strong enough so he created demigods and castes, and finally the most excellent *Dharma*. *Dharma* is the *Kshatra* [strength] of the *Kshatra*, therefore there is nothing higher than *Dharma*. Thenceforth even a weak man rules a stronger with the help of the *Dharma*, as with [the help of] a king. Thus the *Dharma* is what is called the true. Truth and *Dharma* are interchangeable. Hence, if a man speaks the truth they say he speaks the *Dharma*, and if he speaks the *Dharma* they say he speaks the truth. *Bṛ. Up.* i. 4. 11–15 (Also see *S.B.E.* xv, pp. 88–9).

[2] *Ś.B.* v. 4. 5 v. 3. 3. 5. Also *T.B.* i. 7. 10. 'The king is the upholder of *Dharma*, . . . he is to do and speak only that which is right.'

[3] *A.B.* vii. 4. 19.

later to signify, on the practical level, the title brahman for the person who possessed the qualities conveyed by such ideas, and, on the conceptual level, their abstract summation as the immutable universal principle. The word *kshatra* occurs in the Vedas in the sense of dominion or abstract ruling power, as well as in the concrete sense of ruler.[1] The Brāhmaṇas attribute *brahma* power to the brahmans and *kshatra* power to the *kshatriyas*. But apparently it is not the class to which a person belongs that determines the category of his 'strength', rather it is the other way about. Moreover the same person, whether a brahman or a *kshatriya*, may acquire both moral and physical strength.[2] Hence the use of terms like *rājarshi* and *brahmarshi*, 'king-sage' and 'brahman-sage'. Paraśu-rāma was a brahman turned *kshatriya*, Janaka was a *kshatriya* turned brahman; in other words they possessed 'strength' of both types at the same time. Viśvā-mitra was considered a brahman by change in vocation. The Majjhima Nikāya declares 'None is by birth a Brahman, none is by birth no Brahman. By deeds is one a Brahman or no Brahman. By deeds one is a farmer and by deeds an artisan, by deeds a trader too; by deeds one is a servant and a thief, by deeds a soldier and a priest, and even so a king is by deeds.'[3] Aparārka[4] remarks, 'when he who is not a *kshatriya* performs the work of a *kshatriya* [i.e. becomes a king] he should do all this [that a *kshatriya* king has to do] since the maxim is "that by assuming the position or the work of a particular person or thing one receives what is due to that other" [i.e. the non-*kshatriya* turned *kshatriya* should undertake to protect the people and consider himself entitled to receive the tax].' Although the Brāhmaṇas recognize the existence and the importance, even the interdependence, of both *brahma* and *kshatra* qualities the superiority of the former over the latter is made clear when it is stated that the brahman representing *brahma* can do without *kshatra* but not *vice versa*.[5] According to the *Aitareya Brāhmaṇa* the king during the anointment ceremony leaves the throne to bow to the brahman saying, 'verily thus *kshatra* falls under the influence of *brahma*'.[6] In the same text the king is proclaimed protector of *dharma*.[7]

In the Upanishads *brahman*'s most excellent creation is *dharma*, which in one sense describes the class–quality relationship, in another, being identical with truth, it is the very sustenance of things. In the Upanishads too *brahman* attains its classic meaning, it is equated with the absolute, the truth, the ultimate reality.

[1] *Vedic Index*, i. 202.
[2] *Ś.B.* xiii. 1. 5.
[3] ii. 98.
[4] *Yāj.* i. 366.
[5] *Ś.B.* iv. 1. 4 and 6.
[6] *A.B.* viii. 2. 9.
[7] *A.B.* viii. 3. 12.

Varṇa-āśrama-dharma

A new addition to the meaning of *dharma* was made when the Upanishads used it in the sense of duty or expected conduct. Every *āśrama*, stage in life, and *varṇa*, class in society, had a corresponding duty. The *dharma-śāstra* literature and Kauṭilya use the term in this sense as well as to denote law, especially civil law. The *Bhagavad-gītā* is most emphatic about the righteousness of pursuing one's own *dharma*, duty or vocation in life. The king, a *kshatriya* by vocation, would fulfil his *dharma* as much by indulging in war, commendably of a righteous type, as by ensuring conditions in which each member of society could satisfactorily perform his duty.

Dharma in Buddhism

The rise of Buddhism marks a further important and distinctive development in the evolution of the concept of *dharma*. The idea of *dharma* pervaded Buddhism in all its aspects. The theory of dependent origination or the law of becoming was *dharma*; the momentary configuration of events that constituted this evolution were *dharmas*; the enunciation of the four noble truths and the eightfold path that lay at the basis of Buddhism set in motion the 'wheel of *dharma*'; the very essence of *Mahāyāna* was described as *dharma-kāya*; and *Nirvāṇa* itself may be described as integration in *dharma* in its all-pervasive Buddhist connotation. As the eightfold path had to be lived consciously, *dharma* also comprised Buddhist individual and social ethics and morality for both laity and monks.

Dharma in early Mauryan polity

It was this aspect of the Buddhist *dharma* which first slowly seeped through Indian social ethics and then, about three centuries after the Buddha, showed its remarkable fruition as an instrument of polity under the inspiration of Aśoka. Aśoka's policy was not a reaction to the hard-headed Kauṭilyan tradition. The concept and application of *dharma* being so capable of evolution and adaptation, there was no need for it. However ruthless Kauṭilya's advice may be to protect king, kingship, and kingdom, his code of *dharma* for the king, the man, so that he might be a better king, was as exacting as that envisaged by any pre-Buddhist or Buddhist moralist. Thus, 'whoever has not his organs of sense under his control will soon perish . . .', and 'Restraint . . . can be enforced by abandoning lust, anger, greed, vanity (*māna*), haughtiness (*mada*), and over-joy (*harsha*).'[1] What was to be the king's aim? 'In the happiness of his subjects lies his happiness; in their welfare his welfare; whatever pleases himself he shall not consider as good, but whatever pleases his subjects he shall consider as good.'[2] Kauṭilya's king is unsparing of rival kings and is allowed all means, fair or foul, of annihilating them, but he

[1] *Artha.* i. 6. [2] Idib. i. 19.

is advised to prefer peace to war,[1] and righteous conquest to demonic conquest. While he is exhorted to act according to his *dharma*, the king is required to keep his people from swerving from their *dharma* of class and stage of life. But there is a *dharma* common to all: 'Harmlessness, truthfulness, purity, freedom from spite, abstinence from cruelty, and forgiveness.'[2] How is the king to achieve his aim? He is required to be ever active, ever wakeful, ever energetic. If a king is energetic, his subjects will be equally energetic. A king's discipline (*vrata*) is his readiness to action (*utthānam*).[3]

The three types of conquest *dharma*, *lobha*, *asura*

The desire for power or sometimes for the political or economic viability of a kingdom was reconciled with the ideal of *dharma* by classifying the conquerors in three categories. Kauṭilya[4] defines them as *dharma-vijayin* (righteous conqueror), *lobha-vijayin* (greedy conqueror), and *asura-vijayin* (demonic conqueror). The first type of conquest requires only obeisance, the second seeks land and wealth, the third claims, in addition, the vanquished king's closest kin and even his life.

The *Mahā-bhārata*[5] advises that conquests should be made according to *dharma*. The Pāṇḍavas desired only submission and tribute or gifts from the conquered.[6] Harsha's declaration on the commencement of his *dig-vijaya* campaign shows that he sought only obeisance and tribute from the defeated kings.[7]

Kauṭilyan and Aśokan views on polity compared and contrasted

Kauṭilya's *Artha-śāstra* and Aśoka's edicts arouse very different sentiments regarding the nature of these two sets of cultural–political data. Indeed, their approach to such vital matters as acquisition of territory and attitude to other kings is entirely dissimilar.[8]

While the ideal of righteous warfare existed in the *Kauṭiliya*,[9] Aśoka's *dharma-vijaya*, or conquest by *dharma* without war, was an entirely new concept. He applies the term to his gains in the extreme south and among the Greek kingdoms of Syria, Egypt, Cyrene, Macedonia, and Epirus,

[1] Op. cit. vii. 2. [2] Ibid. i. 3.
[3] Ibid. i. 19.
[4] Ibid. xii. 1. [5] *Śānti*. 96. [6] *Sabhā*. 26–32.
[7] *H.C.* text, p. 194; trans., pp. 187–8. On the occasion of his daughter's marriage, kings, subordinate to Prabhākara-vardhana, rendered personal service and gave presents: *H.C.* text, p. 142; trans., p. 124.
[8] Several factors may account for it. Aśoka and his grandfather Chandra-gupta Maurya, for whose benefit Kauṭilya is said to have written, lived in dissimilar political circumstances. Kauṭilya, moreover, was one of a long line of political theorists, whose debt he acknowledges and whose tradition he carries forward, albeit with many and bold changes. A political treatise, furthermore, should list possibilities as well as actualities. Kauṭilya may therefore be expected to cater for the needs of all kings, in diverse situations, at all times. Aśoka's experiment, on the other hand, although it grew out of past tradition, was unique, personal, and applicable to a given situation.
[9] *Artha*. xii. 1.

'borderers even as far as at [the distance of] six hundred *yojanas*'.[1] Aśoka appealed to posterity that they 'should not think that a fresh conquest ought to be made, [that] if a conquest does please them they should take pleasure in mercy and light punishments, and [that] they should regard the conquest by morality as the only [true] conquest'.[2]

Both Kauṭilya and Aśoka emphasize the importance of the same fundamental principles of goodness and progress in human character. However, Aśoka takes the ideal an immense step forward by incessantly reminding not only the king (i.e. himself) of the necessity of their implementation but also the people through the written and spoken word. We give below some citations from Aśoka's edicts to illustrate our point.[3] 'What does *dharma* include? [It includes] few sins, many virtuous deeds, compassion, liberality, truthfulness, [and] purity.'[4] 'But even one who [practises] great liberality, [but] does not possess self-control, purity of mind, gratitude, and firm devotion, is very mean.'[5] 'Whoever is fatigued in the administration [of justice] will not move and rise; but one ought to move, to walk, and to advance in the administration [of justice].'[6] 'For I am never content in exerting [*utthāna*] myself . . .'. 'But the root of that [i.e. of the welfare of all men is] this, [viz.] exertion [*utthāna*] . . .'. 'But it is difficult to accomplish this [welfare of all men] without great zeal [*parākrama*].'[7]

Gods in royal epithets

We may refer here to the use of the epithet *devānaṁ-priya*, 'the beloved of the gods', by Aśoka. It has been cited as an example in support of the concept of the king's divinity in ancient India; that being one of the gods he was dear to them. An obvious interpretation would, in fact, be that he was not one of them. The usage emphasizes, we think, the familiarity in which gods were held at that time. *Devānaṁ-priya* was a popular honorific similar to *bhavān*, *āyushmān*, etc.[8] It seems that a number of Indian and Ceylonese kings of the Mauryan period used it.[9] In the typical Sanskrit style the lofty word also had a humble, in this case comical, meaning: fool or simpleton. In any case, in later ages when the stock of the institution of kingship was higher, kings expressed their vanity through *deva*-less titles such as *vikram-āditya*, 'sun[10] of valour',

[1] Thirteenth Rock Edict. The Kauṭilyan *yojana* is stated to be 5·114 miles.
[2] Thirteenth Rock Edict. Our references are to E. Hultzsch in *C.I.I.* i, Introd. and text.
[3] Cf. citation from the *Artha-śāstra* given above, p. 116.
[4] Pillar Edict II.
[5] Seventh Rock Edict.
[6] Jaugada (first separate) Rock Edict.
[7] Sixth Rock Edict.
[8] Patañjali's *Mahā-bhāshya* on Pāṇini, ii. 4. 56, Hema-chandra, *Abhidāna-chintāmaṇi*, iii. 17.
[9] Eighth Rock Edict; *Dīpa-vaṁśa*, xi. 25–9.
[10] In the sense of 'shining star', not 'sun-god'.

bāl-āditya, 'morning (rising) sun,' *pratāpa-śīla*, possessor of power,' and, in the case of Harsha, *śīla-āditya*, 'sun of virtue,'.[1] The Kushāṇa title *deva-putra*, 'son of gods,' on the other hand carries the sense of divinity, and was probably inspired by their Central Asian heritage which found a supporting climate in India.

Dharma as the Universal law, the social law, and as the guiding spirit

It may be said that by the end of the B.C. period a threefold meaning of *dharma* had evolved. It was conceived on the one hand as an inherent law of the universe, inviolate and ever active, fixed and operating at the same time. On the other hand it was equated with man-made laws and institutions. These two extremes were so to say connected by yet another concept of *dharma*, the contribution mainly of Buddhism, that which encompassed man as an individual, as a social being, and in *nirvāna*. The content of truth or reality is present in *dharma* of all categories, from the mundane to the metaphysical.

Dharma in the *smṛitis*

The early Vedic and Buddhist thought on the subject of *dharma* and its application to polity may be further pursued in the *smṛiti* literature and the Jātakas. One of the significant works in the former category is the *Mānava-dharma-śāstra*, or *Manu-smṛiti*.

Manu

Like his Vedic predecessors Manu too uses *dharma* both in the general sense of righteousness and in the particular sense of social rules and court laws. Equating *dharma* with truth in the chapter on civil and criminal law he says, '*Dharma* slain verily slays, [but] *dharma* protected protects; therefore *dharma* is not to be injured. May not injured *dharma* slay us!'[2]

The ethical content of *dharma* is given in the following words: 'Steadfastness [*dhṛiti*], patience [*kshamā*], self-control [*dāma*], honesty [*asteya*], purity [*śaucham*], restraint of the senses, wisdom [*dhī*], learning, truth, absence of anger, are the ten marks of *dharma*.'[3]

As a guide for practical living, what is man to regard as *dharma*? 'The entire Veda is the root of *dharma*, [so also] the thought and usage [*smṛiti-śīla*] of those who know, also the conduct [*āchāra*] of the good [*sādhu*], as well as satisfaction of [one's] self.'[4]

Dharma in *tri-varga*

Dharma, the guiding star of life, in the sense of virtue, is the foremost of the *tri-varga*, the three categories *dharma*, *artha*, and *kāma*, which lead one to the ultimate aim of life, *moksha*—freedom or reintegration with the infinite. Good results, however, are contingent upon good conduct in the cycle of birth and rebirth, *karma* or actions being the determining factor. The law of *karma* applies to gods as well as mortals.

[1] The Buddhist term *śīla* is much more comprehensive than this English equivalent.
[2] *Manu.* viii. 15.
[3] Op. cit. vi. 92.
[4] Op. cit. ii. 6.

Moksha does not come from inaction; in fact, the three objects of life, the *purushārthas*,[1] involve living life fully and busily in all its aspects, in a disciplined manner. *Artha*, the acquisition of wealth, and *kāma*, enjoyment through the senses, if obtained and applied according to the laws of *dharma* will help one to attain the ultimate goal, *moksha*.

Artha According to the treatises on polity the king's primary concern should be with *artha*. This term too is much more comprehensive than is generally recognized, especially in the context of polity. The word is as old as the *Ṛig-veda*. It derives from the root *ṛi*, which means 'to go', 'to move', 'to emit', or from *arth*, perhaps a derivative root of *ṛi*, meaning 'to desire', 'to request'. *Artha* also denotes wealth, motive, or purpose. Though second on the list of the four objects of life of the ancient Indian, it was of vital importance to the individual, to the community, and to the king who protected them. *Artha-śāstras*, i.e. works on the science of polity, claim great antiquity in the history of Sanskrit literature. The *Atharva-veda* refers to *artha-śāstra* as an *upa-veda* (subsidiary) of the *Ṛig-veda*. Kauṭilya[2] and Kāmaṅdaka[3] both state that various works on the subject existed before they composed theirs.[4] *Artha*, therefore, had acquired a wide connotation over a long period of time. Kauṭilya, the earliest extant authority on the subject,[5] envisages *artha* as comprehending the entire material aspect of life, without an efficient management of which no non-material ends could be pursued. 'The subsistence of mankind is termed *artha*; the earth which contains mankind is termed *artha*; the science which treats of the means of acquiring and maintaining the earth is the *artha-śāstra*, science of polity.'[6] Indeed, the *Kauṭilīya* and similar works cover not only political ground but such subjects as would be treated today under the headings law, economics, and morals. Concluding his work, therefore, Kauṭilya justifiably says: 'Thus this

[1] In modern usage the word denotes manly effort.

[2] *Artha*. i. 1. 'This *artha-śāstra* is made as a compendium of almost all the *artha-śāstras* which, in view of acquisition and maintenance of the earth, have been composed by ancient teachers.'

[3] Kāmaṅdaka, i. 6. 'Kāmaṅdaka does obeisance to Vishṇugupta, who extracted the nectar of Nīti-sāra from the vast ocean of Nīti-sāra works.'

[4] Some of the names that have come down to us are the schools of the Mānavas, Bārhaspatyas, Aushaṇasas, Ambhīyas, and Parāśaras, and the individual authors, Bhāradvāja, Viśālāksha, Piśuna, Kaunpadanta, Vātavyādhi, Bahudanti-putra, Kāmaṅdaka, and Śukra. According to the *Mahā-bhārata* Brahma himself was the founder of the science of *artha*. His work was abridged by Śiva, and several writers, such as Indra, Bṛihaspati, Ushaṇas, Manu, Bhāradvāja, etc., followed in that tradition.

[5] The *Artha-śāstra* of Kauṭilya as it exists is ascribed to a date somewhere between the fourth century B.C. and A.D. 300 but most authorities are agreed that its political thought derives validity from Chandra-gupta Maurya's times, i.e. the fourth century B.C.

[6] *Artha*. xv. 1.

śāstra . . . is composed as a guide to acquire and secure this and the other world.'

Kauṭilya wants his king to enjoy in an equal degree the three pursuits of life, *dharma*, *artha*, and *kāma*—which are mutually interdependent.[1] 'Any one of these three, when enjoyed to an excess, hurts not only the other two, but also itself.' Other writers on the subject may have their opinions about the ascendancy of *dharma* over *artha*,[2] but 'Kauṭilya holds that *artha*, and *artha* alone, is important, inasmuch as *dharma* and *kāma* depend upon *artha* for their realization'.[3]

Manu ordains that *artha* and *kāma*, when they go against *dharma*, should be abandoned.[4]

In the *Mahā-bhārata*, Nārada inquires from Yudhishṭhira if he is fulfilling his duties as a king: 'Are you increasing your wealth? Is your mind rooted in *dharma*? Is *dharma* being fulfilled according to *artha* and *artha* according to *dharma*? Are these two not being obstructed by *kāma*? Are you observing these three in their proper place and time?'

The *Bārhaspatya Sūtra* on *artha*

The *Bārhaspatya Sūtra*, an *artha-śāstra* work placed very close to our period, expresses similar views on the importance of *artha*. This text, said to be posterior to Kāli-dāsa, and most probably anterior to the *Kāmandakīya*, is only remotely related to the ancient treatise of Bṛihaspati.[5] The author of the *Bārhaspatya Sūtra* advises the king to possess *artha*, using the term interchangeably with wealth. 'Who has store of *artha* has friends and righteousness and knowledge and merit and prowess and intelligence. By one without wealth *artha* cannot be acquired, as an elephant by one without an elephant. In wealth is rooted the world, and therein are all things. A man without wealth is a dead man and a *chāṇḍāla*.'[6]

Daṇḍa

Like the rest of humanity, the king's aim too is *moksha*. His means is specified as *artha*, which he should acquire with the help of the tool of *daṇḍa*. *Daṇḍa* again is a specialized term in ancient Indian polity. Its literal meaning is staff or rod, secondarily it means punishment; but political treatises attribute to it a much wider connotation, and use it as a symbol of kingly authority. In fact *daṇḍa* becomes synonymous with the science of government, inasmuch as it keeps the people of the

1 *Artha*. i. 7.

2 Here one or two passages, contaning the opinions of other writers on the subject, seem to have been omitted in the text as we have it.

3 *Artha*. i. 7.

4 *Manu*. iv. 176.

5 *Bār. Sūtra*, trans. by F. W. Thomas. See p. 18 for the translator's view on the date of the work and p. 8 (including footnote) for Bhagavad-datta and Jai Deva's opinion.

6 *Bār. Sūtra*, vi. 7–12.

kingdom and of the neighbouring territories in their proper place, under pressure of authority and power. Kauṭilya and other writers on statecraft use this term in the sense of 'fine' and 'army' as well.[1]

Kauṭilya on *daṇḍa*

Most writers on the subject confine *daṇḍa* to the sphere of practical politics, but Kauṭilya attaches to it an ethical connotation. *Daṇḍa*, according to him, is rooted in or dependent on discipline (*vinaya*). Only those who are possessed of such mental faculties as obedience, listening, grasping, retentive memory, discrimination, inference, and deliberation can benefit by the study of the sciences, and discipline can be imparted only to those who are possessed of such qualities. Sciences, he says, shall be studied by the prince and their precepts strictly observed under the authority of teachers who have specialized in them. In view of maintaining efficient discipline, he shall always keep company with the aged scholars of sciences, in whom alone discipline has its firm root.[2] Kauṭilya then points out that success in discipline depends on the restraint of the organs of senses.[3] The foremost authority on *artha*, the science of polity, therefore, while deeming *daṇḍa* or authority to be the very essence of government, bases its success in the intellectual and moral competence of the wielder of that instrument.

Daṇḍa-nīti has been elaborately dealt with by the authors of the *Manu-smṛiti* and the *Mahā-bhārata*, both of whom use the term interchangeably with *rāja-nīti*, the science of government, and *rāja-dharma*, the king's code.

Manu on *daṇḍa*

According to Manu, *daṇḍa* 'is a king, he is a man'[4] (i.e. he is manly). Let a king knowledgeable in *dharma*, *artha*, and *kāma* use *daṇḍa* properly and discerningly,[5] for *daṇḍa* regulates society,[6] and the king, a *kshatriya*, should protect society according to justice.[7] 'A king properly exercising authority [*daṇḍa*] prospers in all three [virtue, wealth, and pleasure]; but a sensual, unfair, and base [king] verily perishes by authority.'

'For authority, very glorious, and hard to be borne by the undisciplined, destroys a king, together with his kin, when he has indeed departed from *dharma*.'

[1] Writers have translated the term *daṇḍa* variously as justice, restraint, punishment, chastisement, etc. Of the two original meanings of *daṇḍa*, rod and punishment, the former is obviously the older. *Rāja-daṇḍa*, or the king's rod, must have originated as the symbol of his over-all authority. Since all other rights such as justice, punishment, etc., issue from authority, we consider it to be the most appropriate English synonym for the term in this context.

[2] *Artha*. i. 5.

[3] Ibid. 6.

[4] *Manu*. vii. 17: *sa rājā purusho daṇḍaḥ*.

[5] Ibid. vii. 26.

[6] Ibid. 18–24.

[7] Ibid. 2.

'[A king who is] pure, truthful, and a follower of the treatises, who has good helpers and is prudent is capable of exercising authority.'[1]

'The chief duty of a *kshatriya* is simply the protection of the people, for a king who receives the recompense [tax] specified is bound by law[2] [i.e. by his duty to protect in return for what he receives].' This view occurs time and again in several works and, as P. V. Kane remarks, the ancient Indian standpoint appears to have been that taxation and protection must go hand in hand.[3]

The *Mahā-bhārata* on *rāja-dharma* and *daṇḍa*

The *Mahā-bhārata* epic, centred on the great Kaurava–Pāṇḍava war, includes a chapter entitled *Śānti-parva* or 'the Book on Peace', which contains the political philosophy of the time, as expounded by the highly esteemed fallen warrior Bhīshma. The date of the epic is hard to determine, but the ideals expounded and the practices described pertain to a period when royal contests were common, an attempt was being made at large-scale conquest and consolidation, leadership of a king was considered essential for achieving it, and emergency measures were deemed justifiable to end emergency conditions.

While *dharma*, 'the supreme law' in its general meaning, is defined and exalted in other sections of the epic, the *Śānti-parva* concerns itself, among other things, with *rāja-dharma* or the king's code. Kingship is regarded as so indispensable an institution and the ruler's duties are so comprehensive that all *dharmas* are said to merge in *rāja-dharma.* It is declared that 'the welfare, good rains, sickness, calamities, and death among people owe their origin to the king'.[4] An equally wide connotation is given to *daṇḍa-nīti*, or 'the way of authority', by equating it with *rāja-dharma.* Like the Buddhist texts, the *Mahā-bhārata* takes the view that originally, in the most perfect epoch, there was no king nor *daṇḍa*; that the science of polity was created when men fell from their high standards.[5] 'But now *daṇḍa-nīti* controls the four classes, so as to lead them on to the performance of their duties, and, when it is employed by the ruler

[1] *Manu.* vii. 27, 28, 31.

[2] Ibid. 144. Or, '[Only] the king who enjoys the assigned recompense [and no more] acts according to *dharma*': *nirdishṭa phala bhoktā hi rājā dharmeṇa yujyate.*

[3] *Hist. Dh.* iii, pp. 36–9: P. V. Kane quotes copiously to support his statement: 'The king being hired for the sixth part (that he takes as tax) should protect the subjects' (*Baudh. Dh. Sūt.* i. 10. 1); 'every one when giving wealth does so with reference to a purpose related to himself and there is no purpose except one's protection that is intended in rendering taxes' (Aparārka on *Yāj.* i. 366); 'The king shares half of that evil which the subjects do when not protected by the king, since he takes taxes (from the people)' (*Yāj.* i. 337); 'a king who protects . . . receives the sixth part of the merit [*puṇya*] of the subjects' (*Yāj.* i. 334). According to the *Rāmāyaṇa* (iii. 6, 14) the king was required to protect forest hermits even though they paid no taxes, for he shared the merit of their good deeds.

[4] *Śānti.* 141. 9–10.

[5] See below, p. 125.

properly, it makes them desist from non-*dharma*.'[1] It is suggestive that Sarasvatī, the goddess of learning, is said to have created *daṇḍa-nīti*.[2] Apparently it was considered to be a deliberately formulated and benevolent science of government.[3]

The *Mahā-bhārata* distinguishes between desirable behaviour in normal times and in difficult times, terming the latter *āpad-dharma* or expected conduct in times of adversity. The king is advised to exercise any amount of harshness or duplicity in an emergency: for example, 'one should inspire confidence in one's enemy by some means which appear to be true, but one should strike him down at the right moment when he takes a wrong step,'[4] and 'one should be very courteous in speech, but like a razor at heart'.[5]

According to Bṛihaspati there is only one science and that is *daṇḍa-nīti*.[6] 'The king who abandons the science of *daṇḍa* is sure to land himself in misery, as a moth burns itself in a flame through ignorance.'[7]

Kāmaṅdaka on *daṇḍa*

Kāmaṅdaka furnishes us with a very precise definition of *daṇḍa* and *daṇḍa-nīti*, giving a clear idea of the function of the state as seen by a late-ancient writer on polity. '*Dāma* [control, restraint] is called *daṇḍa*,' he says, 'the king is called *daṇḍa* because *dāma* is centred in him'. He continues, '... the *nīti* [rules] of *daṇḍa* is called *daṇḍa-nīti*, and *nīti* [from the root *nī*] is so called because it leads [guides] people.'[8] The *Śukra-nīti-sāra* repeats the definition,[9] and adds '*Nīti-sāra* aims at social well-being and leads on to the welfare of mankind. It is admitted to be the very source of *dharma*, *artha*, and *kāma*, and hence a means to *moksha*. Therefore it is for the king to study always the *śāstra*, the knowledge of which helps him to overcome his enemies, and himself to become the source of delight to his people.'[10]

Orthodoxy versus heterodoxy

The opinion of the heterodox schools on the origin of kingship, and consequently on the relationship between king and subject, is different from the general *śruti* and *smṛiti* views on the subject. That is to be expected. The beginnings of the Vedic literature go back to a more primitive age, its range in time, space, and contents is greater, and its approach to problems is many-sided. On the other hand the heterodox

[1] *Śānti*. 69. 76.
[2] Ibid. 122. 25.
[3] Quoting from Viśva-rūpa on *Yāj*. (i. 350), P. V. Kane paraphrases the contents as '... then the gods made *dharma* (i.e. *daṇḍa*) his [the king's] friend'. *Hist. Dh.* iii, p. 33.
[4] *Śānti*. 140. 44.
[5] Ibid. 140. 13.
[6] *Bṛ*. i. 3.
[7] Ibid. i. 112.
[8] Kāmaṅdaka, ii. 15.
[9] *Śukra*. i. 157. It is a late treatise on polity. (See below, p. 167 n. 7.) In concurring with earlier texts it demonstrates continuity of tradition in various fields.
[10] Ibid. i. 5–6 and 12.

schools, such as the Lokāyata, Sāṅkhya, and Buddhist, are more compact, specialist, and unequivocal.

The Lokāyata, an atheist school: its views on knowledge, creation, society, and kingship

The Lokāyata, although little known, expressed its views on a variety of subjects. Also called Chārvāka after its legendary founder, the school was already well established in the sixth century B.C. Its latest text to have survived belongs to the eighth century A.D. That its dialectics was powerful and its theories were popular is evident from the strong and censorious criticism levelled against it by its opponents, Hindu, Jaina, and Buddhist. Lokāyata is uncompromisingly atheist. It declares that the sole source of reliable knowledge is direct sense perception. It does not believe in the existence of any invariable cause or consequence of an event. The universe, according to Lokāyata, came into existence from the fortuitous combination of atoms of matter from the four primary elements.

As may be expected the Lokāyata views on society and state follow from their materialistic and atheistic postulates It is stated that as the blood of the same colour flows through the veins of the brahman and the *chāṇḍāla* each is equally entitled to the opportunities of pleasure, the goal of life. To demolish belief in a higher power or divinities it is also declared that there is no being superior to an earthly monarch and that the latter should be duly recognized (established) by the people (*loka-siddho bhaved rājā*). The king in other words held office at the people's pleasure.

Buddhist views on kingship

The Buddha's views on questions related to polity are in line with his general view of the cosmos. Since he did not believe in God as the superhuman source of all motivation and activity of man, his ideas on the beginnings of existence and on the development of the first human beings and their institutions are different from those that would proceed from a pantheistic or monotheistic basis. The earliest beings, according to the Buddha as recorded in his *Dialogues*, had subtle bodies, a notion reminiscent of the Upanishadic and Sāṅkhya views and indeed very similar to that expounded by the Jainas. In the beginning all was purity and happiness. Later lust and greed arose, leading to sexual activity, private property, and violence, and so to the need for authority to regulate society. Hence the election of the *mahā-sammata*. The commentaries explain the term as '[one who is] approved by a great [assembly]'. In his capacity as the leader and organizer, the *rājā*, the *mahā-sammata*, was to maintain order in society in return for a fixed portion of produce to be given to him by the people. The etymological explanation of *rājā*, from the verb *rañjayati*, 'he pleases',[1] is not correct but is psychologically

[1] *Nirukta*, ii. 3, derives *rājan* from *raj*, 'to shine', while Bṛihaspati as quoted in the Rāja-dharma-kāṇḍa of *Kṛitya-kalpa-taru*, i, p. 5, traces it to both *rāj* and *rañj*.

revealing, whether intended to convey that the king was expected to please his people by good government or that the people were pleased with themselves for having created a useful institution.

In addition to the overriding influence of his over-all view of the universe in the formulation of particular theories regarding kingship, etc.: the Buddha's actual experience as the member of a state of republican type may also have influenced his approach to the origin of this institution. Later Buddhist thought continued the early tradition and is most succinctly represented in the *Chatuḥ-śatikā*, a second-century work of the *Mādhyamika* philosopher Ārya-deva.[1] He first puts forward some prevalent views on kingship, such as 'the king's pride in himself is justified because all undertakings proceed from him'. Then follows a commentary concluding with the following remarks: 'What arrogance is thine [O king!], thou who art a *gaṇa-dāsa* [slave of the people or a servant of the governmental organization] and who receivest the sixth part [of the produce] as thy wages.'[2] Ārya-deva then proceeds to assert the superiority of the principle of *dharma* over the sages' interpretation of it. 'The wise man', he writes, 'should not conform to all the doings of the sages, since even among them exist grades of bad, intermediate, and good.'[3] The commentary informs us that this is the author's reply to those who believe that the king who slays people in accordance with the law laid down by the sages (*ṛishi-praṇīta dharma*) incurs no sin.[4]

A sociological–psychological examination of the various stages in the development of political ideas would put them in clearer perspective.

The era of mythology: the mingling of gods and humans in political and social institutions

The earliest Vedic theories about kingship, class, and other human institutions, as well as about natural phenomena, were propounded in the era of mythology when the world of gods and demons and other celestial beings was a kind of symbolic reality to be part enjoyed, part revered and emulated. Naturally the origin of most social institutions, even if they were devised for utilitarian purposes, was sought in the world of gods, who mingled with the humans but were more fascinating and powerful than the latter. Gods were made in the image of man and given many superhuman attributes. Before long, words denoting human status worthy of great respect would be considered complete only with the addition of the honorific *deva*, 'god'; thus *guru-deva*, 'teacher

[1] *H.C.I.P.* iii, p. 381.

[2] *Chatuḥ.*, p. 461.

[3] Ibid., p. 462.

[4] The Tibetan translation of the *Chatuḥ-śatikā* gives us the name of the commentator, Chandra-kīrti. Chandra-kīrti is well known by the commentary on the works of his spiritual teacher, Nāgārjuna, the founder of the Mādhyamika school. His own work, the *Mādhyamaka-avatāra*, exists only in Tibetan. He writes beautiful prose.

who is god-like', *muni-deva*, 'seer who is god-like'. The name of a god as symbolic of his function might also be used as a type-name for men in similar position, such as *Indra* for king, *Bṛihaspati* for preceptor, and others. It is in this background that the legends about the origin of the institution of kingship may be viewed. As may be expected the early Brāhmaṇas and Upanishads trace the beginnings of the first king in the wars between gods and demons.[1]

The era of inquiry: man and the universe

As the Vedic civilization became more sophisticated, gods (as distinct from God) began to occupy a secondary place. The charm, freshness, and naïveté of the earlier period gave way to an awareness of something more profound regarding the true nature of things. A nagging feeling developed in man to know, to understand, and to explain what he saw and felt. This led to metaphysical speculation and the Upanishadic literature was born.[2] While inquiry persisted and intellect became keener, a new dimension to thought was added by the reasoned approach of the heterodox sects of the sixth century B.C. Many of the schools such as Lokāyata, Sāṅkhya, Jainism, and Buddhism were atheistic. Some of these, as well as other systems, postulated an atomic nature of the universe and evolutionary development of matter. Lokāyata was unequivocal regarding the non-existence of God or gods. Sāṅkhya based its philosophy on the two fundamental principles of *purusha*, pure consciousness, and *prakṛiti*, the prius of the whole material and psychical order of phenomena. Jainism and Buddhism made no reference to God; regarding gods they took the view that they were subject to the same laws as human beings. Even the theistic schools of the period, such as Yoga, did not necessarily prove the existence of God by the cosmological argument or on the grounds of differentiation in the nature of the substance underlying the universe. Rather it based it on the theory that the knowable attributes of that nature such as knowledge, time, space, etc., were limited by degrees of minimum and maximum, and that the entity in which they could be contained in their full scope and extent should be termed God.

The new intellectual upsurge expressed intself in all walks of life. As with regard to the cosmos and to man's inner problems, so with regard to his role as a social and political being, a more rationalistic, although

[1] *A.B.* i. 3.3 . *T.U.* i. 5.

[2] Generalizations are never exact and the early and later Vedic periods may only loosely be thus described. In certain cases some of the earlier pieces are examples without peer in the history of philosophic speculation, such as the Ṛig-vedic hymn of creation (x. 129). On the other hand some of the Upanishads contain material best described as superstitious.

still often allegorical, interpretation of phenomena was put forward, characterized by an open-mindedness and elasticity which admitted of change and new interpretations.

The momentum inherent in such an approach kept Indian society vitalized for nearly a millennium. When it subsided and turned into set tradition, stagnation began, followed by degeneration. Yet the emaciated flow of original thought manifested its potential spasmodically in the remainder of the ancient period after the Guptas, while in the medieval period, quickened by external stimulation, it became a steady stream carrying out successful experiments in synthesis in the fields of religion, literature, art and architecture, polity and economy.

The earliest era of mythology and wonderment diverged into two trends, one that followed the letter and turned it into belief, the other that followed the spirit and through continuous questioning and inquiry became creative and elastic, qualitatively as well as quantitatively. Hence we find the coexistence of superstitious and pragmatic political thought sometimes in different studies, sometimes in the same texts. Even writers of the latter type catered for the unthinking or for the too troublesome by excessively stressing the importance or the power of the state, alternating such statements with almost contradictory ones for their more critical readers. In times of political instability, whether caused by internal or external factors, even the independent-minded may do well to heed the supremacy of the state represented by the king over society, its constituents, and its various institutions. It seems that, as much as for any other reason, the specific slant of the *rāja-dharma* sections of the *smṛitis* was caused by an effort on the part of the *smṛiti-kāras* to emphasize political authority to a people (including themselves) who allocated to the state only a secondary place in the scheme of things, and regarded society, and finally *dharma*, as primary. This sense of values may in fact have always presented a problem to writers on polity. The tenor of their assertions may also have been guided by their own temperament and view of things as well as perhaps by the qualities and attitude of the contemporary ruler, who must have served as an example even in theoretical studies of state and government. Above all, the current political situations would have influenced the views of the authors who may have wanted to register their counsel not only for peaceful but also for disturbed times from the viewpoint of both the people and the king.[1]

[1] There is support from P. V. Kane on the last point, 'the apparently inconsistent dicta . . . are delivered from two different standpoints and are addressed to different persons . . . to the people . . . [and to] the king and his advisers' (*Hist. Dh.* iii, p. 27).

If in their works the *smṛiti* writers continued to give priority to brahman interests this was not necessarily because they themselves might belong to that class but also because their audience wanted to see the superior position reserved for the brahmans, who represented the values which were rated highest by both author and reader, the values, that is, of learning, integrity, piety, etc., rather than, say, of toughness, aggressiveness, or shrewdness. Whatever the case may be, the *smṛiti* writers themselves were products of their environment.

The modern scholars, therefore, who cannot read between the lines in the *smṛiti* literature miss the point. Manu's statement that the king is made up of parts of the gods, *Indra*, *Yama*, Wind, Sun, etc.,[1] is far from being indicative of the omnipotence of the king. As distinguished from God, gods were many and fallible, and controlled by their own *karma* or acts. As Manu states in complementary verses, the king who acted unwisely or unrighteously wrought his own as well as his people's ruin. By registering both the powers and the checks of the king in strong terms Manu serves more than one purpose. He impresses the credulous, he satisfies the critical, and he emphasizes upon both the importance of government. In spite of its second position, *artha*, 'state' (one of the many meanings of this versatile concept), was indispensable, especially in the troubled conditions which may have characterized Manu's own age and region. Moreover, his statement regarding the king being made up of parts of the gods is simply an enlargement of the Vedic habit of identifying a god-name with a function, as well as an example of the usual hyperbole, with every generation a shade stronger, that attaches to an ancient idea become conventionalized. That such remarks are to be understood figuratively, not literally, is shown by the fact that the *Śukra-nīti-sāra* describes the king as made up of parts of *rākshasas* (demons) if he is an oppressor of his people.[2] Passages of this type show that myth in the form of metaphor was made to serve the cause of reason.

Polity in the post-A.D 400 period

So far we have mainly concentrated on the development of political concepts in the period before *circa* A.D. 400, referring only incidentally to later literature. This brief survey was necessitated by the fact that the basic concepts of state and society as man's instruments for his highest fulfilment took shape and became established in this creative period of Indian history. With the passage of time the needs of the ever-evolving society were fulfilled in the light of new conditions, but always along the line of these deep-rooted traditions. Later political literature and institutions follow from this background.

[1] *Manu*. vii. 4–7. [2] *Śukra*. i. 70.

We shall now examine some of the more important political works composed after A.D. *c.* 400, because of their close proximity to Harsha's period. As noted before, this age abounded in *smṛiti* literature and commentaries of earlier texts. Some of the *smṛitis* are concerned with human conduct generally, but most are purely legal textbooks, dealing with such rules of jurisprudence as pertain to marriage, property, assault, defamation, and so on.[1]

The *smṛiti* of Kātyāyana

The *smṛiti* of Kātyāyana not only occupies the foremost place in the various works of jurisprudence composed between A.D. 400 and 600, but, by virtue of its closeness to Harsha's age, is our best guide to how society was governed and laws administered by the successors of the Guptas, including Harsha and his predecessors. The fact that many rules of Kātyāyana's *smṛiti* survive in modern schools of Hindu law testifies to their practical application at the time they were written down. Since Kātyāyana liberally borrows from his forerunners in the *smṛiti* tradition as well as from writers on polity, such as Kauṭilya, we must assume that many of his laws had long been current. It also proves that it is erroneous to regard the works of Kauṭilya and Kāmaṅdaka as wholly theoretical expositions of polity.

Kātyāyana's *smṛiti* has reached us in the form of quotations in the works of about a dozen later writers. It deals with various subjects, such as the position of the king, courts of justice, judicial procedure, criminal law, laws of partition and inheritance, laws of debt, etc. In several places Kātyāyana quotes from or enlarges upon Manu, Yājña-valkya, Nārada, and Bṛihaspati, etc., but he also introduces many new ideas and rules in jurisprudence, such as those on *strī-dhana* (a woman's personal property), the constitution of the court of justice, and judicial procedure.[2]

The king's rights and functions

'The king', says Kātyāyana, 'is . . . the lord of the land but never of other kinds of wealth; therefore he should secure the sixth part of the

[1] The important *dharma-śāstras* or *smṛitis* composed between the date of the *Manu-smṛiti* and the eighth century A.D. are listed below. The dates adopted are those given by P. V. Kane in his *History of the Dharma-śāstras*, vols. i, iii, and iv.

Yājña-valkya	A.D. 100–300
Nārada	A.D. 100–400
Parāśara	A.D. 100–500
Bṛihaspati	A.D. 300–500
Kātyāyana	A.D. 400–600
Devala	*c.* A.D. 400
Pitāmaha	A.D. 300–700
Pulastya	A.D. 300–700
Hārita	A.D. 400–700
Asahāya's commentary on *Nārada-smṛiti*	A.D. 600–750

[2] For details see *Hist. Dh.* i, pp. 213–21; also *H.C.I.P.* iii, pp. 359–63.

fruits of land but not otherwise at all.'[1] He may take his due share of tolls, taxes, and fines, etc.[2] When attending a court of justice the king should dress simply.[3] Before resorting to royal edict he is advised to give judgment on the basis of judicial proof and usage, in that order except in special circumstances.[4] Kātyāyana's court consisted of 'incorruptible and diligent assessors', 'brahmans . . . well versed in the meaning of sacred texts and the science of politics', and 'merchants who form a group or guild'.[5] If unable to try cases himself, he should appoint a learned brahman to take his place. The members of the court should turn the king away from injustice should he give orders to that effect.[6] Apparently he was expected to heed the opinion of his advisers. An interesting point about judicial procedure as laid down by Kātyāyana is the differentiation between complete and summary trials. Bṛihaspati, Vyāsa, etc. use the term *jaya-patra* for judgement given after both kinds of trial, but Kātyāyana reserves it for a verdict given in cases in which claims are cast off for various reasons without a thorough trial. Judgment pronounced after the usual stages of a trial had been gone through is described as *paśchāt-kāra* or refutation.[7] The term was known to Kauṭilya but had fallen into disuse until Kātyāyana revived it.

Hārīta on the king

Several other jurists of the period, whose views have survived only in the form of quotations in later compilations, comment on the powers and functions of the king. Hārīta requires him to be well versed in the *śāstras* and acquainted with the duties of the (three upper) *varṇas* and of those outside them.[8] The king should also know the characteristics of *vyavahāra* (judicial proof) and when giving judgment act according to all this. According to Pitāmaha, 'where no document exists, nor [proof of] possession, nor even witnesses, in such a case an ordeal need not be resorted to; there the authority is the king. For disputes of doubtful aspect... the king is the authority, since he is the overlord of everything.'[9]

The *niti-sāra* of Kāmaṅdaka

Written on the lines of the *Kauṭilīya*, Kāmaṅdaka's *nīti-sāra* provides us with a comparatively full study of polity at the time of the decline of the Guptas. Its date, however, is still a subject of controversy and needs to be discussed in detail.

The date of the *Kāmaṅdakīya*

Manmath Nath Dutt, writing in the late nineteenth century, maintained that on the basis of the possession of a version of the *Kāmaṅdakīya*

[1] *Kāt.* 16.
[2] Ibid. 947–8.
[3] Ibid. 55.
[4] Ibid. 43.
[5] Ibid. 57–9.
[6] Ibid. 72–8.
[7] Ibid. 259–65.
[8] Verse preserved in the *Smṛiti-chandrikā* composed by Devaṇa Bhaṭṭa, p. 51. The term *prakṛiti* is used for those outside the three *varṇas*, as explained in the following verse by Pitāmaha quoted in the same work.
[9] Op. cit., p. 98.

by the Hindus of Java, who were obliged to go to Bali in the early fourth century A.D., the Indian *Kāmaṅdakīya* may be said to have been written before that date.[1] Rajendralal Mitra in his Preface to the *nīti-sāra* also subscribes to the same view and dates the work about the beginning of the Christian era. The fact that Kāmaṅdaka declares himself to be a disciple of Chāṇakya, i.e. Kauṭilya, also weighed with Dutt in dating the *nīti-sāra* in proximity to the work which was its ideal. But he also observes, 'Indeed, had it [*nīti-sāra*] to be judged by its metres alone, they would have justified the inference that its origin is due to a much later age than that of Kālidāsa.'

The possibility of a later period of composition for the *nīti-sāra* is in fact the established opinion of writers today, though they have not been able to agree on a specific date. According to T. Ganapati Sastri the *nīti-sāra* must have existed before *c.* A.D. 550,[2] since Daṇḍin, of the latter half of the sixth century, cites Kāmaṅdaka at the end of the first chapter of the *Daśa-kumāra-charita.* As Bhava-bhūti, of the seventh or eighth century A.D., gave the name Kāmaṅdakī to a female ascetic conversant in the art of diplomacy, it is surmised that Bhava-bhūti knew of Kāmaṅdaka and his work on polity. A. B. Keith dismisses the theory of the *Kāmaṅdakīya*'s early existence on the basis of the Bali tradition but admits that its date can be determined only vaguely.[3] According to him the *Kāmaṅdakīya* is not known to the Pañcha-tantra in its oldest form, nor to Kāli-dāsa, nor even to Daṇḍin, the first chapter of whose book he suspects to be a later interpolation. The name Kāmaṅdakī for a character in Bhava-bhūti, he declares, may have some significance but is not a dependable argument. Yet he raises no strong objection against the case presented by some scholars that Kāmaṅdaka was a contemporary of Varāha-mihira, the astronomer and mathematician who lived around A.D. 550. Keith's own view that the *Kāmaṅdakīya* was composed in *c.* A.D. 700 is obviously erroneous as he bases it on the assumption that Vāmana, who refers to Kāmaṅdaka, lived in *c.* A.D. 800,[4] although on the basis of I-tsing's evidence Vāmana may be reliably placed in *c.* A.D. 660.[5] Keith is aware of this information,[6] and it remains inexplicable as to how

[1] Kāmaṅdaka, trans.: Preface.

[2] The *nīti-sāra* of Kāmaṅdaka with commentary, ed. by T. Ganapati Sastri: Preface.

[3] *A History of Sanskrit Literature*, p. 462.

[4] Ibid., p. 463.

[5] Vāmana's commentary on Pāṇini's *sūtras*, the *Kāśikā-vṛitti*, was the most popular Sanskrit grammar in the time of I-tsing (A.D. 671–95 abroad; 673–87 in India). The Chinese pilgrim records that Jayāditya, the co-author with Vāmana of the *Kāśikā-vṛitti*, died in *c.* A.D. 661–2 (I-tsing, pp. 175–6).

[6] *History of Sanskrit Literature*, p. 429.

he could have overlooked it when making his assertion regarding Kāmaṅdaka's date only thirty-four pages later in the same book.

P. V. Kane, in his first volume of the *History of Dharmaśāstra*,[1] assigns Kāmaṅdaka to the third century A.D., but in the third volume of the same work Kāmaṅdaka's *nīti-sāra* is dated A.D. 400 to 600.[2] According to G. V. Devasthali the treatise was probably composed in the period A.D. 700–50.[3]

We believe that the *Kāmaṅdakīya* should be assigned to the period *c.* A.D. 450–550 on the following grounds. This period witnessed the composition of various *smṛiti* and *nīti* texts of similar quality, such as the writings of Kātyāyana, Pitāmaha, Devala, etc., which were mostly derivative and generally of lower stature and lesser importance than the earlier works, such as those of Manu and Yājña-valkya. Judging by its literary style the *Kāmaṅdakīya* appears to be later than the works of Kālidāsa. Kātyāyana explicitly mentions the names of several *dharmaśāstra* and *smṛiti* writers, such as Manu, Bhṛigu, Gautama, and Bṛihaspati, while his knowledge of Kauṭilya and Nārada, etc., is shown indirectly by several of his verses. He does not, however, mention Kāmaṅdaka, probably because the latter was his contemporary or too recent an authority to be acknowledged, or perhaps posterior to him in time. Daṇḍin, of the latter half of the sixth century, mentions Kāmaṅdaka at the end of his first chapter of the *Daśa-kumāra-charita*, and there is no convincing reason to believe that this portion is a later interpolation. The first chapter, we feel, is an integral part of the book, for it would be extremely difficult to follow the rest of the story without it. From references in the *Mahā-bhārata*, Vāmana, and Bhava-bhūti it seems certain that the *Kāmaṅdakīya* had been composed before the time of Harsha.[4] By the medieval period Kāmaṅdaka's name had passed into the traditional list of ancient Indian *nīti-* and *smṛiti*-writers, and he is quoted alongside Nārada, Bṛihaspati, and Kātyāyana in Hemādri's *Chaturvarga-chintā-maṇi*, a work of the thirteenth century. He may, therefore, have written his treatise within a century prior to Harsha.

The synopsis of the *Kāmaṅdakīya*

Being the only detailed text on polity near to our period, Kāmaṅdaka's *nīti-sāra* needs to be examined closely. The book consists of thirty-six chapters,[5] in contrast to the 180 of the *Artha-śāstra* of Kauṭilya. In fact, the *Kāmaṅdakīya* is a metrical version of the *Kauṭilīya* excluding the

[1] p. 91. [2] p. xviii.

[3] *H.C.I.P.* iii, p. 300.

[4] The greater body of the *Mahā-bhārata* is ascribed to the last two or three centuries B.C., but the epic has earlier and later strata which are hard to date.

[5] T. Ganapati Sastri's edition with 20 *sargas* and 36 *prakaraṇas*.

latter's chapters on civil law and the departments of administration. The arrangement and classification of Kāmandaka's material, however, are more convenient and precise than Kauṭilya's, and compensate to some extent for his lack of originality. It must be noticed, however, that, though Kāmandaka takes his inspiration mainly from Kauṭilya and acknowledges his debt to the latter, the influence of the political thought of the *Mahā-bhārata* is also apparent in his work.[1] U. N. Ghoshal holds the same view in as far as Kāmandaka follows the example of the *Mahā-bhārata* in citing authoritative precedents for the justification of his Machiavellian principles of statecraft.[2]

First of all, the author states his motive in writing the *nīti-sāra*: 'we shall inculcate, out of our love for the science of polity, a series of short and significant lessons to kings, directing them regarding the acquirement and preservation of territory . . .'.[3]

In the thirty-six chapters of his book, Kāmandaka deals with various aspects of statecraft, which may be broadly classed as follows: importance of the king; education of the prince; protection of the established order of society; duties of master and servant; duties of subjects; the seven constituent elements of the state—king, minister, country, fortified city, treasury, army, and ally,[4] conduct of *maṇḍala*—the circle or orbit of a king's near and distant neighbours, both friends and foes; dealings with friends and enemies, including alliances, deliberations, and annihilation of the enemy; duties of envoys and spies; army, invasions, and warfare.

Kauṭilya, whose views are echoed in the *Kāmandakīya* in the relevant sections, states the king's aim and defines his strength in precise terms. The attainment of the goal, or success (*siddhi*) is identified with well-being (*sukhaṁ*). Three types of powers are listed as essential for achieving this end: strength through knowledge constitutes the power of deliberation, that through treasury and army is defined as power of mastery or sovereignty, that through valour and vigour is termed the power of vitality. Success may be described accordingly: success through deliberation, through mastery or sovereignty, and through vitality.[5]

The three-pronged means of attaining the successful end were ap-

[1] Kāmandaka, xv. 16: 'Rulers of the earth doing good [kindness] to the people grow in prosperity; their growth depends on the growth of the people and their ruin on these latter's ruin.' Cf. *Śānti*. lxxi. 26–9: 'In a thousand years the king expiates the sin which he commits in one day by his failure to protect his subjects from fear'; op. cit. cxxxix: 'The king who does not protect his subjects is truly a thief.'

[2] *H.C.I.P.* iii, p. 341; and *A History of Hindu Political Theories*, p. 220.

[3] Kāmandaka, i. 7–8.

[4] Ibid., iv. 1; *svāmī, amātya, rāshṭra, durga, kosha, bala,* and *suhṛit*.

[5] *Artha*. vi. 2.

parently used singly or collectively and, judging from the way they are listed, perhaps in that order of preference by the conqueror, the central figure of the *maṇḍala*, aiming at paramount sovereignty. The conqueror should, moreover, remember that for securing his aim peace was better than war, and in war, righteous conquest requiring only acknowledgement of his sovereignty was better than conquest for greed, which entailed seizure of the land and wealth of the vanquished, or from the worst type of conquest, the demonic, which deprived the defeated foe of his family and his life as well.

The *maṇḍala* system

The topic of *maṇḍala* needs some elaboration, for we believe that Harsha's empire furnishes the most vivid available example of the application, although naturally not in entirety, of what at first sight appears to be a purely schematic composition on a political chessboard. While we do not believe that the *maṇḍala* scheme is in every detail a description of actual conditions at any given time, it does seem on the whole to be an exposition of some very commonsense principles in statecraft, for example, the assumption that the kingdom in the immediate neighbourhood may be suspected of jealousy and animosity while the one beyond it may generally be considered friendly, or that 'to win the good graces of his circle of states' the suzerain should satisfy all the allies in a successful campaign with booty, himself being content with victory only.[1] The *maṇḍala* orbit was twelve strong, which is no doubt an arbitrary number to represent various possible relationships in diplomacy. Their order too, although logical, may not always be expected to remain the same.

The composition of the *maṇḍala* is described by Kauṭilya[2] and Kāmaṅdaka[3] as follows:

1. *Vijigīshu*, the conqueror, desirous of *dig-vijaya*, i.e. conquest of the four quarters, by war or favourable alliance is the focal point of the circle.

In geographical order, the five kings in front of his kingdom are listed as:

2. *Ari*—the enemy.
3. *Mitra*—the friend of the *Vijigīshu* or conqueror.
4. *Ari-mitra*—friend of the enemy.
5. *Mitra-mitra*—the friend's friend of the conqueror.
6. *Ari-mitra-mitra*—the friend's friend of the enemy.

Rearward, in geographical order, are:

7. *Pārshṇi-grāha*—a rearward enemy.
8. *Ākranda*–a rearward friend.

[1] *Artha.* vii. 5. [2] Ibid. vi. 2. [3] Kāmaṅdaka, viii.

9. *Pārshṇi-grāhā-sāra*—friend of the enemy in the rear.
10. *Ākrandā-sāra*—friend of the friend in the rear.

The circle was completed by:

11. *Mādhyama*—the intermediary, situated close to the conqueror and to the latter's immediate enemy.
12. *Udāsīna*—the neutral, situated beyond the territory of all those enumerated above and in a position to help or resist the conqueror, his enemy, and the intermediary, singly or all together.

It will be seen that the adjacent state is considered hostile, while the one beyond it is considered friendly throughout the circle. Next to the *vijigīshu*, the *udāsīna* is the strongest existing power. He is in no need of a diplomatic alliance. *Mādhyama* is intermediate in strength, being inferior to the *udāsīna* but superior to other powers. *Vijigīshu*, the aspirant to paramount sovereignty, should, through diplomacy, maintain his primacy in this circle of kings.

Inter-state relations among the twelve kings are based on the 'sixfold' policy:[1]

1. *Saṅdhi*—treaty of peace, or alliance.
2. *Vigraha*—war.
3. *Āsana*—neutrality.
4. *Yāna*—preparing for attack without declaring war.
5. *Saṁśraya*—seeking protection of another.
6. *Dvaidhī-bhāva*—double policy, or making peace with one and waging war against the other.

'Of these, a wise king shall observe that form of policy which, in his opinion, enables him to build forts, to construct buildings and commercial roads, to open new plantations and villages, to exploit mines and timber and elephant forests, and at the same time to harass similar works of his enemy.'[2]

Saṅdhi, peace or alliance

When advantages to be derived from both appear equal, peace is preferred to war, 'for disadvantages, such as the loss of power and wealth, sojourning [staying away from home, *pravāsa*], and sin, are ever attending upon war.'[3]

Alliance is advisable when the two rivals are enjoying, or labouring under, similar conditions. There are two kinds of alliance, one between

[1] *Artha*. vii. 1; cf. Kāmaṅdaka, ix–xi.
[2] *Artha*. vii. 1.
[3] *Artha*. vii. 2; cf. Kāmaṅdaka, ix. 73–5.

equals and the other between the subordinate and his overlord. Both kinds may be entered into with or without war and it is not without significance that the same term *saṅdhi* is applied to either situation.

Advice to a conqueror

To create the right conditions for peace after victory, it is expected of the conqueror that 'he should never covet the land, things [property], and sons and wives of the king slain by him; he should reinstate in their own estates [positions] the relatives of the kings slain. He should install in the kingdom the son of the king killed in action; all conquered kings will, if thus treated, loyally follow the sons and grandsons of the conqueror'.[1]

The conqueror is warned that the state of peace and interstate relations would be jeopardized if the above advice is not heeded.

> But the circle (of kings) being frightened, rises to destroy one who were to kill or imprison those who have submitted and covet their land, property, sons, or wives. And those ministers, who are under his control in their own lands, become frightened of him and resort to the circle. Or, they themselves seek to take his kingdom or life. And therefore, kings, protected in their own territories by means of conciliation, become favourably disposed towards the king, remaining obedient to his sons and grandsons.[2]

'We have joined in peace': the declaration of this oath was considered sufficient by some policy-makers to make an alliance immutable, sometimes reinforced by swearing by symbols of life, strength, and prosperity such as seeds, the brick of a fort wall, or gold. Others advised 'peace with a security', i.e. with hostages ranging from holy men to princes of the royal family. A princess as a hostage, incidentally, was considered an advantage to the giver, for she generally caused trouble to the receiver.[3]

Terms of an unequal alliance

An alliance sought by an inferior king imposed on him conditions of various grades of severity. He might be required to lend his overlord part or the pick of his army accompanied by himself, or the commander, or the heir apparent, or another unspecified person. Other types of agreement preferred by the inferior required payment of money, an immense quantity or that capable of being carried by a man on his shoulders, or secession of territory productive or barren, or payment of land produce.[4]

A conquered king, moreover, was expected to seek his overlord's permission in several matters, political, military, and economic. He might not, without sanction, build forts, install an heir apparent, celebrate

[1] *Artha*. vii. 16; cf. Kāmaṅdaka, x. 6, 7, 8, 10.
[2] *Artha*. vii. 16.
[3] *Artha*. vii. 17; cf. Kāmaṅdaka, ix. 6, 72.
[4] *Artha*. vii. 3; cf. Kāmaṅdaka, ix. 5, 15, 17, 18.

marriages (perhaps those leading to political alliances), trade in horses, capture elephants (both important for the army), march against an enemy, or hold tournaments and other martial sports. On all occasions of worship he should cause people to pray for the long life of the protector.[1] This served the purpose of reminding the people of the ultimate authority of the paramount sovereign. In the epigraphic records of subordinate kings, the name of the overlord was recorded before their own.

The significance of the *maṇḍala*

Thus on the one hand the paramount sovereign curbed the political and economic powers of his homagers, on the other he sought to remove irritants that might disturb peace and political equilibrium. Considering such factors as limitations of communications (although they could vie with any other network of the pre-industrialization period), human psychology, and the ideal of *dharma* in polity, it was at once a practical, psychologically sound, and idealistic approach to let the vanquished king retain his throne. Under such conditions the system of loose political hegemony worked admirably as long as there was a strong central monarch whom all acknowledged as their paramount sovereign. His conquered allies felt reasonably satisfied with their partial rights and responsibilities, and guarded their own and, as a corollary, their overlord's interests, by keeping at bay an outside enemy beyond the periphery of the *maṇḍala*. A protective alliance with the overlord gave them security against any outside attack.[2] The paramount sovereign on his part felt safe to rule over comparatively content subordinates, many of whom, especially the heirs of the defeated kings directly appointed by him, acted as the centre's glorified governors. Any ambitious monarchs beyond the *vijigīshu*'s *maṇḍala* held their peace at the sight of a large and homogeneous though loose confederation.

Effect on the people of the conquered territory

As for the people of the conquered territories, the continuation of the familiar ruling dynasty made them feel psychologically safe and unperturbed, and the lowering of its status hardly affected them. The slight change of emphasis in governmental policy regarding political and economic matters influenced but a few. Engaged in their respective *varṇ-āśrama-dharmas* or class-wise vocations, the people of the conquered territory went about their own lives with no provocation or incentive to engage in a counter-attack.

The utility of social organisation into classes

The conventional method of warfare, with military retinues made heavy and homely by physical comforts of all kinds, and more import-

[1] *Artha*. vii. 15; Kāmaṅdaka, xi. 29.

[2] The Kings of Valabhī in the west and of Kāma-rūpa in the east, with Pulā-keśin and Śaśāṅka as the hostile neighbours in the respective regions, furnish good examples of subordinate kings of this category in Harsha's *maṇḍala*.

antly the *varṇ-āśrama-dharma* injunctions, limited serious loss from war. Obviously fighting caused some disturbance to the whole of society, but the country's decentralized political system coupled with the social 'class' structure mitigated the harm considerably. While descriptions exist of damage to the countryside by advancing armies, it was in the conqueror's own interest not to inflict undue injury upon land he sought to make his own. Similarly the people of the region under attack would, except in special circumstances, be willing to transfer their ultimate loyalty from the local ruler to the conquering suzerain for the sake of continuation of good rule. Because, in the final analysis, the ruler was the instrument for good rule, and the people were expected to be good individuals and good members of society rather than good subjects in the sense of political patriots. Consequently we find that literary works such as the *Daśa-kumāra-charita* of the sixth century A.D., though composed in comparatively unsettled political periods, give an over-all impression of the bustle and activity of normal times. Like the contribution of the civil service in providing stability in the administrative sphere in some modern states, the discipline of *varṇ-āśrama-dharma* conduced to equilibrium and steadiness in most spheres of the state's life.

The conqueror's attitude towards new subjects

It was expected of the people that they should devote their energies to their respective tasks, as indeed it was expected of their king, independent or subservient, that he should enable them to do so. The *vijigīshu* was not to upset the conquered peoples in any way nor to force his own ways and beliefs on them. Rather he was specifically advised to 'adopt the same mode of life, the same dress, language, and customs as those of the people', and to follow them in the faith with which they celebrate their own religious and regional festivals.[1]

Regional indigenous law and custom were brought into harmony with the general cultural concepts that belonged to and were adhered to by the country as a whole. Indeed, another dimension might be added to the existing complex to incorporate a new idea or institution. Normally, however, the choice available in all spheres of human action was so wide that little more than a shift in interpretation would be necessary to incorporate them.

Maṇḍala and loose political organisation

The *maṇḍala* political situation was ever-present and ever-expandable because the *vijigīshu*, the aspiring conqueror, could apply it before, during, and after conquest. When the next immediate neighbour, initially considered an enemy, had been vanquished or won over as an ally, his territory in effect becoming a part of the *vijigīshu*'s empire, the

[1] *Artha*. xiii. 5.

state of natural rivalry shifted to the kingdom adjacent to the previous one and so on until the conqueror's ambition or resources were exhausted or were exceeded by those of the natural enemy.

What were the motives for expansion? The ideal of universal kingship had been created not only to cater for the ambition of kings. Rather kingship was there to realize the ideal for the sake of common good. An expansionist policy might be adopted solely with that purpose in mind. Yet the king was a human being and lived, moreover, in an era of the king's exaltation. He possessed the instruments of power which he could employ for personal vainglory, but being the symbol of the state he could identify his whim with the noble cause of his subjects' interest. At other times even an attempt at justification might not be needed, a king's ambition being considered sufficient reason, indeed, an impressive one, for a policy of aggression. In fact, war might even be indulged in as a royal sport.

The *maṇḍala* political situation was transferable: the claim to paramount sovereignty was not limited to one dynasty or one region. On an indication of decline in the emperor's power one or more of his subordinates might begin to assert themselves and start thinking in terms of their own *maṇḍala.* It may be safe to assume that when strength could back them memories of past defeats were used as incentives for revenge, although such thinking was morally insupportable, as the ideal of *chakravartī* and therefore of his efforts at expansion was recognized by all. But, as invariably happens, principles would become confused with persons, and successes and defeats in war would be treated as personal achievements and humiliations. Moreover, the freedom and the power granted to the subordinate in the name of *dharma-vijaya*, that is, in the interests of personal goodwill and political and social equilibrium, might ironically goad him to make a bid for power. It is clear that the righteous method of expansion had its practical drawbacks and that the virtues of the *maṇḍala* system in one situation became its weaknesses in the other.

A loose, accomodating imperial aegis is yet another example of diversity in unity in Indian culture, in this case in the political field. It was the most natural system that could have evolved in a land where each member of society, horizontally and vertically, was expected to act according to his own *dharma.* Unity came from the common basic approach to life, that of an active acceptance of diversity.

Political concepts, too, developed along this line of thought. The coexistence of the *chakra-vartin* ideal with the recommended *dharma* method of conquest illustrates the point. Ancient Indian political science was partly influenced by geographical circumstances but primarily it was a conscious direction of theory and practice in accordance with a system of cultural values.

Nor did these values remain static. Even if they conformed to the pivotal idea of *dharma* in all ages, they changed form, sometimes because of changes in the social and economic milieus, sometimes causing such changes. This led to the emergence of different political and administrative patterns in different periods.

A final assessment of Harsha's policies and early-medieval Indian polity will be made against the background of this discussion.

VI

HARSHA'S ADMINISTRATION

General picture of the times from contemporary sources

A BRIEF general picture of the times from contemporary sources should serve as a comparatively authentic commentary on the efficiency of the administrative system of the period. We shall follow these observations with a summary characterization of Harsha, the man at the helm of affairs, and finally discuss at length the political set-up and the governmental organization in various fields.

The Gupta age compared with Harsha's period

The semi-historical and literary records of the period depict a people still creative and lively, who welcomed diversity and nonconformity and who under a liberal government enjoyed liberty of expression. The upward trend of the Gupta times, however, had gone. Pedantry and ornament had taken the place of simplicity, freshness, and boldness. Conditions of security had to some extent weakened and the law, though still mild, had become comparatively rigorous to meet the somewhat lower standards of behaviour caused perhaps by the absence of a strong central authority for a century with corresponding loss of prosperity. While it is true that the exceptionally high Gupta standards would be hard to measure up to by any given dynasty, it is apparent that the peak had been passed.

Hsüan-tsang's general remarks

The account of Hsüan-tsang, as preserved in the 'Records' and the 'Life', gives on the whole an impression of general well-being in Harsha's reign. 'The administration is honest, and the people live together in harmony', observes the pilgrim in his introductory description of India.

Crime and justice

He continues: 'When occasionally the rebels and the wicked transgress the statute law of the country and plot against the rulers and superiors, after the facts are brought to light, they are put into prison but without any corporal punishment. They are no more considered members of the community and are left to live or die .... In the trial of criminals no

Taxation

torture is used.' In the section on revenue and taxation the Chinese traveller records that the government was 'tolerant'; official requirements were, therefore, reduced to a minimum. There was no registration of families. People were contentedly engaged in cultivating their land. Land tax was no more than one-sixth of the produce. Hsüan-tsang first remarks that there was no (regular?) *corvée* but then goes on to add that it was moderate and that the taxes were light. Perhaps he is referring to the provision of labour in lieu of taxes.[1]

People's temperament

On the people themselves Hsüan-tsang expresses his opinion freely, calling them harsh, quarrelsome, trustworthy, or gentle as the case may be in his individual descriptions of the various provinces he visited, but he also appears to have formed an over-all opinion of Indians which he relates in his general account of the country. 'The people,' he says, 'although rather hot-tempered, are upright and sincere [simple?]. They never take anything wrongfully and often yield to others more than fairness requires. . . . They do not practise treachery and abide by their oaths.' We learn from him that the standards of personal hygiene were high and the brahmans and *kshatriyas* led 'clean, pure, simple, and frugal lives', although in the very next sentence the pilgrim describes the various ornaments with which they adorn themselves. The Indian polysyllabic language and alphabetic script so different from the mono-syllabic and ideographic Chinese seem to have appealed to Hsüan-tsang. Capable of appreciating Sanskrit he compliments the people of mid India on their 'explicit and correct' speech, 'harmonious and elegant' expression, and 'clear and distinct' intonation. Equally, he denounces the degenerate style of the neighbouring 'countries'. He is perhaps deprecating the use of the popular but not chaste *prākṛits* and *apabhraṁśa*.

Dress and hygiene

Language

Description of Kanauj

Kanauj, Harsha's capital, impressed the Chinese visitor. He remarks on its lofty structures, beautiful gardens, and tanks of clean water. The abundance of fruit and flowers in the city and its exotic merchandise, valuable and in large quantities, draw his comment. The inhabitants, he notes, were well off and contented, some families being particularly wealthy. 'The people are honest and sincere. They are noble and gracious in appearance . . . They apply themselves much to learning', remarks the Chinese scholar, adding further that they were very keen on discourses on religious subjects, which they conducted with great clarity. In fact in all contemporary works there are numerous references to the traditional practice of public assemblies for discussion and debate among men of learning of various schools of religious thought.

Education

Education was widespread and scholarly life was vigorous. Hsüan-tsang's visit, aimed at accumulating Buddhist learning, which involved studies not only in religion but also in grammar, logic, epistemology, and certain sciences, is itself a proof of it. In north India, Kashmir, Valabhī,

[1] See below, pp. 204–5.

Banaras, and Nālandā were the great centres of learning in Harsha's time, with many lesser ones no doubt, such as Kanauj, Prayāga, Jālandhara, etc., connected with state and religious activities. Indeed, the high tempo of intellectual activity continued until the end of the twelfth century when the armies of Bakhtyār Khiljī ravaged the eastern monastic universities.[1] A modern Chinese scholar, Liang Chi-chao, has traced in his indigenous sources names of 162 visitors from China to India between the fifth and eighth centuries A.D.[2] The flow continued in the following period. Examined alongside other evidence, Hsüan-tsang's detailed account of the Nālandā establishment throws much light on various aspects of education in India.[3] Constant vigilance and a spirit of enquiry and doubt on the pupils's part appear to have been as important a requirement as regard and veneration for the teacher.[4] The curriculum at Nālandā comprised Buddhist and Hindu religious and secular subjects and is probably indicative of the general practice at such establishments over a very long period of time in ancient India.[5] Centres of learning in Kashmir and at Nālandā and Kāñchī attracted as much interest from the outside world as did the Indian centres of trade.

Economic activity

Economic activity within the country and with foreign lands, although

[1] New universities were founded and old ones patronized by the Pālas, who rose in east India in the eighth century A.D. and who ruled, although with dwindling fortunes towards the end, until the twelfth century A.D. Vikrama-śīlā, Jagaddala, and Uddantapurī won great renown as centres of learning under the Pālas.

[2] The untranslated researches of Liang Chi-chao are summarized in a paper *Chinese sources of Indian history* by Lo Lia-chuen submitted to the Indian Historical Records Commission (Silver Jubilee Session), 1948. See S. Dutt in *2,500 Years of Buddhism*, ed. P. V. Bapat, p. 185.

[3] 'Life', pp. 110–12; Beal ii, pp. 102 ff.; Watters ii, pp. 164 ff. Nālandā's connection with Buddhism appears to go back to the time of the Buddha himself (Watters ii, p. 166 n. 2). A *vihāra* about 20 miles to the west of Nālandā is said to have been founded by the last descendant of King Bimbi-sāra (Watters ii, pp. 105–7). Aśoka's name too is associated with Nālandā. The 'Life' and the 'Records', moreover, declare that the monastery was founded by one King Śakr-āditya. The names of his descendants who continued to build at the site are registered as Budha-gupta, Tathā-gata-rāja, Bālāditya, and Vajra. A King of mid India added another *sangh-ārāma*. The 'Life' also states that the monastery was 700 years old at the time of Hsüan-tsang's visit (A.D. 637). These statements make it clear that although it is not possible to trace the history of Nālandā with great accuracy it is safe to assume its antiquity and continuity. Archaeological remains from the site date from the fifth century A.D. to the end of the twelfth century. In Harsha's time the monastery and the university were certainly at the height of their fame. When Nālandā declined, the near-by new Buddhist university of Vikrama-śilā, patronized by the Pālas, came into prominence.

[4] Beal i, p. 79; ii, pp. 170–1; Watters i, p. 160; ii, p. 165; *Mahā-vagga*, i. 25. 20, and i. 36. 12.

[5] 'Life', p. 112; I-tsing, pp. 176–7; *H.C.* text, pp. 236–7; trans., p. 236; Beal i, pp. 78–9; Watters i, pp. 154–60. The *Hsi Yü Chi* includes Hsüan-tsang's observations on the syllabus for a child of six, and on the variety of subjects that an advanced student was expected to master. A brahman's repertoire probably consisted of most of these subjects as well as the Vedas.

never seriously interrupted, would have been furthered by the mobilizing of resources of the vast territory united under the political leadership of Harsha. It may be expected that economic motives reinforced Harsha's political considerations in manipulating a superior alliance with Valabhī and Kāma-rūpa and in conducting the Orissa campaign. There are a few specific and many incidental references in contemporary records that throw light on the material condition of the people in Harsha's kingdom.

Hsüan-tsang remarks on the taxes being light. He also observes, 'Tradesmen go to and fro bartering their merchandise after paying light duties at ferries and barrier stations.'[1] More than once the traveller refers to the presence of rare and valuable merchandise in cities. Describing Banaras he says, 'the inhabitants were very numerous and had boundless wealth, their houses being full of rare valuables'.[2] In Kanauj he noticed 'rarities from strange lands'.[3]

Inland trade and foreign contacts

Both the 'Life' and the 'Records' make numerous references to the use of the Ganga as a highway, which indicates the presence of commercial centres all along the river. Ocean travel was popular. Hsüan-tsang records about Su-la-chʻa (Surat) that as it 'was on the highway to the sea all its inhabitants utilized the sea and were traders by profession'.[4] Notices of political embassies from Indian kings to the Roman court cease only with the decline of the Roman empire: the last two were sent to the court of Justinian in A.D. 530 and 552. Contacts with the Persians to be traced back to very remote beginnings continued to flourish. Hsüan-tsang[5] attests to the thriving state of Hinduism and Buddhism in Lang-kie (ka)-lo which was subject to Persia. The script used by the people and, with some differences, the spoken language too are stated to be like those of India. This description is followed by an account of Persia (Po-la-sse) based on report. The country is said to abound in *deva* temples. The pilgrim generally uses this term for Hindu sanctuaries but in this case it may also apply to Zoroastrian houses of worship. The presence of Buddhist monks, moreover, is recorded, and their preference for the *sarvāsti-vādin* school indicates Buddhism's early arrival in Persia. The continuity of the Buddhist tradition in this region over a very long period is attested by both archaeological and literary evidence. It was a Parthian prince An Shih-kao (second century A.D.) who made the first organized effort to translate the Buddhist canon into Chinese. Mani, the founder of Manichæism (third century A.D.), was influenced by

[1] Watters i, p. 176.
[2] Ibid. ii, p. 47.
[3] Ibid. i, p. 340.
[4] Ibid. ii, p. 248.
[5] Beal ii, pp. 277–9; Watters ii, pp. 257–8.

Buddhism. Manichæan manuscript fragments written in Iranian and old Turkish contain Buddhist episodes. The tenth-century Muslim scholar al-bīrūnī records the presence of Buddhism, in former times, in Khorasan, Persia, Iraq, and neighbouring countries up to the borders of Syria.

Indian embassies to Persia during the reigns of Khusru I (531–79) and Khusru II (591–628) are reported in the works of the Arabic historian Ṭabarī (839–923) and the Persian poet Firdausi (tenth century), who made use of earlier Pahlavi (middle Persian) sources. The westward journey of the *Pañcha-tantra*, a Sanskrit book of stories, began in the sixth century A.D. with a translation into Pahlavi; and then into Syriac.[1] Arab and Persian historians make numerous references to Indian ships in the Persian Gulf, the Red Sea, and possibly in the Mediterranean. The first Muslim fleet appeared in Indian waters in A.D. 636. The Arabs, who had become particularly active after the rise of Islam, met Indian traders at every step. The existence of brisk trade along the Central Asian route on the one hand, and with south-east Asia on the other, is attested by the use of land and sea routes from China by Fa-hsien, Sung-Yun, Hsüan-tsang, I-tsing, and a host of other travellers. Bāṇa twice refers to shields made of *kārda-raṅga* leather used as far apart as in the Panjab and Assam.[2] The leather, apparently obtained from an island of that name in the Indonesian archipelago, makes a novel addition to the long list of articles of trade between India and south-east Asia.[3]

Evidence of trade with the western regions and with south-east Asia

Trade with Central Asia and China

A kind of Chinese silk, *chīn-āṁśuka*, known from an earlier reference in Kāli-dāsa's *Śakuntalā*, is often mentioned by Bāṇa, which shows that the material was still being traded.[4] A Chinese-style coat, *chīna-cholaka*, appears to have entered India via Central Asia, perhaps with the Śakas.[5]

[1] The Pahlavi version was translated into Arabic in the eighth century A.D. The latter into Greek in the eleventh century A.D., into Persian in the twelfth, and into Hebrew, Latin, and Spanish in the thirteenth. There followed more translations in German, Turkish, Old Slavonic, Czech, Italian, and English. According to J. Hertel over 200 versions of the *Pañcha-tantra* are known to exist in more than 50 languages. Their range extends from Java to Iceland.

[2] *H.C.* text, pp. 207 and 217.

[3] The commentator (op. cit., p. 217) remarks that Kārda-raṅga was the name of a country. Other sources seem to corroborate the information provided by the *Harsha-charita*. The *Mañju-śrī-mūla-kalpa* enumerates Karma-raṅga among the islands of the Indian ocean. Varāha-mihira in his *Bṛihat Saṁhitā* (14. 9) includes Charma-dvīpa (Leather Island) in his list of the southern islands. S. Lévi and P. C. Bagchi (*Pre-Aryan and Pre-Dravidian in India*, p. 106) identify Kārda-raṅga with Charma-raṅga and locate it in the Indonesian archipelago. See V. S. Agrawala, p. 156.

[4] *H.C.* text, pp. 36, 167, 242; also see V. S. Agrawala, p. 78.

[5] *H.C.* text, p. 207; also see V. S. Agrawala, p. 151.

Mostly it would have been tailored from Indian cloth but it is possible that, if it was associated with some special Chinese material, a demand for the same must have existed among the rich and the finicky. An active trade in horses existed between India and Central Asia, as demonstrated by Bāṇa's mention of the fine steeds from Kamboja (the Pamir region along the river Oxus) and Pārasīka (Sassanian Iran) in Harsha's stables.[1] They may have been bought or exchanged with the better breeds of Indian horses from Vanāyu (Vaziristan), Āraṭṭa (the Panjab), Bhāradvāja (northern Gaḍhwal), and Sindhu-deśa (along the river Indus where it meets the five rivers), once again referred to in the *Harsha-charita*. Intercourse with Tibet had never been closer and continued to grow until it consummated in the historic departure for Tibet of the Buddhist scholar Dīpaṅkara Śrī-jñāna (Atiśa) in the eleventh century.

Trade with Africa

The purely literary works of the period, Daṇḍin's *Daśa-kumāra-charita*, 'Adventures of the Ten Princes', written not long before Harsha's time, and the latter's own plays give ample evidence of abundant trade and brisk economic activity. Among other countries, Indian merchants exchanged their wares with an island named *Kāla-yavana dvīpa*, by which Africa may be meant. The story of Harsha's *Ratn-āvalī* points to flourishing trade with Ceylon.

General prosperity

The impression of prosperity in the country is confirmed by several incidental references in the 'Life' and the *Hsi Yü Chi*. Hsüan-tsang saw many statues of the Buddha made of gold. The common man would contribute to the construction of *sanghārāmas* in order to provide benefices for monks who impressed him.[2] Wherever he went the Chinese pilgrim received liberal hospitality and was continually offered gifts which, being a scrupulous Buddhist monk, he never accepted. Mention by Hsüan-tsang of the scores of Buddhist and Hindu temples in every city he visited points to great activity in matters religious, social, and educational, the three purposes served by such premises. Apparently the establishments were beginning to get richer than was desirable, for I-tsing, the Chinese observer of half a century later, remarks, 'It is unseemly for a monastery to have great wealth, granaries full of rotten corn, many servants, male and female, money and treasures hoarded in the treasury without using. . . .'[3]

Architecture

Bāṇa's account of Rājya-śri's marriage reveals the variety and extent of the arts and crafts that were practised in the country. Light is also thrown on city planning and architecture. The description in the

[1] *H.C.* text, p. 62; trans., p. 50.
[2] 'Life', p. 97.
[3] I-tsing, p. 194.

Harsha-charita refers mainly to Prabhākara-vardhana's capital, where houses appear to have been single or multi-storeyed, whitewashed or plastered with stucco. There is reference to the polishing of 'mosaic floors of red lead', apparently in the King's palace, as well as to the painting of pictures, presumably on walls. These latter were a part of the face-lift given to the city on the festive occasion of the wedding.

Hsüan-tsang was impressed by the height of the structures.[1] He records that houses were made of stone, brick, or wood, and their flat roofs were covered with planks, thatching, or burnt or unburnt tiles. Like Bāṇa, he too refers to walls plastered with lime and painted or carved doors, walls, and ceilings. The floors when unpaved seem to have been coated with a mixture of straw, clay, and cow-dung, as is still done in some present-day villages, and, according to Hsüan-tsang, 'strewn with flowers of the season'. Of the houses of the Buddhist laity the pilgrim says they were 'sumptuous inside and economical outside'. Almshouses, rest-houses, gardens, and fresh-water tanks were common features of a city. The city streets apart from the highways seem to have been narrow and zigzag.[2]

Life in a forest district

The daily bustle and activity of a city come through most vividly in Bāṇa's description of Ujjayinī in his *Kādambarī*,[3] while life in a forest dwelling in the Vindhya region is portrayed in minute detail in the *Harsha-charita*.[4] The inhabitants of this settlement in the heart of a dense forest are shown hard at work. The village economy was balanced: hunting, extensive cultivation, and metal crafts were carried on side by side. Administration appears to have been well organized; there were public refreshment arbours and watchmen on duty who guarded the valuable village woodland from trespassers. But in thick jungle the authorized timber-fellers from the neighbouring region were not safe from thieves, for fear of whom they would wear ragged clothes. Incidents of robbery in secluded areas are also attested by Hsüan-tsang. As the records of the

[1] Multi-storeyed buildings had been common in India from very early times. But the Nālandā structures seem to have been exceptionally tall and repeatedly draw comment on that account. Hsüan-tsang speaks of the four-storeyed outside courts at the establishment ('Life', pp. 111–12). The Nālandā inscription (*E.I.* xx. 45) describes the *vihāras* with 'spires [that] lick the clouds . . . like a garland hanging up high'. A legend preserved in a Tibetan history, written in the eighteenth century, records the presence of a nine-storeyed library building at Nālandā called the Ratnodadhi (the ocean of jewels): *Pag-sam-jon-zang*, ed. by S. C. Das, p. 92, translation provided by Dr. Lokesh Chandra. See S. Dutt, *Buddhist Monks and Monasteries in India*, p. 343 n. 2.

[2] This description is mainly based on Hsüan-tsang's remarks on towns and houses in his general account of India: Beal i, pp. 73–5; Watters i, pp. 147–8. Some details have been obtained from the 'Life' or from other parts of the 'Records'.

[3] Trans. pp. 210 ff.

[4] *H.C.* text, pp. 227–30; trans., pp. 225–9.

Gupta period, both Chinese and indigenous, are free from any such references it seems that conditions of public safety deteriorated after the decline of the great empire. It seems that the more remote parts of Harsha's empire did not recover from this state.

Harsha, the king and the man

From ancient times, until the advent of the modern 'democracies', a very important factor that has contributed towards making an administration efficient, and a reign great and successful has been the ruler's own personality. It will therefore be well to form an estimate of Harsha as a man and as a king before discussing the general notions of monarchy in the seventh century and the details ot Harsha's administrative system. It must be remembered, however, that while each king was unique as an individual, and if strong and able made an imprint on government and even on society in many ways, as a king he was expected to act as an archetype. Harsha's policies and attitudes regarding, for instance, religion, learning, or interstate relations were the attitudes and policies expected of any Indian monarch although moulded both consciously and inevitably in the matrix of his times. A portrait of Harsha, a particular king, however notable, is therefore also a portrait of any king of the period.

Ambitious, strong, and favoured by circumstances

According to the *Harsha-charita*, Harsha was a promising youth well trained in the traditional princely arts. The incident of the deathbed bequest of royalty to Harsha, the younger son, by his father, followed by Rājya-vardhana's renunciation of the throne and Harsha's deep regret over it not made vocal, are all matters of puzzling significance suggestive of some unworthy act of ambition on Harsha's part which never came to light because of Rājya-vardhana's early death. Harsha's personality must have been strong to have inspired confidence and loyalty in his ministers at the very outset of his reign. The veteran commander of the forces, Siṁha-nāda, advised him to embark on a comprehensive scheme of conquest, while Bhaṇḍi secured the approval of the ministers of Kanauj for Harsha's accession to their vacant throne.

Politically shrewd

The Vardhana aspirant acted shrewdly in connection with the Maukhari kingdom. Partly out of brotherly affection but also no doubt because of practical considerations Harsha gave priority to the rescue of his sister, the fugitive queen of the late King of Kanauj, even though it meant having to depute somebody else to lead his important expedition. For, although the armies of Sthāṇv-īśvara had saved Kanauj from falling into the hands of the King of Mālava, and Harsha was the elder brother of the widow of the King of Kanauj, the Maukhari kingdom had to be occupied cautiously, with sufficient popular and supernatural support.

The effect of escorting the unfortunate Queen safely back to the capital may not have been overlooked. Rājya-śrī's presence beside him gave Harsha the right to protect her, and her deceased husband's kingdom. We learn from Hsüan-tsang that strong attachment to his family was put forward as an argument in favour of Harsha's succession to the throne of Kanauj.[1]

Industrious

Harsha was a hard-working king. According to Hsüan-tsang his day was divided into three periods, of which one was devoted to 'affairs of government' and two to 'religious works'. While the affairs of state may refer to the more secular aspects of administration, religious works may be understood to have included a variety of other state activities. Thus the establishment of hospitals or educational centres, the provision on highways of free rest-houses, drink stalls, and fruit-bearing or shady trees, the arrangement of philosophical debates, the performance of plays with moral themes, and the distribution of charity, would all be regarded as acts of religious merit. The pilgrim pays high tribute to Harsha's piety and industry: 'He forgot sleep and food in his devotion to good works.' 'He was indefatigable . . ., the day was too short for him.'[2] Discounting the element of exaggeration in such statements Harsha appears to have been an industrious king well occupied both by state duties and by his literary and artistic pursuits, for he was a man of versatile interests.

In touch with the people

In spite of Bāṇa's imposing description of the royal court with 'hundreds' of tributary chiefs waiting long periods for an audience, or Hsüan-tsang's account of the grand procession on the occasion of the sixth quinquennial assembly at Prayāga, Harsha does not appear to have been too far removed from his people nor too forbidding to the subordinate kings of his *maṇḍala.* The Chinese pilgrim speaks of frequent tours of inspection by the King, some of which may have been in the traditional incognito manner. It was the practice to make charity grants and issue official royal charters on such occasions. Harsha thus would have come into contact with the man in the street, with various donees, and with his provincial administrative officials.

Bāṇa vividly portrays the scene of the King's military march, an occasion utilized by people not only for watching pageantry but also for conveying their compliments or complaints to the King. Some farmers whose ripe grain had been plundered, presumably by some members of the expedition, are depicted as censuring their sovereign in words such as: 'Where's the King?', 'What a king', 'What right has he to be King?'

[1] Beal i, p. 211. Also see above, p. 80. [2] Watters i, p. 344.

This brings home firstly the unruliness of camp followers[1] or soldiers, secondly the desperation of the aggrieved who could easily have been beaten up for such utterances before they could reach the ears for which they were intended, and lastly the fact that the people could venture on and the King could put up with such severe public criticism. Occurring at the beginning of his career, if we rely on Bāṇa's testimony, such an event reflects the general relationship between the king and the people which Harsha accepted rather than a new practice that he initiated. However, the incident of his attempted assassination that occurred towards the end of Harsha's reign, when according to Hsüan-tsang he neither panicked nor got angry but questioned and pardoned the offender, brings out his personal qualities and indicates his own approach to king–subject relations.

The story of Bāṇa's own meeting with Harsha depicts him as a human, warm-hearted individual who was interested enough in his people to entertain a prejudice against a man of no great importance, and anxious to gain his acquaintance after dismissing the suspicions against him. It was probably Harsha's lively disposition and love of learning that made him seek the friendship of a poet with an interesting past. At any rate the episode throws light on his attitude towards his subjects.

Harsha was equally anxious to interview Hsüan-tsang, whose first refusal to meet the request he gracefully accepted until one of his subordinate kings was obliged by the pilgrim. This naturally enraged Harsha, not so much against the guest as against the host, who was suitably reprimanded. On meeting them later, however, he was most kindly disposed towards Hsüan-tsang and behaved towards his feudatory as if nothing had happened.

The fact that Harsha was personally familiar with his extensive empire must have added to his ability as an administrator. A knowledge of local geography as well as of the temperament of the people living in the different regions would have helped him in a correct choice of local governors. As a prince, Harsha had travelled in the north-west, acting as a kind of rearguard to his brother's army engaged in chastising the Hūṇas. Immediately after becoming King of Sthāṇv-īśvara he traversed most of the Vindhya region in search of his sister. In the six years following his accession Harsha, covered with his troops the 'five Indias' from east to west, inspecting some kingdoms and subduing others. From time to time throughout his reign he invaded new territories, and it appears that he

[1] *H.C.* text, p. 210; trans., p. 207: 'Quick, slave, with a knife cut a mouthful of fodder from this bean field: who can tell the fate of his crop when we are gone?'

made it a rule to inspect his domains and give fresh orders on his journeys. We find him encamped at Maṇi-tārā,[1] in riverside villages along the route from Sthāṇv-īśvara to Kanauj,[2] at Vardhamāna-koṭi,[3] and at Pinṭhika.[4] On his way back from the victorious campaign in Orissa he stayed for a considerable period at Kajaṅgala.[5] Harsha's regular five-yearly assemblies were held at Prayāga. Hsüan-tsang observes: 'If it was necessary to transact state business, he employed couriers who continually went and returned. The King also made visits of inspection. During the tours he had no permanent abode.'[6] He attended to official matters in temporary buildings.

Though Harsha travelled frequently and moved in great state, as is evident from contemporary accounts, there are unfortunately no monuments which might remind us of his 'travelling palaces'. They were built from perishable materials. When he held court at Kajaṅgala Harsha had a temporary structure put up which was burnt on his departure.[7] The 'Life' records that the two thatched halls built at Kanauj for accommodating scholars of various schools to hold a discussion with Hsüan-tsang were 'lofty and spacious, each capable of seating a thousand persons'. On the occasion of the sixth quinquennial assembly at Prayāga a whole township of temporary structures was constructed. Bāṇa and Hsüan-tsang's biographer also attest to the impressive formalities observed on important occasions. Describing the Prayāga celebration Hui Li states that a special ceremonial distinguished the Emperor's march from that of any other king of the realm. Harsha was always accompanied by several hundred drummers who beat one stroke on their golden drums for every step taken. These drums were called the regulating-pace-drums (*chieh-pu-ku*).[8]

Relations with subordinate kings and feudatories

The periodic assemblies of various kinds attended by subordinate kings, courtiers, and common people of all classes served many purposes. On the one hand they brought together, from various parts of the country, people of different vocations and beliefs, on the other they provided the King with another source of contact with his subjects. Regular summonses to assemble, made innocuous by the declared object

[1] In Avadh, see *H.C.* text, p. 57 has Maṇi-pura; trans., p. 46.

[2] *H.C.* text, pp. 203 and 225; trans., pp. 198 and 223.

[3] See the Baṅskhera plate: *E.I.* iv. 208 ff.

[4] See the Madhu-ban plate: *E.I.* i. 67 ff.

[5] Beal i, p. 215, and ii, p. 193; Watters i, p. 348, and ii, p. 183; *C.A.G.I.*, p. 548, Cunningham, identifies it with modern Kankjol in Rajmahal, E. Bihar.

[6] *Hsi Yü Chi* text v. 5a (cf. Beal i, pp. 215 and 218 n. 36; Watters i, p. 344); 'Life', pp. 177 and 185, etc. See also *H.C.* text, p. 203; trans. p. 198.

[7] *Hsi Yü Chi* text x. 4b and 5a; Beal ii, p. 193.

[8] Cf. 'Life', p. 173.

of the assemblies, reminded the tributary kings of Harsha's supreme authority, the order of precedence in the ceremonial marches, etc., indicating, it appears, the status of each. Periodic personal audiences with important tributary rulers, of which there appear to have been over twenty in *c.* A.D. 643, must have proved useful administratively, for such rulers in many ways had the same functions as the centrally appointed governors in a more centralized system of government. Of the vast number of *sāmantas* and *mahā-sāmantas*,[1] the petty subservient chiefs, who are often referred to by Bāṇa, some may have served as courtiers, others as administrative officials, yet others may have been allowed to enjoy independent internal government on condition that they pay a regular tribute of an agreed kind. An illuminating passage in the *Harsha-charita*[2] refers to the presence of different kinds of feudatories at Harsha's Maṇi-tāra encampment visited by Bāṇa. There were, firstly, the 'conquered enemy *mahā-sāmantas*', towards whom the King was now favourably disposed. The commentary on the word *nirjitaiḥ*, 'conquered', of the phrase, indicates that it was intended to rehabilitate them.[3] There were, moreover, lesser kings who, overawed by Harsha's power, had come to pay him homage, and yet others who had come to see him out of attachment or devotion. In a florid stretch of similes a little later in the same text,[4] V. S. Agrawala[5] detects a confirmation of these categories and compares them with those mentioned in Samudra-gupta's Prayāga inscription.

The events and episodes related by both Bāṇa and Hsüan-tsang show that Harsha achieved the right balance in his relationship with the subordinate kings. He gave them due honour and importance, yet kept his distance. The policy ascribed by Bāṇa[6] to a King of Kāma-rūpa is typical of the political relations of the period between the sovereign and his vassals and may well apply to Harsha: '... he took away the conch-shells of the lords of the armies,[7] not their jewels; ... seized the majesty of monarchs,[8] not their hardness.' Kāli-dāsa, in his *Raghu-vaṁśa*,[9] ascribes the same policy to Raghu, who, he says, deprived Mahendra of his glory but not of his territory.

The discourse between Harsha and the ambassador of Kāma-rūpa, as given in the *Harsha-charita*, is indeed a clever piece of diplomatic conversation, and is indicative of the relations which were maintained

[1] See below, pp. 159 ff.

[2] *H.C.* text, p. 60; trans., p. 48.

[3] Lallanji Gopal interprets the phrase *śatru mahā-sāmantaiḥ* as '*sāmantas* of the enemy kings who fighting for their overlords were defeated and captured': *J.R.A.S.*, pts. 1 and 2 (1963), 34.

[4] *H.C.* text, p. 72; trans., p. 59.

[5] p. 45.

[6] *H.C.* text, p. 220; trans., p. 217.

[7] Or 'lords of rivers' = oceans. The use of the conch-shells was a sign of independent rule.

[8] Or 'mountains'.

[9] iv. 43.

between Kumāra and Harsha throughout the latter's reign.[1] The 'Life' relates an incident in which the King of Kāma-rūpa, when he insolently refused to part company with his Chinese guest and sent the message, 'the King can take my head but not the master of the law', was peremptorily asked by Harsha to send his head with the messenger.[2] Not long after this incident, however, Kumāra of Kāma-rūpa was given the honour of walking beside his sovereign in the grand quinquennial procession at Prayāga.

It was probably because of Harsha's special treatment of the two Mālava princes, Kumāra-gupta and Mādhava-gupta, that we do not hear of the Later Guptas until after Harsha's death. The King of Kashmir was made to yield the Buddhist relic merely by a show of force. It was a diplomatic victory; Harsha was wise enough not to earn his enmity nor to incur losses which he probably could not afford by a full-scale war. The alliance with Valabhī, of great importance because of its geographical position from the viewpoint of both trade and military strategy, was secured by giving to Dhruva-bhaṭṭa[3] his daughter in marriage. Harsha seems to have been on friendly terms with the kings of neighbouring countries, to whom he wrote asking them to extend facilities of travel and residence to Hsüan-tsang.[4] He also had diplomatic contact with the Chinese emperor.

Courage and composure

Among personal qualities Harsha possessed courage and chivalry. Bāṇa states that he saved a king from the grip of an elephant, presumably regardless of the risk involved.[5] We have already mentioned the incident recorded by Hsüan-tsang of the attempt on his life, his composure on the occasion, and the subsequent amnesty.

Literary and artistic talents

Harsha had literary and artistic talent and was a patron of learning. He is credited with three plays, a grammar, and at least two extant poems.[6] Bāṇa and several other writers, including Jaya-deva of the eleventh century, have paid high tribute to his ability as a poet. He may

[1] *H.C.* text, pp. 219 ff.; trans., pp. 216 ff.

[2] p. 172. Watters i, p. 349, in apparently making use of the information supplied by the 'Life'. The *Hsi Yü Chi* text, iv. 5a (cf. Beal i, p. 216) mentions only one message in authoritative language which was complied with.

[3] T'u-lu-p'o-po-t'a (Dhruva-bhaṭṭa) of Chinese sources, Dhruva-sena II, Bālāditya of Valabhi records. Also see above p. 52.

[4] Harsha 'commissioned four *Ta-kwan* (*official guides*) to accompany the escort: they call such officers Mo-ho-ta-lo [Mahā-tāras?]. The king also wrote some letters on fine white cotton stuff and sealed them with red wax (*or composition*), which he ordered the *Ta-kwan* officers to present in all the countries through which they conducted the Master, to the end that the princes of these countries might provide carriages or modes of conveyance to escort the Master even to the borders of China.' 'Life', pp. 189–90.

[5] *H.C.* text, p. 91; trans., p. 76.

[6] R. K. Mookerji, *Harsha*, pp. 148–59; A. B. Keith, *A History of Sanskrit Literature*, p. 215; *J.R.A.S.* (1903), 703–22; R. S. Tripathi, *History of Kanauj*, pp. 180–7.

well have composed the verses in his Baṅskhera and Madhu-ban inscriptions, the former bearing a beautiful florid signature explicitly stated to be Harsha's own. Obviously he practised calligraphy.[1] On Bāṇa's testimony Harsha also appears to have been a lute-player of some reputation.[2] I-tsing relates that Harsha versified his play *Nāg-ānanda*, and had it set to music and performed in order to popularize Buddhist ideals.[3] He probably directed its production himself. The pilgrim also records the great popularity of the Viśvāṅtara opera composed by one Chandra of eastern India.[4] It may not be wrong to surmise that full of admiration for this medium of Buddhist instruction I-tsing took the *Nāg-ānanda* with him to China, if his predecessor Hsüan-tsang had not already done so. From China the play appears to have travelled to Japan, where it survives to the present day as part of the Bugaku theatre. It is almost certainly the world's oldest opera still being performed.[5]

Patronage to learning

A reference in I-tsing's records gives some indication of the prolific literary activity of the times, encouraged and patronized by Harsha. 'Once King Śīlāditya, who was exceedingly fond of literature, commanded, saying: "Ye who are fond of poetry, bring and show me some pieces of your own tomorrow morning." When he had collected them they amounted to five hundred bundles.' Many of these poems were the Jātakas which were versified, sung, and acted, and which, according to I-tsing, taught the Buddhist doctrine to the common people in a manner which had great appeal for them.

[1] Bāṇa (*H.C.* text, p. 66; trans., p. 53) in his description of the royal elephant uses a complicated simile referring to florid signatures (*vibhrama kṛita hasta sthiti*) engraved on donative inscriptions. Bāṇa's statement could not be better verified than in the specimen on the Baṅskhera plate.

[2] *H.C.* text, pp. 73 and 75; trans., pp. 61 and 63.

[3] I-tsing, p. 163.

[4] For references to Viśvāṅtara Jātaka in Chinese sources see Étienne Lamotte, *Le Traité de la grande vertu de sagesse de Nāgārjuna* (Mahā-prajñā-pāramitā-śastra) ii, p. 714.

[5] From the end of the sixth century until the twelfth, teams of Japanese musicians continually visited China and Korea to acquaint themselves with foreign music. In A.D. 612, a Korean named Mimashi brought to Japan the Gigaku form of dance and music which he had learnt in China. The features of its masks now stored in temples in Nara, the prominence given to the lion and the snake devouring the Garuda (Japanese Karura) bird in its themes, and some of its musical features make it evident that the Gigaku owed much to Indian origins. Its successor, the Gagaku school of music, with its dance form the Bugaku, incorporated even more Indian features, Buddhism giving added impetus to their popularity. In 752, on the occasion of the consecration of the large Buddha image at the newly built Tōdaiji temple of Nara, hundreds of foreign musicians performed. Some of the musical instruments and masks from that occasion are still preserved, and the dances are performed on formal occasions especially in the imperial palace. Among these the Japanese Bugaku Ryo-o musical dance theme preserves, according to Takakusu, a part of the Nāgānanda (*Hôbôgirin*, Tokyo–Paris, 1929–37, pp. 150–7).

As might be expected Harsha had a nucleus of renowned literary men at his court. Among the poets Bāṇa and his relative Mayūra are well known. The name of a third one, Mātaṅga Divākara, is recorded by Rāja-śekhara, a critic and dramatist of *c.* A.D. 900. Mātaṅga is styled a *chāṇḍāla*, and is probably rightly identified with the Jaina writer Māna-tuṅga in competition with whose hymns to Sūrya, Bāṇa wrote those in praise of Chaṇḍī.[1] A *chāṇḍāla* poet's presence at Harsha's court proves that the lowest social status did not detract from the worth of an able man. There may well have been witticisms at Mātaṅga's expense, and, indeed, he himself may have joined in the fun, but he was accepted all the same as a peer by the courtiers, and honoured for his literary talent by the King.

Hsüan-tsang makes a lengthy statement to the effect that Harsha held men of noble conduct and distinguished ability in high esteem and demonstrated it by honouring them in various ways, such as by leading them to the 'lion's throne' (i.e. to the highest seat of honour) and by receiving instruction from them. But his regard for intellectual attainment was high, and, 'if any one, though distinguished for purity of life, had no distinction for learning, he was reverenced but not highly honoured'. Harsha was always bestowing gifts on the pious and the learned. The 'Life' records an offer by him of the revenue of eighty large towns to a versatile scholar named Jaya-sena,[2] and to Hsüan-tsang a present of 10,000 pieces of gold, and three times as much silver and other things.[3] Being believers in simplicity and non-possession, however, neither would accept the gifts.

Attitude towards religion

Harsha's plays are valuable evidence on the general conditions of the times in addition to providing a guide on their author's beliefs and character. The plots of the *Ratnāvalī* and the *Priya-darśikā* are simple and similar, and the blessings of Śiva, Vishṇu, and Indra are invoked in both the plays. The *Nāg-ānanda*, from its maturity, appears to have been composed last. It has a Buddhist theme and Buddha is the deity invoked for blessings. This is a unique case in Sanskrit drama. The appearance of the Hindu goddess Gaurī in the play, as the gracious boon-giver, points not only to Harsha's own mixed religious beliefs, but also to the liberal tendency of the times. Harsha's quinquennial assemblies further confirm his adherence to both Hinduism and Buddhism, which were beginning to show increasing signs of convergence. The assemblies were

[1] Cf. G. P. Quackenbos, *The Sanskrit Poems of Mayūra*, pp. 10 ff.
[2] 'Life', p. 154.
[3] Ibid. p. 180.

in the Buddhist tradition[1] but were held at the holy Hindu site of Prayāga. Donations distributed on the occasion benefited followers of all sects. Harsha celebrated six of such assemblies, which proves his early attachment to Buddhism.

His kingly ideal

The dramatist king shows his concern for the welfare of his kingdom in all the three plays. The opening and the closing stanzas of the *Ratnāvalī* seek God's blessing on the king and his subjects. The closing stanzas of the other two plays are also prayers for God's grace on the land and its people. In the *Nāg-ānanda* the king beseeches the following boon from the goddess: 'May the clouds in due season let loose their showers. . . . May they clothe the earth with green harvests in a continual succession! And may all my people accumulating good deeds, and freed from all calamities, rejoice with minds untainted by envy, tasting unbroken pleasure in the society of relations and friends.'

This traditional ideal of the kings of ancient India, of a happy people enjoying the fruits of their ruler's efficient administration, was, thus, also the ideal of Harsha's hero.

General estimate

The picture of Harsha that emerges from a collective scrutiny of contemporary sources is, over and above all, that of a king. His knowledge and understanding of various faiths, his notably charitable disposition, his love of learning, his accomplishments in the fields of art and literature, all combined to enhance his worth as a king. Harsha was ambitious, industrious, a tireless soldier though a benevolent conqueror, a moderately good administrator but no great innovator of policies, and fond of pomp and show. On the whole, from a combination of strength from authority, mellowness from his catholic religious beliefs, and sensitivity from his love of literature and art, he must have had a poised personality.

We shall follow this estimate of Harsha by a discussion of the political institutions of the day and the details of his administrative machinery.

Mode of government: hereditary monarchy

Hereditary monarchy was the prevailing form of government in the seventh century, though we may trace in Hsüan-tsang's records a vestige of the once flourishing 'republics' that lasted until the invasions of the Hūṇas. They were certainly still there in Samudra Gupta's day, and he

[1] Beal's (i, p. 214, and 'Life', p. 184) rendering *moksha* for the original *Wu-che ta hui* (*Hsi Yü Chi* text, v. 4b) is not correct. *Wu-che* literally means 'without bar', i.e where no one is excluded. The term is used for the Buddhist five-yearly assemblies. Soothhill gives the Sanskrit equivalent as *Pañcha* (*vārshika*) *parishad*. Also see P. Pelliott, *T'oung Pao* 26 (1929), pp. 184–5 and 258–9 and 28 (1931), pp. 432–4. For Fa-hsien's reference to the *Pañcha-parishad*, see J. Legge, *The Travels of Fa-hsien*, p. 22. According to Buddhist texts, the first quinquennial assembly was held by Aśoka; cf. J. Przyluski, *La Légende de l'empereur Aśoka*, p. 262; and É. Lamotte, *Le Traité de la grande vertu de sagesse de Nāgārjuna* i, p. 106.

does not appear to have suppressed them. Writing about the administration of Kapila-vastu, the pilgrim says: 'There is no supreme ruler; each of the towns appoints its own ruler.'[1] The traditional local system of government may have been allowed to continue in Kapila-vastu by virtue of its being the birthplace of the Buddha, but its autonomous communities must have assimilated most of the characteristics of the administrative methods applied in the neighbouring regions ruled by a centralized monarchy. Kapila-vastu, therefore, though well within the boundaries of Harsha's empire, probably continued to enjoy a special kind of local self-government. It was, however, a small and unimportant city in the seventh century, desolate and sparsely populated according to Hsüan-tsang.

Kapila-vastu a sentimental relic of the old republics

We have earlier dealt with the institution of kingship as represented in the *artha-śāstra* and *dharma-śāstra* political texts, and have related incidents from the *Harsha-charita* and the Chinese writings which describe the actual conduct of the king and the people towards each other. There is one explicit statement in Bāṇa's *Kādambarī* which throws light on both the theory and the practice of kingship. It offsets the views expressed in some of the *smṛitis*. 'Only weak and foolish monarchs', says the author, 'are taken in by the flattery of roguish courtiers. By looking upon himself as having alighted on earth as a divine being with a superhuman destiny, though in reality subject to all mortal conditions, the stupid king only wins the contempt of his people.'[2]

Grandiloquent titles

The accepted title of a great king in Harsha's days was *parama-bhaṭṭāraka mahārāj-ādhirāja*, 'the noblest, the supreme king of kings'. It was inherited from the Gupta empire. Paramount sovereignty in the seventh century, however, did not connote what it did a few hundred years earlier. By Harsha's period kings of little consequence were beginning to style themselves in grandiose fashion. The use of the title *parama-bhaṭṭāraka mahārāj-ādhirāja* for the grandfather, father, and brother of Harsha in the latter's inscriptions is indicative of the trend, even if the early Vardhanas were only posthumously so honoured by Harsha to stress the importance of his lineage. In any case, kings at this time, almost as soon as they entertained the idea of universal conquest and achieved the foremost position among rivals, began using high titles.[3] The use of *parama-bhaṭṭāraka mahārāj-ādhirāja* for Harsha him-

[1] Beal ii, p. 14.

[2] Condensed from *Kādambarī*, pp. 81–2.

[3] We give below some examples of this practice:

(*a*) Śarva-varman (*c.* A.D. 560–5 to 585) in his Asirgarh inscription (*C.I.I.* iii, pp. 219–21) styles himself and his father Īśāna-varman *mahārāj-ādhirāja*, while the

self, however, is quite justified from the record of his conquests and the extent of his empire. The epithet *sakal-ottarā-path-eśvara*, 'the lord of the entire north', bestowed on him by his adversary Pulā-keśin II further strengthens the authenticity of his claim.

The crown usually passed to the eldest son, who was installed as *yuva-rāja*, heir apparent, on coming of age. In a few cases a younger son was selected for succession if he definitely surpassed the elder in ability. In western India the practice of brother-to-brother succession was known. When all the brothers were dead the crown passed to the eldest son of the eldest brother.[1] The practice was common among the western *kshatrapas*. In the period of our study the Maitrakas of Valabhī sometimes followed it. The female members of the royal family seldom figure prominently in the affairs of state. The statement in the *Fang-chih* that Harsha was 'administering the government in conjunction with his widowed sister'[2] is not, we think, indicative of a general practice, but shows that if an aspiring claimant to a foreign throne was related to its widowed and childless queen not on her husband's but rather on her parents' side he thought it wise to give her a special status. According to the 'Life', Rājya-śrī 'of great intelligence . . . was sitting behind the king . . . as she heard the Master of the Law extolling the doctrine of the Great Vehicle . . . she was filled with joy, and could not cease her praises.'[3] Thus her ability, her connection with Kanauj, her unfortunate circumstances, and her support for Harsha may all have combined to secure for Rājya-śrī a position uncommon for the female members of royalty.

The lesser kings

The lesser kings of the period were knows as *rājās* and *mahārājas*. Independent in the internal administration of their territories they generally owed allegiance to a suzerain. Hsüan-tsang's political description of the kingdoms he visited, states with their own rulers and dependencies, testifies to this political set-up. Kings subordinate to Harsha are variously referred to by Bāṇa as *rājā*, *bhūpāla*, *pārthiva*, *kumāra*, *kshiti-pāla*, *loka-pāla*, *nṛi-pati*, *nara-pati*, etc. *Sāmanta* and *mahā-sāmanta*

queens of four generations from Śarva-varman's mother upwards are styled *bhaṭṭārikā*.

(*b*) In his two Mandār Hill rock inscriptions (*C.I.I.* iii, pp. 211–12) the Later Gupta king, Āditya-sena (*c.* A.D. 650–75) uses the title *mahārāj-ādhirāja* for himself, and for his queen the epithets *parama-bhaṭṭārikā* and *mahā-devī*.

(*c*) The Maitraka ruler Śīlāditya VII in his Alīnā copperplate inscription dated A.D. 766–7 (*C.I.I.* iii, pp. 171–91) styles all kings of his dynasty from Dhara-sena IV (*c.* A.D. 645–50) onwards as *parama-bhaṭṭāraka*, *mahārāj-ādhirāja*, or *parameśvara* and *chakra-vartin*.

[1] Rapson, *Catalogue of the Indian Coins* (Āndhras, Western Kshatrapas, etc.), p. cliii.

[2] See Watters i, p. 345.

[3] 'Life', p. 176.

were other very common titles of the period, and the epigraphic and literary sources of Harsha's period abound in references to them. Generally speaking they were of lower status than *rājā* and *mahārāja* and it is not uncommon to find the more powerful *sāmantas* and *mahā-sāmantas* using the additional title *mahārāja*. The question of the status and functions of the different grades of title-bearers from the *sāmanta* to the *mahārāja* is complex because the connotation of the terms changed over a period of time. From post-Gupta days onwards, with the modification in the political and administrative set-up it changed particularly rapidly. The powers and function of the dignitaries now often overlapped, creating many new types. This makes the task of definition very difficult.

The various categories of Harsha's subordinates

It is clear that Harsha had tributary kings belonging to different categories. Bhāskara-varman of Kāma-rūpa and Dhruva-bhaṭṭa[1] of Valabhī were his most important subordinate allies, as is apparent from Hsüan-tsang's account of the Prayāga assembly.[2] Situated on the two extremities of Harsha's empire and bordering on the kingdoms of two of his formidable enemies, Śaśāṅka and Pula-keśin, Kāma-rūpa and Valabhī were in a class by themselves. Others who would have occupied important positions among Harsha's subordinates were: Pūrṇa-varman of Magadha, in all probability a scion of the Maukhari family, and therefore entrusted with the administration of an important province, Udita, the King of Jālandhara, 'the royal city of North India',[3] and a border kingdom, and the Later Gupta prince Mādhava-gupta, whose family returned to prominence only after Harsha's death. Each one of these, however, we believe, stood in a different relationship to the centre. Mādhava-gupta appears to have been the King's personal companion and adviser. Udita, apparently independent with regard to the internal administration of Jālandhara, also officiated as Harsha's minister for Buddhist affairs.[4] Pūrṇa-varman, in charge of the centrally situated and rich province of Magadha, would have had to conform more closely to the central administrative system.[5] Kāma-rūpa and Valabhī may have presented the centre with valuable periodic gifts or conceded special trade rights. Jālandhara submitted tribute and services in other forms referred to above. Magadha, however, must have provided the centre with regular yearly income from land and other sources. We know from the description of the Prayāga and Kanauj assemblies that there were

[1] Dhruva-sena II, Bālāditya.
[2] Beal i, pp. 217–18; 'Life', pp. 177, 185.
[3] 'Life', p. 190.
[4] Beal i, p. 176; Watters i, p. 296.
[5] Cf. A. S. Altekar's remarks on Gupta administration: *N.H.I.P.* vi, p. 280.

approximately twenty tributary kings of fairly important status in Harsha's empire.[1] But 'the small princes of neighbouring states and their chief ministers' who were honoured from time to time for their zeal in good works,[2] probably belonged to the lower *rājā* and *mahā-sāmanta* category.

The non-Aryan *sāmantas*

The forest chiefs of the Vindhyas were another group of feudatories in Harsha's empire. Scattered references in the *Harsha-charita* cumulatively point to the tributary status of the *aṭavī-rājya*.[3] Once again the type and degree of their subordination to the centre seems to have been governed by their geographical, historical, cultural, and economic circumstances. Situated in the heart of the country the Vindhy-āṭavī tract figures in the documents of many of Harsha's predecessors. Samudragupta's Allahabad inscription[4] records his subjugation of *āṭavika rājās*. More important from our point of view, however, because of its dating and the clues it provides to the location of the *aṭavī-rājya*, is the Khoh grant of A.D. 528–9 of the Parivrājaka *mahārāja* Saṁkshobha.[5] It states that Saṁkshobha's father, Hastin, ruled over the inherited kingdom of Ḍabhālā (later Ḍahālā) together with the region included in the eighteen *aṭavī-rājyas*. Fleet places Hastin's territories in the direction of 'Bundelkhand, Baghelkhand, Riwa, and other neighbouring parts of the Vindhya range'.[6] Bāṇa explicitly connects an *āṭavika sāmanta* with the Vindhya region. In his Sanskrit–English dictionary, Monier Williams defines *Vindhyāṭavī* as the forest 'which appears to have spread at one time from near Mathurā to the Narmadā'. V. S. Agrawala gives the limits of the *aṭavī-rājya* as the River Chambal in the west and the Son in the east.[7]

In direct contact with the central authority, at least from Early Gupta times, the forest kingdoms had taken to some open-field cultivation but maintained side by side large timber reserves.[8] Judging by the description of the hermitage in the *Harsha-charita* their economic management seems to have been typical of the jungle habitations of the times. Aryan in their culture, the chiefs of the *aṭavī-rājya* of the Vindhyas were ethnically non-Aryan. Probably they retained some of their original community organization. A fair amount of autonomy in internal administration is

[1] Beal i, p. 218; *Hsi Yü Chi* text, v. 6a: The original conveys between 20 and 30 countries; 'Life', pp. 177, 178, 186.

[2] *Hsi Yü Chi* text, v. 4b; cf. Beal i, p. 215; Watters i, p. 344.

[3] *H.C.* text, p. 58; trans., p. 46; text, pp. 231-3, trans., pp. 230–2. The former reference seems to record the various categories of Harsha's feudatories, one being that of the *aṭavī* kings. See below, p. 190 n. 2, and pp. 199–201.

[4] *C.I.I.* iii, no. 1.

[5] Ibid., no. 25.

[6] Ibid., p. 13, n. 7.

[7] p. 189.

[8] *H.C.* text, pp. 227–30; trans., pp. 225–9.

apparent from the mention of a *śabara* army general described as master of the Vindhyas and leader of all village chiefs. With regard to their representation at the court, however, the forest chiefs conformed to the usual governmental pattern as indicated by Bāṇa's reference to an *āṭavika sāmanta*. They contributed their share to the central economy by supplying, among other things, elephants for the elephant corps, a particularly strong wing of Harsha's army. The Vindhya jungles were still one of the best sources of elephant supply.[1]

The *maṇḍala* in action

With a few important subordinate allies, more than a score of high-ranking tributary kings, some hundreds of *sāmantas* and *mahā-sāmantas*, and border friends who vaguely emerge from our sources, interstate relations under Harsha's government fell into four or five different categories, most of them on a horizontal but some on a vertical level. The office of the *mahā-sāndhi-vigrahika*, the minister for alliances and hostilities who conducted these relations, must have been entrusted to one most wise and shrewd at the same time. It may be presumed that he also advised the King on the admission and disptach of foreign embassies.

There does not appear to have been an ally of equal status in Harsha's *maṇḍala*. The tribute paid by his subordinates took different forms, depending apparently on the classification to which they belonged.[2] All must have been treaty-bound not to form military alliances with the suzerain's adversaries, to assist him in defensive or offensive wars or in both, to grant unhindered passage through their territories, etc.[3] Periodic visits of homage on special occasions sufficed from some tributary rulers; with others matrimonial alliances were concluded.[4] Some conquered kings were required to present one or more sons for attendance on the suzerain, who, of course, treated them well.[5] Regular gifts or express tribute in cash or kind were received from others.[6] Some were

[1] See below, p. 190.

[2] Kauṭilya in his *Artha-śāstra*, Book vii, Chs. 3, 16, and 17 discusses the various types of tribute paid by the conquered king. Relations between the conqueror and the conquered were conducted in the same vein in Harsha's time, as is apparent from contemporary sources.

[3] It is not possible to give concrete examples of such treaties. But Harsha's position with regard to Kāma-rūpa and Valabhī, bulwarks, respectively, against Śaśāṅka and Pula-keśin, would imply this.

[4] Because of limited materials we are obliged to repeat our examples. Both the above statements again apply to the Kings of Kāma-rūpa and Valabhī.

[5] The Mālava princes Kumāra-gupta and Mādhava-gupta served the Vardhanas in this capacity.

[6] Various gifts from Bhāskara-varman to Harsha are recorded by Bāṇa (*H.C.*, Ch. vii) when the former sought a treaty by alliance through his envoy. It is safe to presume that Bhāskara-varman and Dhruva-bhaṭṭa as well as other subordinate kings made presents to their suzerain from time to time. There is, of course, reference to wedding

expected to acknowledge their subordinate status in their grants and charters and to use the suzerain's own era or that used by him, others would not be under any obligation to observe these forms.[1] Some would be required to obtain the centre's permission to assign revenues in their own territories while others would be allowed their own feudatories to whom they could issue grants.[2] Some might enjoy the simple title *sāmanta* yet issue grants and charters, others styled *rājās* served as the centre's administrative officers.[3]

The *Sāmanta* institution

In his recent study on *sāmanta*, Lallanji Gopal[4] traces the history of the term and points out that in the beginning when applied to villages it meant a neighbouring cultivator, and when used in connection with kingdoms it denoted a neighbouring king.[5] Later by a process of association the term came 'to be applied to those neighbouring kings who had been made subordinate'. As has been discussed in the last chapter it was a recommendation of Indian polity that a monarch aiming at paramount sovereignty should accept subordinate alliances from those who would seek them, and conquer those who offered resistance, but preferably reinstate them in their thrones as tributary kings. Both kinds of relations were covered by the term *sandhi*, peace or alliance. The neighbouring kings or *sāmantas* were naturally the first to feel the brunt of the conqueror's might and to be made tributary. In time the term came to be applied to subordinate kings even when distant, as well as

Sāmanta—the conquered lesser king

gifts for Rājya-śrī 'from many a king' (*H.C.* text, p. 142; trans., p. 123). One of Harsha's ancestors is stated to have made the *mahā-sāmantas* subject to tax (*karadīkṛta*) (*H.C.* text, p. 100; trans., p. 85), the nature of which is not specified.

[1] The Balasore copperplates of *mahā-pratīhāra mahārāja sāmanta* Bhānu-datta (*I.H.Q.* xi. 611 ff., and *E.I.* xxiii. 197 ff.) were issued for the enhancement of the religious merit of his overlord Śaśāṅka. They are dated, most probably, in the regnal years of the latter.

[2] There are extant inscriptions which show that the feudatories of the Vākāṭakas, Kadambas, and Guptas required their overlords' sanction for alienating revenues in their territories. (*C.I.I.* iii, pp. 235 ff.; *I.A.* vi. 31–2; *I.H.Q.* vi. 53.) On the other hand the Nirmaṇḍ (Panjab) copperplate of *mahā-sāmanta mahārāja* Samudra-sena (*C.I.I.* iii. 286 ff.) dated A.D. 612–13, probably in the Harsha era, refers to the existence of his own *sāmantas* (line 1). The Maitraka *mahā-sāmanta* Dhruva-sena I (*c.* A.D. 525–50), a feudatory probably of the Guptas, was the acknowledged overlord of the Gārulakas (*E.I.* xi. 17).

[3] The Maitrakas when still holding the title *sāmanta* issued grants (*I.A.* xv. 187). Śaśāṅka is entitled *mahā-sāmanta* on the Rohtas-garh seal mould (*C.I.I.* iii., pp. 283–4), casts from which were meant to be attached to copperplate charters. King Udita of Jālandhara, who is referred to as *rājā* ('Life', pp. 189–90), was appointed inspector of Buddhist affairs in the 'five Indias' by the King of Mid India, by whom evidently Harsha is meant (Beal i, p. 176).

[4] *J.R.A.S.*, pts. 1 and 2 (1963), pp. 21–37. I gratefully acknowledge the use of this article to confirm some of my own conclusions.

[5] By derivation (from *sam-anta*: Monier Williams, *Sanskrit–English Dictionary*) *sāmanta* means 'bordering', 'neighbouring', 'being on all sides'.

***Sāmanta*—the government officer**

to the petty rulers who enjoyed status and power similar to those of such kings. The conquered and reinstalled *sāmantas* often acted as administrative officers of the centre. In the inscriptions the list of officers to whom the grants are addressed includes *sāmanta* together with *rājā* before *kumār-āmātya*, *viṣaya-pati*, and *bhogika*.[1] As Gopal remarks, their being addressed even before governors and other high officers of the state indicates their status.

***Sāmanta*—a title**

It is apparent, however, that *sāmanta* was also used as an honorific title. In the inscriptions of the period *sāmantas* or *mahā-sāmantas* are given more than one official designation,[2] which shows that not only *sāmanta* but also some of the other appellations were sinecures. The titles *sāmanta* and *dūtaka* often go together.[3] The latter was a high officer or delegate who conveyed the king's command about the grant of land to local officers.

***Sāmanta*—a courtier**

A work of the twelfth century A.D., the *Aparājita-prichchhā*,[4] states that a king bearing the epithet *mahārāj-ādhirāja parameśvara* is expected to have a certain number of lesser rulers and other office-bearers in attendance at his court, among them 16 *mahā-sāmantas*, 32 *sāmantas*, and 160 *laghu-sāmantas*.[5] This may have been the minimum technical requirement commensurate with the dignity of a paramount sovereign in the later period. The unofficial number at least at Harsha's court appears to have been much larger. In the *Kādaṁbarī*, in a vivid palace scene, Bāṇa describes how a multitude of *sāmantas* who had received lustration[6] were indulging in the pleasant diversions of music, poetry, painting, chess, flirtation, etc. The qualification of lustration indicates that they were *sāmantas* of high status.

It seems that for prestige alone powerful kings supported a number of hangers-on who in their turn voluntarily or otherwise accepted an easy life with a decorative status.

The *sāmantas* of various ranks in the *Harsha-charita*

The *Harsha-charita* abounds in references to *sāmantas*. Some

[1] *E.I.* iii. 6; ix. 40; xv. 19; xxiii. 13; and xxviii. no. 34 (B).

[2] Harsha's Madhu-ban grant (*E.I.* vii. no. 22); the inscription of Maitraka Dhruva-sena I (*I.A.* iv. 105).

[3] e.g. Harsha's Madhu-ban grant (*E.I.* vii. no. 22); the Valabhī plate of Dhara-sena II (*J.B.B.R.A.S.* (N.S.) i. 24).

[4] 'Questionnaire by Aparājita' is a minutely detailed treatise on ancient-Indian architecture addressed to the divine legendary architect Viśva-karman by its author Bhuvana-deva. The editor, Popadbhai Ambashankar Mankad, assigns the work to the twelfth or the first half of the thirteenth century (Introd., pp. ix–xii).

[5] *Ap. Pṛi.*, p. 196, 78. 32–4. Others whose presence is required are 4 *maṇḍaleśas*, 12 *māṇḍalikas*, 400 *chaturaṅśikaś*, 12 *daṇḍa-nāyakas*, and 2 *pratīhāras*.

[6] *Kādaṁbarī*, pp. 193–4: *mūrdhā-bhishiktena sāmanta lokena*. Lustration (*abhisheka*) and not crowning was the important part of an Indian king's installation ceremony, hence our above rendering of the term.

sāmantas appear to have paid obeisance by visiting the royal capital on specific occasions when their services were needed.[1] Among those who resided at court some were of higher rank than others; their wishes were highly respected.[2] Those low in the scale might stand in attendance, waving *chowries* or acting as doorkeepers. Bāṇa refers to a large number of conquered enemy *mahā-sāmantas* in the royal camp who were probably waiting to be assigned their new duties. The accepted practice seems to have been to treat them with consideration and respect.[3] All the same perhaps in their first audience with the King they might be expected to acknowledge their loss of status by appearing with downcast faces, beards grown long in mourning, *chowries* in hand, and sword-blades hanging from their necks.[4] At one place in the *Harsha-charita*, Bāṇa uses the term *prati-sāmanta*, possibly a more specific term for the *sāmantas* of enemy kings.[5]

The *sāmanta* —an addition to the armed strength

Sāmantas were expected to assist their suzerain in time of war,[6] but they were not created for that purpose. Apart from the standing army which the king had, additional soldiers for special military expeditions or policing purposes appear to have been obtained by announcing payment for the work entailed.[7]

The *kula-putras* frequently mentioned in the *Harsha-charita*[8] were probably sons of friendly *mahā-sāmantas* or of feudatory *rājās* who had been sent to the suzerain's household in accordance with the conditions of subordination.

It appears that by Harsha's time the practice of donating land or land tax for religious purposes had been extended to the secular sphere, which contributed to the strengthening of the *sāmanta* institution.

[1] *Sāmantas* with their wives travelled from great distances to serve Prabhākara-vardhana at the time of Rājya-śrī's marriage: *H.C.* text, p. 143; trans., p. 124. Some of those present at the time of the King's last illness (*H.C.* text, p. 155; trans., p. 138) may have come on special visits.

[2] *H.C.* text, p. 178: '*anatikramaṇīya vachanaiḥ upasṛitya pradhāna-sāmantaiḥ* . . .', 'approached by the chief *sāmantas* whose words were not to be transgressed.' Cowell and Thomas (p. 168) translate the first words as 'inoffensive' but also suggest the alternative meaning 'not to be resisted'.

[3] *H.C.* text, p. 60: '*nirjitaiḥ śatru-mahā-sāmantaiḥ*'. The commentary explains the first word to connote this.

[4] The appearance is suggested through a series of similes. *H.C.* text, p. 60; trans., p. 48.

[5] *H.C.* text, p. 200.

[6] *Mahā-sāmantas* accompanied Rājya-vardhana on his campaign against the Hūṇas (*H.C.* text, p. 150; trans., p. 132). Harsha's invading armies comprising 'all the soldiers of the kingdom' (Beal i, p. 213) appear to have included *sāmantas*, for, recording his success against Harsha, Pula-keśin in the Aihoḷe inscription refers to Harsha's feet as covered with the rays of the jewels of the diadems of hosts of feudatories (*E.I.* vi. 1).

[7] *Hsi Yü Chi* text, ii. 10a; Beal i, pp. 87–8; Watters i, pp. 176–7.

[8] *H.C.* text, pp. 130, 155, 161, 165, 169, 173, 202, 225, etc.

The king's rights over land

However, the king's capacity to donate land was limited. *Smṛiti*-writers and commentators, from Jaimini in the pre-Christian era to Manu,[1] Śabara, and the writer of the *Vyavahāra-mayūkha* in the seventeenth century, appear to hold that the ownership of land rested in the cultivator, the king being entitled to a share of the produce for the protection he afforded.[2] Supporting his own views, Nīla-kaṇṭha, the writer of the *Vyavahāra-mayūkha*, states,

> therefore it is said in the sixth chapter of Jaimini that the whole earth cannot be given away by the emperor and a province by a feudatory chief. The ownership in the several villages and fields on the entire earth or in a province belongs to the holders of the land alone, while kings are entitled only to collect taxes. Therefore when kings now make what are technically called gifts of fields, no gift of land (soil) is effected thereby, but only provision is made for the maintenance of the donee (from the taxes which are alienated by the king). Where however houses and fields are purchased from the holders thereof (by the king) he has also ownership (over the fields, etc.) in those cases and he in such cases secures the full merit of the gift of land (if he makes a gift of such fields).[3]

But Bhaṭṭa-svāmin, the commentator on the more authoritarian *Artha-śāstra*, states that the king was the owner of all water and land. On the other hand a little earlier the same text clearly differentiates between crown lands and private lands.[4]

Generally speaking land that was waste or not cultivated belonged to the state. In the inscriptions of the Gupta period we come across passages which show that the state owned small fields of cultivated land termed *rājya-vastu*.[5] Break in the line of inheritance, default in the payment of taxes, or direct purchase from the owner made such land the king's property. Frequently it was donated in charity. As Altekar remarks, in such cases 'Donees . . . acquired full ownership of the land and not a right to its land-tax, in fact they were often not exempted from it. When, however, entire villages were given away in charity, what was donated was the right to receive the royal dues.'[6]

Land or/and land-tax as salary

Manu and Bṛihaspati recommended a practice, apparently for good government, which in later times may have reinforced the *sāmanta* institution, especially when the functions and titles of the state's administrative officials and those of the *sāmantas* became combined.

[1] ix. 44. It is stated that the field belongs to him who uproots the stems of trees and shrubs (*sthāṇu-chchheda*) from waste or uncultivated land (*kedāram*). This and other verses indicate that Manu considered the cultivator to be the owner of arable land.

[2] For a documented exposition of the above view see *Hist. Dh.* ii, pt. 2, pp. 865–9.

[3] Op. cit., p. 866.

[4] *Artha.* ii. 24.

[5] *E.I.* viii. 235.

[6] *N.H.I.P.*, p. 361.

According to Manu[1] a king should appoint heads for towns numbering one, ten, twenty, a hundred, and a thousand. As subsistence they were to take, respectively, from the head of ten towns upwards, two *kula*[2] of land, ten *kula* of land, a town, and a city. A minister of the king was to supervise their work and to guard the people against any maltreatment. While no epigraphic evidence has yet come to light to show the existence of such a practice in the Gupta period, certain terms in the Pāla inscriptions such as *dāśa-grāmika* (head of ten villages)[3] seem to corroborate the statements in the law books.

Sāmanta **as a rank for lesser kings**

In the late-medieval period *sāmanta* appears to have become established as a designation, however low in the scale, in the hierarchy of rulers. The earlier encyclopaedias, such as the *Māna-sāra* of *c.* A.D. 500,[4] the *Amara-kosha* of the post-Gupta period,[5] and the *Anekārtha-samuchchaya* of the sixth or seventh century A.D.,[6] do not mention *sāmanta* in this context. But the term is included in lists enumerating kingly ranks in later works such as the *Aparājita-prichchhā* of the twelfth or thirteenth century[7] and the *Śukra-nīti-sāra* of an even later date.[8]

[1] vii. 115–24, Bṛihaspati repeats the advice, Br. xix. 44. The head is variously designated by Manu as *pati*, *adhi-pati*, *adhyaksha*, and *īśa*, most probably without any technical distinction.

[2] *Kulam* '(as much land as suffices for one) family', is really a technical term which Medhā-tithi explains by *ghaṅta*, a term known 'in some districts'. Govinda, Kullūka, Nārāyaṇa, and Rāghav-ānanda state that it is the double of a 'middling plough', i.e. as much as can be cultivated with twelve oxen, while Nandana interprets it by 'the share of one cultivator'. See G. Bühler's trans. of the *Manu Smṛiti*, p. 235 n. 119.

[3] See *History of Bengal*, i (ed. R. C. Majumdar), p. 277.

[4] The question of the date is discussed by the editor Prasanna Kumar Acharya in the Preface, p. vi.

[5] According to legend Amara, the author of the *kosha* was one of the nine 'jewels' at the court of Vikram-āditya, but he probably lived later.

[6] Date suggested by K. G. Oka in his Introduction, p. vi.

[7] Date ascribed by its editor, Popadbhai Ambashankar Mankad in the Introduction, pp. ix–xii.

[8] In a recent study L. Gopal has shown it to be a nineteenth-century work (*B.S.O.A.S.* 25, pt. 3 (1962), 524–56). However, as it is written in the tradition of the ancient *smṛitis* and has quotations from earlier works, e.g. the *Mahābhārata* and the *Kāmandaka-nīti-sāra*, the *Śukra-nīti* obviously incorporates material applicable to earlier periods along with that pertaining to contemporary conditions. It would therefore still yield some useful information on early medieval history. But the new thesis that it is a very late work is so striking that for the next few years historians of early and medieval India may tend to underrate the usefulness of the *Śukra-nīti-sāra*. It may therefore be well to quote Gopal's concluding remarks on the evaluation of the work in the context of the Indian practice of *smṛiti*-writing. 'The legal traditions in India', he writes, 'reveal flexibility in the sense that the commentaries and digests . . . aimed at from time to time adapting the laws to changed conditions by new interpretations, rearrangement, or cataloguing with a particular emphasis in view. . . . The *Śukranīti* differs from these medieval legal writings in that it is presented as an original work . . . In this respect it seems to be in the tradition of the *smṛitis* known under the name of Manu, Yājñavalkya, and other sages. . . . the author of the present *Śukranīti* cannot

Land allotment to *sāmantas*

It is also clear from the later works that ownership of land and political status had become closely associated. The eleventh-century *Kathā-sarit-sāgara*[1] contains several references to *sāmantas* being installed in that position by the king who bestowed on them villages, gold, umbrellas, and vehicles. If they earned the king's displeasure, the *sāmantas* were replaced.[2] It is recorded by Śukra[3] that the erring *sāmantas* were deprived of their status (*hīna-sāmanta*) and of some other rights and honours but continued to get maintenance.

Income from land of a *sāmanta*

According to the *Aparājita-pṛichchhā*[4] a *sāmanta* had an income of 10,000 *kārshā-paṇas*. Śukra[5] states it to be from 100,000 to 300,000 silver *kārshā-paṇas*. From the use of various terms for plough to denote the extent of territory[6] we know that land was measured in terms of ploughs, i.e. according to the capacity of a plough, pulled by a given number of cattle, to till a certain acreage. When donating their income from land kings declared the extent of territory in plough measures.[7] Apparently the incomes of the *sāmantas* denote their authority over corresponding territorial units; thus a *sāmanta* with a 100,000-*kārshā-paṇa* income would obtain his revenue from the same number of plough units of land, which according to Śukra[8] were equivalent to 1,250,000,000 elbow measures, i.e. 625,000,000 square yards or approximately 133,333 acres. A twelfth- or thirteenth-century *sāmanta* would be entitled to his 10,000-*kārshā-paṇa* income from 13,333 acres on the basis of Śukra's area definition, while a seventh-century *sāmanta*, who no doubt had an even smaller income, perhaps 1,000 *kārshā-paṇas* as suggested by a reference in the *Harsha-charita*,[9] had rights over an area of 1,333 acres.

Land endowments for charity by Harsha

Harsha seems to have made numerous land endowments in his time. His Baṅskhera and Madhu-ban inscriptions[10] bear testimony to grants for religious purposes. Bāṇa speaks of the donation of 100 villages of 1,000 ploughs each to brahmans by Harsha at the beginning of his first

be charged with forgery. He produced a *nīti* text which was brought up-to-date by incorporating even the most recent information, and used the name of Śukra because of his reputation as one of the foremost authorities on *nīti*, according to ancient convention which even to his own day had not wholly disappeared.'

[1] *Kathā*. xviii. 126–30; xxx. 137–8; xlix. 61–2; liii. 72.

[2] Op. cit. xlii. 115. [3] 1–189. [4] 82. 5–10. [5] 183.

[6] The term *sīra* for plough was in use in Harsha's time: *H.C.* text, p. 203, '*sīra sahasra saṁmita sīmnāṁ grāmāṇāṁ śataṁ*'; trans., p. 199, 'a hundred villages delimited by a thousand ploughs'. The Ikshvāku inscriptions of the third century A.D. from the Āndhra region (D. C. Sircar, *Select Inscriptions*, pp. 219–31) employ the term *hala* for plough. *Manu*. vii, 119, uses *kula* probably for the same purpose (see above, p. 167 n. 2). Difference in period, locality, or measurement may have determined the term for plough in each case.

[7] e.g. *H.C.* text, p. 203; trans., p. 199. [8] 193–5.

[9] *H.C.* text, p. 203; trans., p. 199. [10] *E.I.* i, no. 11; iv, no. 29.

military undertaking.[1] Towards the latter part of his reign, apparently after the successful Orissa campaign, Harsha is reported to have made an extravagant but unaccepted offer of 'the revenue of 80 large towns' in that province to the Buddhist scholar Jaya-sena.[2]

Secular land grants by Harsha

But the 'Records' suggest that Harsha may also have made land grants for secular purposes. In his general description of Indian administration, which may be taken to apply to Harsha's empire, Hsüan-tsang says that royal land was divided into four categories assigned to four items of expenditure: government expenses and state worship, endowment to ministers, rewards to men of distinguished ability, and charity to 'heretics'.[3] Again it is stated that ministers and officials each had their appropriate share of land so that they could rely on it for support.[4] It is possible that the complex working of the typically Indian *sāmanta* institution confused the Chinese observer. As noted earlier many important administrative officers of the state were subordinated *sāmantas* who had their own territorial possessions, income from which under the changed circumstances may have been considered as their salary for the administrative duties they performed for the state. The majority, of course, were not thus employed and paid their share to the centre in other forms, such as regular or periodic gifts of gold, valuable commodities, elephants, military help in time of war, or hostages who served as courtiers. Some may have enjoyed cultivator's rights over their land and paid the regular one-sixth of the produce in the form of tax to the state. Thus while allowing the *sāmantas* to enjoy their high status Harsha may also have safeguarded the interests of the treasury. As for creating new *sāmantas* Harsha may not only have bestowed the honorific title to raise the prestige of some of his important cash-salaried officials but may also have used land or land tax instead of cash as the mode of payment to bring some officers in line with the real *sāmantas*.

Sāmantas as state employees

Sāmantas as state tenants

Difficulties in reconstruction of administrative organization

We have no systematic account of the machinery of central or local government in Harsha's period. The Gupta administrative organization which in many ways served as the model for seventh-century governments has itself to be reconstructed on the basis of scattered materials. Hsüan-tsang's memoirs, affected by the usual handicaps and advantages of a foreign observer, contain a fair amount of information on the general aspects of administration but very little on the actual functioning of the government. The information that we pick up in this connection from

[1] *H.C.* text, p. 203; trans., p. 199. [2] 'Life', p. 154.
[3] *Hsi Yü Chi* text, ii. 10a; cf. Watters i, p. 176; Beal i, p. 87.
[4] *Hsi Yü Chi*, op. cit.; cf. Watters i, p. 177; Beal i, p. 88.

Bāṇa's works, with incidental notices of official titles and designations in their original form, sometimes along with their corresponding functions, is much more valuable. *Smṛitis* supply some useful data regarding high administrative functionaries and on legal procedure, while inscriptions afford the most dependable material on contemporary administrative practices.

Hsüan-tsang refers to the practice of maintaining 'archives and records [for which] there are separate custodians. . . . The official annals and state-papers are called collectively *ni-lo-pi-t'u* [or *ch'a*]; in these good and bad are recorded, and instances of public calamity and good fortune are set forth in detail.'[1] Such records are perhaps irretrievably lost.

There is, however, sufficient information at our disposal to spur us to tackle the incomplete jigsaw puzzle it creates. A few vital and comparatively well defined designations are supplied along with a number of inconsequential or vague ones. Some examples of the more definitive terms are *mahā-sāndhi-vigrah-ādhikṛita*, the minister of interstate relations, and the *mahāksha-paṭal-ādhikṛita* or the keeper of the accounts. Among the less important are the different designations for a host of personal attendants of the king, the queen, and the heir apparent. While some gaps in the puzzle may be filled fairly safely on the basis of Gupta or post-seventh-century records such as the resuscitation of the *rahasi-niyukta*, king's personal officer whose services must have been greatly in demand by Harsha, others had better be left blank until further material comes to light.

Our sources supply us with over fifty designations, that may be applied to members of the king's administrative staff and military officers, from the highest to the lowest. While the army personnel was connected with the usual three wings, the infantry, the cavalry, and the elephant corps, the civilian staff looked after a wide range of subjects such as the court and the royal household, the central and local administrative offices, the departments of law, taxation, religious and social welfare, etc.

We attempt, below, a reconstruction of the pattern of Harsha's administration on the basis of reasonable inference and direct proof.

King, council, and the central secretariat

The King at the helm of affairs controlled the machinery of government with the help of a central ministry and a secretariat comprising

[1] *Hsi Yü Chi* text, ii. 5b; Watters i, p. 154 (Beal i, p. 78), *Ni-lo-pi-t'u, Nīla-piṭa* or Blue Chest. It is not unusual to find that certain colours become associated with certain functions. *Peṭa* and *piṭaka* are synonyms for *piṭa*. The three divisions of Buddhist literature, perhaps from being stored originally in three containers, came to be known as *tripiṭaka*. This and the present reference indicate that it was traditional practice to preserve religious and secular documents.

various departments. The latter exchanged business with the regional secretariats in a precise or a generalized manner depending on the nature of the matter concerned or on the type of relation in which the region concerned stood to the centre. The permanent headquarters of all state departments must have been situated at the capital. Judging by Hsüan-tsang's reference to the *nīla-piṭa*, the official annals and state papers, the central secretariat probably housed the written records of its business with all the regional centres, which would in turn have stored their own corresponding local documents.

There appears to have been a general superintendent of the offices who with his various assistants carried out multiple liaison tasks. He maintained rapport among various departments, between the King and the departments, between the centre and the directly administered provinces, and between the centre and the various close and distant members of the *maṇḍala*. South-Indian inscriptions mention an officer by the title of *sarv-ādhyaksha*, over-all supervisor, whose duty was to convey orders of the central government to the provincial and district officers through 'carriers of royal commands'.[1] We read of *adhyakshas* in the *Harsha-charita* as officers in charge of their special commissions.[2] The use of the term in this context seems to be a survival from the days of the *Kauṭilīya*, when it implied an administrative civil servant.

The central council of ministers

The central ministry is called in some sources the *mantri-parishad*. *Smṛitis* and inscriptions of all periods refer to ministers as *mantrin*, *sachiva*, or *amātya*, although in certain contexts the different terms may have been employed discriminatingly.[3] The strength of the ministry appears to have varied from approximately eight to twenty, depending on the needs of the state.[4] It appears that a council composed of members from all the four classes or castes was preferred or perhaps even required. According to the *Mahā-bhārata* the king should have 37 *sachivas*: 4 brahmans, 8 *kshatriyas*, 21 *vaiśyas*, 3 *śūdras*, and 1 *sūta* versed in the Purāṇas.[5] It is also declared that the king should not have less than three

[1] *E.I.* viii. 162: '*Sarvādhyaksha vallabha śāsana sañchāriṇaḥ*'. Pallava, Vākāṭaka, and Kadamba inscriptions, see *I.A.* v. 155; vi. 25; *E.I.* xxii. 172.

[2] *H.C.* text, p. 227: '*Yathā adhikāramādikshat adhyakshān*'.

[3] In the period of our study *mantrin* is freely used in the *Kāmandakīya*, e.g. iv. 41; xiii. 23; also *E.I.* x. 71. For *sachiva* see *C.I.I.* iii, no. 35, *l.* 16. *H.C.* text, p. 199 uses *mantri*, *sachiva*, and *amātya* for minister, apparently without distinction. Also see below, p. 175.

[4] *Artha.* i. 15 and Kāmandaka xi. 67–8 state that the schools of Manu, Bṛihaspati, and Uśanas required respectively 12, 16, and 20 members to constitute the *parishad* but Kauṭilya held that the number should be determined by the state's interests. *Manu.* vii. 54 suggests seven or eight. Many authorities advised the king neither to act alone nor to seek the advice of too many ministers but rather to consult three or four (*Rāmāyaṇa* ii. 100, 71; *Sabhā.* 5. 30, 18; *Artha.* i. 15).

[5] *Śānti.* 85. 7–9.

mantrins[1] and that he should discuss policies with eight of them.[2] Hsüan-tsang's account of local kingdoms refers to rulers of all classes.

On the basis of Watters's translation of the *Hsi Yü Chi*, U. N. Ghoshal suggests,[3] in our opinion unjustifiably, that there may have been a smaller and a larger state council at Kanauj at the beginning of Harsha's reign. Watters's paraphrase of the text runs as follows: 'The *statesmen* of Kanauj, on the advice of their leading man Bāni (or Vāni), invited Harshavardhana, . . . to become their sovereign', and further, 'the *ministers of state* pressed Harshavardhana to succeed . . . .'[4] The two relevant sets of characters *liao shu* and *fu-ch'en chih shih*[5] for ministers, etc., have no precise English equivalents. In their Chinese usage too they are general, undefined terms employed to convey several meanings. The first term may be used for officials, subordinates, colleagues, or statesmen, the second for ministers and officials or men in charge of affairs. One may hazard the guess that the second term stands for a formal body of counsellors or *mantrins* while the first, more vague and general, for *sāmantas*, an institution not easily appreciated by a foreigner and therefore difficult to render in a foreign tongue. By Harsha's time the *sāmantas* had become a regular feature at royal courts and some highly esteemed ones tendered advice on important matters, 'their words not to be transgressed'.[6] They appear again and again in the *Harsha-charita*, sometimes as the King's solicitous well-wishers in times of personal distress, at other times as members of a regular court presided over by the king.[7] Harsha's inscriptions depict them as administrative officers also. With the passage of time the deliberative as well as the administrative role of the *sāmantas* appears to have become firmly established. The colophon of a manuscript from Pattan dated A.D. 1170 refers to the rule of a *sāmanta-mantrin* over a *paṭhaka*, an administrative unit.[8] As has been noticed, 'Soḍḍhala in his *Udaya-sundarī-kathā* maintains a difference between the *mantrins* and the *sāmantas* and observes that while the king discussed with his *mantrins* the conduct of ideal kings of the past, such as Pṛthu, Bharata, and Bhāgīratha, he deliberated the actions of turbulent enemies with the *sāmantas*.'[9]

[1] *Śānti*. 83. 47. [2] Ibid. 85. 11. [3] *H.C.I.P.* iii, p. 349.

[4] Watters i, p. 343. Our italics. Beal i, p. 211, translated the terms in question as *ministers* and *chief ministers and magistrates*. Also see above, p. 80.

[5] *Hsi Yü Chi* text, v. 3a. [6] *H.C.* text, p. 178; trans., p. 168.

[7] Ibid., text, pp. 72, 155, 178; trans., pp. 59, 138, 168.

[8] L. B. Gandhi, *Catalogue of Manuscripts at Pattan* i, p. 105.

[9] Mrs. K. K. Gopal, 'The Assembly of the Sāmantas in Early Medieval India', *J.I.H.* xlii, pt. 1 (April 1964), 249. Soḍḍhala was a Valabhī Kāyastha of Lāṭa who lived at the court of a King of Konkaṇ around A.D. 1000.

Thus, the 'statesmen' or the *liao-shu* of Kanauj who 'invited Harsha-vardhana . . . to become their sovereign' may have been the *sāmanta* members of the court, one of whose functions appears to have been to exert influence at the time of succession.

While most members of the central ministry may also have been heads of departments such as army, revenue, public welfare, etc., some, esteemed for their experience, learning, or wisdom, may have acted only as *mantrins* or counsellors. Siṁha-nāda, a friend of Prabhākara-vardhana and 'far advanced in years', but still enjoying the title *senā-pati* or commander of the forces, apparently from his younger days of active service, seems to have acted in a purely advisory capacity in his old age.[1]

Military proficiency of ministers

It appears that a good many of the central ministers along with their specific qualifications were also expected to possess military skill in Harsha's time as in the Gupta period. Pṛithvī-sheṇa, at first a *mantrin* of Kumāra Gupta, later assumed the office of *mahā-balādhikṛita* or great officer of the forces.[2] According to the *Harsha-charita* Bhaṇḍi accompanied or led the Vardhana forces on crucial occasions. His military competence, coupled with the fact that he was closely related to the royal family and had been in its service for many years, must have secured for him a prominent place in the central council. Hsüan-tsang refers to him as 'the great [or important] minister Po-ni, whose power and reputation were high and of much weight' and who guided the 'ministers and officials' of Kanauj in the choice of Harsha as king.[3] Although we do not come across any official designations for Bhaṇḍi in the indigenous sources, he may well have held the titles *mantrin* and *mahā-balādhikṛita*.

As the *mantrin* so the *mahā-sāndhi-vigrah-ādhikṛita*, the minister of peace and war or of interstate relations, may have been trained for military duties. Samudra Gupta's *sāndhi-vigrahika* Hari-sheṇa held two additional titles, *kumār-āmātya* and *mahā-daṇḍa-nāyaka*, the latter a military designation.[4] Presumably Harsha's *mahā-sāndhi-vigrah-ādhikṛita* Avanti too could lead an army. The royal commandant of the elephant corps or *gaja-sādhan-ādhikṛita*, Skanda-gupta, mentioned by Bāṇa may well be the same as the *dūtaka*, *mahā-pramātāra*, *mahā-sāmanta* Skanda-

[1] He is portrayed as advising young Harsha on a suitable course of action after the death of Graha-varman and Rājya-vardhana. *H.C.* text, pp. 188–93; trans., pp. 180–6.

[2] *E.I.* x. 71, '*prthviṣeṇaḥ mantrī . . . anantarañca Mahābalādhikṛta*'.

[3] *Hsi Yü Chi* text, v. 3b. Also see above, p. 80.

[4] Also capable of being interpreted as a legal designation, the term was mostly used as a military title. Inscriptions use synonyms for the term meaning exclusively 'leader of the army' (Kargudari inscription of Vikramāditya VI and Tailapa II: *I.A.* x. 252). The Bala-gaṁve inscription of Saṅkama-deva (*I.A.* v. 46) defines *daṇḍa-nāyaka* as *samasta-senā-agresara* or 'leader of the whole army'.

gupta referred to in Harsha's Baṅskhera plate. The bestowal of multiple titles on the same person indicates that a few competent men were often assigned more than one post, though not always in allied fields. The fact that the King shared many of their responsibilities may have made it possible for the officers to look after more than one job. All the same, if civilian and military offices were delegated to the same man, a temporary suspension or reallocation of duties would have been necessary in times of war, which took place every so often. This must have affected efficiency adversely. It seems, however, that many of the credentials were only technical labels of distinction. The assumption is supported by the example of Dhruva-sena I of Valabhī, who held five titles: *mahā-sāmanta*, *mahā-pratīhāra*, *mahā-daṇḍa-nāyaka*, *mahā-kārtta-kṛitika*, and *mahārāja*.[1]

The *mahā-sāndhi-vigrah-ādhikṛita*, the minister of peace and war or interstate relations

The office of *mahā-sāndhi-vigrah-ādhikṛita* was perhaps the most onerous of all, requiring, one may presume, the guidance of the complete 'sixfold' state policy with *sandhi* and *vigraha* as two of its main constituents. Although we find the policy first enunciated in Kauṭilya's *artha-śāstra*, the designation *sāndhi-vigrahika* does not appear until the Gupta period. Presumably the Mauryan king was his own *sāndhi-vigrahika*, while the Gupta monarchs broadened the base of governmental responsibility by instituting this new office. By the seventh-century titles had become more grandiloquent. Harsha's minister of peace and war or of interstate relations, Avanti, was known as *mahā-sāndhi-vigrah-ādhikṛita*. He was probably assisted by some lesser *sāndhi-vigrahikas*. In later times some kingdoms of the Deccan are known to have employed several *sāndhi-vigrahikas*, each responsible for relations with a particular region.[2] In addition to the regulation of interstate relations, Harsha's *mahā-sāndhi-vigrah-ādhikṛita* may also have advised him on the exchange of political, cultural, and commercial missions with China, a region beyond the usually contemplated limits of a king's *maṇḍala*.

Kumār-āmātya

The title of *kumār-āmātya* may sometimes have been honorary, but appears generally to have carried with it some administrative responsibilities. The two components of the word taken separately mean respectively prince or boy, and minister,[3] but the literal meaning of the compound is 'a counsellor of the prince'. It has also been interpreted as 'one who was in the service of the king from the time when he was a boy.'[4] Some scholars consider that *kumār-āmātyas* were princes of royal

[1] *I.A.* iv. 105.

[2] *E.I.* xiii. 41, where a Chālūkya officer is said to have held, among other titles, that of *Kannaḍa-sāndhi-vigrahika*.

[3] Bühler translated it as 'princes and ministers': *I.A.* iv. 175; *E.I.* iv. 74.

[4] Bloch, *E.I.* x. 50 n. 2.

blood '(who) formed a council of the nobles, and were consulted by the ruling chiefs on points of imperial importance'.[1] The early assumption, based on the literal meaning of the compound, that *kumār-āmātyas* were ministers to princes has long been discarded because there is clear inscriptional evidence that *kumār-āmātyas* served ruling monarchs.[2] We suggest that the term was originally designed to describe princes of royal blood who carried out the duties of an *amātya*. It may also have served the purpose of differentiating *amātyas* who were *kumāras*, i.e. princes, from *rāj-āmātyas*, i.e. *amātyas* who were *rājas* by title or function. At some stage an *amātya* with the appellation *kumāra* may have signified a minister who had the same dignity as a *kumāra*. In time, of course, the etymological meanings of the titles disappeared and they could be bestowed on commoners as well.

In Maurya and Sāta-vāhana times *amātyas* were a class of high-ranking officers from among whom were selected important ministers. The inscriptions of our period, however, appear to use the term for officers of a lower grade. The Khoh copperplate (A.D. 475–6) of *mahārāja* Jaya-natha, for instance, records that a certain *amātya* was also a *bhogika*.[3] The latter class of officers were probably responsible for collecting *bhoga*, the state's share of land produce in kind. Fleet considers *bhogika* to be a technical title, possibly connected with the territorial term *bhukti*.[4] Judging from another inscription[5] the *bhogika* ranked lower than the *sāmanta* but higher than the *vishaya-pati*. The technical title therefore does not place the *amātyas* in a very high category of officials. The son of a *bhogika*, the grandson of an *amātya* and *bhogika*, and the great-grandson of an *amātya*, Sūrya-datta attained, however, the high office of *mahā-sāndhi-vigrahika*.[6] Bāṇa informs us that among the various courtiers at Sthāṇv-īśvara, such as princes of noble descent, venerable advisers, and brahmans versed in law and *dharma*, were also 'anointed *rājās* who were *amātyas*'.[7] The context suggests that, in this case at least, *amātya* was a title of honour and not an administrative designation.

[1] Ibid. xi. 176.

[2] *A.S.I.A.R.* (1903–4), p. 107; *parama-bhaṭṭāraka-pādīya kumār-āmātya* or '*kumār-āmātya* in service of the emperor'. The *kumār-āmātya* attached to the heir apparent is designated *yuva-rāja-pādīya kumār-āmātya* in the same inscription. Hari-sheṇa and Pṛithvī-sheṇa, ministers respectively of Samudra Gupta and Chandra Gupta II, held the title *kumār-āmātya*.

[3] *C.I.I.* iii, no. 27.

[4] Op. cit., p. 100.

[5] Kāvi grant of Jaya-bhaṭa II: *I.A.* v. 114, l. 8.

[6] *C.I.I.* iii, nos. 21 and 22.

[7] *H.C.* text, p. 173. Cowell and Thomas (p. 162) translate the phrase, inaccurately we think, as 'anointed counsellors of royal rank'. It was, in fact, the full-fledged anointed *rājās* who held the title *amātya* and not the other way about. Moreover, inscriptions of our period use the term *mantrin*, not *amātya*, for counsellor.

In his Baṅskhera and Madhu-ban grants Harsha addresses his command to various title-holders listed in the following sequence: *Mahā-sāmanta*, *Mahārāja*, *dauḥssādha-sādhanika*, *pramātāra*, *rāja-sthānīya*, *kumārāmātya*, *uparika*, *vishaya-pati*, *bhaṭa*, *chāṭa*, *sevaka*, etc. The place of the *kumār-āmātyas* in the list indicates not only that they held administrative posts but also their position in relation to other officers.[1]

Several inscriptions reveal that *kumār-āmātyas* worked as district officers in charge of divisions of *bhuktis* which were governed by *uparikas*.[2] Other records show that they served as subordinates of *mahā-daṇḍa-nāyakas*.[3] That they were lower in rank than the *mahā-bal-ādhikṛitas* is attested by the fact that Pṛithvī-sheṇa, a minister of Kumāra Gupta I, was at first a *kumār-āmātya*; after some approved service he was promoted to the higher office of *mahā-bal-ādhikṛita*.[4] Pṛithvī-sheṇa also held the important office of *mahā-sāṅdhi-vigrahika* or minister of interstate relations. It is indicative of the importance of the rank of *kumār-āmātya* that it was retained after the acquirement of other offices. That such high offices were bestowed on *kumār-āmātyas* also, signifies that they were an able and competent class of officers.

As A. S. Altekar observes, 'It seems that *Kumārāmātyas*, to a great extent, resembled the modern [British-period] I.C.S. officers, who sometimes work in the district, sometimes in the provincial or central secretariat and sometimes become members of the government itself. Higher posts of ministers and generals were filled . . . from their cadre.'[5] True of the Gupta times, this remark largely applies to Harsha's period as well.

Rahasi-niyukta, the king's private secretary

In the inscriptions of the Gupta period we meet an officer called the *rahasi-niyukta*. The term may be translated very nearly as private secretary. Kings in ancient India were often on the move either on tours of inspection or on distant military campaigns. Certain state business was transacted during this period, very often including the issue of charity grants of land or income from it. The kings gave oral orders[6] which were taken down by *rahasi-niyuktas* or private secretaries, who passed them on for recording and execution to the appropriate departments.[7]

[1] Two grants, those of Dhara-sena II of Valabhī (*C.I.I.* iii, no. 38) and Jīvita-gupta II of Magadha (op. cit., no. 46), also provide examples of similar nature. Their orders of sequence have little in common with each other or with that in Harsha's grants nor, indeed, do they indicate any systematic listing in ascending or descending order. However, in all of them *kumār-āmātyas* appear alongside fairly high officers such as the *rāja-sthānīya*, *uparika*, and *mahā-pratīhāra*, which points to their importance.

[2] *E.I.* xv. 130; xvii. 193, 347; xx. 61; xxi. 8.

[3] *A.S.I.A.R.* (1911–12), 32.

[4] *E.I.* x. 52.

[5] *N.H.I.P.* vi, p. 282.

[6] *E.I.* vi. 38; *C.I.I.* iii, p. 155.

[7] '*Sva mukha ājñyāyā abhilikhitaḥ rahasi-niyukteṇa* (*na*) *chullena*': *E.I.* xix. 103.

Literary and epigraphic records show that during his frequent journeys Harsha issued orders of various kinds. At the commencement of his first military campaign in A.D. 606, camped at the outskirts of Sthāṇvīśvara, Harsha made a grant of a hundred villages, 'his commands for the day' being stamped by 'a new made golden seal with a bull for its emblem'.[1] Copper and clay seals of Harsha with bull emblems have been discovered respectively at Sonpat in the Panjab and Nālandā in Bihar. Examples of some other orders which Harsha is said to have issued when on the move are his two messages to the King of Kāma-rūpa regarding Hsüan-tsang,[2] and his letters 'on fine white cotton stuff and sealed . . . with red wax'[3] issued to facilitate the Chinese pilgrim's return journey. There was thus a clear need for a functionary of the type of the *rahasi-niyukta*, and, although we do not come across the designation in contemporary records, the familiar Gupta office associated with such tasks is very likely to have existed in Harsha's time as well. In an inscription of Bhāskara-varman of Kāma-rūpa,[4] the subordinate ally of Harsha, we meet with numerous official titles, one of which, the *ājñā-śataṁ prāpayitā*, may have carried some of the responsibilities of the *rahasi-niyukta*.

Pratīhāras and *mahā-pratīhāras* are another class of officers who figure prominently in records from Gupta to post-Harsha times.[5] In charge of court procedure and royal audiences, the *mahā-pratīhāra* or the chamberlain appears to have been an officer of high status. Bāṇa describes the chief of all the *mahā-pratīhāras* in extravagant terms.[6] Dhruva-sena I of Valabhī, although holder of various high titles such as *mahārāja* and *mahā-daṇḍa-nāyaka*, also carried the title *mahā-pratīhāra*.[7] *Pratīhāra*

There were several categories of *pratīhāras*, depending on their rank and where they were posted. The *Harsha-charita* speaks of *bāhya*, or outer (-court), and *antara*, or inner (-court), *pratīhāras*, of *mahā-pratīhāras*, each of whom appears to have been in charge of a number of *pratīhāras*, and of a *dauvārika*, a rank that does not appear elsewhere, the chief of all the *mahā-pratīhāras*.[8] The *pratīhāras* accompanied the King during journeys, as is evident from Bāṇa's reference to them[9] in the account of the meeting at a military encampment between Harsha

[1] *H.C.* text, p. 203; trans., p. 199.
[2] 'Life', p. 172.
[3] Ibid., pp. 189–90.
[4] *E.I.* xii. 65; xix. 118 ff.
[5] *H.C.* text, pp. 62, 214, etc.; trans., pp. 50, 211, etc.; *I.A.* iv. 105; *C.I.I.* iii, no. 39.
[6] *H.C.* text, pp. 61–2; trans., pp. 49–50.
[7] *I.A.* iv. 105.
[8] *Mahā-pratīhārāṇāṁ anantaraḥ*: Ibid., text, p. 62.
[9] Ibid., text, p. 214; trans., p. 211.

and the envoy from Kāma-rūpa. There were special *pratīhāra* quarters at such halting-places.[1]

Skandhā-vāra, the royal quarters

We are able to reconstruct from the *Harsha-charita* an approximate plan of the royal quarters manned by the *pratīhāras*. The whole campus, called the *skandhā-vāra*, was approached from the main street.[2] It was divided into two broad sections. The first or outer section, called the *bāhya-kakshyā*, is described as crowded with the camps of tributary kings with their gifts of elephants, horses, camels, umbrellas, and chowries. Along with such kings aspiring for an audience with their sovereign also waited the conquered enemy *mahā-sāmantas*; envoys from distant countries, natives of different places, *mlechchhas* from regions bordering the sea, as well as followers of multifarious religious callings.[3]

On leaving this outer section the visitor encountered the *pratīhāras* who guarded and regulated procedure in the inner section, comprising the palace complex or *rāja-kula*. It was at this junction that Bāṇa was introduced by his royal escort Mekhālaka to the chief of all the *mahā-pratīhāras*, the *dauvārika* Pāri-yātra.[4]

The *rāja-kula* was staffed by *antara-pratīhāras*.[5] It consisted of various sections. The first section (adjoining the *bāhya-kakshyā*—the outer court) accommodated the King's favourite beasts, pedigree elephants and horses.[6] Beyond that were three *kakshyās*,[7] or courts, which appear to have been used as the halls of public audience. On the occasion of Bāṇa's own meeting with Harsha they are described as swarming with lesser kings.[8] The same part of the palace is described again in a gloomier vein as it looked at the time of Prabhākara-vardhana's last illness.[9]

Elsewhere termed *āsthāna-maṇḍapa*[10] or *sabhā-maṇḍapa*,[11] these courts

[1] *Pratīhāra-bhavana*: Op. cit., text, p. 218.
[2] Op. cit., p. 153.
[3] Op. cit., p. 60.
[4] Bāṇa's description of Pāri-yātra is of great interest. In all likelihood he was a native of Pāri-yātra, a region that is mentioned as a target for conquest by Harsha (*H.C.* text, p. 214; trans., p. 210). From the description of his dress and manners Pāri-yātra appears to have been an Indianized foreigner: 'a tall man fair . . . clothed in a . . . jacket with his waist tightly bound by a girdle . . . with his topknot bent down to the ground, lifting his white turban as a token of respect . . .' (Op. cit., pp. 61–2; trans., pp. 49–50).
[5] Op. cit., text, p. 60.
[6] Op. cit., pp. 62–9.
[7] '*Samatikramya . . . triṇi kakshyā-ṅtarāṇi . . .*': Op. cit., p. 69, and '. . . *tritīyaṁ kakshyāntaraṁ*': op. cit., p. 154.
[8] *H.C.* Op. cit., p. 69.
[9] Op. cit., text, pp. 154–5; trans., pp. 137–8.
[10] Op. cit., text, pp. 172, 186, 190, 214.
[11] Op. cit., pp. 194, 201.

were also used for making important declarations and for ministerial conferences of a less confidential nature.[1]

Beyond the three *kakshyās* or courts lay the King's hall of special audience, the *bhuktā-sthāna-maṇḍapa*,[2] where Bāṇa was presented to Harsha. The hall received its name for being used for lounging after meals. Situated in the interior it was presumably also used for deliberations of a more secret nature.

The next and final section of the palace was the double-storeye *dhavala-gṛiha*, or White House, containing the King's private apartments, a flight of steps leading to the royal bedroom on the upper floor.[3] Numerous *pratīhāras* and attendants served in the inner apartments, which appear to have been lavishly staffed. In the exceptional circumstances of Prabhākara-vardhana's illness, and perhaps normally too, the vestibule in the White House was guarded by *vetra-grāhīs*, cane- or mace-bearers.[4] *Pratīhāras* saw to it that the stairs leading to the patient's bedroom were negotiated noiselessly. Other staff mentioned in the same context are *chāmara-grāhī* (chowrie bearers), *kañchukī* (old man in charge of the women's apartments or attendant furnished with armour), *aṅga-rakshaka* (bodyguard), *shiro-rakshaka* (head bodyguard), and so forth.

Apart from the King, the Queen, the royal princes, and princesses also had their own personal attendants.[5]

Religion and social welfare

From Hsüan-tsang's statement that the King divided his day into three parts, one devoted to matters of government and two to religious affairs,[6] the latter including social and educational undertakings looked upon as acts of spiritual merit, one would expect to find mention of several designations for officials concerned with religious and public-welfare duties. In the Gupta inscriptions we read of the *vinaya-sthiti-sthāpakas*,[7] whose Mauryan prototype were the *dharma-mahāmātras*. For Harsha's period, however, although we find numerous references to undertakings in the field, from the building of hospices to the famous quinquennial assemblies, we hardly come across any designations of officers connected with the work. The King of Jālandhara is stated to

[1] Following the news of Rājya-vardhana's death, the veteran Siṁha-nāda gave advice to Harsha in the *āsthāna*. At the same place Harsha instructed his 'minister of war and peace' to proclaim his intention of a *dig-vijaya* march: *H.C.* text, pp. 186–94; trans., pp. 177–88.

[2] '. . . *triṇi kakshyāṅtarāṇi chaturthe bhukt-āsthāna-maṅḍapasya* . . .': Op. cit., text, p. 69; trans., p. 56.

[3] Op. cit., text, pp. 123, 159; trans., pp. 104, 143.

[4] Op. cit., text, p. 155.

[5] For Queen Yaśo-vatī, op. cit., text, pp. 164–5; trans., p. 151: for Prince Rājya-vardhana, op. cit., text, p. 176; trans., p. 165.

[6] Watters i, p. 344; Beal i, p. 215.

[7] See *N.H.I.P.* vi, p. 279.

have been appointed by Harsha as the 'sole inspector of the affairs of religion (*the Three Gems*) throughout the five Indies';[1] this indicates the existence of a specific department for the purpose with a hierarchy of officials. In connection with the donated villages called *agra-hāras* we come across the term *agra-hārika* in Gupta records, meaning officers who regulated the affairs of such villages.[2] Bestowed on students, on brahmans, who according to custom gave free education to a number of students, on monasteries, which were both religious and educational institutions, and on learned scholars, many land grants were an instrument in the promotion of learning. Whether the Crown alienated land for limited or unlimited duration or the income from it, the transaction needed state supervision as long as the donee's rights lasted. Both of Harsha's grants employ the term *agra-hāra* for donated villages. The officer who conveyed the king's command about the grant to local officers was called *dūtaka* and might carry additional titles such as *mahāsāmanta* and *mahārāja*. *Dūtaka* in this context was not necessarily a permanent post. In fact generally it was a temporary assignment given to any person of rank who acted as the king's representative at the transfer of the land.

Contemporary evidence on Harsha's acts of piety shows that a considerable number of staff would have been employed for tasks ranging from animal protection to recreational activities, such as plays and recitations that emphasized ethical virtues. I-tsing refers to the composition of the Jātakas in verse for the purpose of teaching 'the doctrine of universal salvation in a beautiful style, agreeable to the popular mind and attractive to readers'.[3] A poetical song composed by one Chandra of East India, which told the story of the Viśvāṅtara Jātaka, was sung and danced to by the people throughout the five countries of India. This may apply not only to I-tsing's time but also to the slightly earlier period of Harsha. It is also recorded that Harsha versified his *Nāg-ānanda*, a play with a Buddhist theme, had it set to music and performed, and 'thus popularized it in his time.'[4] The opera was first taken to China and then to Japan, where it is performed to this day as a part of the Ryo-o theatre.[5]

Exaggerating perhaps a limited ban on the consumption of meat or on hunting by Harsha, Hsüan-tsang states that the King decreed punishment without pardon for 'eating of meat' or 'killing of life'. 'In all the highways of the towns and villages throughout India he erected hospices

[1] Beal i, p. 176; cf. Watters i, p. 296.
[2] *C.I.I.* iii, pp. 52 and 257 n.
[3] I-tsing, p. 163.
[4] Op. cit., p. 164.
[5] See above, p. 155.

provided with food and drink, and stationed there physicians, with medicines for travellers and poor persons . . . to be given without . . . stint.' 'Every year he assembled the *śramaṇas* from all countries, and . . . bestowed on them the four kinds of alms [food, drink, medicine, clothing].' 'Constantly in his travelling palace he would 'provide delicious rare food for men of all sorts of religions . . .'

Not only did Harsha shower material favours on the deserving but his piety extended to the promotion of religion and learning through arranging debates, bestowing honours, and so forth. Hsüan-tsang relates: 'he decorated the throne of the law and extensively ornamented the oratories. He ordered the priests to carry on discussions, and himself judged of their several arguments. . . . He rewarded the good and punished the wicked, degraded the evil, and promoted the men of talent.'

Harsha set a high example in munificence. 'He regularly held the Quinquennial Convocation; and gave away in religious alms everything except the material of war.'[1] On these occasions he distributed his favours freely to the poor and the needy, and to all religious sects. Hsüan-tsang's account of the celebration attests the catholic religious attitude of the times. The quinquennial assemblies were perhaps one of the most spectacular features of Harsha's reign and judging from their description they must have entailed long and careful preparation, second only to that needed for a military campaign. In spite of the absence of mention of any specific designations connected with tasks promoting piety, education, the arts, and public welfare, except Hsüan-tsang's reference to the 'sole inspector of Buddhist affairs', it is safe to assume that a large staff looked after these duties of the state.

Law and justice

Some idea of the administration of law in Harsha's time may be obtained from contemporary *smṛiti* literature, Kātyāyana's work (A.D. 400–600) being the nearest to our period.

Law and judicial procedure received ample attention from scholars in ancient India and the well-developed system of Hindu jurisprudence had already gone through a long period of evolution by Harsha's time.

Even in the early Vedic age the judicial had become separated from the executive or political function, as is evident from the mention of the purely legal designation *praśna-vivāka* in the Brāhmaṇas. It is obviously related to *prāḍ-vivāka*, the term used for judge in the Kātyāyana *smṛiti*. *Praśna* and *prāḍ*, derived from the root *prachh*, mean respectively 'question' and 'questioner'. *Vivāka* from the root *vach* denotes 'one who

[1] Watters i, p. 344 (*Hsi Yü Chi* text, v. 4b); also see above, p. 157 n. 1.

speaks out or analyses'. The term *prāḍ-vivāka* is a *dvandva* compound meaning 'questioner and discriminator'.

When the king could legislate

The king was the fountain (i.e. the distributor) of justice and the highest court of appeal. His legislative action, however, was extremely limited. Law issued from (*a*) the Veda, *Dharma-śāstra*, and related literature; (*b*) customs; (*c*) usages of husbandmen, traders, artisans, etc.; (*d*) ratiocination; and (*e*) the opinions delivered by the assembly of the learned.[1] The king or the chief judge was required to decide according to the rules of the *dharma-śāstra* and, in the absence of texts, in accordance with the recognized custom of the country. Bṛihaspati, however, declares that 'a decision should not be given by merely relying on the text of the *śāstra*; when consideration of a matter is divorced from reason and common sense, loss of *dharma* results'.[2] Kātyāyana clearly condemns the neglect by the king of the established sources of law in preference to his own decision, which should only be applied in the last resort:

> If a king decided [a case] by his own fiat where there is a text . . . it causes ruin to the prople . . . but in the absence of *smṛiti* texts he should carry out [judicial administration] according to the usages [lit. the views of the country]. . . . The usages established in a country by the approval of its people and that are not in direct conflict with Veda and *smṛitis* should be recorded in writing under the seal of the king.[3]

King's role as head of justice

All writers on law stress that the king should be easily accessible to those seeking justice.[4] Megasthenes[5] confirms that such was the case in the time of Chandra-gupta Maurya, while Hsüan-tsang's general comments on Harsha's industry with regard to his administrative duties point to the same conclusion.

The jurists also declared that a king who punished the innocent or let off the guilty incurred sin.[6] When the king could not personally attend to the administration of justice he was expected to appoint a learned judge and three *sabhyas* (junior members of the court of justice) for the purpose.[7] Kātyāyana prescribes that the judge should be restrained, born of a good family, impartial, not repellent (or harsh in his manners), steady, afraid of the next world, highly religious, assiduous, and free from hot temper.[8] His designation in Harsha's period may have

[1] *Gaut.* xi. 19–25.
[2] *Bṛ.* quoted by Aparārka, p. 599.
[3] *Kāt.* quoted by Aparārka, p. 599.
[4] *Rāmāyāṇa*, vii. 53–4; *Anu.* 6–38; *Artha.* i. 19; *Śukra.* iv. 5–8.
[5] *Frag.* xxvii, pp. 70–1.
[6] *Manu.* viii. 128.
[7] *Manu.* viii. 9–10; *Yāj.* ii. 3; *Kāt.* 63; *Śukra.* iv. 5. 12.
[8] See *Hist. Dh.* iii, p. 271.

been *prāḍ-vivāka*,[1] *dharm-ādhikarin*,[2] or *dharm-ādhyaksha*.[3] *Aksha-darśaka* was another synonym of *prāḍ-vivāka*.[4]

Courts of justice

The court of justice was called *dharma-sthāna*,[5] *dharm-āsana*,[6] and, in the days of the Guptas and Harsha, *adhikaraṇa*[7] or *dharm-ādhikaraṇa*, the latter, according to Kātyāyana, being 'the place where the truth of the plaint [lit. the cause or root of dispute] is discussed according to the rules of the sacred law'.[8]

Apart from courts at the capital, which may have been presided over by the king or the chief judge, judicial assemblies of the third sort enumerated by Bṛihaspati[9]—those furnished with the king's signet ring—must also have existed. Law courts were held in towns and villages and Bṛihaspati also mentions movable courts[10] which suggest the circuit courts of English law.

Definition and scope of lawsuit

An important term in ancient Indian law is *vyavahāra*, which is used in various senses in the *sūtra* and *smṛiti* works. It is applied to 'transaction or dealing', 'a dispute, a lawsuit', 'legal capacity to enter into transactions', and 'the means of deciding a matter'. Kātyāyana gives two definitions of *vyavahāra*, the first of which, 'that which removes various doubts',[11] is based on etymology and places intellectual and ethical demands on the purpose and function of law. His second interpretation of the term as lawsuit is simpler and more conventional. A *vyavahāra-pada* means the 'topic or subject-matter of litigation or dispute'. Such

[1] *Gaut.* xiii. 26, 27, 31; *Nār.* i. 35; *Bṛ.* (quoted by Aparārka, p. 602); *Kāt.* 68.

[2] As in the twelfth century A.D. work the *Mānas-ollāsa*, ii. 2. v. 93.

[3] As in the thirteenth or fourteenth century A.D. work the *Rāja-nīti-ratnākara*, p. 18.

[4] *Amara.* 2, 8, 5.

[5] *Śaṅkha-likhita*, quoted in *Smṛiti-chandrikā* ii, p. 19.

[6] *Nārada.* i. 34; *Manu.* viii. 23; *Śukra.* iv. 5. 46.

[7] *Vākya-vidāṁ adhikaraṇa vichāraḥ*: *H.C.* text, p. 78; trans., p. 65. Punningly the statement may be referred to the scholars of Mīmāṁsā (the commentator Śaṅkara explains *vākya-vidāṁ* as *mīmāṁsaka*), who pondered over the intricacies of their system, or to the skilled in speech, or knowers of the subject-matter (*vākya-vidāṁ*), i.e. lawyers, or legal officers who dealt with court cases. In the Gupta times the term *adhikaraṇa* was applied both to government offices (from which comes the word *karaṇi* for clerk) and to law courts. For a vivid description of the efficient handling of a law-case by a *prāḍ-vivāka*, V. S. Agrawala (p. 49 n. 1) refers to the *Pada-tāḍitakaṁ* section, p. 9 of the *Chatur-bhāṇi-saṁgraha*.

[8] *Kāt.*, quoted in *Smṛiti-chandrikā* ii, p. 19.

[9] *Bṛ.* i, verse 2.

[10] Op. cit., verses 2–3.

[11] *vi* = various, *ava* = doubt, *hāra* = removing. See *Hist. Dh.* iii, pp. 246–7. Strictly speaking, the etymology may be considered fanciful but the persistence with which the *smṛitis* repeat it (*Kātyāyana* quoted in *Vyavahāra Mātṛikā*, p. 283; *Parāśara Mādhavīya* iii, p. 7; and Kullūka on *Manu.* viii. 1) indicates the high standards expected in a court of justice. A similar example exists wherein the etymology of the word *rājā* is traced from the verb *rañjayati* (he pleases) once again flouting the rules of language but showing what was expected of the king.

subjects may broadly fall under two headings, civil and criminal, cases of both types being tried in the same courts.

Vyavahāra is stated to be *chatush-pād* or having four feet, named by some as *dharma* (moral law), *vyavahāra* (judicial proof), *charitra* (popular usage), and *rāja-śāsana* (king's edict), by others as the plaint, the reply, the proof (*kṛiyā*), and decision (*nirṇaya*). Kātyāyana states them to be plaint, reply, *pratyā-kalita* (decision as to where the burden of proof lies), and proof.[1]

According to P. V. Kane, 'Dharma and the other three are really the four feet of nirṇaya (final decision), which is one of the four stages of a law-suit (vyavahāra) and so only in a secondary or far-fetched sense they are the four pādas of vyavahāra.'[2] Each of these four is said to be of two kinds. A decision is said to be arrived at by *dharma* (i) when the guilty party makes an admission, and (ii) when judgment is by ordeal; by *vyavahāra* (i) when witnesses, both human and documentary, are used, and (ii) when decision is given against the party whose reply is tainted with faults; by *charitra* (i) when *anumāna* or possession and presumptions are relied on, and (ii) when the uses of a region, village, or family (written down in the census records of the king),[3] conforming to the *smṛiti* or not, are adhered to, and finally in the case of a deadlock by *rāja-śāsana* or the king's decision, which should be opposed neither to *smṛiti* nor to usage. It is stated that each later one of the four methods nullifies the preceding one, but Kātyāyana explains that this is so only in some cases.[4]

Court procedure

The decision by *vyavahāra*, or judicial proof, was arrived at after the following procedure.[5] The plaintiff, not necessarily the one who informed the court first, but the one who suffered greatest loss of wealth or bodily injury, was first allowed to put forward the plaint (*pūrva-paksha*). The defendant then answered it (*uttara*).[6] Thereafter both parties submitted evidence to support their stands.[7] Interrogation and deliberation as to burden of proof by the judges followed this (*pratyā-kalita*), and finally judgment was delivered (*kriyā-pāda*). Kātyāyana differentiated between judgment after a complete trial, and judgment before all the stages of

[1] *Kāt.* 31 quoted by Aparārka, p. 616.

[2] *Hist. Dh.* iii, p. 260.

[3] Ibid., p. 261.

[4] *Kāt.* 43 quoted in *Vyavahāra-prakāśa* of Mitra-miśra.

[5] *Kāt.* 31.

[6] Ibid. 158. Reply was of four kinds—admission, denial, a special plea, and a plea of former judgment. A complete definition of Kātyāyana's rule is given in K. V. R. Aiyangar, *Additional Verses*, no. 12.

[7] *Kāt.* 219–44. Evidence was of three kinds: documents, witnesses, and possession, as well as reasoning and ordeals. Kātyāyana says that if the litigant fails by relying on weak grounds he cannot raise the question again on other and stronger grounds: see *res judicata* in *Modern Law*.

the trial had been gone through. This implies that some cases were judged summarily, without going through all the steps of legal procedure.

An interesting feature of the legal system of our period is that the institution of pleaders was just beginning to make its appearance, though they did not at this time enjoy an established status. Asahāya's commentary on the *Nārada-smṛiti*[1] (A.D. 600–750) quotes a case where the judge rebuked a brahman for advocating the cause of a third party in return for a fee. It may be that he was especially reprimanded because he was a brahman, who, according to the ethics of his class, should not accept fees for such services.

Pramātāra

Harsha's Madhu-ban inscription mentions a new administrative office, that of *mahā-pramātāra*, which is not to be found in the Gupta records. This designation, which was also perhaps a title, seems to have been created some time in the sixth or seventh centuries A.D., because it is found elsewhere only in the records of the Maitrakas of Valabhī[2] and in the Baijnath *praśasti* dated *c.* A.D. 800.[3] According to R. S. Tripathi[4] the *pramātri*, or the *pramātāra*, was probably entrusted with justice. U. N. Ghoshal[5] connects the office with the department of land survey, whereas G. Bühler[6] takes it to mean a 'spiritual counsellor' on the basis of etymology.[7]

It seems to us that the function of the *pramātṛi*, or the *pramātāra*, was to interpret the *dharma-śāstras* for the king in court,[8] or to perform the same function as an officer in a law court. If his office was, in addition to being connected with law and *dharma*, also associated with land survey, the *pramātṛi* would, indeed, be a most qualified officer to witness the execution of a religious document, such as the Madhu-ban grant, recovered from a tenant who had been enjoying the property through a forged deed.

Police

Certain titles and designations occurring in the *Harsha-charita* and contemporary inscriptions appear to be meant for police officials. Terms including the word *daṇḍa*, meaning army, fine, rod (of chastisement), authority, etc., are capable of being interpreted as military, judicial, or police designations.[9] While *mahā-daṇḍa-nāyaka* was a military rank or

[1] iv. 5. [2] Grant of Khara-graha II of Valabhī: *I.A.* vii. 76.
[3] *E.I.* i. 102. [4] *History of Kanauj*, p. 140.
[5] *H.C.I.P.* iii, p. 348. [6] *E.I.* i. 118.
[7] Monier Williams describes the *pramātṛi* as 'one who has a correct notion or idea'. A. A. Macdonnell substitutes 'judgement' for 'idea'. Other meanings given by both are 'authority' and 'performer of the mental operation resulting in a true conception'. V. S. Apte, adds 'proof' also to the list of meanings.
[8] One Bhṛiṅgaka was attached as *pramātṛi* to the King of Kashmir: Baijnath Praśasti, *E.I.* i. 102. [9] See *C.I.I.* iii, p. 16 n. 5.

office,[1] the *daṇḍika* (chastiser, punisher) and *daṇḍa-pāśika* (holder of the noose of punishment) of the inscriptions[2] are almost certainly police designations. The *daṇḍīs* (rod-wielders) of the *Harsha-charita*,[3] shown as maintaining order among the crowd anxious to see the king in the military procession, were obviously carrying out police duties. From the literal meaning of his designation the *chaur-oddharaṇika* (one who is entrusted with the extermination of the thieves) too was apparently a police officer. The title appears in the inscriptions of many Gupta-period dynasties of northern India. The same may be said of the *dauḥssādha-sādhanika* (accomplisher of difficult tasks) of Harsha's inscriptions, although R. G. Basak renders the term as 'poster or superintendent of villages'.[4] The ordinary members of the police force were called *chāṭa* and *bhaṭa*. In the *Harsha-charita* the compound *chāra-bhaṭa* is used for soldiers in the vanguard of the infantry.[5] Like the *daṇḍī* and the *vetrī* this is probably another case of junior officers qualified for both civil and military duties.[6] Two terms that accidentally appear in the description of a romance in the *Harsha-charita*, *sañchāraka* and *sarva-gataḥ*,[7] could have been technical designations for couriers in Harsha's period. The former simply means 'messenger' but is also used in an inscription for state servants who seem to have been specifically assigned the task of carrying messages.[8] The latter, literally meaning 'one who could reach anywhere', may have been applied to members of a confidential courier service required to keep the king in touch with the people's condition, conduct, criticisms, views, etc.

Courier service

The army—composition

The army, of course, was another indispensable institution of the state. According to Hsüan-tsang it comprised four wings, the infantry, the cavalry, the chariots, and the elephants.[9] Apparently the Chinese scholar is reproducing the theoretical list, for chariots were out of use even in Gupta times. Bāṇa's detailed description of the royal campus does not make any reference to chariots. When inspecting his army the King is said to have been riding an elephant.[10]

Included boats

Harsha's forces, however, did include boats, a fact that has surprisingly escaped general notice. Both the Baṅskhera and Madhu-ban inscriptions

[1] See above, pp. 173–4.
[2] Deo-Barnark inscription of Jīvita-gupta II: *C.I.I.* iii, no. 46, and Maliya Inscription of Dhara-sena II: op. cit., no. 38.
[3] *H.C.* text, pp. 208 and 212; trans., pp. 204 and 208.
[4] *E.I.* xii. 43, 141.
[5] *H.C.* text, pp. 205, 207.
[6] Also see below, pp. 191–2.
[7] *H.C.* text, p. 35; trans., p. 27.
[8] '*Sarvā-dhyaksha vallabha śāsana saṅchariṇaḥ*': *E.I.* viii. 162.
[9] Beal i, p. 82.
[10] *H.C.* text, p. 207; trans., p. 203.

open with a reference to the 'great camp of victory [containing] boats, elephants and horses'.[1]

In days when there was nothing faster than the horse as means of communication, rivers played a very important part as highways, arteries of commerce, and strategic bulwarks. The Ganga that flowed across the heart of Harsha's empire was extensively used for all these purposes, as is apparent from the many references to private and state vessels. In addition, consequent upon the extension of Harsha's authority over Valabhī and parts of Orissa, the state's trade and military departments might have owned or held rights over ocean-going ships.

Recruitment, war- and peacetime duties

Hsüan-tsang is our informant on the method of military recruitment. In his general account of India he states: 'the men of valour are selected to be warriors. The profession is hereditary so that they have been able to exhaust the art of war. When they are garrisoned they guard the palaces, when there is war they act as a brave vanguard.'[2] Elsewhere he notes, 'for stationing in faraway places and expeditions, and guard duties round the palace [variant, camp] only so many men are recruited as are necessary for work. After proclamation of the reward the pay is there to await the men.'[3]

It is apparent that the general practice was to maintain a large standing army. It rendered multiple services during both peace and war. The sentinel at the palace, the royal stables' officer, the member of an armed guard keeping watch over a frontier post, the mace-bearer clearing the way for the king's mount in the military procession, the soldier on horse, foot, or elephant, all were members of the royal army. Allotment of specific duties during peacetime would have served to mitigate the psychopathic desire to indulge in war, which generally overcomes a standing militia. In addition to soldiers who were recruited to expand the forces in event of war, the feudatories were expected to rally to their suzerain's help with their own armies. There was no conscription. The appropriate number of men were invited to join the army by promise of a reward or a certain salary.[4] After the expedition some of the troops may

[1] *E.I.* i. 72; iv. 210.

[2] *Hsi Yü Chi* text, ii. 7b: cf. Beal i, p. 82; Watters i, p. 171.

[3] *Hsi Yü Chi* text, ii. 10a: cf. Beal i, pp. 87–8; Watters i, pp. 176–7.

[4] *Hsi Yü Chi* text, ii. 10a: Hsüan-tsang's statement, 'after the proclamation of the reward the pay is there to await the man' may be interpreted in two ways: (*a*) The act of enlistment itself was rewarded; (*b*) soldiers were recruited for a salary which was announced at the outset. The second meaning is more likely because the following sentence in the text refers to payments in kind to some other government employees. We find Beal's (i, pp. 87–8) and Watters's (i, pp. 176–7) translations of the passage unsatisfactory.

have been disbanded. They would, presumably, return to family professions. On the whole, however, the size of Harsha's army appears to have steadily increased with the passage of time.

Hsüan-tsang's statement about the military profession being hereditary is, we think, a reference to the traditional association with war of the *kshatriyas*, who may have provided a good number of soldiers. Indeed, many non-*kshatriyas* after an appreciably long association with the profession, may have come to be classed as *kshatriyas*.

Size of the army

The need for mobilizing the army arose immediately on Harsha's accession to the throne of Sthāṇv-īśvara. In the words of Hsüan-tsang, he declared to his assembled ministers: 'I have not yet avenged my brother and the neighbouring countries are not yet brought to submission; while this is so my right hand shall never lift food to my mouth.' He then ordered that all the soldiers of the kingdom be assembled and drilled in readiness for a military campaign. With '5,000 elephant soldiers, 20,000 cavalry, and 50,000 foot soldiers' he subdued the five Indias in six years. 'Having thus enlarged his territory, he increased his forces; he had 60,000 elephant soldiers and 100,000 cavalry.[1] Close on thirty years his arms reposed . . . .'[2]

Elephant corps

An incidental simile by Bāṇa refers to the several-*āyuta*-strong elephant corps of Harsha.[3] As an *āyuta* is equal to 10,000, Hsüan-tsang's figure of 60,000 may not be too far from the truth.

Harsha's huge army was in keeping with the ancient custom, which to some extent was determined by the method of warfare. While a chariot in Maurya days carried, including the driver, three men, an elephant carried four,[4] all of whom did not do the actual fighting.

The twelvefold increase in the elephant corps points to the importance of the beast for military purposes in the seventh century. As

[1] The infantry is not mentioned again, probably because it remained the same in size.

[2] *Hsi Yü Chi* text, v. 4b. Our phrase 'close on' is a literal translation of the original. Beal (i, p. 213) conveys the sense when he interprets it 'after thirty years his arms reposed'. But Watters (i, p. 343) is incorrect when he renders: '[Harsha] reigned in peace for thirty years without raising a weapon.' Other contemporary evidence also tells us that Harsha's military activity continued practically throughout his reign.

[3] *H.C.* text, p. 76; trans., p. 63.

[4] Strabo, xv. 52; Aelian, xiii. 10; Pliny, vi. 19; and Plutarch, *Alex.*, Ch. 62, record the strength of the Nanda and Maurya armies. Mahā-padma Nanda had a force of 80,000 horse, 200,000 foot, 8,000 chariots, and 6,000 elephants. Chaudra-gupta Maurya raised the numbers of the infantry to 600,000 and of elephants to 9,000 but reduced the cavalry to 30,000. The Portuguese chronicler Núñez states that Kṛishṇa Deva Rāya of Vijaya-nagara led against Raichur an army of 703,000 infantry, 32,600 cavalry, and 551 elephants, besides camp-followers (R. Sewell, *A Forgotten Empire*, p. 147). The powerful Āndhra kingdom, however, maintained only a small army of 100,000 infantry, 2,000 cavalry, and 1,000 elephants (Pliny, vi. 19).

V. S. Agrawala points out,[1] it was a natural reaction to the earlier Gupta emphasis on cavalry. The Śakas' partiality for the horse may have influenced the Guptas. Kāli-dāsa's works testify to the strong cavalry force of the latter. The various smaller kingdoms that arose on the ruins of the Guptas searched for new effective methods of warfare in their bid for supremacy. The numerous lesser kings probably took to fortifying their territories, which could be overpowered only by storming the fortresses for which elephants would be suitable rather than horses. Bāṇa's metaphorical description of Harsha's favourite elephant Darpa-śāta as 'a moving hill-fort with its high frontal-globes as so many towers', as 'an iron wall indented with thousands of arrows', and as 'Time in his buttings'[2] confirms the above assumption. With high wooden towers[3] securely fastened to their backs the elephants were used as mobile fortresses. From the towers the soldiers would manœuvre their weapons, including nooses of various kinds.[4] The Sassanians too used their elephants in the same way.[5] Prabhākara-vardhana's and Harsha's campaigns were directed against the various contenders for power who had been strengthening their military techniques for some time. Above all, perhaps, the strength of the elephant corps of his most formidable adversary, Pulā-keśin, induced Harsha to make corresponding improvements in his own armed forces before waging a war of aggression which he, however, lost. Hsüan-tsang records that Pula-keśin, relying on the strength of his heroes and elephants, treated his neighbouring countries with contempt.[6] His 'martial heroes who led the van of the army in battle went into conflict intoxicated and their war-elephants were also made drunk before an engagement'. In his general description of Indian armies, the Chinese observer informs us that the elephants' destructive power was increased by covering them with strong armour and attaching sharp spurs to their tusks.[7] Bāṇa's similes for Harsha's special elephant reveal the various uses to which the beast was put in the battlefield. He was '. . . Varuṇa in the noose which he held in his hand . . . Yama's net in entangling his

[1] pp. 38–41 and 127–32.

[2] *H.C.* text, p. 68; trans., p. 55.

[3] Op. cit., text p. 68. '*Uchcha kumbba kūṭ-āṭṭālaka vikaṭaṁ sañchāri giri durgaṁ*'.

[4] Ibid.: '*Hasta pāś-ākrishṭishu yama vāgurāṁ . . . .*'

[5] 'The reserve of the [Sassanian] army was formed of elephants from India, which inspired the Romans with a certain amount of terror. They carried great wooden towers full of soldiers . . .

'The Sassanians knew the use of the ram, the *ballista*, and movable towers for attacking strongholds, and when defending them they used to catch the ram in a slip knot (the *kamand* or lasso) . . .'. Clément Huart, *Ancient Persia and Iranian Civilisation*, trans. M. R. Dobie, pp. 151–2.

[6] Also see Watters ii, p. 239.

[7] *Hsi Yü Chi* text, ii. 7b (Beal i, pp. 82–3; Watters i, p. 171).

enemies . . . Time in his buttings, Rāhu in his grip, Mars in his crooked movements, a circling torch in his rapid rounds.'[1] The elephants, apparently, were trained to create havoc in the adversary's camp by ramming, crushing soldiers in their trunks, and calculatingly going amok.

It seems that Harsha employed all possible means to acquire elephants. They arrived as presents, as revenue, as booty, as fines, as fee for a first audience, as essential gifts with each embassy, as circus beasts, as new acquisitions from the forests, and in special consignments from officers of elephant reserves and the Vindhyan *śabara* settlements.[2]

The list of officers employed in the elephant stables is a long one and is yet another indication of the importance attached to the elephant corps in Harsha's time. The chief *mahouts* were known as *mahāmātras*[3] and are depicted as training the elephants in various manœuvres by displaying stuffed leathern dummies. Elephants used only for riding were trained to walk in different ways, their instructors being known as *ādhoraṇas*.[4] Servants called *karpaṭī*[5] and *leśika*[6] supplied the beasts with fodder. The old elephants, of little use for other purposes, were especially adorned to add to the gaiety of processions. Their *mahouts* were simply called *ārohas* or riders.[7] The *nishādins* exercised the animals. Elephant-doctors were styled *ibha-bhishag-vara*,[8] the end of the compound being indicative of their honoured position. Certain officers of the elephant corps were called *pīlū-pati* or elephant-masters. Their seniors were known as *mahā-pīlūpati*. Corresponding officers in the cavalry were *aśva-pati* and *mahāśva-pati*.

Cavalry Harsha's cavalry received careful attention. Pedigree horses were imported from Vanāyu (Vaziristan), Āraṭṭa (Vāhīka or Panjab), Kaṁboja (Pamir region), Bhāradvāja (northern Gaḍhwāl), Sindhu-deśa (Sindh *Doab*), and Pārasīka (Sassanian Iran). Bāṇa mentions horses of six different colours in the King's stables. The *taṅgaṇa* type, famous for their smooth and steady gait,[9] are believed to have been obtained from

[1] *H.C.* text, p. 68; trans., p. 55.

[2] Information collated from *H.C.* text, pp. 58, 196, and 231–3. The terms *palli-parivṛiḍha*, *araṇya-pāla*, and *aṭavī pāla* are apparently all synonyms for the Vindhyan forest officers.

[3] *H.C.* text, p. 196, trans., p. 190. The modern *mahāvat* or *mahout* are apparently derived from *mahāmātra*. In the days of the Mauryas, the *mahāmātras* were important officers of high rank serving in executive, judicial, and military posts. It is surprising that the term came to be applied to elephant-keepers in Harsha's time. We do not find the *mahāmātras* serving in any other capacity. The 'Life' (p. 189) describes Hsüan-tsang's official escorts as *mo-ho-ta-lo* or *mahattaras*.

[4] *H.C.* text, p. 196.

[5] Op. cit., pp. 52, 196, and 213.

[6] Op. cit., pp. 65 and 211.

[7] Op. cit., p. 67.

[8] Op. cit., p. 196.

[9] *H.C.* text, p. 206; trans., p. 201.

northern Gaḍhwāl.[1] Agrawala identifies their riders, the *khakkhaṭas*, with an ancient tribe of the central Panjab.[2] Horses of especially good breeds are referred to in adjectives pertaining to their build, habits, and special distinguishing features, exhibiting a good knowledge of the old-established veterinary science.[3] A pedigree horse is described in detail. Referred to several times as the King's 'loved ones' (*vallabha*), Harsha's favourite horses, like the elephants, were kept in an inner part of the camp while the more ordinary types had stables outside. Some of the stable officials were known as *sthāna-pāla*[4] and *vallabha-pāla*. Bāṇa refers to them in the account of Harsha's military procession; the commentator describes them as *aśva-pāla* or grooms.[5] Men with the designation *patti* are shown as leading the King's favourite horses in the procession.[6]

The *kramelaka-kulaiḥ*,[7] or herds of camels, translated by Cowell and Thomas as 'troops of camels',[8] are taken by R. S. Tripathi as a possible reference to a fighting wing of the army,[9] but a later mention makes it clear that the animals were used as beasts of burden like oxen and asses.[10]

Infantry

A description of the infantry is given in Hsüan-tsang's general account of India.

> They are light and fierce, only the brave are selected for it. They bear a big shield and hold a long spear. Sometimes they carry sabres and swords and dash to the front of the formation. All the weapons are very sharp and pointed. They are expert in the use of spears, shields, bows, arrows, sabres, swords, battle axes, lances, halberds, long javelins, and various kinds of slings, having been drilled in them for generations.[11]

The footmen in the van of Harsha's army, called *chāra-bhaṭa*,[12] coated

[1] Parashuram K. Gode, 'Taṅgaṇa horses . . . in *Harsha-charita*', *Proceedings of the Indian History Congress*, Eighth Session, p. 66.

[2] V. S. Agrawala, p. 146.

[3] *H.C.* text, p. 62; trans., p. 50.

[4] The modern *thān* for cowshed probably derives from *sthāna*.

[5] *H.C.* text, p. 205 commentary. V. S. Agrawala, however, describes the *sthāna-pālas* as officers in charge of fortresses or posts of some kind.

[6] *H.C.* text, p. 205; trans., p. 200.

[7] *H.C.* text, p. 58.

[8] *H.C.* trans., p. 46.

[9] *History of Kanauj*, p. 131 n. 1.

[10] *H.C.* text, p. 210; trans., p. 206.

[11] *Hsi Yü Chi* text, ii. 8a; cf. Watters i, p. 171; Beal i, p. 83.

[12] The *chāra-bhaṭas* of the *Harsha-charita* are no doubt the same as the *chāṭa-bhaṭa* or *bhaṭa-chāṭa* of the inscriptions, including those of Harsha. It appears, however, that the term was used variously in different regions and at different times. In his translations of Harsha's inscriptions Bühler renders *bhaṭa-chāṭa* as 'regular and irregular' soldiers. Fleet follows Bühler's interpretation. He also demonstrates that *chāṭa* is not governed by *bhaṭa* (*C.I.I.* iii, p. 98 n. 2). In other contexts and with regard to different inscriptions the term has been translated as 'soldiers against robbers' or members of the police (Bhagwanlal Indraji, *I.A.* ix. 175 n. 41); *chāṭa* has been rendered as 'head of the *parganā* responsible for the internal management of the district for the collection of

their bodies with thick unguents,[1] either for adornment, or to render the grip difficult in hand-to-hand combat, or as protection against infection and injury. They also carried round leathern shields.[2]

The *daṇḍa-dharas* or staff-bearers are shown 'heralding [the King's] appearance and clearing the way'.[3] Officers with a similar designation and function, the *vetra-grāhis*, carrying light sticks or canes, tried to keep the sightseers, complainants, and favour-seekers from besieging the King when on the march.[4] The *vetrīs* are also represented as guarding the entrance to the inner apartments in the royal palace. Apparently these officers carried out police and bodyguard duties during both peace and war, but, unless their roles were later altered, they do not seem to have taken part in the actual fighting. Hsüan-tsang's soldiers who 'when in garrison guarded the palace but in war acted as a brave vanguard',[5] may have been selected from amongst the *chāra-bhaṭas*.

Army officers

A few military designations appear in Bāṇa's account of Harsha's army, and the existence of others may be inferred from the frequency of their mention in contemporary or near-contemporary inscriptions. To the latter category belongs *mahā-daṇḍa-nāyaka*.[6] The existence of the *mahā-bal-ādhikṛita* may be assumed from the mention of *bal-ādhikṛita* in the *Harsha-charita*.[7] Sometimes only a technical title,[8] it is quite clearly an office, not a rank, in Bāṇa's description. V. S. Agrawala suggests that the *bal-ādhyaksha*, the same as the *bal-ādhikṛita*, was in charge of a *vāhinī*, comparable to a modern battalion.[9]

In the *Harsha-charita* the *bal-ādhikṛita* is depicted as giving orders to the *pāṭī-pati*.[10] The latter is an obscure compound and the comparatively long explanation in the commentary does little to make the meaning clear.[11] Cowell and Thomas, basing their interpretation on this, give

revenue and the apprehension of criminals' and *bhaṭa* as his official subordinate (J. P. Vogel, *Antiquities of the Chamba State*, pt. i, pp. 131–2), and both as 'ordinary members of the police force' (A. S. Altekar, *N.H.I.P.* vi, p. 277).

[1] *H.C.* text, p. 205; trans., p. 200.

[2] Ibid., text, p. 207; trans., p. 203. Another interesting reference to the use of leather occurs in the 'Life' (p. 189), where it is stated that Hsüan-tsang accepted from the King of Assam a useful travelling-garment, 'a cape called *ho-la-li*, made of coarse skin lined with soft down'.

[3] *H.C.* text, p. 208; trans., p. 204.

[4] *H.C.* text, p. 212; trans., p. 208.

[5] *Hsi Yü Chi* text, ii. 7b.

[6] See above, pp. 173–4; also *C.I.I.* iii, p. 16 n. 5; *H.C.I.P.* iii, pp. 349 ff.

[7] *H.C.* text, p. 204; trans., p. 199.

[8] See Fleet, *C.I.I.* iii, p. 109.

[9] p. 143, n. 3.

[10] *H.C.* text, p. 204.

[11] Ibid., commentary: '*pāṭī bahu-parivāra-purusha-gṛihīto nivāsa-bhūbhāgaḥ, kulaputraka-samūha ityanye. Peṭakaṁ tatsamūhaḥ, "pāṭhipati" iti pāṭhe pāṭhipatayaḥ prati-niyata-svasthāna-pari-rakshiṇaḥ.*' This suggests that the *pāṭī* or *pāṭhī-patis* were either persons commanding the bands of élite troops or deputed to guard forts or other establishments of the king and his nobles.

perhaps the most satisfactory rendering by translating *pāṭī-pati* as 'barrack superintendents'.[1]

The title *senā-pati*, or chief of the army, for Siṁha-nāda, is almost certainly used as a sinecure for a veteran soldier,[2] but it proves the existence of the office. There must, moreover, have been *mahā-senā-patis* as in the Gupta days, who were in charge of a number of *senā patis*. The King was the supreme head of all the armed forces.

The army's informal character

The army was made bulky by the presence of the King's and the feudatories' harems.[3] Nor were the pleasures of the palate neglected. In the army procession were 'bearers of kitchen appurtenances with goats attached to thongs of pig-skin, a tangle of hanging sparrows and fore-quarters of venison, a collection of young rabbits, potherbs, and bamboo shoots, buttermilk pots protected by wet seals . . . baskets containing a chaos of fire-trays, ovens, simmering pans, spits, copper saucepans, and frying-pans'.[4]

Indeed, an army march, at least in its early stages, far from being a spectacle of efficiency charged with tension, was characterized by ease and interest in the normal affairs of life. The frequency of such undertakings perhaps necessitated that they be treated in this manner. This together with humanizing factors such as the presence of women, and the use, not of machines, but of emotion-betraying animals as mounts and beasts of burden would have prevented the soldiers from going through a metamorphosis of personality in wartime.

The behaviour of the members of the retinue, although just at the time of departure, reflects perhaps the general atmosphere of the camp. Bāṇa records the 'multitudinous babble' that went on among the crowd.

> Friend, you hobble like a lame man, while the vanguard here is coming furiously upon us. Why are you hurrying the camel? Don't you see, you pitiless brute, the child lying there? Rāmila, darling, take care not to get lost in the dust! Don't you see the barley-meal sack leaks? What's the hurry, Go-ahead? Ox, you are leaving the track and running among the horses. Are you coming, fishwife? You female elephant, you want to go among the males.

Pace of travelling

The army travelled approximately nine miles a day, because we are told the the beginning of Harsha's march was announced by beating the drum as many times, eight in this case, as the number of *krośas* expected to be covered.[5] Following Manu, Śukra considers 2,000 yards

[1] Ibid., trans., p. 199. [2] Ibid., text, pp. 188 and 190; trans., p. 180.

[3] See Ibid., text, p. 205; trans., p. 200: 'The carriages of the high-born nobles' wives were . . .'; also ibid., text, p. 206, trans., p. 201: *aṅtaḥpura kariṇī* = seraglio elephants.

[4] Ibid., text, p. 211; trans., p. 208. [5] Ibid., text, p. 203; trans., p. 199.

as the length of a *krośa*.[1] On the authority of Kauṭilya, Harsha's army, from the point of view of the mileage covered by it, would be considered slightly below the army of the best quality, which was supposed to cover two *yojanas*, or just over ten miles a day.[2]

Units of administration —the *désa*

The empire was organized into convenient divisions for administrative purposes. It seems that in Gupta times the largest territorial units such as Surāshṭra and Mālava were called *deśa*.[3]

It was probably the territory directly administered by Harsha which is stated by Hsüan-tsang to have comprised the 'five Gauḍas' or 'five Indias' associated with Sārasvata (eastern Panjab), Kānya-kubja (Kanauj), Gauḍa (western Bengal), Mithilā (northern Bihar), and Utkala (northern Orissa).[4] But there is no reason to suppose that the divisions had any administrative basis.

Hsüan-tsang's seventy 'countries' of varying sizes measured in circuits

Hsüan-tsang states that India comprised seventy 'countries',[5] which is approximately the number he lists within Indian boundaries. He records the extent of each in terms of its perimeter, only rarely giving the distance from east to west and north to south, which makes it impossible to calculate with any exactness the area of the unit. The figures vary from 1,000 *li* (200 miles) in circuit for Lamghan and Koṅgoḍa, to 10,000 for Ṭakka and Kāma-rūpa, which gives some idea of the wide range of sizes involved. It is also interesting to note that the tiny 'country' of Chīnā-pati in the Panjab, with a circuit of 2,000 *li*, lay between the mighty Ṭakka and Jālandhara, the latter 1,000 *li* from east to west and 800 from north to south. In the same way Koṅgoḍa had neighbouring states the circuits of which were seven times (Uḍra) and five times (Kaliṅga) its own. While the powerful kingdoms may have approved of the smaller ones for their 'buffer' value, they may also have been led to respect the latter's territorial integrity for reasons of their military power, strong allies, dynastic prestige, or the recognized rules of war and peace.

[1] *Śukra*. 1–194.

[2] *Artha*. x. 2.

[3] Skanda Gupta's Junāgaḍh inscription (A.D. 456): *C.I.I.* iii, p. 59, lines 6 and 8—'*sarvveshu deśeshu vidhāya goptṛin*' and '*yo me praśishyān nikhilān Surāshṭrān*'. It should be remembered, however, that at different times and in different regions the term *deśa* was used indiscriminately for large provinces or small districts. Yaśo-dharman's Mandsor inscription of A.D. 533–4 (*C.I.I.* iii, p. 152) records that a *rāja-sthānīya* (viceroy) was assisted in the administration of his many *deśas* (districts) by his own *sachivas* (ministers). The grants of Amma II of A.D. 945–6 (*I.A.* vii. 16; viii. 74) describe the kingdom of the eastern Chālukyas as *Veṅgi-deśa*. Elsewhere (*I.A.* viii. 79; xiii. 213) the same territory is called *maṇḍala*.

[4] See above, pp. 83–5.

[5] Beal i, p. 70.

The measurements given by Hsüan-tsang offer little or no indication of area,[1] but as he considers the territorial units worthy of being described as countries and divides the whole subcontinent into seventy of them they may have ranged in size from the *vishaya* to the *deśa*, the intervening division being the *bhukti*. Writing about the Gupta period A. S. Altekar[2] compares the *vishaya* and the *bhukti* in size respectively with the modern district and Commissioner's Division.[3]

The *bhukti*, *vishaya*, *paṭhaka*, and *grāma*

Harsha's Bañskhera inscription mentions four territorial units. It records the grant of a *grāma*, a village situated in the western *paṭhaka* of a *vishaya* that lay in the *bhukti* of Ahichchhatrā (Ram-nagar, U.P.). The Madhu-ban copperplate speaks of the *grāma*, *vishaya*, and *bhukti*, but omits the *paṭhaka*. The latter term is not mentioned in the Gupta records but occurs in an eighth-century Maitraka inscription from Valabhī,[4] and in the form *peṭha* in the sixth-century Khoh inscription from central India.[5]

The *deśa* and its governor

While there is no evidence to show that Harsha divided his kingdom into *deśas*, it is not improbable that some provinces of his empire may have been administered much in the same way as the Gupta *deśa*. Magadha, associated after Harsha's death with the Later Guptas, may well have been one such territory governed at Harsha's behest by his dependent, the Later Gupta prince Mādhava-gupta.

The Gupta records inform us that *deśas* were administered by governors appointed by the king. Their rights and responsibilities were considerable, and they must have been the king's trusted officers. Their designation may have been *rāja-sthānīya*, meaning the king's representative,[6] and they probably enjoyed the title *kumār-āmātya*.[7] Although the sequence is of little value in solving the problem of titles and their relative importance, it may be mentioned that in Harsha's grants the *rāja-sthānīya* is placed before *kumār-āmātya* and *uparika*, and after *mahā-pramātāra*. There was really little discrimination in the use of designations and titles. For example, if an *uparika* considered himself powerful enough, he styled himself *uparika-mahārāja*, as in some

[1] A territory with a circuit of 1,000 *li* or 200 miles, even if it were a regular figure might have, depending on its length and breadth, an area of $199 \times 1 = 199$ sq. miles (if oblong), to 2,500 sq. miles (if square), to approximately 3,218 sq. miles (if circular).

[2] *N.H.I.P.* vi, p. 283.

[3] A district has an average area of 4,430 sq. miles. A Commissioner's Division consists of four to six districts. See *Imperial Gazetteer of India*, iv, pp. 48–9.

[4] *C.I.I.* iii, no. 39.

[5] Ibid., no. 31.

[6] Kshmendra's *Loka-prakāśa*, Ch. iv, describes a *rāja-sthānīya* as 'he who carries out the object of protecting subjects and shelters them'.

[7] See above, pp. 174–6.

west-Bengal grants of the fifth and sixth centuries A.D,[1] or a strong and deserving governor of a *bhukti* might be given the designation *rāja-sthānīya* by the king. If prince of royal blood, the *rāja-sthānīya* might style himself *mahārāja-putra deva-bhaṭṭāraka*. The provincial governors had a free hand in internal administration and guarded the king's interest in relation to any neutral neighbours. Probably all the departments of the centre had their replicas in the provinces.

The Junāgaḍh rock inscription of Skanda-Gupta,[2] despite its formal panegyric, succeeds in giving us a fairly clear picture of the provincial administration of the Guptas which served as the model for later kings. It records the repairing of an embankment by Chakra-pālita, the able and popular governor of Surāshṭra, who carried out his multifarious duties in the following manner:

> He caused distress to no man in the city, but he chastised the wicked.
> Even in this mean age he did not fail the trust of the people.
> He cherished the citizens as his own children and he put down crime.
> He delighted the inhabitants with gifts and honours, and smiling conversation, and he increased their love with informal visits and friendly receptions.[3]

The *bukhti* and its governor

The *bhuktis* were governed by *uparikas*, who again were appointed by and responsible to the emperor himself. They figure in both the Baṅskhera and the Madhu-ban grants of Harsha. As is apparent from other inscriptions the governors of *bhuktis* were also designated *bhogika*, *bhoga-pati*, *gopta*, *uparika-mahārāja*, and also *rāja-sthānīya*.[4] Some of these terms point to the fiscal duties of the governor of a *bhukti*. The heads of districts, or *vishayas*, were known as *vishaya-patis*, and under the Guptas were mostly appointed not by the centre but by the governor of the *bhukti*. Such a system relieved the pressure of work on the centre and provided provincial governors with initiative. Delegated by a strong king, power and responsibility would engender confidence and satisfaction in his officers, under a weak king, however, the policy might lead to undesirable results. The Gupta practice was probably continued by Harsha, although as his empire was smaller he might sometimes have made such appointments himself. Often the *vishaya-pati* had the status of *mahārāja*, *kumār-āmātya*, or *āyuktaka*,[5] possibly conferred upon him

The *vishaya* or district and its officers

[1] *E.I.* xv. 130 ff. This tendency appears from the time of Budha Gupta. Under Kumāra Gupta I the title was simply *uparika*.

[2] *C.I.I.* iii, no. 14.

[3] A. L. Basham's rendering of the relevant verses in *The Wonder that was India*, p. 104.

[4] *C.I.I.* iii, no. 14; *E.I.* xv, no. 7. The Dāmodar-pur copperplates.

[5] Copperplate grant of Budha Gupta: *E.I.* xv. 138.

by the monarch himself. This is significant as the bestowal of titles of honour on the *vishaya-pati* by the king established direct contact between them, without prejudicing the authority of the governor of the *bhukti* who appointed the former.

The *vishaya-pati* had his office, called *adhikaraṇa*, in the chief town of the district, which was called *adhishṭhāna*.[1] In this office must have been preserved the regional *nīla-piṭa*, Hsüan-tsang's 'official documents containing good and bad, public calamity and good fortune'. The person in charge of the official registers was called *pusta-pāla*, literally the book-keeper, who listed the precise dimensions of land, both cultivated and uncultivated. Details of the state wastelands were also recorded, for we learn that the district authorities had to be consulted in the event of a change of ownership.

A class of officers called the *aksha-paṭalika* seems to have been responsible for the legal aspect of land transactions. There were *aksha-paṭalas* of district as well as village status. Etymologically the term may be associated with matters of law. The *Amara-kosha* declares *aksha-darśaka* to be a synonym of *prāḍ-vivāka*, a legal officer.[2] The *aksha-paṭala* is known to us as the superintendent of accounts in the records and audit office. The list of his duties is very exhaustive in both scope and detail. As may be expected, the subject of land transactions is one of them. In time his duties may have become more specialized. The nature of his work, however, would always involve the *aksha-darśaka* in several departments. The spurious Gayā plate of Samudra Gupta mentions that the land deed was drawn up by the order of an *aksha-paṭal-ādhikṛita*.[3] Similarly Harsha's Baṅskhera grant was 'inscribed at the command of the *mahāksha-paṭal-ādhikaraṇ-ādhikṛita* Bhānu'.[4] Several *aksha-paṭalikas* in the states and districts and *gram-āksha-paṭalikas* in the villages kept local records, and acted as liaison officers with the centre.

The district council

That the district administration had a representative character is demonstrated by several copperplate inscriptions of the Gupta period.[5] We learn that the district officers worked in cooperation with the *adhishṭhān-ādhikaraṇa* (municipal board) or with the *vishay-ādhikaraṇa* (district office). The municipal board had a popular character. It consisted of about twenty members called the *vishaya-mahattaras*.[6] The

[1] Dāmodar-pur copperplates: *E.I.* xv. 130 ff.; xvii. 193 ff.

[2] *Amara*. 2, 8, 5. Also see above pp. 181–3.

[3] *C.I.I.* iii, no. 60, p. 257.

[4] *E.I.* iv. 211.

[5] *E.I.* xv. 113 ff., xvii. 193 ff., Dāmodar-pur copperplates; *I.A.* xxxix. 195 ff. Faridpur plate III.

[6] We also read of *rāshṭra-mahattaras* in Śankara-gaṇa's inscription. An interesting reference in the 'Life' (p. 189) to the designation *mahattara* indicates that they acted

most prominent (*puroga*) among them were the chief banker (*nagara-śreshṭhin*), the chief trader (*sārtha-vāha*), the chief artisan (*prathama kulika*), and the chief scribe (*prathama-kāyastha*). Judging from the word *prathama*, 'the first', affixed to their designations, the latter two seem to have been the heads of their guilds. From the occupations of the important members of the council it may be surmised that urban interests got precedence over rural. No doubt the remaining members of the council represented the other aspects of district life and may have been quite unconnected with any guilds.

The district law court

The districts had their own law courts. The seals of the office of *nyāy-ādhikaraṇa*, *dharm-ādhikaraṇa*, and *dharma-śāsan-ādhikaraṇa* found at Nālandā and Vaiśālī[1] may have been issued from the courts of justice which existed at these places. There were certain other kinds of courts as well. The guild system being so developed, the traders had their own courts where disputes among members were settled. Bṛihaspati[2] advises the king to let certain classes of people be tried according to the rules of their own professions. Among these are mentioned cultivators, artisans, money-lenders, dancers, and followers of certain religious sects. Courts were conducted in forests for the semi-nomadic foresters, in camp for warriors, in caravans for merchants. According to Bṛihaspati,[3] '[Meetings of] kindred companies [of artisans], assemblies, [of cohabitants, i.e. people living in the same place], and chief judges are declared to be resorts for the passing of a sentence', the importance of the authority of these courts being in the ascending order. The right of appeal to higher courts existed: 'Judges are superior in authority to meetings of the kindred and the others; the chief judge is placed above them, and the king is superior to all.'[4]

Grāma or village

The smallest unit of administration was the village, *grāma*. As today, villages varied widely in size. Both a cluster of a dozen households and a dozen of such clusters may be called *grāma*. Various inscriptions of the Gupta period indicate that the jurisdiction of the village authorities extended over houses, streets, markets, cremation grounds, temples, wells, tanks, wastelands, forests, and cultivable lands. Land was measured by *sīmā-karas*. The village boundaries were demarcated by walls and ditches, which also offered protection against intruders.[5] Agriculture

as official escorts for Hsüan-tsang on his return journey. Harsha had furnished them with despatches for the rulers of the various countries through which they passed so that the party might be provided with travelling facilities, 'even to the border of China'.

[1] *M.A.S.I.*, no. 66, 52–3; *A.S.I.A.R.*, 1913–14, p. 128; and *E.I.* xi. 107.

[2] *Bṛ.* i. 25–6.

[3] Ibid. i. 29.

[4] Ibid. i. 31.

[5] *E.I.* xix. 130.

was the main occupation. Cattle rearing, weaving, pottery, carpentry, working in metals, and such other employment as was supplied by the natural resources of the village provided the inhabitants with other means of livelihood.

The village headman, known as *grāmeyaka* or *grāma-ādhyaksha*, was in charge of village administration. We do not know how he was appointed. Beni Prasad's view that 'Probably, heredity, informal village opinion and government approval were jointly responsible for his selection'[1] seems to be correct. The headman was assisted in his work by various officials, of whom two categories are mentioned in the *Harsha-charita*.[2] At the first camp in the course of his march, Harsha is said to have been approached by a *grām-āksha-paṭalika* accompanied by his staff of *karaṇis*, clerks, for the King to place a seal on a land grant with his own hand. A specimen of such a document is fortunately available to us in Harsha's Sonpat seal.[3] The *Harsha-charita* also mentions *mahattaras*.[4] It is clear from Gupta period records that they were the village elders, who formed an unofficial council to help the headman in duties of administration. The *ashṭa-kul-ādhikaraṇa* shown as working in collaboration with the *grāmika* (headman), *kuṭumbins* (householders), etc., in the northern Bengal inscriptions of the Gupta period was probably composed of the *grāma-mahattaras*. This rural board was the village counterpart of the *vishaya adhishṭhāna-adhikaraṇa* or the district municipal board. In central India the unofficial council of the village headmen was called, in Gupta times *pañcha-maṇḍalī*, in Bihar the *grāma-jana-pada*. A large number of seals of the village *jana-padas*, used for stamping official documents, have been found at Nālandā belonging to the Later Gupta period.[5] The elders were probably selected by common consent on the basis of their age, ability, integrity, wealth, etc. The village government looked after all local matters concerning houses, streets, markets, temples, wells, tanks, cremation grounds, cattle, pasturages, forests, arable and unarable lands. There were popular *panchayat* courts which with the help of village elders tried all the civil and petty criminal cases. The right of appeal to higher courts was permitted.

The economy and administration of a forest settlement

If Bāṇa's versatile pen had chosen to write about any ordinary village instead of a forest settlement we should have possessed a very realistic picture of life in this basic unit of administration. Instead we get from

1 *The State in Ancient India*, p. 297.
2 *H.C.* text, p. 203; trans., p. 198.
3 *C.I.I.* iii, no. 52.
4 *H.C.* text, p. 212; trans., p. 208.
5 *M.A.S.I.*, no. 66, 45–9.

him a vivid description of a community that lived in a remote area with few of the benefits that accrue from the usual appurtenances of civilization. The Śabara habitation portrayed in the *Harsha-charita*[1] was situated in the Vindhya region. Its inhabitants lived both by hunting and by farming. Their wealth of flora and fauna as well as cultivated products provided the villagers and neighbouring inhabitants with various occupations. Timber was one of the principal means of livelihood. It was regularly collected from the forest and sold in towns. Flax, hemp, wax, honey, *lāmajjaka* (a kind of reed), peacock feathers, and several other cultivated and natural products were also a source of income. A variety of fruit- and flower-bearing trees, such as the *aśoka*, *keśara*, mango, and betel-nut, as well as the timber-yielding *deodar*, were grown or flourished wild. Bird-snaring was as popular as beast-hunting, and intricate traps and nooses were used for the purpose. At least two varieties of rice—the *shashṭika*, so called because it ripened in sixty days,[2] and the *nala*—were cultivated. Cotton was obtained from the pods of the *seemul* tree even as today, and sugar-cane plantations were common. Among artisans, the blacksmith is mentioned.

Thick vegetation and earth 'as stiff as black iron' made farming a strenuous occupation, and peasants laboured hard with spades to carve out small fields. The apportionment of rice-patches and threshing-ground was done in raised voices.[3] Reclaimed land was treated with manure and was ploughed by oxen.

As was common practice, there were in the forest settlement wayside amenities for travellers' rest and refreshment. In every direction at the entrance to the woods were drinking-arbours which supplied the tired and the thirsty with cool fragrant water or sweetened beverage. Seasonal easy-growing fruit-trees supplied additional sustenance.

The inhabitants of this forest village are depicted as hard-working, self-sufficient, and well-organized. Their houses were widely spaced. Walls, which were made of bamboo and reed, were decorated with pigment and flowers. Orchards and gardens abounded in decorative as well as useful trees. Fruit, vegetables, dried roots, edible seeds, food-grains, and cotton were stored in large quantities. The surplus after consumption would have been sold or bartered. Wine is referred to and so are pets for pleasure, both birds and animals. Among domestic animals of the more useful type there is mention of fowls and calves.

[1] *H.C.* text, pp. 227–30; trans., pp. 225–9.

[2] See Pāṇini, 5.1.90.

[3] The relevant passage admits of various interpretations. It may also mean that the tillers kept beat with a loud clapper, or, talking noisily, they worked on high ground.

Thieves and wild beasts were the two disturbers of peace. Scaffolds, fences, and sharp-pointed stakes were constructed to keep away the animals. For fear of robbers who hid themselves in the jungle, the wood-cutters avoided wearing decent apparel and went to work in ragged clothes.

Bāṇa makes note of but few officials or dignitaries connected with the forest settlement. He mentions *vana-pāla*, the roving forest guard who watched out for trespassing woodcutters.[1] The *sarva-pallī-patī*, or chief of all the villages, is mentioned, but his duties are not specified. The Śabaras also had some kind of an army led by a *senā-pati*.

Agriculture

The importance of land in contemporary polity cannot be overstated, for although the state treasury was enriched by taxes from various sources the bulk of its income was in the form of land-tax. Consequently the sciences of agriculture and animal husbandry were carefully studied. Apart from references in the Vedic, Buddhist, Jaina, and early Tamil literatures, the *Agni Purāṇa* and the *Vishṇu-dharmottara Mahā-purāṇa* devote regular sections to the subject. The *Charaka* and *Suśruta Saṁhitās* and more especially Varāha-mihira's *Bṛihat Saṁhitā* and the *Kṛishi-saṁgraha* of Parāśara deal with the sciences of agriculture and animal husbandry in a thorough and systematic manner. Many other specialist studies survive, written throughout Indian history. Part of the second book of the *Artha-śāstra* deals not only with agriculture and forestry as applied sciences, their working supervised by state superintendents, but also with the management of land revenue. It contains the greatest detail regarding state supervision of agriculture. We quote from the *Artha-śāstra*, a work very much anterior to our period, because the general principles underlying the particulars are applicable to later times. Often some of the details too occur in later sources.

The superintendent of agriculture or his advisers were expected to have thorough knowledge of the quality of land and of the various kinds of seeds. Forecasts of rain were made by observing the position, motion, and impregnation of Jupiter, from the rise, setting, and movements of Venus, and from modification in the natural appearance of the sun. The sun indicated the successful sprouting of seeds, Jupiter the formation of stalks in crops, and Venus rain. Three types of clouds that rained continuously for seven days, eighty that sent meagre showers, and sixty that were accompanied by sunshine constituted a beneficial pattern.

Rainfall was measured; precise figures are given for dry and moist

[1] *H.C.* text, p. 227; trans., p. 226.

areas in general and for Aśmaka (Panjab) and Avanti (western Madhya Pradesh) in particular. Their proportions to each other are roughly in line with the modern rainfall figures for these areas.[1] Seeds were planted according to the quantity and timing of rainfall, the slant of land, and its position with relation to river, marsh, sea, or mountain.

Agriculture was regulated on a different basis in areas with man-made means of irrigation such as reservoirs and water channels. Land was regularly nourished. The sprouts were fed with a fresh haul of minute fishes and with the milk of the *snuhi* plant (*Euphorbia antiquorum*). Bāṇa refers to wagons of manure in his description of the Vindhyan forest settlement.[2]

The king was advised to encourage production by every means possible. He was to remit taxes or help with grains, cattle, and money, if, ultimately, it swelled the treasury. Co-operative construction works were encouraged, reservoirs were built, facilities were provided for cattle-breeding, plant and cattle diseases were controlled, and protection was provided from dangerous animals, thieves, or official excesses.

Grains and crops were collected as often as they were harvested. Not even chaff was left in the fields. Fields that remained unsown were brought under cultivation by offering special remuneration. Uncultivable tracts were turned into pasture grounds.

Prayer and symbolism too were harnessed in the service of the peasant and the king. 'Salutation to god Prajā-pati Kāśyapa. Agriculture may always flourish and the goddess [may reside] in seeds and wealth.'[3] A handful of seeds were then bathed in water which had a piece of gold immersed in it and scattered in the field.

Land was wealth. When it was state property the king could alienate the earnings from it, donate it completely for charitable purposes, or use

[1] *Artha.* ii. 24. gives 16 *droṇas* for dry land, one and a half times that in wet land, $13\frac{1}{2}$ in the Aśmakas, 23 in the Avantis, and unlimited in the Aparāntas (Konkaṇa) and the snowy regions. R. P. Kangle ii, (p. 171 n. 5) has worked out that, measured by a square-mouthed gauge of 18″ × 18″, 16 *droṇas* would be equal to 25″ of rain. The present-day rainfall figures are under 20″ for lower Panjab and Rajasthan, between 20″ and 40″ for upper Panjab and western Madhya Pradesh, and over 100″ for the Konkan.

Aśmaka has been explained as Mahā-rāshṭra in the commentary *Pratipada-pañchikā* by Bhaṭṭa-svāmin and as Āraṭṭa in the commentary *Śrī-mūla* by T. Ganapati Sastri (*Artha-śāstra*, Trivandrum, 1924–5). It seems that the Aśmakas had two centres, one in the Panjab and one near Pratishṭhāna on the River Godāvarī in Mahārāshṭra. While the majority of our sources connect the Aśmakas with the latter, the *Kūrma Purāṇa* and the *Bṛihat-Sāṁhitā* (Ch. 14) locate them in the Panjab region. Āraṭṭa according to the *Mahā-bhārata* is the land of the five rivers, the Panjab. See *G.D.A.M.I.*, pp. 10, 12–13), Judging by the *Artha-śāstra*'s rainfall figures the *Śrī-mūla* commentary's identification of Aśmaka with Āraṭṭa (Panjab) seems to be correct.

[2] *H.C.* text, p. 229.

[3] *Artha.* ii. 24.

it as a mode of payment or reward.[1] But most importantly, land was the chief recurrent source of the state's income. According to Hsüan-tsang one-sixth of the land produce was the state's share.[2] It was called *bhāga-kara* or *udraṅga*. Harsha's inscriptions recognize both forms.[3]

It was an ancient practice to measure villages for purposes of land-tax in plough measures, i.e. the area that could be turned over with a plough pulled by a given number of oxen. Tax was then fixed on each plough measure. Inscriptions sometimes append numerical adjectives after the names of villages (*Śākambhara sapāda-laksha*). Apparently the numbers denote plough measures in the territory as well as the tax from it in silver *paṇas*.[4] Bāṇa's reference to the area of a village in terms of *sīras*[5] indicates that the land unit was also known by this name among others. The *sīra* of Harsha's time was probably equal to the *kulya-vāpa* of Gupta days. Śankara's commentary on the *Harsha-charita* describes *sīra* as *hala* (plough). The latter term was employed for land units in Andhra in the third century A.D. Manu's commentators state that as much land as could be cultivated by twelve oxen (double of a 'middling plough') was called *kula*.[6] Bāṇa's reference also suggests that an average village measured 1,000 plough units, which according to a late text, the *Śukra-nīti-sāra*, comprised one square *prājā-patya* krośa, 6,250,000 square yards or approximately 1,333 acres.[7]

Land-tax was calculated per plough unit (one and a third acres at one silver *kārshā-paṇa* a month).[8] As a benedictory beginning to his march of conquest Harsha donated to brahmans a hundred villages, each delimited by a thousand ploughs and therefore capable of yielding tax of a thousand silver *paṇas* a month. While we have no figures regarding the income or expenses of the state in Harsha's time, Hsüan-tsang furnishes us with the following information. Writing generally about the country he says that 'royal land' was divided into four categories for meeting the state expenses. It is difficult to say whether Hsüan-tsang means by land the realm generally or the directly government-owned estates. Nor can we be sure if he is referring only to land-tax as the source of income or also to taxes from other sources connected with land. Whatever the case may be the income was expended as follows: 'One for the expenses of the state and ceremonial worship, one for the

1 For views on the king's rights over land, see above, p. 166.
2 Beal i, p. 87; Watters i, p. 176.
3 *E.I.* i. 73, iv. 211.
4 See V. S. Agrawala, pp. 138 and 219.
5 *H.C.* text, p. 203; trans., p. 199.
6 i.e. as much land as sufficed for a family (*kula*): vii. 119.
7 *Śukra.* 1–195.
8 *Śukra.* 1–193.

endowment of ministers, one for rewarding the clever, the learned and the talented, one for acquiring religious merit through sustenance of the heretics.'

A piecing together of fragments of interrelated statements in the *Kauṭilīya*, the *Harsha-charita*, and the *Śukra-nīti-sāra* seems to throw some light on the expenditure on state employees. The Mauryan text records that 'the foreteller, the reader of omens, the astrologer, the reader of Pūraṇas, the storyteller, the bard, the retinue of the priest, and all superintendents of departments' received salaries of 1,000 *paṇas* per month.[1] Harsha gave a village of a thousand ploughs, capable of yielding a similar number of *paṇas* in revenue, to donee brahmans whose status is likely to be similar to the types of professional men mentioned in the *Artha-śāstra*. This leads us to the tentative assumption that at least some of the state employees in Harsha's time were paid salaries similar to those mentioned in detail in the *Artha-śāstra*. It is true that the figures in the *Artha-śāstra* refer to the salaries of government servants while those in the *Harsha-charita* to gifts made to self-employed brahmans. This makes the Mauryan rates appear parsimonious or Harsha's gift extravagant. The gap between the two is narrowed if we consider that Harsha's donation was connected with the very special occasion of the start of a *dig-vijaya* march. The similarity in the vocations of the two sets of recipients also suggests that the state in Mauryan times as well as in Harsha's evaluated their services in a somewhat similar manner.

Hsüan-tsang makes three references to forced labour, or to the lack of it, in one paragraph on Indian administration. That he persistently remarks on it in connection with military service, construction work, and land revenue is probably due to his background, for in China the state made use of it freely, sometimes even forcing the monks to do revenue accounts. With regard to revenue, taxation, and payment for labour in India, he observes:

As the government is tolerant, administrative duties are simple. There is no registration of households, nor is there *corvée* for individuals. Royal land is divided generally into four parts . . . [for defraying various expenses]. For this reason, tax and *corvée* are light, and the people are happy to follow the calling of their forefathers. Those who work as tenant farmers on the royal estate, hold land in proportion to the number of persons in the family, and they pay a tax of one part in six. . . . Official building does not rely on *corvée*, but people are rewarded according to the work they accomplish. For the purpose of manning defences and military expeditions as well as standing guard

[1] *Artha*. v. 3.

on the royal tents [*ch'iung-lu*; or *kung-lu*, palace dwellings] appropriate numbers are invited to join the army, and there is reward waiting to be collected by those who join. . . .[1]

The Indian artisan and the cultivator both paid taxes. The latter contributed his share mostly in the form of land produce but, as Harsha's grants point out, might also be required to provide '[objects of] enjoyment, taxes, gold and so forth, and . . . service'.[2] According to Kauṭilya's *Artha-śāstra*, the dues paid by the country part (*rāshṭra*)[3] comprised taxes raised in the form of one-sixth of the produce, provisions supplied by the people for the army, taxes levied for religious purposes, etc.[4] They may all have been payable at the same time. The unspecified 'taxes' in Harsha's grants probably signify those that were expected in addition to the share of the crops. To make the best use of their specialist skills, however, whole villages might be required to render a specific kind of service or pay a specific kind of tax. The *Artha-śāstra* classifies them as follows: villages exempted from taxation, those that supply soldiers, those that pay their taxes in the form of grain, cattle, gold, or raw material, and those that supply free labour (*vishṭi*) and dairy produce in lieu of taxes.[5] Individual workers, too, of all types, sweepers, watchmen, those who measure grains, slaves, labourers, and so forth, might render *vishṭi*.[6] It was the village accountant's duty to keep record of the exact number of such workers and of the service allotted to each.[7] As the principle of labour in lieu of taxes was recognized, the service required of the cultivator in Harsha's grants may be expected to have been of a well-accepted and reasonable type. An obvious cursory interpretation of such a practice would be the one that Hsüan-tsang presents us with, that forced service was exacted but that it was moderate.

The traditional taxes and fines

Indian sources state that there were eighteen kinds of taxes, of which that on land was the most important, but they do not name the others. A broad term *daś-āparādhaḥ*, or 'ten offences', is used in the context of judicial administration and implies crimes or misdemeanours for which fines were payable.[8] They were classified as follows: three offences of the body: theft, murder, and adultery; four of speech: harsh, untruthful, libellous, and pointless; and three of mind: coveting others property,

[1] *Hsi Yü Chi* text, ii. 10a.
[2] *E.I.* i. 73; iv. 211.
[3] The regions or categories to be taxed were classified under various headings such as country parts (*rāshṭra*), cities or forts (*durga*), forests (*vana*), and so forth. *Artha.* ii. 6.
[4] *Artha.* ii. 15.
[5] Ibid. ii. 35.
[6] Ibid. ii. 15.
[7] Ibid. ii. 35.
[8] Jīvita-gupta II's record mentions donation of proceeds from the ten offences: *C.I.I.* iii, no. 46, p. 213.

thinking of wrong, and devotion to what is not true. It is evident that the term 'ten offences' was more expansive than the needs of judicial administration required. Obviously the offences of the mind could not be punished, while on the other hand murder carried a higher penalty than a fine. Some records of the Gupta period mention taxes on pasturage, hides, charcoal, mines, purchase of fermenting drugs, hidden treasures, deposits, abundance of milk and flowers, and succession of cattle.[1] In view of Hsüan-tsang's statement that taxation was light, Harsha's government probably did not exploit all these sources of income or possibly the Chinese traveller's statement was conditioned by his own national background. He does, however, inform us that 'merchants paid a light tax at ferries and barrier stations'.[2] The collectors of *octroi* duties were probably called *drāṅgikas*.[3]

[1] The Poona plates of the Vākāṭaka queen Prabhā-vatī-guptā: *E.I.* xv, no. 4.
[2] *Hsi Yü Chi* text, ii. 10a; cf. Beal i, p. 87; Watters i, p. 176.
[3] The Maitraka grants mention *drāṅgikas*, see *C.I.I.* iii. p. 165, and *E.I.* xii. 339; also *N.H.I.P.* vi. p. 279.

VII

THE INDO-CHINESE MISSIONS AND THE DEATH OF HARSHA[1]

Sources of information—Chinese

OUR only source of information for the exchange of diplomatic missions between Harsha and the T'ang emperor T'ai Tsung are the Chinese records. They also throw some light on the unsettled political conditions after Harsha's death. These writings are of the nature of official histories, geographical accounts, and pilgrims' travelogues, and often derive their facts from some common informants. So far only a fourteenth-century work, the *Wên Hsien T'ung Kao*, 'Comprehensive History of Civilization', by Ma Tuan-lin,[2] based on an earlier work, the New Tang history of the eleventh century (which in its turn draws on the tenth-century *T'ang Hui Yao*) has been translated in parts into English,[3] and for that reason has received the greatest attention from Indian historians, whose knowledge of foreign languages is generally limited to English. Over six decades after the rendering of Ma Tuan-lin's work, Sylvain Lévi wrote, in 1900, a very erudite paper on the subject[4] utilizing the material in a seventh-century work, the *Fa Yüan Chu Lin*, and in the Old and the New T'ang histories, dated respectively in the tenth and the eleventh

Their availability to the English-language historians

[1] The Chinese sources from which this information is derived were translated in longer or shorter fragments towards the end of the nineteenth century. Advances in various fields of knowledge since then have made it desirable to examine the material afresh. We are deeply indebted to Mr. D. C. Lau of the School of Oriental and African Studies for rendering afresh for us passages previously translated and, what is more significant, for procuring hitherto unknown and unutilized material from new works.

[2] The title of the work has been translated variously. The above is Han Yu-shan's rendering in *Elements of Chinese Historiography* (p. 62). He states that the work is also referred to as an 'Encyclopaedia of Culture'. J. Needham and Wang Ling, in *Science and Civilisation in China* (i, p. 317) translate it as 'Historical Investigation of Public Affairs'.

[3] Anonymous translation in the *Asiatic Journal and Monthly Register for British and Foreign India, China and Australia*, N.S., 20 (May–Aug. 1836), pp. 213–22, 313–16, reproduced in *J.A.S.B.* vi, pt. 1 (1837), 61–75; Burgess's translation of *Ma Tuan-lin* from the French of Julien (*Journal asiatique*, IVme sér. x (1847), pp. 81–121) in *I.A.* ix (1880). Rémusat also rendered Ma twan-lin's account (Bk. 335, fol. 14) into French (*Nouveaux Mélanges asiatiques*, i, pp. 193 ff.).

[4] 'Missions de Wang Hiuen-Ts'e dans l'Inde', *Journal asiatique*, IXme sér. xv (1900), pp. 297 ff., 401 ff.

centuries. Being in French, however, Lévi's translation and conclusions were insufficiently known and used by the Indian, and even the British historians of India. Moreover, omission of certain passages in his rendering leaves Lévi's account incomplete. We give below a fresh translation of the relevant sections from the four above-mentioned sources, and translate for the first time passages on India and Tibet from seven other works that confirm, correct, or add to the information obtained from the former. For greater accuracy in interpretation literalness has been aimed at. The accounts being repetitive have all been included in view of the fact that the translations are being published for the first time. In their chronological order the sources are as follows:

Names and descriptions of works utilized in this chapter

1. *Chi Ku Chin Fo Tao Lun Hêng* (Religious Work)

   Collection of discussions and criticisms of Buddhists and Taoists, ancient and modern.
   T'ang (Preface dated A.D. 661)
   Tao-hsüan (Monk)

2. *Fa Yüan Chu Lin* (Religious Work)

   Collection of anecdotes from the sacred books of Buddhism.
   T'ang (completed A.D. 668)
   Tao-shih (Monk)

3. *T'ung Tien* (Secular Work)

   Reservoir of source material on political and social history.
   T'ang *c.* A.D. 812.
   Tu Yu

4. *Chiu T'ang Shu* (Secular Work)

   Old History of the T'ang Dynasty (A.D. 618 to A.D. 906).
   Wu Tai, A.D. 945
   Ed. Liu Hsü

5. *T'ang Hui Yao* (Secular Work)

   Reservoir of source material on political history of T'ang
   Sung, A.D. 961
   Wang P'u

6. *T'ai-P'ing Yü Lan* (Secular Work)

   T'ai-P'ing reign-period imperial encyclopaedia.
   Sung, A.D. 983.
   Ed. Li Fang
   Yin-te (Index) no. 23

7. *T'ai-P'ing Huan Yü Chi* (Secular Work)

T'ai-P'ing reign-period general description of the world (Geographical Record).
Sung, from A.D. 976 to A.D. 983
Yüeh-shih

8. *Ts'ê Fu Yüan Kuei* (Secular Work)

Collection of material on the lives of emperors and ministers.
Sung, from A.D. 1005 to A.D. 1013
Eds.: Wang Ch'in-jo and Yang I

9. *Hsin T'ang Shu* (Secular Work)

New History of the T'ang Dynasty (from A.D. 618 to A.D. 906).
Sung, from A.D. 1061
Eds.: Ou-yang Hsiu and Sung Ch'i

10. *Tzŭ Chih T'ung Chien* (Secular Work)

Mirror of universal history (from 403 B.C. to A.D. 959).
Sung, A.D. 1084
Ssü-ma Kuang

11. *Wên Hsien T'ung K'ao* (Secular Work)

Historical investigation of public affairs.
Sung, *c.* A.D. 1254, but not published until A.D. 1319
Ma Tuan-lin

The relevant sections from the above sources may be translated as follows:

Translation of relevant passages from the *Chi Ku Chin Fo Tao Lun Hêng*

1. *Chi Ku Chin Fo Tao Lun Hêng*[1]

The envoy to the western countries, Li I-piao returned and memorialized the throne in the twenty-first year of Chên-kuan [A.D. 647].'[2]

From the *Fa Yüan Chu Lin*

2. *Fa Yüan Chu Lin*[3]

According to the biography of Wang Hsüan-t'sê: 'In the third month of

[1] Chüan-C, *Takakusu*, 52, p. 386b: edict ordering Hsüan-tsang to translate Lao-tzü into Sanskrit. S. Lévi, *Les Missions*, etc., p. 308 n. 1, etc. gives his reference: Chap. 2 fir Nanj; éd. jap. xxxvii, 7, p. 20 b.

[2] Although ascribed to both his return and his 'memorializing' the throne, the year 647, according to the dating system employed in the following accounts, will be seen to apply more correctly to 'memorializing'.

[3] *Chüan* 29, p. 98b. The *Fa Yüan Chu Lin* preserves in fragments Wang Hsüan-t'sê's memoirs, known variously as the *Chung T'ien Chu-Hsing Chi* (an account of the journey in central India), *Wang Hsüan-t'sê Hsing-Chuan* (an account of the travels of Wang Hsüan-t'sê), *Hsi Kuo Hsing Chuan* (a description of the journey to the kingdoms

the year seventeen of Chên-kuan [643] of the great T'ang was published an imperial decree which ordered to send on a mission, the senior envoy, *Ch'ao-san-ta-fu* Li I-piao exercising the functions of *Wei-wei*, assistant of the temples and the superior protector of the army,[1] having as his second Wang Hsüan t'sê, the former county magistrate of Huang-shui in the district of Jung, with the mission to escort back officially a brahman guest to his country. In the twelfth month of this year they arrived in the kingdom of Magadha. They travelled over it and visited the lands of the Buddha, and contemplated the surviving remains of the Buddha .... In the nineteenth year [645] on the twenty-seventh day of the first month they arrived at Rāja-gṛiha, climbed Gṛidhra-kūṭa, and set up inscriptions . . .'.[2]

From the *T'ung Tien*

3. *T'ung Tien*[3]

In the Wu-tê period of T'ang [618–27] the four kingdoms of eastern, western, southern, and northern India were all annexed by central India.

In the fifteenth year of Chên-kuan [A.D. 641] its king, whose surname was Ch'i-li-ch'i [śrī?] and whose personal name was Shih-lo-i-to [others say his surname was Śā-li] sent an envoy to present a memorial [to the Chinese throne].

In the twenty-second year [A.D. 648] Wang Hsüan-t'sê the *Yu-wêi-shuai-fu-chang-shih*[4] went as envoy to India. It so happened that Śī-lo-i-to died and the country fell into great disorder. His minister Nā-fu-ti [or *ti*, i.e. King of Nā-fu?] A-lo-na-shun[5] set himself up and then despatched troops to resist Hsüan-t'sê. Hsüan-t'sê fled to the south-west of Tibet and summoned troops by letter from the neighbouring countries. The Tibetans sent out 1,200 crack troops and the kingdom of Nepal more than 7,000 cavalry to serve Hsüan-t'sê. Together with his second in command, Chiang Shih-jên, Hsüan-t'sê led the troops of the two kingdoms and advanced to Ch'a-po-ho-lo city, which was the place where central India is [where the King of central India resided]. In a number of battles they greatly defeated them [the Indians],

of the West), and *Hsi Yü Hsing Chuan* (description of the journey to the Western countries). The original memoirs are unfortunately lost. The *Fa-yüan-chu-lin* also preserves sections of an official compilation the *Hsi Yü Chi* which was based on Hsüan-tsang's *Hsi Yü Chi* and Wang Hsüan-t'sê's memoirs. The official *Hsi Yü Chi* is dated 666 and was extant at least until A.D. 720, as it is mentioned in the catalogue of the Imperial Library Ku-chin-shu-lu, which forms the bibliographical chapter in the *Chiu T'ang-shu*.

[1] For detailed explanation of the complete title *Ch'ao-san-ta-fu, hsing-wêi-wêi-ssŭ-ch'êng, shang-hu-chün*, see R. Des Rotours, pp. 36, 51, and 362–70.

[2] It was the usual practice of overland missions taking this route to wind up their journey by setting up commemorative tablets at the sacred Buddhist site of Gṛidhra-kūṭa. This fact as well as the date of their arrival at Rāja-gṛiha provides for a reasonably adequate period of two years for completing the business of the mission, and indicates that Li I-piao reached home in A.D. 645.

[3] Ch. 193, p. 1040c.

[4] For explanation of the title see R. Des Rotours, pp. 608–19.

[5] Aruṇāśva. For the reading A-na-shun (Arjuna?) see the account in *Ts'e Fu Yüan Kuei*. See below, p. 214 n. 1.

cutting off more than 3,000 heads. Those who jumped into the water and were drowned were almost 10,000. Hsüan-tʻsê captured the concubine[s] and the prince[s] of the king, and others, and took captive 13,000 people, male and female, together with more than 30,000 head of cattle and horses. Upon this India was overawed. The cities, towns, and villages which submitted numbered more than 580. Thereupon, taking A-lo-na-shun as captive, he returned.

From the *Chiu Tʻang Shu* (the Old Tʻang History)

4. *Chiu Tʻang Shu*[1]

(*a*) Basic Annals of Tʻai Tsung[2]

On the day of Kêng-tzu of the fifth month of the twenty-second year [of Chên-kuan] [A.D. 648] *Yu-wêi-chang-shih*[3] Wang Hsüan-tʻsê attacked the kingdom of Ti-na-fu and greatly defeated and captured the King, A-lo-na-shun, and his wife, son, etc. He took captive 12,000 men and women, and over 20,000 oxen and horses, which he presented to the Emperor.

(*b*) Tufan (Tibet)

In the twenty-second year [of Chên-kuan] [A.D. 648] Wang Hsüan-tʻsê, who was *Yu-wêi-shuai-fu-chang-shih*, went as an envoy to the western countries, and was pillaged by central India. Tibet sent crack troops to attack Tʻien Chu with Hsüan-tʻsê and greatly defeated them. [Tibet] sent an envoy to present the victory [to the Chinese emperor].

(*c*) Tʻien Chu (India)

During the reign-period Wu-tê [A.D. 618–27] the country [India] was in great disorder. The succeeding king, Śīlāditya, trained soldiers and gathered together a multitude of people and was invincible wherever he went. The saddles never came off the elephants and the armour never came off the soldiers. After six years the kings of the 'four Indias'[4] all faced north and submitted to him. His fame spread far and wide and his government was well ordered.

In the fifteenth year of Chên-kuan [A.D. 641], Śīlāditya assumed the title the King of Magadha, and sent an envoy to pay tribute[5] [to China]. Tʻai Tsung condescended to send a letter with an imperial seal on it expressing his gracious solicitude. Śīlāditya was greatly overwhelmed and asked his countrymen, saying, 'Has an envoy from Mahā-chīna-sthāna ever come to this country?' They all said, 'Never.' He then prostrated himself and received the imperial letter. Thereupon he sent an envoy to pay tribute. Tʻai Tsung, seeing that his land was very far away, treated the envoy with great courtesy. He further sent Li I-piao, who was *wêi-wêi-chʻêng*, to return the visit. Śīlāditya

[1] *Chüans* 3, 196a and 198; sections: Basic Annals Tʻai Tsung, Tufan, and Tʻien Chu.

[2] The *Hsin Tʻang Shu* has no parallel section.

[3] Administrator in charge of the guard of the right. See R. Des Rotours, pp. 501–21.

[4] The histories, in contrast to the account of Hsüan-tsang who always refers to the conquest of 'five Indias' by Śīlāditya, speak of 'four Indias'. Probably they regard Harsha's own kingdom as the fifth.

[5] See below, pp. 220–1 and 223–4.

sent his great ministers to go outside the city to welcome Li I-piao. Whole cities turned out to watch. Incense was burnt on either side of the road. Śīlāditya, facing east, led his ministers in prostrating themselves to receive the royal letter. He further sent an envoy to present *huo-chu* [fire pearl], *yü-chin*[1] incense, and [cuttings of] the *Bodhi* tree.

In the tenth year of Chên-kuan [A.D. 636] the monk Hsüan-tsang reached the country [India] and took back Sanskrit texts of over 600 *sūtras* and *śāstras*.

Previous to that Wang Hsüan-tʻsê, who was *Yu-shuai-fu-chang-shih*, was sent as an envoy to India.[2] The kings of the 'four Indias' all sent envoys to pay tribute. It so happened that Śīlāditya, the King of Central India died and there was great disorder in the country. His minister, A-lo-na-shun, King of Na-fu, usurped the throne and sent all the barbarian troops to resist Wang Hsüan-tʻsê. Hsüan-tʻsê, with an escort of thirty horsemen, went and fought with them but was no match for them. When all the arrows were used up they were all captured. The barbarians pillaged all the objects offered as tribute by the various countries. Hsüan-tʻsê fled by night to Tibet, which sent 1,200 crack troops together with over 7,000 cavalry from Nepal to go with Hsüan-tʻsê. Hsüan-tʻsê and his second in command, Chiang Shih-jên, led the troops of the two countries and advanced on the capital of Central India. After three days of continuous fighting he greatly defeated them, cutting off over 3,000 heads. Those who jumped into the water and were drowned numbered almost 10,000. A-lo-na-shun abandoned the city and fled. Shih-jên advanced and took him captive, taking prisoner 12,000 men and women and over 30,000 oxen and horses. Thereupon India was overawed. [Hsüan-tʻsê] took A-lo-na-shun back as captive and returned to the capital in the twenty-second year. Tʻai Tsung was greatly pleased and ordered the officials to report this to the ancestral temple . . ., and Hsüan-tʻsê was made *chʻao-san-ta-fu*.

From the *Tʻang Hui Yao*

5. *Tʻang Hui Yao*[3]

In Wu-tê [the period 618–27] the country [India] was in great disorder. The King, Śīlāditya, led his army. The saddles never came off the elephants, the armour never came off the soldiers. In six years the kings of the 'four Indias' all faced north and submitted to him.

In the early years of Chên-kuan the Chinese monk Hsüan-tsang reached their central country [capital?]. The King of India, Śīlāditya, said to Hsüan-tsang: 'I hear that a sage has appeared in China[4] and has composed the music of "the routing of [enemy] formation of the Prince of Chʻin".[5] Try and tell me

[1] *Curcoma longa*: see Mathews's *Chinese–English Dictionary*.

[2] The phrase 'previous to that' causes ambiguity. Apparently Wang Hsüan-tʻsê was *sent* to India 'previous to' Hsüan-tsang's departure from India for China but *arrived* there (India) after it.

[3] *Chüan* 100, section Tʻien-chu (India).

[4] The *Hsin Tʻang Shu* has 'your country', which seems to be a corruption.

[5] Emperor Tʻai Tsung of Tʻang was the former Prince of Chʻin. This music was composed when Tʻai Tsung as Prince of Chʻin defeated Liu Wu-chou.

what sort of person he is.' Hsüan-tsang duly[1] described the sage [-like] virtues of the Emperor. The King Śīlāditya said, 'If what you say is true, I shall myself pay homage to him.'

By the fifteenth year [of Chên-kuan] [A.D. 641] he [Śīlāditya] assumed the title the King of Magadha, and sent an envoy to pay tribute.[2] The Emperor [T'ai Tsung of T'ang] thereupon sent Liang Huai-ching, who was *Yün-ch'i-wei*,[3] to establish relations with the country [India]. Śīlāditya was greatly overwhelmed and asked his countrymen: 'Has an envoy ever come from Mahā-chīna-sthāna?' They all said 'Never'.[4]

By the fourth month of the twenty-second year [A.D. 648] [the Emperor] sent Wang Hsüan-ts'ê, who was *Yü-wêi-chang-chih*, as envoy to India. When he arrived Śīlāditya was dead and there was great disorder in the country. An army was sent to resist him. Hsüan-t'sê fought and was no match for them. So he fled by night to Tibet, which sent 1,200 crack troops, together with 7,000 cavalry of Nepal. Hsüan-t'sê and his second in command, Chiang Shih-jên, led the troops of the two countries and greatly defeated them [India]. [Hsüan-t'sê] came back [to the capital] with the king as captive. T'ai Tsung was very pleased.

6. *T'ai-P'ing Yü Lan*[5] bases its account entirely on the *Chiu T'ang Shu* ('Old T'ang History'), therefore we do not include its translation. From the *T'ai P'ing Yü Lan*

7. *T'ai-P'ing Huan Yü Chi*[6] bases its account entirely on the *T'ung Tien* and need not be reproduced here. From the *T'ai-P'ing Huan Yu Chi*

8. *Ts'ê Fu Yüan Kuei*[7] From the *Ts'ê Fu Yüan Kuei*

(*a*) Fifteenth year of Chên-kuan [A.D. 641]. That year the king of India, Śīlāditya, sent an envoy to pay tribute. The Emperor sent Li I-piao to return the visit.[8] Its [India's] king further sent an envoy to present a big pearl [or fire pearl?], *yü-chin* incense, and [cuttings of] the *Bodhi* tree.

(*b*) Chên-kuan, twenty-second to twenty-fifth moon [A.D. 648]. Wang Hsüan-t'sê, who was *Yu-wei-chang-chih*, attacked the country of Ti-na-fu and greatly defeated them. Previously Hsüan-t'sê was sent as an envoy to the

[1] The *Hsin T'ang Shu* has 'roughly'. [2] See below, pp. 220–1 and 223–4.

[3] 'Director of the cavalry [fast] like the clouds.' For further details see R. Des Rotours, p. 53.

[4] The *T'ang Hui Yao* omits the mention of the three following embassies: from Harsha to T'ai Tsung, from T'ai Tsung to Harsha under the leadership of Li I-piao, and again from Harsha to T'ai Tsung in reply to which came the Chinese mission next mentioned in this source, that led by Wang Hsüan-t'sê.

[5] Ch. 792, section 7 (pp. 9b–10b).

[6] Ch. 183, section T'ien-chü.

[7] *Chüans* 970, 973, 995 (respectively under accounts of the years 15, 22 (fifth month), and 22 (sixth month).

[8] Two previous embassies have been omitted here: from T'ai Tsung to Harsha under Liang Huai-ching and from Harsha to T'ai Tsung, in reply to which Li I-piao was sent.

country of India. It so happened that the King of Central India died, and the country was in great disorder. The King of Na-fu-ti, A-na-shun,[1] set himself up and sent barbarian troops to resist Hsüan-tʻsê. Hsüan-tʻsê escaped by night and reached the western borders of Tibet. He sent out letters to demand troops from neighbouring countries. Tibet sent 1,200 crack troops. The country [read *kuo* instead of *ku*] of Nepal sent over 7,000 cavalry with Hsüan-tʻsê to attack A-na-shun, who greatly defeated him [A-na-shun]. Tibet soon afterwards sent an envoy to present the victory to China.

(*c*) Twenty-second year of Chên-kuan, sixth month [A.D. 648]. Tibet came to present its victory [over India] to China.[2]

From the *Hsin Tʻang Shu* (the New Tʻang History)

9. *Hsin Tʻang Shu*[3]

(*a*) Tibet

In the twenty-second year [of Chên-kuan] [A.D. 648] Wang Hsüan-tʻsê, who was *Yu-wêi-shuai-fu-chang-shih*, was sent as an envoy to Hsi-yü [the western countries] and was ambushed by Chung-tʻien-chu [central India]. Nêng Tsan sent crack troops to follow Hsüan-tʻsê [who] defeated them and came to present the captives [to the Chinese Emperor].

(*b*) India

In the reign-period of Wu-tê [618–27], the country [i.e. India] was in great disorder. The King Śīlāditya led his armies and was invincible. The saddles never came off the elephants and the armour never came off the soldiers. He marched against the 'four Indias' and they all faced north and submitted to him.

It so happened that the Tʻang monk, Hsüan-tsang, arrived in his country. Śīlāditya sent for him[4] and said to him: 'There is a sage who has appeared in your country and composed the "Music of the Routing of [Enemy] Formation of the Prince of Chʻin". Try and tell me what sort of a person he is.' Hsüan-tsang gave a rough description of the godlike military prowess of Tʻai Tsung and how he subdued disorder and caused the four barbarians to submit. Śīlāditya was pleased and said, 'I shall face east and pay homage to him.'

In the fifteenth year of Chên-kuan [A.D. 641] he assumed the title of the King of Magadha and sent an envoy to present a letter. The Emperor [Tʻai

[1] Usually the name is spelt A-lo-na-shun and interpreted as Aruṇāśva. The possibility that the last two syllables may have got interchanged is also taken into account, in which case the name is interpreted as Arjuna. The present reading A-na-shun seems to support the latter interpretation. It is possible that, not being sure whether the sound was 'lo' or 'na', the Chinese put in both syllables, of which 'lo' is dropped here. It may, of course, be a slip in the present case, as no other text employs this spelling.

[2] This notice, in conjunction with the previous one, is most significant as it helps to establish finally the date of Wang Hsüan-tʻsê's return to China in the fifth month of A.D. 648.

[3] *Chüans* 216a (Tibet) and 221a (India).

[4] For our reasons why the statement regarding Hsüan-tsang's arrival in India is immediately followed by that of his meeting with Harsha although several years intervened the two events, see below, pp. 217–9.

Tsung] ordered Liang Huai-ching, who was *yün-chʻi-wei*, as envoy [lit. holding credentials] to convey his gracious solicitude. Śīlāditya was overwhelmed and asked his countrymen whether an envoy from Mahā-chīna-sthāna had ever before arrived in his country. They all replied, 'Never.' (Mahā-chīna-sthāna is the barbarian name for China.) He went out to welcome the envoy and prostrated himself to receive the imperial letter, which he placed on his own head. He then sent an envoy to accompany [the Chinese envoy] to the Chinese court. The Emperor ordered Li I-piao, who was *Wêi-wêi-chʻêng*, to return the visit. The great ministers [of India] went outside the city to welcome him and cities were emptied as the people flocked to watch, and incense was burnt along the way. Śīlāditya led his ministers, facing east, to receive the imperial letter, and sent as tribute *huo chu* [fire pearl], *yü-chin* incense, and [cuttings of] the *Bodhi* tree.

In the twenty-second year [of Chên-kuan] [A.D. 648] the Emperor sent Wang Hsüan-tʻsê, who was *Yu-wêi-shuai-fu-chang-shih*, on a mission to the country [India] with Chiang Shih-jên as second in command. Before their arrival Shih-lo-i-to [Śīlāditya] died, and the kingdom fell into disorder. His minister, the King of Na-fu, A-lo-na-shun, set himself up and sent troops to resist Wang Hsüan-tʻsê. Wang then had an escort of only a few tens of men, so they were overcome and all perished. The objects offered in tribute by the various kingdoms were pillaged. Wang Hsüan-tʻsê escaped and fled to the western frontier of Tibet and summoned armed help from the neighbouring countries. Tibet came with a 1000 soldiers, while Nepal came with 7,000 horsemen. Wang Hsüan-tʻsê disposed his army into groups and advanced as far as the town of Cha [Tʻu]-po-ho-lo.[1] At the end of three days he took it. 3,000 heads were cut off and 10,000 who jumped into the water were drowned. A-lo-na-shun left the kingdom, fled, and gathered together his dispersed troops into battle formation again. Shih-jên took him prisoner and captured and decapitated [his followers] in thousands. The remnant of his people rallied round the king's wife and child and barred the passage to the river, Chʻien-tʻo-wêi. Shih-jên attacked and routed them. He took prisoner the wife and son of the king, and captured 12,000 men and women and 30,000 various domestic animals. He received the submission of 580 cities and villages. The King of eastern India, Shih-chiu-ma [Śrī Kumāra], sent as a gift 30,000 oxen and horses as provisions for the army and also bows, swords, and spears. The kingdom of Chia-mo-lu [Kāma-rūpa] offered curiosities to the Emperor, and a map of the country, and asked for a picture [or statue] of Lao-tzŭ. Wang Hsüan-tʻsê took prisoner A-lo-na-shun and humbly offered him to the Emperor. The officials reported this to the ancestral temples.... Wang Hsüan-tʻsê was promoted to the rank of *Chʻao-san-ta-fu*.

10. *Tzŭ Chih Tʻung Chien*[2]

From the *Tzŭ Chih Tʻung Chien*

Twenty-second year [of Chên-kuan] [A.D. 648], fifth moon. Wang Hsüan-tʻsê,

[1] For the identification of Cha (Tʻu)-po-ho-lo and Ch ien-tʻo-wêi which occurs a few lines later, see below, pp. 227–8.

[2] *Chüan* 199, section India.

the *Yu-wêi-shuai-chang-shi*, attacked the king of Ti-na-fu-ti,[1] A-lo-na-shun, and greatly defeated him. Previously Shih-lo-i-to [Śīlāditya], the king of Central India, had the strongest army. All the 'four Indias' were subject to him. Wang Hsüan-tʻsê went as imperial envoy to India. All the different countries sent envoys to pay tribute to China. It happened that Śīlāditya died and there was great disorder in the country. His minister, A-lo-na-shun, set himself up and sent his barbarian troops to attack Hsüan-tʻsê. Hsüan-tʻsê let his thirty followers fight against them but they were no match for the troops. They were all captured. A-lo-na-shun robbed them of all the tributes from the various countries. Wang Hsüan-tʻsê got away and fled by night. He reached the western borders of Tu-Fan [Tibet] and sent out letters asking for troops from various neighbouring countries. Tu-fan sent 1,200 crack troops. Nepal sent over 7,000 cavalry to go to him. Hsüan-tʻsê and his second in command, Chiang Shih-jên, led the troops of the two countries and advanced to the city of Cha-po-ho-lo, where Central India is. After three days of continuous fighting he greatly defeated them. They cut off more than 3,000 heads, those who were drowned when they jumped into the water were almost 10,000. A-lo-na-shun abandoned the city and fled. Then he collected the remnants of his army and returned to fight with Shih-jên, who again defeated him and captured A-lo-na-shun. The remaining soldiers rallied round the wife and the prince and barred the way at the Chʻien-tʻo-wêi river.[2] Shih-jên advanced and attacked them. He dispersed the troops and captured the wife and the prince and took men and women captives to the number of 12,000. Thereupon India was overawed and 580 cities and villages surrendered. Wang Hsüan-tʻsê came back to [the capital] with A-lo-na-shun and was made *Chʻao-san-ta-fu*.

The *Wên Hsien Tʻung Kʻao* reproduced from the *Hsin Tʻang Shu*

11. *Wên Hsien Tʻung Kʻao* by Ma Tuan-lin[3]

This work reproduces literally the account preserved in the *Hsin Tʻang Shu*.

The above sources together furnish us with many facts which, although always with a pro-Chinese bias, provide us with a coherent story of the exchange of missions between Harsha and Tʻai Tsung. The account of the last mission led by Wang Hsüan-tʻsê reveals the loss of political equilibrium, following Harsha's death, in areas erstwhile under his sphere of influence.

The purposes served by the missions

The Indo-Chinese missions were inspired primarily by political, commercial, and religious motives, and were utilized besides for cultural exchanges in such fields of knowledge as science and philosophy.

[1] See below, p. 227.

[2] In a note it is stated that this river was first to the west and then to the north of the Ganga: see below, p. 228.

[3] *Chüan* 338, section India.

Harsha as 'the King of Magadha' initiated the contact

According to our sources Harsha took the initiative in opening diplomatic relations with T'ai Tsung. It is stated that, on assuming the title 'the King of Magadha' in A.D. 641, Harsha sent an envoy to China. Neither the Indian sources nor even Hsüan-tsang's 'Records' or the 'Life' refer to or suggest any special event in Harsha's career in A.D. 641 with regard to Magdaha. It seems to us that the simple fact of the use of the title 'the King of Magadha' by Harsha in the royal documents carried by his envoy to China in A.D. 641 has happened to be so recorded in the Chinese sources as to give the impression that a noteworthy event such as the assumption of a new title by Harsha took place in that year. That Harsha preferred to be known as the King of Magadha rather than the King of Kanauj, especially in a foreign communication, and for all we know in some hitherto undiscovered internal records as well, is understandable in the light of the reputation that Magadha had come to enjoy as the seat of imperial power from pre-Mauryan days.

Reasons for it: ambition, enthusiasm

Motives both political and of prestige, which a monarch ruling in stability and security could afford to indulge in, as well as intellectual curiosity, may have guided Harsha in opening diplomatic relations with China. A year or so later when he met the Buddhist pilgrim from China, Harsha gave evidence of his interest in and some knowledge of a foreign country by asking Hsüan-tsang: 'The Master comes from China; your disciple has heard that that country has a King of T'sin,[1] whose fame is celebrated in songs and airs set for dancing and music; I never yet knew who this King of T'sin was, or what his distinguished merit was, that led to this distinction.'[2] Hsüan-tsang then related in detail the accomplishments of T'ai Tsung. There is every reason to believe that the Chinese pilgrim is recording a fact. While Harsha with his slight knowledge of China would have been curious to learn more, Hsüan-tsang would have welcomed an opportunity to give vent to his patriotism. Energetic, versatile, and of Buddhist inclinations, Harsha not only showed interest in meeting the Chinese pilgrim many years before he succeeded in doing so, but he also opened diplomatic relations with China, and his second earnest attempt at contacting Hsüan-tsang may partly be attributed to a desire to increase his knowledge of the country he had sent his envoys to.

Did Hsüan-tsang inspire Harsha to open relations with China

Scholars have so far taken the view that Harsha's first embassy to China

[1] Prince of Ch'in, later the Emperor T'ai Tsung.

[2] 'Life', p. 174. Harsha's inquiry makes Hsüan-tsang's eulogistic reply fit in the context. But apparently Harsha already knew something about T'ai Tsung, and we believe that by this time he had already despatched his first official mission to China.

was inspired by his meeting with Hsüan-tsang.[1] The conclusion appeared logical, especially in view of the fact that an ambiguous sequence of events, to be discussed presently in the most easily accessible Chinese account, that of Ma Tuan-lin, seemed to support it. But this view ignores the schedule of dates arrived at on the basis of the more dependable sources, the 'Records' and the 'Life'. A careful calculation of the duration of Hsüan-tsang's sojourns, as he and his biographer note them, places his stay with Harsha at the end of A.D. 642 and early in 643.[2] The 'Life' explicitly states that Hsüan-tsang reached the Chinese capital in the spring of 645. The duration of his return journey from Prayāga, where he attended the sixth quinquennial assembly with Harsha, through north-west India to Khotan, and finally to China can be satisfactorily fitted in only between 643 and 645; it cannot be stretched to fill the period 641 to 645.

Ma Tuan-lin's account of India, as we have remarked earlier, is reproduced verbatim from the *Hsin T'ang Shu*. The relevant passages from the latter have been translated above.[3] It is easy to see how the account can lead to the view that Harsha's first embassy to China was the result of his meeting with the pilgrim. The section (*b*) on India records first the fact of extensive conquests by Harsha in the period A.D. 618–27. It then states, 'It so happened that the T'ang monk Hsüan-tsang arrived in his [i.e. Harsha's] country' but does not give any date for the event. An earlier history, the *Chiu T'ang Shu*, places Hsüan-tsang's arrival in India in A.D. 636.[4] In doing so it is probably referring to his visit to Harsha's capital at Kanauj in that year,[5] for the pilgrim had entered the boundaries of India in *c.* A.D. 630. Whichever of the two dates may be intended by the *Hsin T'ang Shu* to denote Hsüan-tsang's arrival in India, the event, according to it, though not according to the *Chiu*, which is quiet on the matter, was immediately followed by 'Sīlāditya's invitation to Hsüan-tsang',[6] giving the wrong impression that the King and the pilgrim met soon after 630 or 636. Moreover, in his conversation with Hsüan-tsang, Harsha on hearing the praise of T'ai Tsung is reported to have said, 'I shall face east and pay homage to him.' It should be realized that, whether or not Harsha had already 'paid homage' in the form of a mission, he would be made to express his deference once again on the mention of the Chinese emperor. The

[1] Ettinghausen, p. 54; R. C. Majumdar, *H.C.I.P.* iii, p. 120.
[2] *C.A.G.I.*, p. 648; Watters ii, p. 336. [3] See above, pp. 214–15.
[4] See above, p. 212.
[5] *C.A.G.I.*, p. 646 dates Hsüan-tsang's visit to Kanauj in A.D. 636.
[6] See above, p. 214.

T'ang Hui Yao too follows the same sequence of events as the *Hsin T'ang Shu*. Apparently this procedure is adopted by these two histories because of their preference for a topical (first Hsüan-tsang and then the missions) rather than a chronological (arrival of Hsüan-tsang, exchange of missions, meeting of Hsüan-tsang and Harsha, more missions) account. The first mission by Harsha is clearly stated to have been sent in A.D. 641, whereas he did not meet the pilgrim until 642 on the testimony of the 'Life' and the 'Records'. We feel that this evidence has been ignored not only because the date of the meeting cannot be vouched for with absolute certainty but also because of the psychological trap created by an expected result of such a meeting.

The factual details of the six missions exchanged between Harsha and T'ai Tsung, the last arriving after Harsha's death

The *Hsin T'ang Shu* gives the most detailed information, however sketchy, on the exchange of missions between Harsha and T'ai Tsung. The following facts, however, are assembled from several sources. Six missions were sent, three by each ruler, in the short space of less than eight years between A.D. 641 and 648. Most Chinese ambassadors held high titles, both civil and military. Harsha commissioned the first embassy, but no particulars regarding its personnel are recorded. T'ai Tsung reciprocated by sending a mission under Liang Huai-ching.[1] Harsha then sent an envoy 'to accompany [the Chinese envoy] to the Chinese court'. The second Chinese mission is stated to have been decreed in 643.[2] It was led by Li I-piao with Wang Hsüan-t'sê as the second in command, and was 'to escort back officially a brahman guest to his country'. India was not unoften referred to as the country of the brahmans, and the guest in question whether brahman or otherwise was apparently the previous envoy from Harsha. Li I-piao's mission returned via Rāja-gṛiha and Gṛidhra-kūṭa, where commemorative tablets were set up according to established practice. The party reached China in A.D. 645 but T'ai Tsung was at that time engaged in a war with Liao-tung (Manchuria). Li I-piao was therefore not able to 'memorialize the throne' until the twenty-first year of Chên-kuan, i.e. A.D. 647.[3] Harsha sent another embassy following Li I-piao's mission.[4] The last embassy from China, with Wang Hsüan-t'sê as the principal envoy and Chiang Shih-jên as the second-in-command, was sent in the fourth month of the twenty-second year of Chên-kuan (648).[5] On arrival in India in the following month they discovered that Harsha had died. The event had

1 See the *T'ang Hui Yao* and the *Hsin T'ang Shu*.

2 See the *Fa Yüan Chu Lin*.

3 See the *Chi Ku Chin Fo Tao Lun Hêng*.

4 See the *Chiu T'ang Shu*, the *Ts'ê Fu Yüan Kuei*, and the *Hsin T'ang Shu*.

5 See the *T'ang Hui Yao*.

probably occurred not long before, for, with the close liaison that was being maintained between India and China at that time, it may be expected that T'ai Tsung would have learnt of Harsha's death had it occurred very much earlier, and the embassy of 648 would not than have been dispatched to Harsha's court. At the time the first five chapters of the 'Life' were being compiled, between A.D. 648–9[1], Hsüan-tsang apparently knew about Harsha's death, which may have occurred in A.D. 647. The pilgrim's biographer gives us information which is not included in the 'Records'. It is stated that, when in Magadha in A.D. 640, Hsüan-tsang dreamt that Harsha would die after ten years.[2] 'So towards the end of the Yung Hwei period . . . Śīlāditya rāja died . . . . The imperial ambassador, Wang-ün-tse, was at this time making ready to be a witness of these things.'[3] Arthur Waley comments that the original character was probably for seven 'but ten (十) and seven (七) look very much alike in Chinese, and in T'ang texts they are often confused; so perhaps the prophecy was exact'.[4]

On arrival Wang Hsüan-tsê clashed with one A-lo-na-shun, the King of Na-fu (stated variously as Na-fu-ti or Ti-na-fu-ti, which we surmise stands for Tīra-bhukti on the northern borders of Bihar), who it is stated was a minister of Harsha and had usurped the throne. The battle of Cha-po-holo (Champāran?) on the banks of the Ch'ien-t'o-wêi (Gaṇḍakī?) took place in the fifth month of the twenty-second year of Chên-kuan[5] and lasted three days.[6] A-lo-na-shun was taken captive and carried off to China to be presented to the Emperor. The party probably reached China in the sixth month of the twenty-second year of Chên-kuan, for the *Ts'ê Fu Yüan Kuei* first records that Tibet, which had helped Wang Hsüan-t'sê in the battle in the fifth month, 'soon afterwards sent an envoy to present the victory to China'. It then states in the following small section (*c*) the information that Tibet 'presented the victory' to China in the sixth month of the twenty-second year of Chên-kuan (648).

The seventh-century contacts, link in a long tradition

Such is the factual account of the six official embassies exchanged between India and China during the concluding years of Harsha's reign. They are representative of the exceptionally busy intercourse that existed between the two countries from *c.* A.D. 400 to 760, although irregular visits extended well beyond both limits, continuing in the latter direction to about the middle of the eleventh century, when

[1] See Waley, p. 280. [2] 'Life', p. 155. [3] Op. cit., p. 156.
[4] Waley, p. 52. [5] See the *Chiu T'ang Shu.*
[6] See the *Chiu T'ang Shu*, the *Hsin T'ang Shu*, and the *Tzŭ Chih T'ung Chien.*

Muslim expansion in Central Asia and India discouraged the use of overland routes. Of voluntary travellers, hundreds journeyed in both directions, inspired by the zeal of Buddhism. As for the official exchanges, Harsha's practice, itself a continuation of the old tradition, was maintained unabated for over a hundred years, during which period embassies are recorded between China on the one hand and Baltistan, Kapiśa, Uddiyāna, Gandhāra, Kashmir, and Ceylon on the other.

What was the purpose of such embassies?

The political and cultural interest of Harsha–T'ai Tsung embassies

When Harsha opened relations with China he was at the height of his power. His sphere of influence extended almost from one extremity of northern India to the other, and to the River Narmadā in the south. In the south-east his final territorial gains had been made in Orissa around A.D. 640. Politically ambitious, intellectually vigorous, and confident in an over-all atmosphere of activity and well-being which he himself was mainly to be credited for, Harsha may be expected to have opened relations with China for reasons that flow from such conditions. China's interest in Buddhism, manifested through the visits of various monk scholars, and Harsha's own enthusiasm for the faith are likely to have provided extra impetus. Once the process had been started a number of specific interests would have been added to the general ones, although we have but scanty information about them. Exotic articles were exchanged: from the Indian side 'fire pearl' (*huo-chu*) and incense (*yü-chin*, *Curcoma longa*) are stated to have been sent with the third mission. Although the King of Kāma-rūpa sent them to Wang Hsüan-t'sê as a kind of peace offering to ward off trouble, some of his presents are indicative of the items of interest to both parties. He 'offered curiosities', it is recorded, 'and a map of the country, and asked for a picture [or statue] of Lao-tzŭ'.[1] Bhāskara-varman had requested an earlier mission, that led by Li I-piao assisted by Wang Hsüan-t'sê, to obtain for him a Taoist text, the *Tao tê Ching*, of which a Sanskrit translation was made for him.[2]

Harsha's third mission is said to have taken a present of (cuttings of) the *Bodhi* tree. Almost certainly other Buddhist relics as well as works of scholarship must have gone to China through the medium of state embassies. Indeed, accomplished and enterprising men, Hindu, Buddhist, or of other Indian or Chinese creeds, and of religious or secular leanings, may have been deliberately included in the missions, while others may

[1] See the *Hsin T'ang Shu*.

[2] P. Pelliot has translated an account preserved in the *Chi Ku Chin Fo Tao Lun Hêng* (Nanjio, 1471) of the difficulties of the translation work being done: see his paper 'Autour d'une traduction sanskrite du Tao-tö-king', *T'oung Pao* 13 (1912), p. 350.

have been allowed to make use of the benefits of security and the other conveniences available to state-sponsored missions by travelling at the same time. The leader of the third Chinese mission, Wang Hsüan-tʻsê, helped Hsüan-chʻao, a scholar of Sanskrit and of Buddhism, to get back to China. The official Chinese party then returned by another route with the defeated King A-lo-na-shun, who took with him a scholar proficient in arts and magic, Na-lo-mi-si-po-ho, who knew the secret of longevity. Tʻai Tsung was happy to patronize him. A statement by this Indian expert preserves what may be one of the earliest passages on mineral acids.[1]

An important incidental reference concerning Indian chemistry

The *Yo-yang Tsa Tsu* of Tuan Chʻeng-shih, dated *c.* A.D. 860, quotes Na-lo-mi-si-po-ho as having said, 'In India there is a substance called Pan Chha Cho Shui [Pan-Chha-Cho water] which is produced from minerals in the mountains, has seven varieties of different colours, is sometimes hot, sometimes cold, can dissolve herbs, wood, metals, and iron—and if it is put into a person's hand, it will melt and destroy it. The skulls of camels have to be used as recipients for it . . . .'[2]

The study of the Indian knowledge of the sciences by the Chinese

The official history of the Sui dynasty (A.D. 581–628), completed in A.D. 610 by Wei Chêng, contains in its bibliographical catalogue, of which the counterpart is preserved in the *Hsin Tʻang Shu*, the names of numerous books of Indian origin, as signified by the usual title prefix *po-lo-mên* or brahman, on astronomy, mathematics, medicine, etc.[3] The flow of such material continued in the Tʻang period through both official and unofficial channels. One of the important assignments for Li I-piao's mission was to learn the Indian technique of making sugar. The pilgrim scholar I-tsing, who spent twelve years in India (A.D. 673–85), includes in his records three chapters on medicine. The aforementioned monk Hsüan-chʻao returned to India in A.D. 664 under imperial orders to collect medicinal plants and contact famous physicians, one of whom, So-po-mei or Lu-chia-i-to, mentioned in the *Tʻung Chien Kang Mu*,[4] he was able to send to China. But he himself never

[1] Later Arab works refer perhaps to the same chemical as 'alkahest' or universal solvent. In Europe the first reference to mineral acids occurs in a thirteenth-century French Franciscan writing. See G. Sarton, *Introduction to the History of Science*, ii, p. 408; iii, p. 531.

[2] See J. Needham and Wang Ling, *Science and Civilisation in China*, i, p. 212. Footnote *c* on the same page gives the reference to the original—Ch. 7, p. 7a—and notes that the *Chiu Tʻang Shu*, Ch. 3, p. 8a, has a similar passage.

[3] Op. cit., p. 128 n. *b*: Altogether twelve are listed in the *Yin-te* (Index) no. 10 (the index to the bibliographies in all the official histories), including three on astronomy, three on mathematics, and three on pharmaceutics. Unfortunately they are all now lost.

[4] L. Weiger, *Textes historiques*, pp. 1371, 1372, 1374. See J. Needham and Wang Ling, op. cit. i, p. 212 n. *f*.

returned home. The Central Asian route by which he had come became unsafe because of the rising Arab power, and Tibet declared war on China, blocking the eastern route.

The concentration of Indian scholarship at the Chinese capital during the Sui period continued during the seventh and eighth centuries. Indian experts working at the Astronomical Bureau made contributions themselves and inspired those of Chinese scholars, noted amongst whom was the Tantric Buddhist monk I-hsing (A.D. 682–727). The sinicized forms of some of the famous Indian names that have been preserved[1] are Chiayeh Hsiao-wei, who introduced improvements in the calendar some time after A.D. 650, and Ch'üthan Hsi-ta, who became president of the Board and produced the celebrated work on astronomy and mathematics, the *Khai-yuan Chan Ching*, in *c*. A.D. 729, introducing trigonometry, zero, and other innovations. Other exchanges stimulated in China the study of Indian grammar and philology,[2] architecture and sculpture,[3] painting,[4] music,[5] and so forth. Chinese influences too, in many fields, entered India. Hsüan-tsang was entertained with a T'ang-period musical composition by King Bhāskara-varman of Assam in A.D. 638. Some scholars of Chinese civilization suggest the influence of Taoism on Indian Tantric Buddhism.[6]

The superior tone of the Chinese official histories with regard to other countries: India

The Chinese state records, however, when relating the purpose of official missions, use a conventional phraseology to demonstrate the superiority of China over a foreign country, whatever the relative status of the two at a given time. The *Chiu T'ang Shu*, the *T'ang Hui Yao*, and the *Ts'ê Fu Yüan Kuei* declare that Harsha sent the first embassy to China 'to pay tribute'; the *Hsin T'ang Shu* says 'to present a letter'. In contrast China's first mission to India in response to Harsha's approach is stated by the *Chiu T'ang Shu* to be an act of condescension on the part of T'ai Tsung, who sent a letter 'to express his gracious solicitude'. The *Hsin T'ang Shu* also uses the same terminology. The *T'ang Hui Yao* says that its purpose was 'to establish relations with the country [India]'. Harsha's second embassy, according to the *Chiu T'ang Shu*, was again

1 The *Chiu T'ang Shu*, Ch. 33, p. 17a.

2 A. L. Kroeber, *Configurations of Culture Growth*.

3 E. Boerschmann, *Chinesische Pagoden*; G. Combaz, 'L'évolution du Stūpa en Asie', *Mélanges chinois et bouddhiques*, 1932, 2, 163 (Étude d'architecture bouddhique); 1935, 3, 93 (Contributions nouvelles et vue d'ensemble); 1937, 4, 1 (Les symbolismes du Stūpa); A. K. Coomaraswamy, 'Hindu Sculptures at Zayton', *Ostasiatische Zeitschrift*, 1933, 9 (19), 5.

4 P. C. Bagchi, *India and China: a Thousand Years of Sino-Indian Cultural Relations*, p. 163.

5 Op. cit., pp. 165–9.

6 J. Needham and Wang Ling, op. cit. ii, pp. 425–30.

to pay tribute; in the words of *Hsin T'ang Shu* it was 'to accompany [the Chinese envoy] to the Chinese court. Both the *Chiu* and the *Hsin T'ang Shu* record that T'ai Tsung sent his second mission to 'return the visit'; the *Fa Yüan Chu Lin* says, 'to escort back officially a brahman guest to his country.' Harsha's final embassy to T'ai Tsung was, in the words of the *Chiu T'ang Shu*, 'to present *huo-chu* [fire pearl], *yü chin* [incense], and [cuttings of] the *Bodhi* tree'; in those of the *Hsin T'ang Shu*, to 'send as tribute' the above articles. In response to this mission came the Chinese party led by Wang Hsüan-t'sê, who 'was sent as an envoy to the western countries' according to the *Chiu* and the *Hsin T'ang Shu*. At another place the *Chiu T'ang Shu* describes him as the 'envoy to India'. So does the *T'ung Tien*.

Gandhāra

Some other official accounts of the visits of Chinese envoys to foreign countries, whether lesser or comparable in power to China at the time of such contacts, also throw light on the Chinese attitude towards others.[1] One example is to be found in an account of Sung Yun's travels preserved in the 'History of the Temples of Lo-Yang (Honan Fu)'. In A.D. 518 the Wei Empress sent Sung Yun and Hwei Sang, a Buddhist monk, to collect works on Buddhism. The two scholars came as far as Peshawar and Nagara-hāra. In A.D. 520 they were at the court of the King of Gandhāra (Mihira-kula?), a non-Buddhist, and by Sung Yun's account a cruel barbarian. When the Chinese envoy presented his credentials to him, 'the King was very rough with him, and failed to salute him. He sat still whilst receiving the letters.' Greatly annoyed by the king's arrogance Sung Yun is reported to have reproved him in the following words: 'Mountains are high and low—rivers are great and small—amongst men also there are distinctions, some being noble and others ignoble. The sovereign of the Ye-Tha and also of U-chang, when they received our credentials, did so respectfully; but your Majesty alone has paid us no respect.' The king replied,

When I see the King of the Wei, then I will pay my respects; but to receive and read his letters whilst seated, what fault can be found with this? When men receive a letter from father and mother, they don't rise from their seats

[1] Not only official historians, but even the Buddhist monk I-tsing, who pays tribute to Indian medicine in his records, sometimes indulges in similar sentiments. Although the Chinese emperors never ceased to import Indian experts on longevity, and I-tsing himself acknowledges the efficacy of the eight sections of medical science (i.e. *Āyurveda*; see *I-tsing*, pp. 127 and 222), one of which was acupuncture, he says (op. cit., p. 136) 'In the healing arts of acupuncture and cautery and the skill of feeling the pulse China has never been superseded by any country of *Gam*būdvīpa (India); the medicament for prolonging life is only found in China. . . . Is there any one, in the five parts of India, who does not admire China? All within the four seas respectfully receive *the command*.'

to read it. The great Wei sovereign is to me [for the nonce] both father and mother, and so, without being unreasonable, I will read the letters you bring me still sitting down.

Sung Yun, records the 'History', thereupon left without any official salutation. He stayed on in Gāndhāra, however, for some more time.

Majapahit (Indonesia and other countries)

The official histories write in the same vein about China's connections with the empires of the Malay archipelago. The defeat of the Mongol admiral, Yi-kʻo-mu-su, at the hands of the founder of the Majapahit empire, Vijaya Kerta-rājasa Jaya-vardhana, in 1293 is played down. One of the kingdoms that suffered on account of the rise of Majapahit in Java was the Sumatra-based Śrī-Vijaya, the San-fo-tsʻi of the Ming annals. As her fortunes were at a very low ebb in 1376 the *Ma-la-cha* (*Mahārāja*) Wu-li of Śrī Vijaya, afraid of ascending the throne on his own authority, sent envoys to China for the Emperor's support to his claim. The Ming annals record: 'The emperor praised his sense of duty and ordered envoys to bring him a seal and a commission as king of San-fo-tʻsi.' But 'at that time San-fo-tʻsi had already been conquered by Java, and the king of this country, hearing that the emperor had appointed a king over San-fo-tʻsi, became very angry and sent men who waylaid and killed the imperial envoys.' Apparently Majapahit felt strong enough not to brook any violation of its authority in its sphere of influence. Java was too distant from China and the Chinese resources too widely scattered to attempt a military showdown. The Ming emperor had to swallow the grievous insult. The annals state: 'The emperor did not think it right to punish him [the king of Majapahit] on this account', and elsewhere 'the emperor was highly incensed and detained their [Majapahit's] envoys more than a month, with the intention to punish them, but ultimately they were sent back with a letter to their king, in which he was reproved for what he had done.'[1] Instances of this type may be multiplied with examples from Malaya, Burma, Tibet, Korea, or even George III's Britain.[2]

The cordial reception of the embassies and the treatment accorded to distinguished foreign visitors

To return to Indo-Chinese missions, the reception of the envoys was most cordial, presumably at both ends, although we have detailed description only of Harsha's reception of the Chinese delegations. It is comparable to the welcome accorded to high foreign dignitaries in modern times. The arrival of exotic visitors was treated as a festive occasion. Streets were decorated, incense was burnt, citizens turned out

[1] K. A. N. Sastri, *Śrī Vijaya*, pp. 302–3.

[2] Letter to George III by the Ching (Manchu) emperor Chʻien Lung in 1793: A. F. Whyte, *China and Foreign Powers*, p. 41.

to watch the procession, and the King and his ministers ceremoniously received the envoys. Their credentials, official messages, and presents were accepted with traditional gestures of courtesy and politeness. Tʻai Tsung, too, is stated in the *Chiu Tʻang Shu* on one occasion to have 'treated the [Indian] envoy with great courtesy . . . seeing that his land was far away'. The accomplished Indian scholars who accompanied the missions were often put up in the royal palace or in the best official establishments. The aforementioned Na-lo-mi-so-po-ho was invited to live and work in the palace under the charge of the Minister of War.

The adventures of the last Chinese mission of 648 led by Wang Hsüan-tʻsê

Of all the Chinese missions the third, that led by Wang Hsüan-tʻsê in A.D. 648, is described in the greatest detail in our sources. This was Hsüan-tʻsê's second visit to India. Previously he had come to Harsha's court as the junior envoy in Li I-piao's mission decreed in A.D. 643. The *Fa Yüan Chu Lin* states the record of his qualifications at that time as 'the former county magistrate of Huang-shui in the district of Jung'.[1] As the head of the delegation in 648 he is entitled *Yu-wei-shuai-fu-chang-shih.*[2] The second in command of the mission was Chiang Shu-jên.

Its arrival after the death of Harsha and encounter with a newly independent Magadhan governor A-lo-na-shun

The embassy was sent by Tʻai Tsung in the fourth month of the twenty-second year of Chên-kuan (A.D. 648). On arrival they found that Harsha had died and 'the country was in great disorder'. A man stated to be his minister, A-lo-na-shun by name, had 'usurped the throne'. Apparently it was not the throne of Kanauj, because A-lo-na-shun is shown as ruling from Tīra-bhukti in north Bihar. Nor, in view of the vagueness of the Chinese character for the designation, can A-lo-na-shun be for certain identified as Harsha's minister, i.e. counsellor or *mantrin*. A-lo-na-shun may have been an able and powerful man, probably the governor of Tīra-bhukti, in the hierarchy of Harsha's officers in Magadha, who declared himself independent after Harsha's death. It is most unlikely that a minister from Kanauj would have gone and set himself up in a peripheral province if he had intentions of appropriating Harsha's legacy. The Chinese sources are, however, consistent in their statements, for they style Harsha as the King of Magadha, and the ruler of Tīra-bhukti in the vicinity of Magadha as a minister of Harsha who usurped the latter's throne. But A-lo-na-shun overstepped his bounds.

Why did he come into conflict with Wang Hsüan-tʻsê?

[1] See above p. 210.

[2] See the *Tung Tien*, the *Chiu Tʻang Shu*, and the *Hsin Tʻang Shu*. At another place the *Chiu Tʻang Shu* styles him *Yu-shuai-fu-chang-shih*; the *Tʻang Hui Yao* as *Yü-wêi-chang-shih*. For detailed information regarding the title see R. des Rotours, pp. 608–19 and 501–21.

It seems that in his reckless and arrogant mood A-lo-na-shun asked the Chinese delegation to treat him as the legatee of Harsha's empire and present their credentials to him. It was probably on being refused that honour that he attacked them and 'pillaged all the objects offered as tribute by various countries'. The encounter took place in the fifth month of the twenty-second year of Chên-kuan. In the first round A-lo-na-shun had the better of it. All the thirty or so members of the Chinese party were captured. Wang Hsüan-tʻsê fled by night to south-west or, according to some sources, west Tibet. The country was at that time friendly to China and her powerful ruler had been given in marriage a princess by China and one by Nepal. Hsüan-tʻsê succeeded in getting '1,200 crack troops', 1,000 according to other sources, from Tibet and 7,000 cavalry from Nepal, and, 'disposing his army into groups, advanced as far as the town of Cha-po-ho-lo [Champāran]'. The battle raged for three days. 3,000 of A-lo-na-shun's men lost their lives and 10,000 jumped into the water, probably of the Gaṇḍakī, and were drowned. The latter figure appears to be exaggerated. A-lo-na-shun fled, reassembled his troops, and returned for another contest. But he lost again. Shih-jên took him prisoner, killing and capturing his men in large numbers. The remainder of his troops, however, still would not give up. Rallying round the Queen and the prince they barred the passage to the River Gaṇḍakī, perhaps in an effort to seal the city-entrance. Shih-jên finally succeeded in breaking the resistance, capturing, moreover, the Queen and the prince. 12,000 more prisoners are said to have been taken, both men and women, and 30,000 domestic animals were appropriated. 580 cities and villages offered submission. Alarmed by the situation, the subordinate but powerful old ally of Harsha, Bhāskara-varman of Kāma-rūpa, sent presents of 30,000 oxen and horses and of weapons of war, apparently to keep the Chinese off his soil.

Probable causes of conflict

Wang Hsüan-tʻsê's flight to Tibet and return with reinforcements

The battle of Champāran and the defeat of A-lo-na-shun

The Chinese reading of the name of A-lo-na-shun's kingdom as Na-fu, Na-fu-ti, or Ti-na-fu-ti; of his capital as Cha (Tʻu)-po-ho-lo; and of the river on which it was situated as Chʻien-tʻo-wêi have presented difficulties of identification. The kingdom was identified as Tīra-bhukti with fair certainty when the *Tzŭ Chih Tʻung Chien*'s reading Ti-na-fu-ti, in contrast to the Na-fu or the Na-fu-ti of the previously known texts, was discovered. The old Chinese pronunciation 'buk' for 'fu' only strengthened the opinion.[1] N. L. Dey,[2] equating Tīra-bhukti

The identification of A-lo-na-shun's kingdom and capital respectively with Tirhut and Champāran on the River Gaṇḍakī

[1] The suggestions that Na-fu-ti may be a transliteration of *senā-pati* (*Journal asiatique* (1892), p. 338) or that the syllables meant the country of the brahmans (S. Lévi, *Journal asiatique* (1900), p. 300 n. 2) are unsatisfactory.

[2] *G.D.A.M.I.*, p. 35.

or modern Tirhut with Bideha (Videha), gives its boundaries as the River Kauśikī (Kosi) on the east, the River Gaṇḍaka (Gaṇḍakī) on the west, the Himalaya on the north, and the Ganga on the south.

The commentator in the *Tzŭ Chih T'ung Chien* states that the River Ch'ien-t'o-wêi was 'first to the west and then to the north' of the Ganga. The *Hsin T'ang Shu*'s commentator locates Cha-po-ho-lo on the bank of the River Chieh-pi-li, which Ma Tuan-lin identifies with the Ganga. The *Hsin T'ang Shu* adds that the River Ch'ien-t'o-wêi was north of the country of To-wei.

Vincent Smith[1] and C. V. Vaidya[2] equated Cha (T'u)-po-ho-lo with Tirhut (Tīra-bhukti), and the River Ch'ien-t'o-wêi with the River Bāgmatī in Nepal, both of which identifications seem to be incorrect. Neither may Cha-po-ho-lo be identified with Davāka, a possibility brought to notice by S. Lévi.[3] De la Vallée Poussin[4] identified Ch'ien-t'o-wêi with the Ganga(?) and Ch'ieh-pi-li with the River Gogrā. The anonymous translator of *Ma Tuan-lin*[5] equates Cha-po-ho-lo with Champāran, the identification with which we agree but makes a quite impossible suggestion that the Ch'ien-t'o-wêi stands for the Godāvarī. We accept Lévi's identification of the Ch'ien-t'o-wêi with the Gaṇḍakī or the Gaṇḍa-vatī. Tirhut (Tīra-bhukti), Champāran (Cha-po-ho-lo), and Ch'ien-t'o-wêi (Gaṇḍakī) are all in the same region. Apparently Champāran situated on the Gaṇḍakī was a city of the kingdom of Tīra-bhukti in the seventh century A.D. The Chinese sources describe Cha-po-ho-lo as a city of Madhya-deśa (lit. central India) because the toponym indicated the region from the borders of the Panjab to the borders of Bengal. Wang Hsüan-t'sê is said to have been 'pillaged' or 'ambushed by central India'.

The other Chinese interests attended to by Wang Hsüan-t'sê

As we have seen, in spite of the initial losses and early difficulties, Wang Hsüan-t'sê's visit to India ended in success, even if some of his assigned tasks may have remained undone. As noted earlier, he did arrange the return to China of the scholar Hsuan-ch'ao. No doubt he was anxious to depart himself too in order to present his handsome booty to the Emperor. A-lo-na-shun, though a prisoner, appears to have received considerate treatment: he was allowed to take with him a scholar versed in arts and magic. While A-lo-na-shun would have felt privileged to be allowed to take the kind of present that would soften T'ai-tsung's attitude towards him, Wang Hsüan-t'sê would have been

[1] *Early History of India*, pp. 366–7.
[2] *H.M.H.I.* i, pp. 334–5.
[3] *Journal asiatique* (1900), 306 n. 2.
[4] *Dynasties*, p. 110.
[5] *J.A.S.B.* vi. 69.

only too pleased to give him this opportunity, so keen always were the Chinese emperors to meet Indian thaumaturges.

Return to China with A-lo-na-shun in 648 and promotion for services

On presenting the rewards of his success Wang Hsüan-tʻsê was suitably honoured with promotion to the rank of *Chʻao-san-ta-fu.*[1] As the arrival of the Chinese party in the capital is dated the sixth month of the twenty-second year of Chên-kuan, the highly eventful trip of Wang Hsüan-tʻsê was apparently crowded into a period of less than three months.

[1] The same title was held by Li I-piao, in whose mission Wang Hsüan-tʻse went to India as the junior envoy. For details regarding the title see R. des Rotours, pp. 36, 51, and 362–70.

CONCLUSION

Forms of government

THE ancient-Indian political system is characterized by three methods of government: the *saṁgha*, *gaṇa*, or 'republics', of the pre-Maurayan period, some of them lasting until the days of the Guptas; the highly centralized empires of the Mauryan type; and the confederate monarchies of the Harshan pattern.

Aim of the state

The success (*siddhi*) of the state is declared to be well-being (*sukhaṁ*). The most important Indian concept with regard to sovereignty is that of the *chakra-vartī* (a ruler, the wheels of whose chariot roll everywhere without obstruction), or the *dig-vijayī* (the conqueror of various countries in all directions), aiming at the political hegemony of the country demarcated by its natural boundaries of the mountains and the seas.

Political concepts: *chakra-vartī*

The three types of conquest

Another significant political concept is that which is concerned with the methods of obtaining sovereignty. Conquest is classified into three types. *Dharma-vijaya*, or righteous conquest, requires only obeisance; *lobha-vijaya* is conquest for greed, aiming at the acquisition of territory and wealth; and *asura-vijaya*, demonic conquest, is that which does not spare the loser's kin or even his life. Strength is also stated to be of three kinds: of deliberation, mastery, and vitality. Probably they correspond to the three methods of conquest.

Even the Machiavellian books on polity recommend *dharma-vijaya*. Conquest, moreover, may be achieved by peaceful methods which are to be preferred to war. Alliances of different types, from those based on word of honour to those cemented by matrimonial relations, are listed. Significantly, the word *saṅdhi* applies both to peace and to alliance. The righteous conqueror is expected to reinstate the conquered king as well as to respect the ways and customs of the conquered people. Subordinate treaties were based on the merits of each case. Generally subservient to the paramount sovereign, the lesser kings expressed their loyalty in different ways depending on the terms of agreement. To these normal concepts of empire and methods of conquest, Aśoka added a new one, unique in the annals of mankind, that of conquest by *dharma*, the spread of righteous ideas by messengers of peace and goodwill.

Aśoka's *dharma-vijaya*

The *maṇḍala*

Another political concept, that of the *maṇḍala* or circle of kings, envisages the different relationships that could exist among different rulers, especially between the *vijigīshu* (the would-be conqueror) and the other kings, when an expansive empire was being contemplated. In a neat plan, the positions are laid out of the conqueror's enemies, friends, and their respective allies in front and at the rear of his kingdom. The situation, however, was much more fluid than appears at first sight. Not only would the relationships change with every new treaty, thus shifting the position of friend and enemy, but there could be more than one of each, as, indeed, of the 'intermediary' and the 'neutral' of the plan, at the same time. It is, therefore, not the schematic character of the situation that is significant, but rather the common sense underlying the definitions of the constituents of the circle and the description of the likely contingencies that might arise. The discourse on *maṇḍala* is characterized by a most brazen analysis of power politics, in spite of the fact that it recognizes the virtues of peace, righteous conquest, decentralization, and regional freedom.

Indian view of politics

In any case the *maṇḍala* system conforms with the concepts of pan-Indian monarchy and the three types of conquest. There was no fixed centre of the circle of kings in the sense that the *vijigīshu*, the would-be conqueror, could arise in any part of the country. Such a concept made the regional unit, trying to extend its political hegemony over all such units in the country, the centre of the system. It did not revolve round a specific dynasty or a particular capital. The lowest reducible in politics was not the tribe, as in the earliest stages of society, or the nation, as in modern civilization. (In a changed milieu the former had been supplanted by the well integrated village, the professional guild, and the class system which now met the more intimate and immediate needs of man.) Moreover, instead of 'political nationhood', we meet 'cultural nationhood' which might extend well beyond the limits of the 'geographical nationhood', the ancient Indian nation-view being culture-centred rather than politics-centred. Generally, however, a viable regional power would attempt to lead and energize the body politic contained within the mountain and ocean boundaries of the country. Both custom and deliberate policy ensured local autonomy for the conquered, allowing for diversity in unity. The regional political unit in relation to the pan-Indian empire, as the individual in relation to the universal, was the microcosm of the macrocosm, implying the independence and the qualitative sameness of the parts and the whole, and the ability of the two to be reconcilable.

Harsha's political efforts and achievements

Harsha's political ambition and policies were conditioned by the concepts discussed above. He aimed at the sovereignty of the whole country but succeeded in extending his boundaries only up to the

River Narmadā in the south-west and to northern Orissa in the south-east. Both Gujarat and Assam owed him allegiance, while Kashmir respected his might. Harsha's prestige was high enough for him to expect that his official letters asking for Hsüan-tsang's protection would be honoured by the kings through whose territories the pilgrim would pass on his land-trek from India to China through Central Asia. Harsha's political acumen is proved by the fact that he tried to open diplomatic relations with his foreign neighbours. He despatched his first official mission to China in 641, possibly by the Nepal–Tibet route. By 648 Harsha and T'ai Tsung of T'ang had despatched three embassies each, the last arriving in India after the former's death. His political efforts prove that Harsha was inspired by the concept of pan-Indian kingship; his accomplishments show that he succeeded in becoming *sakal-ottarā-patha-nātha*, 'the lord of the entire north', a title bestowed on him by his strongest adversary, Pula-keśin, the Chalūkya King of Mahārāshṭra.

His policies

Harsha acquired his territory by the 'righteous' method of conquest. While the political savants' recommendation of it must have guided Harsha's choice, it also seems to have been dictated by a sensible assessment of his own resources, the strength of those he made tributary, and the current state of political equilibrium. For, although Harsha himself does not appear to have employed brutal methods of expansion, they were in use in his day, as is demonstrated by Śaśāṅka and Deva-gupta's attack on Kanauj. It is possible that in his early career practical considerations played an important part in determining Harsha's policies. Later, political maturity, satiety ensuing from success, and a religious disposition influenced his approach.

A powerful king's relations with the various constituents of his *maṇḍala* needed skilful handling for the greater part of his career, as very often an extensive empire might be acquired only gradually through the years. However, upon accomplishing the aim, the task of maintaining a balance in inter-state relations was less exacting in the case of a centralized empire than in that of a confederation-type union.

An estimate

As Harsha continued to undertake military campaigns almost until the end of his reign, and as his empire was of a confederate type, he needed to exercise his authority with consummate skill. In this he succeeded. Although his numerous subordinates may be classified into five or six categories from the viewpoint of treaty relationships, which depended on the merits of each case, Harsha was able to maintain the correct balance between authoritativeness and friendliness towards them. The territory under his direct administration enjoyed good government.

There is evidence to suggest, however, that Harsha used land or land-tax, instead of cash, as the mode of payment to some of his officers. As for men of religion or learning, they often received royal donations in this form. This slowly led to the fragmentation of land.

Such practices were later to lead to a weakening of the body politic. In times of weak central control, individuals tended to misuse their rights over land or regard temporary allocations as permanent arrangements. This in itself placed difficulties in the way of a conqueror attempting to create a unified kingdom.

Under Harsha, however, these ill effects were not visible. In fact, certain statements in the 'Life' suggest that he was clever enough to relieve the *sāmantas* of some of their excess wealth by expecting them to donate generously to the subjects of the realm on the occasion of the quinquennial assembly. They did so by redeeming the precious gifts given away by the King, which were once again bestowed in charity. Whether this excessive generosity was healthy for the recipients' psychology and the country's economy is another matter. We have no evidence that Harsha took any constructive steps to relieve the pressure on land which was beginning to be felt in spite of the abundant trade. Apparently some political and economic bottle-necks were beginning to affect adversely the investment and circulation of money. Perhaps it was the result of the disappearance of the fine but delicate balance between the reality of an empire and regional autonomy which was the distinguishing feature of the Gupta period. The type and degree of decentralization in the Harsha-type confederate monarchy could be effective for a given period, but was not conducive to prosperity and strength in the long run. Within his lifetime Harsha was able to maintain a splendid *status quo*, even if he did not or could not give a new direction to Indian polity. This, however, need not make us underestimate the extent of his domains. We should determine it in the light of Indian political concepts which recognized subordinate allies in charge of their own territories as part of the empire system. Bound in friendly treaties with the paramount sovereign, they extended to him not only nominal courtesies, but also considerable political, strategic, and economic privileges. From this point of view Valabhī (Gujarat) and Kāma-rūpa (Assam) were part of Harsha's empire.

Harsha's reign may be considered notable for activities in the fields of religion, social welfare, and the arts, although in the case of the latter there is more evidence for achievements in the sphere of literature than in that of architecture.

For the first successor of a local potentate Harsha achieved considerable success. He had the difficult task of building up another empire almost a century after the beginning of the decline of the previous one. His times, moreover, contained the seeds of the downhill trends of the medieval period. But on the whole the contemporary spectrum is bright, so much so that it only seems possible for one with hindsight to notice the weaknesses. All the same Harsha cannot be classed among India's greatest monarchs. He may, however, be regarded as one of the lesser among her great kings.

APPENDIX I

The Harsha Era

IN addition to Harsha's Baṅskhera and Madhu-ban inscriptions,[1] the following records issued by other kings are now generally believed to have been dated according to the Harsha era of A.D. 606.[2]

1. The Shāh-pur Stone Image inscription of Āditya-sena, year 66 (Bhandarkar no. 1393).
2. Peheva inscription of the time of Bhoja-deva (Pratī-hāra), year 276 (Bhandarkar no. 1412).
3. Ahar inscriptions with dates ranging between 258 and 298 (Bhandarkar nos. 1409–11, 1414, 1415, 1417–20).
4. Inscriptions of the Kara dynasty, dated 160, 280, and 287 (Bhandarkar nos. 1404, 1413, 1416).
5. Some inscriptions from Rājasthān, Panjab, and central India, dated 182, 184, and 218 (Bhandarkar nos. 182, 184, 218).
6. Seven dates in a stone inscription found at Kaman (*E.I.* xxiv. 329).
7. An inscription in Hund, dated 169 (*E.I.* xxii. 97).[3]

The fact that Harsha founded an era beginning in A.D. 606 has been almost unanimously accepted by scholars. R. C. Majumdar started a controversy when he expressed the view that this belief rests on very slender foundations.[4] D. C. Sircar, in reply to the above doubt, maintained that there is hardly any worthwhile evidence against the generally accepted view.[5] Without going into the details of the arguments advanced by the two scholars, we shall give our reasons for believing that Harsha started an era beginning in A.D. 606.

Writing about India in the eleventh century, al-Bīrūnī (Abū Raihān) states:

. . . people . . . have adopted . . . the eras of
1. Śrī Harsha
2. Vikramāditya

[1] *E.I.* iv, no. 29; i, no. xi; also Kielhorn, nos. 528 and 529.

[2] We have omitted from our list the two Pratī-hāra records and the Nepalese inscriptions, which have been successfully demonstrated to be dated in the Śaka era, and Māna-deva (or Aṁśu-varman) era. See above pp. 106–8.

[3] V. V. Mirashi wrote an article entitled 'The Harṣa and Bhāṭīka Eras' (*I.H.Q.* xxix. 191 ff.) in which, on the basis of a revised reading of the dates of the Hund inscription, he argued that the Bhāṭīka era, starting in *c.* A.D. 624, was used for dating the aforesaid inscription.

[4] *I.H.Q.* xxvii. 183 ff.; xxviii. 280 ff.

[5] *I.H.Q.* xxvii. 321 ff.; xxix. 72 ff.

3. Śaka
4. Valabha and
5. Gupta

. . . His [i.e. Śrī Harsha's] era is used in Mathurā and the country of Kanoj. Between Śrī Harsha and Vikramāditya there is an interval of 400 years, as I have been told by the inhabitants of that region. However, in the Kashmirian calendar I have read that Śrī Harsha was 664 years later than Vikramāditya. In face of this discrepancy I am in perfect uncertainty . . .[1]

To demonstrate the application of the various eras to a given date, the year 400 of Yazdajird, al-Bīrūnī calculates the commencement of the Harsha era according to the Mathurā and Kanauj tradition,[2] which placed Harsha 400 years before Vikram-āditya, i.e. in 457 B.C. But on the authority of the Kashmir calendar, Harsha being '664 years later than Vikramāditya', the Harsha era should be placed in A.D. 606–7.[3] We think it was this era which was prevalent in al-Bīrūnī's time in Mathurā and Kanauj. It seems that the inhabitants of the region deliberately misguided the Muslim scholar in order to impress him with the antiquity of the era they used. Al-Bīrūnī, though in possession of the correct information through the Kashmir source, naturally placed greater reliance on local tradition, which seemed more authentic on its face value. It is well known that he misunderstood, similarly, the traditions relating to the Gupta era. His critical pen, however, has preserved for us the valuable information he got from the Kashmir Calendar, that 'Śrī Harsha was 664 later than Vikramāditya'.

We shall now examine the basis for accepting A.D. 606 as the date of Harsha's accession to the throne, which event served as the starting point for an era.

The astronomical data provided by the *Harsha-charita* helps us to determine the date of Harsha's birth in A.D. 590.[4] All the circumstances of that period support the view that Harsha ascended the throne at an early age after his elder brother was killed in his early youth. The Harsha era, beginning in A.D. 606, when Harsha would be only 16, is in accordance with this fact.

Hsüan-tsang tells us that when the Buddhist oracle told Harsha to accept the throne of Kanauj he counselled him not formally to ascend the 'lion-throne' nor to call himself *mahārāja*. Harsha, therefore, styled himself *kumāra* Śīlāditya.[5] However, after the subjugation of the 'five Indias' in the following six years as recorded by Hsüan-tsang,[6] Harsha must have assumed full imperial dignity and may have celebrated the event at his capital of Kanauj in A.D. 612. Thus, when it is recorded in the 'Life' that Śīlāditya told the pilgrim in A.D. 643 that he had been the lord of India for thirty years and more, and was about to conduct his sixth five-yearly assembly,[7] the year 612 is apparently looked upon as marking the beginning of Harsha's imperial rule.

1 *Alberuni's India*, trans. by E. C. Sachau, ii, p. 5.
2 Op. cit., p. 7.
3 A. Cunningham makes it 664 − 57 = 607: *Book of Indian Eras*, p. 64.
4 See above, p. 65.
5 Beal i, p. 213; Watters i, p. 343.
6 Ibid.
7 'Life', pp. 183–4.

That Hsüan-tsang was using A.D. 643 as the viewing-point of Harsha's career and not the end of A.D. 646, when the 'Records' were completed,[1] or A.D. 648–9, when the 'Life' was compiled,[2] is also clear from the following statement in the 'Records': 'After six years he [Harsha] had subdued [or repulsed] the "five Indias". Having thus enlarged his territory he increased his forces . . . . Close on thirty years his arms reposed . . . .'[3] The six years were apparently the first half-dozen of the thirty years. The determinant date at the other end of Harsha's career was obviously 612, the addition of 30 to which would bring Harsha's story up to date to 643, the year of the meeting of Hsüan-tsang and Harsha. By then the last territorial gain to Harsha's empire, that of northern Orissa, had been made.

It appears that Hsüan-tsang does not take into account the first six years of Harsha's reign when his imperial titles, which he must have assumed after his father's death, signified his suzerainty over Sthāṇv-īśvara only, and when, as far as Kanauj was concerned, he was only *kumāra*, prince. In view of the fact that Hsüan-tsang makes no comment at all on Harsha's connection with Sthāṇv-īśvara, and takes notice of the exceptional circumstances under which Harsha occupied the throne of Kanauj, as a 'regent', his calculation of the beginning of Harsha's rule from A.D. 612 is not surprising at all. But Harsha, who inherited a considerable kingdom in A.D. 606, and who presumably assumed the imperial titles of *parama-bhaṭṭāraka mahārāj-ādhirāja* of Sthāṇv-īśvara on accession and launched a *dig-vijaya* campaign in the same year, must have reckoned A.D. 606 as the beginning of his reign, an appropriate landmark for the commencement of an era.

[1] Waley, p. 89. [2] Ibid., p. 280.
[3] *Hsi Yü Chi* text, v, 4a.

APPENDIX II

The Coins of Harsha Śīlāditya

IN his *Coins of Medieval India*, published in 1894, A. Cunningham illustrated a coin[1] showing, on the obverse, the figure of a horseman, with the legend 'Harshadeva', and, on the reverse, that of a goddess seated on a throne with a cornucopia in her left hand, which he ascribed to King Harsha-deva of Kashmir, whose association with Kabul[2] induced him to imitate the money of the Śāhī rulers of that kingdom. A. F. R. Hoernle,[3] who seems to have been unaware of this fact, doubted Cunningham's ascription, and suggested that the coin belonged to Harsha of Kanauj, who is also sometimes referred to as Harsha-deva. Moreover, the emblem on the coin, he said, of the horseman with the lance at rest 'is the mark of the early Rajput', and 'the chiefs of Thanesar were Rajputs'. We do not agree with the latter statement; Hsüan-tsang's testimony that Harsha was of the *vaiśya* class is more reliable. Moreover, the identity of the Harsha-deva of the coin with the Harsha of Kashmir is too well attested by facts recorded by Kalhaṇa to admit of any doubt. Richard Burn also observes that Hoernle's attribution of this coin to Harsha 'does not seem quite satisfactory'.[4]

In 1904 an earthen pot, containing one gold, 522 silver, and eight copper coins, was found in the village of Bhiṭaura, district Fyzabad (Avadh). In 1906 Burn wrote a paper on this find, entitled 'Some Coins of the Maukharis and of the Thanesar line',[5] illustrating some specimens of the coins. 248 silver coins of this hoard bear the legend 'Śrī Śaladata' (Śrī Śīlāditya), while nine belong to 'Śrī Pratapaśala' (Śrī Pratāpa-śīla). Of the remaining pieces, thirty-two silver coins are of the Maukhari kings and one of a king named Harśa (not Harsha). Names of kings, and in many cases dates also, have disappeared from 192 coins. The gold coin is of the later Indo-Scythian type, the copper coins are of Pratāp-āditya II of Kashmir, and, of the four remaining silver coins, three are 'Varāha drammas' and one is of uncertain type.

The 518 silver coins are of the Gupta silver type; that is, they bear a large head with a date on one side, and a peacock on the other, with a long inscription. On seven coins the head faces the right, as on the Gupta coins, while on the others, which include all the coins of Śīlāditya and Pratāpa-śīla, it faces the left. The inscriptions round the peacock in every case but one read

[1] Plate 5, no. 21, pp. 36–7 and 46.

[2] Rāja-taraṅgiṇī, vii, 956, 1550, 1571, 1579. Kalhaṇa informs us that Harsha's chief queen, Vasanta-lekhā, belonged to the Śāhī dynasty.

[3] *J.R.A.S.* (1903) 547. He seems to have noted the fact of Harsha-deva's connection with Karṇāṭa only.

[4] *J.R.A.S.* (1906) 847.

[5] Ibid. 843–50.

'*Vijitāvaniravanipati-śri*-[name]-*devo-jayati*'. The vowels are only marked in a few types.

We concur with Burn that 'it . . . seems reasonable to identify Pratāpaśīla [of the coins] with Prabhākaravardhana, and Śīlāditya with Harṣa'.[1] Burn, however, does not argue a case for this identification, and the ascription has been accepted only half-heartedly by scholars, who have probed into the question no further than to quote the authority of Burn.[2] We, on our part, believe that Burn's ascription, though not backed by lengthy or reasoned argument, is correct, and is supported by the following facts.

The Chinese sources inform us that Harsha adopted the title Śīlāditya on his accession to the throne of Kanauj. Though the indigenous sources do not mention Harsha as Śīlāditya they honour Prabhākara-vardhana with the *biruda* 'Pratāpa-śīla', which disposes us to treat the Chinese evidence regarding Harsha's title as perfectly authentic. Harsha records his father's *biruda* in his inscriptions, and it seems reasonable to expect that he used his own also for official purposes. He may well have issued his coins in the name Śīlāditya, especially if his father also used his own *biruda* for marking his coinage, which we believe he did, as we agree with Burn that the Pratāpa-śīla coins of the Bhiṭaura hoard are to be attributed to Prabhākara-vardhana.

The two dated coins of Pratāpa-śīla raise certain problems. Each date consists of three symbols. The topmost is the letter 'sa', and one would ordinarily expect this to represent the hundreds, as the other symbols are apparently 10 and 1 or 11. The only symbol for a number which resembles 'sa' is, however, that used for 40, but no symbol for hundreds, resembling this letter, is to be found. The coins of Śīlāditya show clearly that the 'sa' cannot be 40. Therefore it seems that 'sa' stands for *saṁvat*. The 'sa', on Śīlāditya's coins, which invariably appears as the highest symbol, is also to be taken for *saṁvat*. The regnal years on Harsha's inscriptions which we know to be dated in the Harsha era are also preceded by the word *saṁvat*, which no doubt stands for the Harsha *saṁvat*. The point cannot therefore be raised that 'sa', representing *saṁvat* on the Śīlāditya coins, stands for a long-established era, such as the Vikrama or the Gupta, which need not have been referred to by its full name. We believe that, as well as in his inscriptions, Harsha used '*saṁvat*' for his own era on the coins, abbreviating the word owing to their small size.

The figure 11 on Pratāpa-śīla's coins and the dates ranging from 1 to 33 on those of Śīlāditya indicate that the two monarchs used different eras. It may well be that Prabhākara-vardhana, who was the first king of his family to merit the status of a *mahārāj-ādhirāja*, celebrated his attainment by starting an era, a practice which was very much in fashion in those days. Harsha founded yet another era in A.D. 606, probably to commemorate his success in securing the throne of Kanauj, and seems to have issued his first coins under

[1] Op. cit., 847.

[2] e.g. R. S. Tripathi, *History of Kanauj*, p. 117, writes: 'If the Śīlāditya coins found in the Bhiṭaura hoard . . . are to be attributed to Harṣa, as has been done by Sir Richard Burn . . . .'

the newly acquired title Śīlāditya.[1] The date 11 on Pratāpa-śīla's coins is quite in keeping with the length of Prabhākara-vardhana's reign which started in *c.* A.D. 580 and terminated in A.D. 606. New coins may have been issued by Prabhākara-vardhana to celebrate the birth of his second son, Harsha, in A.D. 590, when he had been on the throne for nearly a decade. It is well known that coins were generously distributed among the populace on festive occasions. The date 33 on Śīlāditya's coins is compatible with the duration of Harsha's reign, which we believe lasted for about forty years from A.D. 606 to 647.

From a comparison of the coins of the Maukharis and those of Śīlāditya and Pratāpa-śīla, it is clear that, though the general appearance of the Gupta-type coins was retained by the two dynasties, the established tradition of a continuous dating was repeatedly flouted.

The site of the hoard containing so many coins of Śīlāditya, and the fact that Pratāpa-śīla's and Śīlāditya's coins have been found together, also favours the identification of the two kings with Prabhākara-vardhana and Harsha. Though several Śīlādityas ruled from Valabhī in the sixth, seventh, and eighth centuries, the coins of the Bhiṭaura hoard may be most satisfactorily ascribed to Harsha Śīlāditya of Kanauj.

It will be well to examine here the arguments put forward by Hoernle[2] in repudiation of Burn's ascription.

Hoernle states that before attributing the Śīlāditya coins to Harsha it must be proved that he had assumed that title officially. He argues that as neither Bāṇa nor other Indian sources mention this *biruda* of Harsha, and as Hsüan-tsang is our sole authority on this point, it appears that Harsha was known by this title only in 'Buddhist monkish communities'.

One may comment in passing that if, as Hoernle believes, Harsha was popularly known by this *biruda* amongst Buddhist communities only, the chances are greatly reduced of finding a reference to this *biruda* by Bāṇa, who was a brahman. However, Hoernle's argument is better refuted by the fact that Harsha is referred to as Śīlāditya not only by the Buddhist monk who was a pious pilgrim, but also by the diplomatic envoys who had been deputed by the Chinese emperor to carry out official business. They, at least, may not be expected to have obtained their information only from the 'Buddhist monkish communities'. We believe that the Śīlāditya coins of the Bhiṭaura hoard are the available indigenous evidence of the official use of the title Śīlāditya by Harsha, who seems to have followed his father's tradition in issuing his coinage under a *biruda*.

Hoernle attributes the coins of Pratāpa-śīla and Śīlāditya to a king possessing both these names, known to us from the *Rāja-taraṅgiṇī*.[3] Speaking of Pravara-sena, Kalhaṇa says that 'he replaced Pratāpaśīla, also called Śīlāditya, the son of Vikramāditya, who had been dethroned by enemies in the kingdom of his father'. This Vikram-āditya is identified with Yaśo-dharman of Mālava,

[1] Beal i, p. 213; Watters i, p. 343. [2] *J.R.A.S.* (1909) 446 ff.
[3] Book III, verse 330.

who is credited in the Mandasor inscription[1] with extensive conquests as far as the Himalayas, and Śīlāditya with his son of the same name.[2]

Hoernle writes that 'the discovery of coins in the names of Pratāpaśīla and Śīlāditya is a striking confirmation of the truth of the old Indian tradition'. According to his reckoning, Pratāpa-śīla Śīlāditya's rule lasted 'from about 580 to 608, or 612, that is from the death of Vikramāditya (Yaśodharman) to the great victory, or to the coronation of Harshavardhana'. This gives us a period from 26 to 32 years.[3] But we know that Burn reads the latest date on Śīlāditya's coins as 33. There are thirteen coins with this date. On fourteen more coins the symbol for 30 is fairly certain, but the unit is gone or very doubtful in every case. These coins may be of the year 32, but they may well have been of the years after 33. In any case, as the longest duration ascribed to Pratāpa-śīla Śīlāditya by Hoernle is thirty-two years, the Śīlāditya coins issued at least until the year 33 cannot be ascribed to the Pratāpa-śīla Śīlāditya of Hoernle's identification. Moreover, there is little likelihood that a king named Pratāpa-śīla Śīlāditya should have chosen his latter name for use on a large number of coins for most of his regnal years but should have suddenly reverted to the former name for the coins issued in his eleventh year. This is, however, not a conclusive argument, because we are making this suggestion only on the basis of the coins so far discovered.

But Hoernle is not in the least disturbed by the fact of this discrepancy in the dates he ascribes to Pratāpa-śīla Śīlāditya and those yielded by the coins of Śīlāditya. He writes that it 'creates no difficulty for the exact length of the period is, of course, uncertain'. About the date 33, considered to be quite certain by Burn, he remarks that one has to be very cautious about the indifferently preserved figures.

Hoernle puts forth the third and the last argument in favour of his theory as the 'possible connection of the still unexplained "aulikara" crest of Yaśodharman with the curious crescent-like object on the head of the king on those coins'. It seems to have escaped Hoernle's notice that the crescent appears on both the Maukhari and the Śīlāditya coins. It appears on the Gupta coins also, accompanied by other marks.[4] Apparently both the Maukharis and the Vardhanas retained this symbol, which was one of the minor features of the Gupta-type coin they copied. Neither the Maukharis nor the Vardhanas were *chandra-vaṁśī* kings. The Maukharis are specifically stated to be the descendants of the hundred sons of Aśva-pati, who was blessed with such abundant progeny by Manu Vaivasvata.[5] The Maukharis thus were *sūrya-vaṁśīs*. The Vardhanas belonged to neither of the two traditional royal families.

[1] *C.I.I.* iii, no. 33.

[2] Hoernle, *J.R.A.S.* (1903) 545 ff.

[3] Hoernle's identification of Pratāpaśīla-Śīlāditya as the son of Yaśodharman is, incidentally, almost impossible if Kalhaṇa's chronology is followed. Yaśodharman was evidently at the height of his power in A.D. 532 (*C.I.I.* iii, p. 154), and it is most unlikely that he could have survived until A.D. 580.

[4] Allan, *Catalogue of the Coins of the Gupta Dynasties and of Śaśāṅka, King of Gauda* (in the British Museum), pp. 89 ff. (Kūmāra Gupta I's coins), 119 ff. (Skanda Gupta's coins).

[5] The Harāhā inscription: *E.I.* xiv. 110 ff.

Hoernle's arguments thus prove too weak to refute the ascription of the Śīlāditya coins of the Bhiṭaura hoard to Harsha.

We shall conclude the discussion with a brief description of the coins of Pratāpa-śīla and Śīlāditya.[1]

Pratāpa-śīla: The peacock's head is to the left on all nine coins. The crescent on the king's head is about the centre of the top (instead of at the crown as it is usually in the Maukhari coins), and each horn terminates in a knob. We have earlier referred to the reading of the dates and the fact that the vowels are omitted in spelling his name.

Śīlāditya: The name is usually written 'Śrīśaladata', vowels being very rarely given. On a few coins the final letters are more clearly *-tya*. The crescent on the head has also various forms and positions. The dates on many of the coins are varied and present considerable difficulty, as the symbols differ from the ordinary forms. Burn, however, is positive in his reading of the sign 'sa' as the highest symbol and the symbols 30+1 and 30+3. On the basis of their dates and number, the coins may be classified as follows:[2]

	Date	*Number of Coins*
1.	1 (?)	1
2.	6 (?)	10
3.	10 (?)	10
4.	20 (?)	6
5.	25 (?)	1
6.	30 (?)	4
7.	31 (?)	3
8.	31	24
9.	33	30
10.	3–	14
		103
11.	Illegible dates	181
	Total	284

Six coins of Śīlāditya are preserved at the British Museum, of which three were presented to it in 1906 by the Government of the Central Provinces, India. The remaining three were given it by Nelson Wright, one in 1910 and two in 1929. The dates are clearly read 'sa' (*saṁvat*) on two coins[3] and the tens figure '3' is clear on a third one.[4] Thus the readings on these coins are in accordance with Burn's observations on the coins of Śīlāditya.[5]

We have not been able to find out whether the then Central Provinces Government came into possession of the coins as the result of a local discovery,

[1] For a full description see Burn, *J.R.A.S.* (1906) 745–7, on which we base this brief account giving the salient points of the coins.

[2] Most dates are accompanied by a query mark, as Burn finds the readings doubtful.

[3] One from the 1906 group and the other of 1910.

[4] One of the two coins presented in 1929. The dates on the remaining three coins are very doubtful or illegible.

[5] These coins were kindly examined for us by Professor A. K. Narain of the Banaras Hindu University.

or whether it was given a share of the large Bhiṭaura hoard of which a portion was presented by it to the British Museum. The most regrettable practice of distribution without labelling was quite common in those days. However, if the coins presented by the Central Provinces Government belong to that province, they are a secondary evidence of the extension of Harsha's empire in that region. The importance of this possibility should not be exaggerated, however, first because we are not sure of the find-spot of the coins in question and, secondly, because coins are the most easily portable objects.

APPENDIX III

The Various Readings of Dates on Maukhari Coins

Name of king	Rapson, *Indian* Coins, p. 27	Cunningham, *A.S.I.R.* ix, p. 27, xvi, p. 81	Smith, *J.A.S.B.* 1894, pp. 193–4	Fleet, *Ind. Ant.* xiv, p. 68	Burn, *J.R.A.S.* 1906, pt. ii, pp. 843 ff.	Brown, *Catalogue of the coins of the Guptas and the Maukharis, etc. in the Provincial Museum, Lucknow*, 1920 pp. 29 ff.	Dikshit, as cited by Aravamuthan pp. 102 ff.
Iśāna-varman	54, 55	55? or 155 or 257	54	40, 60, 70, or 5	4x?	4x x x 5?	245, 257 54, 55, 57
Śarva-varman			58		234? 23x?	(2)34 (2)3x	258, 259, 25x, 58
Avanti-varman					250, 57? or 67? 71	250, –57, –70	260, 26x, 67, 71

Note. N. G. Majumdar (*I.A.* xlvi, pp. 125 ff.) writes: 'The date-marks on the coins of Śarva-varman have totally disappeared and as such it is impossible to say at what particular dates these coins were issued.'

GENEALOGICAL TABLES

Genealogical Table of the Vardhanas

Pushpa-bhūti

|

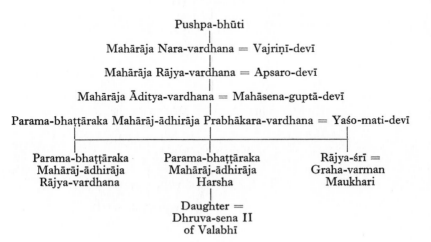

Mahārāja Nara-vardhana = Vajriṇī-devī

|

Mahārāja Rājya-vardhana = Apsaro-devī

|

Mahārāja Āditya-vardhana = Mahāsena-guptā-devī

|

Parama-bhaṭṭāraka Mahārāj-ādhirāja Prabhākara-vardhana = Yaśo-mati-devī

Parama-bhaṭṭāraka Mahārāj-ādhirāja Rājya-vardhana	Parama-bhaṭṭāraka Mahārāj-ādhirāja Harsha	Rājya-śrī = Graha-varman Maukhari
	| Daughter = Dhruva-sena II of Valabhī	

Genealogical Table of the Later Guptas

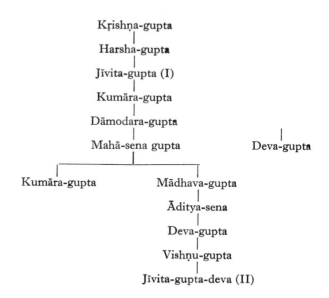

- Kṛishṇa-gupta
  - Harsha-gupta
    - Jīvita-gupta (I)
      - Kumāra-gupta
        - Dāmodara-gupta
          - Mahā-sena gupta
            - Kumāra-gupta
            - Mādhava-gupta
              - Āditya-sena
                - Deva-gupta
                  - Vishṇu-gupta
                    - Jīvita-gupta-deva (II)

- Deva-gupta

Genealogical Table of the Maukharis of Kanauj

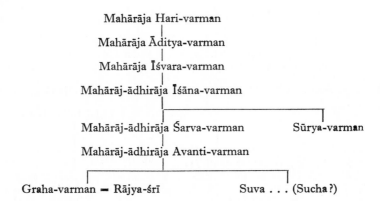

Mahārāja Hari-varman
|
Mahārāja Āditya-varman
|
Mahārāja Īśvara-varman
|
Mahārāj-ādhirāja Īśāna-varman
|
- Mahārāj-ādhirāja Śarva-varman
  |
  Mahārāj-ādhirāja Avanti-varman
  |
  - Graha-varman = Rājya-śrī
  - Suva . . . (Sucha?)
- Sūrya-varman

Genealogical Table of the Maitrakas of Valabhī

- (1) Senā-pati Bhaṭārka
  - (2) Senā-pati Dhara-sena I
  - (3) Mahārāja Droṇa-siṁha
  - (4) Mahārāja Dhruva-sena I
  - (5) Mahārāja Dhara-paṭṭa
    - (6) Mahārāja Guha-sena
      - (7) Mahā-dhirāja Dhara-sena II
        - (8) Mahārāja Śīlāditya I, Dharm-āditya
          - Ḍera-bhaṭa
            - Śīlāditya
              - (15) Śīlāditya II
                - (16) Śīlāditya III
                  - (17) Śīlāditya IV
                    - (18) Śīlāditya V
                      - (19) Śīlāditya VI, Dhru-bhaṭa
            - (14) Khara-graha II Dharm-āditya
            - (13) Dhruva-sena III
        - (9) Khara-graha I
          - (10) Dhara-sena III
          - (11) Dhruva-sena II, Bālāditya (Dhruva-bhaṭṭa)
            - (12) Parama-bhaṭṭāraka Mahārāj-ādhirāja Dhara-sena IV

Note. According to Fleet's arrangement (*C.I.I.* iii, no. 39), rulers (15) to (19) are Śīlāditya III to Śīlāditya VII. The father of no. (15) although he did not rule has been called Śīlāditya II.

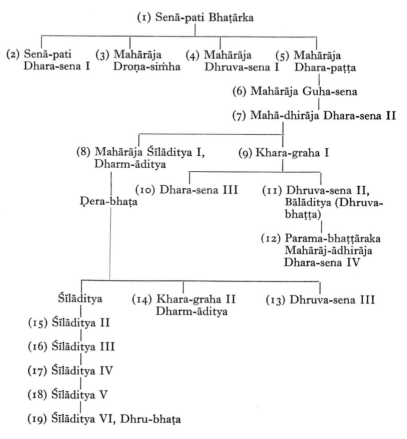

Genealogical Table of the Chālukyas of Vātāpi

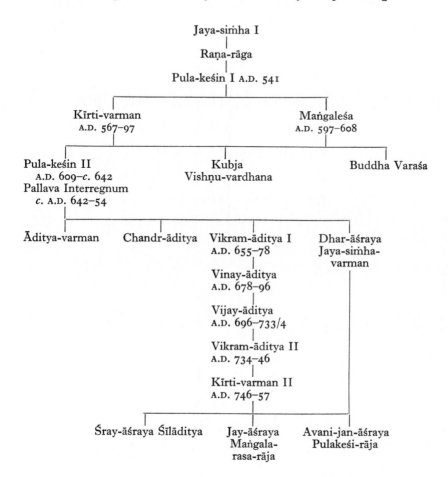

- Jaya-siṁha I
  - Raṇa-rāga
    - Pula-keśin I A.D. 541
      - Kīrti-varman A.D. 567–97
      - Maṅgaleśa A.D. 597–608
        - Pula-keśin II A.D. 609–*c.* 642; Pallava Interregnum *c.* A.D. 642–54
          - Āditya-varman
          - Chandr-āditya
          - Vikram-āditya I A.D. 655–78
            - Vinay-āditya A.D. 678–96
              - Vijay-āditya A.D. 696–733/4
                - Vikram-āditya II A.D. 734–46
                  - Kīrti-varman II A.D. 746–57
          - Dhar-āśraya Jaya-siṁha-varman
            - Śray-āśraya Śīlāditya
            - Jay-āśraya Maṅgala-rasa-rāja
            - Avani-jan-āśraya Pulakeśi-rāja
        - Kubja Vishṇu-vardhana
        - Buddha Varaśa

Genealogical Table of the Pallavas of Kāñchī

Siṁha-varman, *c.* A.D. 550–75
|
Siṁha-vishṇu, *c.* A.D. 575–600
|
Mahendra-varman I, *c.* A.D. 600–30
|
Nara-siṁha-varman I, *c.* A.D. 630–68
|
Mahendra-varman II, *c.* A.D. 668–70
|
Parameśvara-varman I, *c.* A.D. 670–95
|
Nara-siṁha-varman II, *c.* A.D. 695–722
|
Parameśvara-varman II, *c.* A.D. 722–30
|
Nandī-varman II Pallava-malla, *c.* A.D. 730–96

BIBLIOGRAPHY

Abhidāna Chintāmaṇi of Hema-chandra, *see* Hema-chandra.

Acharya, G. V., *The historical inscriptions from Gujarat*, 3 vols., Bombay, 1933–8.

Aelian: *On Animals*, tr. Scholfield, A. F., 3 vols., (Loeb) London, 1958–9.

Agrawala, V. S., *Harsha-charita — Ek Sāṅskṛitik Adhyayan* (in Hindi), Patna, 1953.

—— *India as known to Pāṇini—a study of the cultural material in the Ashṭ-ādhyāyī*, Lucknow, 1953.

Aitareya Brāhmaṇa of the Ṛig Veda, tr. Haug, M., S.B.H., Allahabad, 1922.

—— tr. Keith, A. B., *Aitareya and Kaushītaki Brāhmaṇas*, H.O.S., vol. xxv, Cambridge, Mass., 1920.

Aiyangar, K. V. Rangaswami, *Some aspects of ancient Indian polity*, 2nd ed., Madras, 1935.

—— *Rāja-Dharma*, Adyar, Madras, 1941.

—— 'Additional verses of Kātyāyana on Vyavahāra' in *A volume of studies in indology presented to Prof. P. V. Kane*, Poona, 1941, pp. 7–17.

—— *Aspects of social and political system of Manu-smṛiti*, Lucknow, 1949.

—— *Some aspects of the Hindu view of life according to Dharma-śāstra*, Baroda, 1952.

Aiyangar, K. V. Rangaswami, Commemoration volume, Shashṭiabdapūrti Commemoration Committee, Madras, 1940.

Aiyangar, S. Krishnaswamy, *Evolution of Hindu administrative institutions in south India*, Madras, 1931.

Aiyer, C. P. Ramaswami, *Indian political theories*, Madras, 1937.

—— *The philosophical basis of Indian legal and social systems*, Madras, 1949.

al-Bīrūnī, Abū al Raihān Muhammad ibn Ahmad, *Tahqīq mā li'l-Hind*, tr. Sachau, E. C., as *Alberuni's India*, London, 1888.

Allan, J., *Catalogue of the coins of the Gupta dynasties and of Śaśāṅka, King of Gauḍa* (in the British Museum), London, 1914.

—— *Catalogue of the coins of ancient India* (in the British Museum), London, 1936.

Altekar, A. S., *State and government in ancient India*, Banaras, 1949.

—— *Sources of Hindu Dharma in its socio-religious aspects*, Sholapur, 1952.

Amara-siṁha, *Nāma-liṅg-ānuśāsana* or *Amara-kosha*, ed. Sharma, A. D., and Sardesai, N. G., Poona, 1941.

Anekārtha-samuchchaya of Śāśvata, *see* Śāśvata.

Aparājita-pṛichchhā of Bhuvana-deva, *see* Bhuvana-deva.

APARĀRKA or APARĀDITYA, *Aparārka-Yājñavalkīya-dharmaśāstra-nibandha*, 2 vols., Poona 1903–4.

ĀPASTAMBA, *Dharma-sūtra*, tr. Bühler, G., S.B.E., vol. ii, pt. 1, Oxford, 1879.

ARAVAMUTHAN, T. G., *The Kaveri, the Maukharis and the Sangam age*, Madras, 1925.

ARRIAN, *Anabasis of Alexander* and *Indica*, tr. McCrindle, J. W., as *Ancient India as described by Megasthenes and Arrian*, London, etc., 1877; *The invasion of India by Alexander the Great . . .*, London, 1896; Robson, E. I., *History of Alexander. Indica*, 2 vols., (Loeb) London, 1929–33.

ĀRYA-DEVA, *Chatuḥ-śatikā*, ed. Hara-prasad Shastri (*Memoirs of the Asiatic Society of Bengal*, vol. iii, no. 8, pp. 449–514), Calcutta, 1914.

Ārya Mañju-śrī-mūla-kalpa, ed. and tr. Jayaswal, K. P. (text and translation with commentary), *The imperial history of India*, Lahore, 1934.

Asahāya (See Nārada, *Dharma-śāstra*).

AŚOKA, *Edicts*, ed. Hultzsch, E., Corpus Inscriptionum Indicarum, vol. i *Inscriptions of Aśoka*, Oxford, 1925.

Atharva-veda Saṁhitā, tr. Griffith, R. T. H., 2 vols., Banaras, 1916–17.

—— ed. Satavalekar, S. D. 3rd ed., Surat, 1957.

BAGCHI, PRABODH CHANDRA, *India and China*, Bombay, 1950.

BALLĀLA, *Bhoja-prabandha*, Sanskrit text with a commentary by Kedaranatha Sharma, Banaras, 1956.

—— —— tr. Gray, H. L., New Haven, Conn., 1950.

BĀṆA-BHAṬṬA, *Harsha-charita* (with the commentary of Śaṅkara), ed. Kasinatha Pandurang Parab, 5th ed., Nirnaya Sagara Press, Bombay, 1925.

—— —— The commentary of Raṅga-nātha, Madras Government MSS. Collection, no. R. 2703.

—— —— ed. Kane, P. V., Bombay, 1918, and 2nd edn., Delhi, etc., 1965.

—— —— tr. Cowell, E. B. and Thomas, F. W., London, 1929.

—— —— tr. (Hindi) Chaudhuri, S. 2 vols., Kathautia, Bihar, 1948, 1950.

—— *Kādambarī*, ed. Kane, P. V., Bombay, 1920.

—— —— tr. Ridding, C. M., London, 1896.

BANERJI, R. D. *History of Orissa*, 2 vols., Calcutta, 1930–1.

—— *The age of the imperial Guptas*, Banaras, 1933.

BAPAT, P. V., ed., *2,500 years of Buddhism*, Delhi, 1956.

BARNETT, L. D., *Antiquities of India*, London, 1913.

BARTHÉLEMY-SAINT-HILAIRE, JULES, *Buddhism in India*, tr. Laura Ensor as *Hiouen Thsand in India*, Calcutta, 1952.

BARUA, K. L., *History of Kāmarūpa*, Shillong, 1933.

BASAK, R. G., *History of north-eastern India* (c. A.D. *320–760*), Calcutta, 1934.

BASHAM, A. L., *The wonder that was India*, London, 1954.

BAUDHĀYANA, *Dharma-sūtra*, ed. A. Chinnasvami Shastri, Banaras, 1934.

BUDHĀYANA, tr. Bühler, G., S.B.E., vol. xiv, pt. 2, Oxford, 1889.

BENDALL, C., *A journey of literary and archaeological research in Nepal and northern India during the winter of 1884–5*, Cambridge, 1886.

BENI PRASAD, *Theory of government in ancient India*, Allahabad, 1927.

—— *The state in ancient India*, Allahabad, 1928.

Bhagavad-gītā, Sanskrit text with Hindi translation, Gita Press, Gorakhpur, 22nd reprint, V.S. 2017 (1958).

—— tr. Edgerton, F., H.O.S., vols. xxxviii–xxxix, Cambridge, Mass., 1944.

—— tr. Radhakrishnan, S., London, 1948.

Bhandarkar, D. R., Commemoration volume, ed. Law, B. C., Calcutta, 1940.

BHANDARKAR, R. G., *Early history of the Dekkan*, 3rd ed., Calcutta, 1928.

Bhandarkar, R. G., Commemoration volume, Bhandarkar Oriental Research Institute, Poona, 1917.

Bhoja-prabandha of Ballāla, *see* Ballāla.

BHUVANA-DEVA, *Aparājita-pṛichchhā*, ed. Mankad, P. A., Baroda, 1950.

Bodhi-chary-āvatāra of Śānti-deva, *see* Śānti-deva.

BOERSCHMANN, E., *Die Baukunst und religiöse Kultur der Chinesen.* III: *Chinesische Pagoden*, Berlin and Leipzig, 1931.

Bṛihad-āraṇyaka Upanishad, tr. Swami Madhavananda, Almora, 1950.

BṚIHASPATI, *Dharma-śāstra*, tr. Jolly, J., S.B.E., vol. xxxiii, Oxford, 1889.

—— —— reconstructed by Aiyangar, K. V. Rangaswami, G.O.S., Baroda, 1941.

Bṛihaspati-sūtra (*Bārhaspatya Artha-śāstra*), tr. Thomas, F. W., Lahore, 1921.

Bṛihat-saṁhitā of Varāha-mihira, *see* Varāha-mihira.

BROWN, C. J., *Catalogue of the coins of the Guptas, Maukharis, etc. in the Provincial Museum*, Lucknow, 1920.

—— *The coins of India*, London, 1922.

BÜHLER, J. G., *Indian palaeography*, ed. Fleet, J. F., I.A., vol. xxxiii, Bombay 1904.

Cambridge history of India, vol. i, ed. Rapson, E. J., Cambridge, 1922.

Cambridge history of India, vol. ii, unpublished text consulted.

Chach Nāmā of Muhammad Alī i. Hamīd i. Abū Bakr Kūfi, *see* Muhammad Alī i. Hamīd i. Abū Bakr Kūfi.

CHAṆḌEŚVARA, ṬHAKKURA, *Rāja-nīti-ratnākara*, ed. Jayaswal, K. P., 2nd ed. Patna, 1936.

CHATTERJI, G. S., *Harsha-vardhana* (in Hindi), 2nd ed., Allahabad, 1950.

Chhāndogya Upanishad, tr. Ganganatha Jha, Poona, 1942.

COOMARASWAMY, A. K., *Spiritual authority and temporal power in the Indian theory of government*, New Haven, Conn., 1942.

CSOMA (S.) K., *Tibetan studies*, ed. Ross, E. Denison, Calcutta, 1912.

CUNNINGHAM, A., *The coins of medieval India*, London, 1874.

—— *Book of Indian Eras*, London, 1889.

CUNNINGHAM, A., *The coins of ancient India from the earliest times to the seventh century*, London, 1891.

—— *The ancient geography of India*, ed. Surendranath Majumdar Sastri, Calcutta, 1924.

DANDEKAR, R. N., *History of the Guptas*, Poona, 1941.

DAṆḌIN, *Daśa-kumāra-charita*, ed. Kale, M. R., Bombay, 1917.

DASGUPTA, S. N., *A history of Indian philosophy*, Calcutta, 1922–55.

—— *A history of Sanskrit literature: classical period*, Calcutta, 1947.

DES ROTOURS, R., *Traité des fonctionnaires* (*et*) *Traité de l'armée*. Trad. de la *Nouvelle Histoire des T'ang*, chs. 46–50, 2 vols., Leiden, 1947–8.

DEVAṆṆA BHAṬṬA, *Smṛiti-chandrikā*, ed. Gharpure, J. R., Bombay, 1918.

DEY, N. L., *Geographical dictionary of ancient and medieval India*, London, 1927.

Dhamma-pada, tr. Müller, F. Max., S.B.E., vol. x, pt. 1, Oxford, 1881.

—— tr. Radhakrishnan, S., London, 1950.

Dīgha-Nikāya, tr. Rhys Davids, T. W. and Carpenter, J. E., *Dialogues of the Buddha*, 3 vols., S.B.B., London, 1899, 1900, 1921.

Dīpa-vaṁsa, ed. and tr. Oldenberg, H., London, 1879.

DIKSHITAR, V. R. R., *Hindu administrative institutions*, Madras, 1929.

—— *The Mauryan polity*, Madras, 1932.

—— *Gupta polity*, Madras, 1952.

DREKMEIER, C., *Kingship and community in early India*, Stanford, California, 1962.

DUTT, SUKUMAR, *Buddhist monks and monasteries in India*, London, 1962.

DVIVEDI, HAZARI PRASAD, *Bāṇa-bhaṭṭa kī ātma-kathā* (historical novel in Hindi), Allahabad, 1946.

ELLIOT, Sir H. M., and DOWSON, J., *History of India as told by its own historians: the Muhammadan period*, 8 vols., London, 1867–77; vol. ii reprinted with contributions by Mohammad Habib, Hodiwala, S. H., and Khaliq Ahmad Nizami, Aligarh, 1952.

ETTINGHAUSEN, M. L., *Harṣa Vardhana, empereur et poète, etc.*, London, 1906.

FA-HSIEN, (*Tzŭ*) *Chi Yu T'ien-chu Shih* (the Shaman Fa-hsien's account of his travels in India), tr. Legge, J., *A record of buddhistic kingdoms*, etc., Oxford, 1886.

—— —— Giles, H. A., *The travels of Fa-hsien* (A.D. 399–414) or *Record of buddhistic kingdoms*, Cambridge, 1923.

FLEET, J. F., see *Gupta Inscriptions*.

FUNG YU-LAN, *History of Chinese philosophy*, vols. i and ii, tr. Bodde, Derk, London, 1937, 1953.

GADRE, A. S., *Important inscriptions from the Baroda state*, Baroda, 1943.

GANDHI, L. B., ed., *A descriptive catalogue of MSS. in the Jain Bhandars at Pattan*, 2 vols., Baroda, 1937.

GANGOPADHYAYA, D. C., *The eastern Chalukyas*, Banaras, 1937.

Gauḍa-rāja-mālā, ed. Chanda, R. P., Rajshahi, Bengal, V.S. 1319 (1912).

Gauḍa-lekha-mālā, ed. Maitreya, A. K., Rajshahi, Bengal, V.S. 1319 (1912).

Gauḍa-vaho of Vākpati, *see* Vākpati.

GAUTAMA, *Dharma-sūtra*, ed. Srinivasacharya, L., Mysore, 1917.

—— tr. Bühler, G., S.B.E., vol. ii, Oxford, 1879.

GHOSHAL, U. N., *A history of Indian political ideas*, Bombay, 1959, originally published as *A history of Hindu political theories*, Oxford, 1927.

—— *The agrarian system in ancient India*, Calcutta, 1930.

—— *Studies in Indian history and culture*, Calcutta, 1957, originally published as *The beginnings of historiography and other essays*, Calcutta, 1944.

—— *History of Hindu public life*, Calcutta, 1945.

GHURYE, G. S., *Caste and class in India*, 2nd ed., Bombay, 1957; first published as *Caste and race in India*, New York, 1932.

GNOLI, R., *Nepalese inscriptions in Gupta characters*, Rome, 1956.

GONDA, J., *Notes on Brahman*, Utrecht, 1950.

—— *Epithets in the Ṛgveda*, The Hague, 1959.

—— *Ancient Indian kingship from the religious point of view*, Leiden, 1966.

GOPALAN, K., *The history of the Pallavas of Kāñcī*, Madras, 1928.

Gupta Inscriptions, ed. Fleet, J. F., Corpus Inscriptionum Indicarum, vol. 3, *Inscriptions of the early Gupta kings and their successors*, Calcutta, 1888.

HAN YU-SHAN, *Elements of Chinese historiography*, California, 1955.

Hari-vaṁśa Purāṇa of Jina-sena Sūri Punnāṭa, *see* Jina-sena Sūri Punnāṭa.

Hari-vaṁśa Purāṇa of Svayaṁbhū-deva, *see* Svayaṁbhū-deva.

HARSHA (Śīlāditya), *Liṅg-ānuśāsana*, ed. Venkatarama Sharma, V., Madras, 1931.

—— *Nāg-ānanda*, ed. Karmarkar, R. D., Poona, 1919.

—— —— tr. Boyd, P., London, 1872.

—— —— tr. Wartham, H., London, etc., 1911.

—— —— ed. and tr. Kale, M. R., Bombay, 1953.

—— *Priya-darśikā*, tr. Nariman, G. D., William Jackson, A. V., and Ogden, C. J., New York, 1923.

—— —— ed. Ramachandra Mishra, Banaras, 1955.

—— *Ratn-āvalī*, ed. Joglekar, K. M., Hedvi, 1907.

—— —— ed. and tr. Devadhar, C. R., and Suru, N. G., 2nd ed., Poona, 1954.

HEESTERMANN, J. C., *The ancient Indian royal consecration*, The Hague, 1957.

HELD, G. J., *The Mahābhārata: an ethnological study*, London and Amsterdam, 1935.

HEMA-CHANDRA, *Abhidāna-chintā-maṇi*, ed. Muniraj Jayanta Vijaya, Bhavnagar, 1920.

—— *Kāvy-ānuśāsana*, ed. Parikh, R. C., Bombay, 1964.

HEMA-CHANDRA, *Trishashṭi-śalākā-purusha-charita*, tr. Johnson, Helen M., 4 vols. Baroda, 1931–54.

HEMĀDRI, *Chatur-varga-chintā-maṇi*, ed. (Pandit) Siromani, B. C., 4 vols., Calcutta, 1873–1911.

History and culture of the Indian people, ed. Majumdar, R. C., and Pusalker, A. D., Bharatiya Vidya Bhavan Series: vol. i, *The Vedic age*, London, 1951; vol. ii, *The age of imperial unity*, Bombay, 1951; vol. iii, *The classical age*, Bombay, 1954; vol. iv, *The age of imperial Kanauj*, Bombay, 1955.

HSÜAN-TSANG, *Ta T'ang Hsi Yü Chi* (compiled by Pien Chi), collated text, Peking, 1955.

—— —— tr. Beal, S., *Buddhist records of the western world*, 2 vols., London, 1906.

—— —— ed. Watters, T., *On Yuan Chwang's travels in India*, 2 vols., ed. after his death by Rhys Davids, T. W., and Bushell, S. W., London, 1904–5. *See also* Julien, S.

HUART, C., *Ancient Persia and Iranian civilization*, tr. Dobie, M. R., London, 1927.

HUI-LI: *Ta Tz'u-u-ên Ssu San-tsang Fa-shih Chuan* (*Life of the Master of the Law, Tripitaka, of the Great Monastery of Motherly Love*), tr. Beal, S., *The Life of Hiuen-Tsiang*, London, 1911. *See also* Julien, S.

HULTZSCH, E., *see* Aśoka.

I-TSING, *Nan-hai-chi-kuei-nai-fa-ch'uan* (*A record of Buddhist practices sent home from the Southern Sea*), tr. Takakusu, J., *A record of the Buddhist religion as practised in India and the Malay Archipelago* (*A.D. 671–695*), Oxford, 1896.

IYENGAR, P. T. S., *History of the Tamils to A.D. 600*, Madras, 1929.

JAIMINI, *Mīmāṁsā-sūtras*, tr. Thadani, N. V. (with original Sanskrit text), Delhi, 1952.

—— —— tr. of Śabara-svāmin's commentary by Ganganatha Jha, G. O. S., Baroda, 1933–6.

Jain Bhandars at Pattan, A descriptive catalogue of MSS. in the; *see* Gandhi, L.B.

Jātakas, tr. Cowell, E. B., Cambridge, 1895–1913.

JAYA-DEVA, *Prasanna-rāghava*, ed. Paranjpye and Panse, Poone, 1894.

—— —— ed. and tr. (Hindi) Sesha raja Sharma, Banaras, 1956.

JAYASWAL, K. P., *Manu and Yājña-valkya: a comparison and a contrast*, Calcutta, 1930.

—— *History of India* (Nāga-Vākātaka imperial period, A.D. 150 to 350), Lahore, 1933.

—— ed. *Ārya Mañju-śrī-mūla-kalpa*, tr. as *An imperial history of India*, Lahore, 1934.

—— *Hindu polity*, 2nd ed., Bangalore, 1943.

JĪMŪTA-VĀHANA, *Vyavahāra-mātrikā*, ed. Asutosh Mookerjee, Sarasvati, *Memoirs of the Asiatic Society of Bengal*, vol. iii, no. 5, pp. iii, 277–353, Calcutta, 1912.

JINA-SENA SŪRI PUNNĀṬA, *Hari-vaṁśa Purāṇa*, Māṇika-chandra Digaṁbara Jaina Grantha-mālā, Bombay, 1930.

JOUVEAU-DUBREUIL, G., tr. Dikshitar, V. R. R., *Ancient history of the Deccan*, Pondicherry, 1920.

JULIEN, S., *Histoire de la vie de Hiouen-thsang et de ses voyages dans l'Inde*, Paris, 1853.

—— *Mémoires sur les contrées occidentales . . .*, Paris, 1857–8.

KĀLIDĀSA, *Abhijñāna Śākuntalaṁ*, ed. Pischel, R., H. O. S., vol. xvi, 1922.

—— —— tr. Ryder, A. W., *Śakuntalā and other works*, London, 1912.

—— —— ed. and tr. Kale, M. R., Bombay, 1957.

KALHAṆA, *Rāja-taraṅgiṇī*, tr. Stein, M. A., Westminster, 1900.

KĀMANDAKA, *Nītisāra*, ed. Mitra, Rajendralal, Calcutta, 1884.

—— —— tr. Dutt, M. N., Calcutta, 1896.

Kāma-sūtra of Vātsyāyana, *see* Vātsyāyana.

KANE, P. V., *History of Dharma-śāstra*, vols. i–v, Poona, 1930–62.

—— ed. the *Harsha-charita* of Bāṇa-bhaṭṭa, chs. 1–8 (with introduction and notes), Bombay, 1918, and 2nd ed., Delhi, etc., 1965.

—— *History of Sanskrit poetics*, 3rd ed., Delhi, 1961.

KARAKA, D. F., *History of the Parsis including their manners, customs, religion and present position*, 2 vols., London, 1884.

Kathā-sarit-sāgara of Soma-deva, *see* Soma-deva.

KĀTYĀYANA, *Dharma-śāstra*, ed. Bandyopadhyaya, N. C., Calcutta, 1927.

Kātyāyana-smṛiti-sāroddhāra, Kātyāyanasmṛti on Vyayahāra law and procedure, text reconstructed, trans., notes, and introduction by Kane, P. V., Bombay, 1933. (*See also* Aiyangar, K. V. Rangaswami.)

Kaumudī-Mahotsava of Vijjakā, *see* Vijjakā.

KAUṬILYA, *Artha-śāstra*, tr. Shamasastry, R., 6th ed., Mysore, 1960.

—— —— text, trans., and a study, Kangle, R. P., 3 parts, University of Bombay, 1960, 1963, 1965.

Kāvy-ānuśāsana of Hema-chandra, *see* Hema-chandra.

KEITH, A. B., *A history of Sanskrit literature*, Oxford, 1928.

KEITH, A. B. and MACDONELL, A. A., *Vedic index of names and subjects*, London, 1912.

KHARE, J. H., *Sources of the mediaeval history of the Deccan*, vol. i, Poona, 1935.

KOSAMBI, D. D., *The culture and civilisation of ancient India in historical outline*, London, 1965.

KRAMRISCH, STELLA, *The art of India*, London, 1954.

Kṛitya-kalpa-taru of Lakshmī-dhara Bhaṭṭa, *see* Lakshmī-dhara Bhaṭṭa.

KROEBER, A. L., *Configurations of culture growth*, Berkeley and Los Angeles, 1944.

KSHEMENDRA, *Bṛihat-kathā-mañjarī*, ed. (Pandit) Śiva-datta, M., and Parab, K. P., Bombay, 1931.

KSHEMENDRA, *Loka-prakāśa*, ed. Pt. Jagaddhar Zadoo, Srinagar, 1947.

Kural, tr. Pope, G. U., *The Sacred Kural*, London, 1886.

—— tr. Dikshitar, V. R. R., *Tiru-kkural*, Madras, 1949.

—— tr. Aiyar, V. V. S., *The Kural*, Tiruchirapalli, 1952.

LA VALLÉE POUSSIN (Louis de), *Dynasties et Histoire de l'Inde depuis Kanishka jusqu'aux invasions musulmanes*, Paris VIe, 1935.

LAKSHMĪ-DHARA BHAṬṬA, *Kṛitya-kalpa-taru*, vol. xi, *Rāja-dharma-kāṇḍa*, ed. Aiyangar, K. V. Rangaswami, Baroda, 1943.

LAMOTTE, E., *Le Traité de la Grande Vertu de Sagesse de Nagarjuna* (*Mahā-prajñā-pāramitā-śāstra*), 2 vols., Louvain, 1944, 1949.

LANDON, P., *Nepal*, 2 vols., London, 1928.

LAW, B. C., *Tribes in ancient India*, Lahore, 1926.

—— *The historical geography of ancient India*, Paris, 1954.

Law, B. C., Commemoration volume, ed. Bhandarkar, D. R., Sastri, K. A. N., and others, 2 vols., Calcutta and Poona, 1945–6.

LAW, N. N., *Studies in ancient Hindu polity*, London, 1914.

—— *Interstate relations in ancient India*, London, 1920.

—— *Aspects of ancient Hindu polity*, Oxford, 1921.

LÉVI, S., *Le Népal*, 3 vols., Paris, 1905–8.

MACDONELL, A. A., *A history of Sanskrit literature*, London, 1900.

MADHU-SŪDANA, *Bhāva-bodhini see* Bühler, G., I. A., vol. ii, pp. 127–8.

Mahā-bhārata (see also *Bhagavad-gītā*), tr. Dutt, M. N., Calcutta, 1895–1905.

—— tr. Roy, P. C., 2nd ed., Calcutta, 1919–35.

—— critical edition; eds. Sukthankar, V. S., Belvalkar, S. K., and others; vol. vii, *Bhīshma-parvan* (Belvalkar, 1945–7); vols. xiii–xvi, *Śānti-parvan* (Belvalkar, 1949–54), Bhandarkar Oriental Research Institute, Poona, 1927– in progress.

MAHALINGAM, T. V., *South Indian polity*, Madras, 1955.

MAITY, S. K., *Economic life of northern India in the Gupta period*, A.D. *300–500*, Calcutta, 1958.

Majjhima-Nikāya, tr. Lord Chalmers, *Further dialogues of the Buddha*, 2 vols., S.B.B., London, 1926–7.

MAJUMDAR, R. C., ed., *The history of Bengal*, vol. i, Dacca, 1943.

—— *Ancient India*, Banaras, 1952.

—— gen. editor, *History and culture of the Indian people*, 11-volume project, Bharatiya Vidya Bhavan, Bombay, 1951– in progress.

—— *The classical accounts of India*, Calcutta, 1960.

MAJUMDAR, R. C., and ALTEKAR, A. S., *A new history of the Indian people*, vol. vi (*The Vākāṭaka-Gupta age*), Lahore, 1946.

MAMMAṬA, *Kāvya-prakāśa*, ed. Karmarkar, B. D., 6th ed., Poona, 1950.

—— —— tr. Ganganatha Jha, Allahabad, 1925.

Mānasāra, ed. and tr. Prasanna Kumar Acharya, vol. iii, *Mānasāra on architecture and sculpture*; vols. iv and v, *Architecture of Mānasāra*, London, etc., 1933.

MĀNAS-ŌLLĀSA, *see* Someśvara III.

MANU, *Dharma-śāstra*, ed. Jolly, J., London, 1887.

—— tr. Burnell, A. C., *The ordinances of Manu*, London, 1884.

—— tr. Bühler, G., *The laws of Manu*, S.B.E., vol. xxv, Oxford, 1886.

—— tr. (with notes) Ganganatha Jha, 5 vols., Calcutta, 1922–9.

Mārkaṇḍeya Purāṇa, tr. Pargiter, F. E., Calcutta, 1904.

Matsya Purāṇa, tr. Basu, B. D., Allahabad, 1916.

MAYŪRA, *Sanskrit poems by Mayūra*, Quackenbos, G., New York, 1917.

MCCRINDLE, J. W., *Ancient India as described by Megasthenes (fragments of the Indika of) and Arrian (first part of the Indika of)*, Calcutta 1877.

—— *The commerce and navigation of the Erythraean Sea, being a translation of the Periplus Maris Erythraei*, Calcutta, etc., 1879.

—— *Ancient India as described by Ptolemy, being a translation of* [the relevant parts of the] *Geography*, Calcutta, etc., 1885.

—— *Ancient India as described in classical literature*, Westminster, 1901.

MEES, G. H., *Dharma and society*, The Hague, 1935.

MEGASTHENES, *see* McCrindle, J. W.

MERU-TUṄGA, *Prabandha-chintā-maṇi*, tr. Tawney, C. H., Calcutta, 1899.

MITRA-MIŚRA, *Vīra-mitrodaya (Vyavahār-ādhyāya* only) revised by Maithili Pandita; ed. Babu Rama, Kidderpore, 1815.

MOOKERJI, R. K., *Harsha*, London, 1926.

MORAES, G. M., *Kadamba-kula*, Bombay, 1931.

Mudrā-rākshasa of Viśākha-datta, *see* Viśākha-datta.

MUGALI, R. S., *The Heritage of Karṇāṭaka*, Bangalore, 1946.

MUHAMMAD 'ALĪ I. HAMĪD I. ABŪ BAKR KŪFĪ, *Chach Nāmā*, tr. Mirza Kalich-beg Fredun-beg, 2 vols., Karachi, 1900, 1902.

MUNSHI, K. M., *The glory that was Gurjara-deśa* (*A.D. 550–1300*), Bombay, 1954.

NAGOJI, *Kāvya-pradīp-oddyota*, ed. Chandorkar, D., Poona, 1898.

NĀRADA, *Dharma-śāstra*, as *The Institutes of Nārada together with copious extracts from the Nāradabhāshya of Asahāya and other standard commentaries*, ed. Jolly, J., Calcutta, 1885 (shorter version).

NĀRADA and BṚIHASPATI, *Dharma-śāstras* as *The Minor Law-books*, tr. Jolly, J., S.B.E., vol. xxxiii, Oxford, 1889 (longer version).

NEEDHAM, N. J., and WANG LING, *Science and civilization in China*, Cambridge, 1954–65.

Nīti-vāky-āmṛita of Soma-deva Sūri, *see* Soma-deva Sūri.

Nirukta of Yāska, *see* Yāska.

OJHA, G. H., *Bhāratīya Prāchīna Lipi-mālā*, Ajmer, 1918.

Pañcha-tantra, tr. Williams, A., *Tales from the Pañcha-tantra*, Oxford, 1930.

PANIKKAR, K. M., *Śri Harsha of Kanauj*, Bombay, 1922.

—— *The origin and evolution of kingship in India*, Baroda, 1938.

PĀṆINI, *Asht-ādhyāyī*, ed. and tr. Vasu, S. C., 2 vols., Allahabad, 1891–8.

PARĀŚARA, *Dharma-śāstra*, with the commentary of Sāyaṇa Mādhavāchārya, ed. Vaman Sastri Islāmapurkar, 3 vols., Bombay, 1893–1919.

PARGITER, F. E., *Purāṇa text of the dynasties of the Kali age*, London, 1913.

PATAÑJALI, *Mahā-bhāshya*, ed. and tr. Chatterji, K. C., Calcutta, 1957.

Periplus Maris Erythraei, *see* McCrindle, J. W.

PETECH, L., *A study on the chronicles of Ladakh* (*Indian Tibet*), Calcutta, 1939.

—— *Mediaeval history of Nepal, c.* 750–1480, Rome, 1958.

PIRES, E. A., *The Maukharis*, Madras, 1934.

PLINY (Plinius Secundus), *Natural history*, trs. Rackham, H., Jones, W. H. S., and Eichholz, D. E., 11 vols., (Loeb) London, 1938–62.

PLUTARCH, *Moralia*, tr. Babbitt, F. C., and others, 15 vols., (Loeb) London, 1927–49.

—— *The parallel lives*, tr. Perrin, B., 11 vols., (Loeb) London, 1914–26.

Prabandha-chintā-maṇi of Meru-tuṅga, *see* Meru-tuṅga.

PRINSEP, JAMES, *Essays on Indian antiquities*, London, 1858.

PRZYLUSKI, J., *La Légende de l'empereur Açoka*, Paris, 1923.

PTOLEMY, *Geography*, *see* McCrindle, J. W.

RADHAKRISHNAN, S., *The Hindu view of life*, London, 1927.

—— *Eastern religion and western thought*, London, 1939.

—— *Indian philosophy*, London, 1948.

Rāja-nīti-ratnākara, *see* Chaṇḍeśvara Ṭhakkura.

Rāmāyaṇa of Vālmīki, ed. Varamasarma Vashishtha, Banaras, 1957.

—— tr. and ed. Dutt, M. N., Calcutta, 1891–3.

—— tr. Griffith, R. T. H., Banaras, 1895.

—— tr. Shastri, Hari Prasad, London, 1952–9.

RAPSON, E. J., *Catalogue of the Indian coins*, London, 1897.

RAWLINSON, H. G., *Intercourse between India and the Western world*, Cambridge, 1916.

RAY, H. C., *The dynastic history of northern India*, 2 vols., Calcutta, 1931, 1936.

RAYCHAUDHURI, H. C., *Political history of ancient India*, 4th ed., Calcutta, 1938, 6th ed., 1953.

REGMI, D. R., *Ancient Nepal*, Calcutta, 1960.

RÉMUSAT, J. P. A., *Nouveaux Mélanges asiatiques*, 2 vols., Paris, etc., 1829.

RIEPE, DALE, *The naturalistic tradition in Indian thought*, Seattle, Washington, 1961.

Ṛig-veda Saṁhitā, with the commentary of Sāyaṇa, ed. Müller, F. Max, 6 vols., London, 1849–74.

—— tr. into English by Griffith, R. T. H., 2 vols., 2nd ed., Banaras, 1896, 1897.

Ross, Sir E. Denison, Memorial volume, ed. Katre, S. M. . . . and Gode, P. K., Bombay, 1939.

ROTOURS, R. DES., *see* Des Rotours, R.

SALETORE, R. N., *Life in the Gupta age*, Bombay, 1943.

—— *Ancient Indian political thought and institutions*, New York, 1963.

SAMPURNANAND, *Samrāṭ Harsha-vardhan* (in Hindi), Bombay, V.S. 1977, 1920.

SANKALIA, H. D., *The University of Nālandā*, Madras, 1934.

—— *The archaeology of Gujarat*, Bombay, 1941.

ŚĀNTI-DEVA, *Bodhichary-āvatāra*, with commentary *Pañjikā* of Prajñākaramati, ed. La Vallée Poussin, Louis de, Calcutta, 1901–14. French tr., Paris, 1907. *Also* ed. Vaidya, P. L., Darbhanga, 1960.

SARTON, G., *Introduction to the history of science*, 3 vols., Baltimore, 1927–47.

SASTRI, K. A. NILAKANTA, *The theory of pre-Muslim Indian polity*, Madras, 1912.

—— *History of Śrī Vijaya*, Madras, 1949.

—— *Factors in Indian history*, Waltair, 1949.

—— *A comprehensive history of India*, vol. ii, *The Mauryas and Satavahanas, 325 B.C.–A.D. 300*, Madras, etc., 1957.

—— *Age of the Nandas and Mauryas*, Banaras, 1952.

ŚAŚVATA, *Anekārtha-samuchchaya*, ed. Oka, K. G., Poona, 1918.

—— —— ed. Narayan Nathji Kulkarni, Poona, 1929.

Śata-patha Brāhmaṇa, pts. i–v, tr. Eggeling, J., S.B.E., vols. xii, xxvi, xli, xliii, xliv, Oxford, 1882–1900.

SEN, B. C., *Some historical aspects of the inscriptions of Bengal*, Calcutta, 1942.

SEN, D. C., *History of Bengali language and literature*, Calcutta, 1911.

SEWELL, ROBERT, *A forgotten empire*, London, 1900.

—— *Siddhāntas and the Indian calendar*, Calcutta, 1924.

SHAH, C. L. J., *Jainism in northern India*, London, 1932.

SHARMA, R. S., *Aspects of political ideas and institutions in ancient India*, Delhi, 1959.

—— *Indian Feudalism: c. 300–1200*, Calcutta, 1965.

SHASTRI, J. L., *Political thought in the Purāṇas*, Lahore, 1944.

SINGHAL, C. R., *Bibliography of Indian coins*, pt. 1, ed. Altekar, A. S., Bombay, 1950.

SINHA, B. P., *The decline of the kingdom of Magadha* (*cir.* A.D. *455–1000*), Patna 1954.

SINHA, H. N., *Sovereignty in ancient Indian polity*, London, 1938.

SIRCAR, D. C., *Select inscriptions bearing on Indian history and civilization*, vol. i, Calcutta, 1942.

—— ed. *Land system and feudalism in ancient India*, Calcutta, 1966.

SMITH, V. A., *Catalogue of coins in the Indian Museum, Calcutta*, vol. i, Oxford, 1906.

—— *Early history of India*, 4th ed. Oxford, 1924.

Smṛiti-chandrikā of Devaṇṇa Bhaṭṭa, *see* Devaṇṇa Bhaṭṭa.

SOḌḌHALA, *Udaya-sundarī-kathā*, ed. Dalal, C. D., and Krishnamacharya, E., G.O.S., Baroda, 1920.

SOMADEVA, *Kathā-sarit-sāgara*, tr. Tawney, C. H., 2 vols., Calcutta, 1880–4.

SOMA-DEVA SŪRI, *Nīti-vāky-āmṛita*, ed. Soni, P. L., 2 vols., S. B. H., Bombay, 1923, 1933.

SOMEŚVARA III (Bhū-loka-malla), *Mānas-ōllāsa* (or *Abhilasit-ārtha-chintā-maṇi*, ed. Shrigondekar, G. K., G.O.S., no. 28, Baroda, 1925.

STRABO, *Geography*, tr. Jones, H. L., 8 vols., (Loeb) London, 1917–33.

Subhāshita ratna bhāṇḍāgāra, ed. Parab, K. P., 5th ed., Bombay, 1911.

Subhāshit-āvalī of Vallabha-deva, *see* Vallabha-deva.

ŚUKRA, *Nīti-sāra*, ed. Oppert, G., Madras, 1882.

—— —— tr. Sarkar, B. K., S.B.H., Allahabad, 1914.

SVAYAṀBHŪ-DEVA, *Hari-vaṁśa Purāṇa*, relevant references in Jain, J. P., *The Jaina sources of the history of ancient India*, Delhi, 1964, pp. 201–2, and *H.C.I.P.*, vol. iv, Bombay, 1955, pp. 217 and 219.

Taittirīya Brāhmaṇa, ed. Mitra, R. L., 3 vols., Calcutta, 1859.

Taittirīya Saṁhitā (the Veda of the Black Yaju School), see *Yajur-veda.*

Taittirīya Upanishad, ed. Röer, E., (Bibliotheca Indica) Calcutta, 1850.

TAKAKUSU, J., *Taisho Issaikyō*, Tokyo, 1924– .

TAKAKUSU, J., and LÉVI, S., *Hōbōgirin. Dictionnaire encyclopédique du Bouddhisme* . . ., Tokyo–Paris, 1929–37.

TĀRĀ-NĀTHA, tr. as *Mystic tales of Lāmā Tārā-nātha* by Datta, B. N., Calcutta, 1944.

Tā'rīkh-i-Mā'ṣūmī, tr. Malet, G. G., Bombay, 1855.

THAPAR, R., *Aśoka and the decline of the Mauryas*, London, 1961.

Thomas, F. W., Memorial volume, Eastern and Indian studies, ed. Katre, S. M., and Gode, P. K., Bombay, 1939.

Tirukkural, see *Kural.*

TOYNBEE, ARNOLD J., *A study of history*, vol. x, London, etc., 1954.

TRIPATHI, R. S., *History of Kanauj to the Moslem conquest*, Banaras, 1937.

Tuḥfat ul Kirām, tr. Lt. Postans in *J.A.S.B.*, vol. xiv, 1845.

Udaya-sundarī-kathā of Soḍḍhala, *see* Soḍḍhala.

UPADHYAYA, V. D., *Gupta Sāmrājya kā Itihās* (in Hindi), Allahabad, 1939.

The *Upanishads*, tr. and ed. Müller, F. Max, S.B.E., vols. i and xv, Oxford, 1879, 1884.

Upanishads, The Principal, ed. Radhakrishnan, S., London, 1953.

VAIDYA, C. V., *History of medieval Hindu India*, vol. i, Poona, 1921.

Vājasaneyi Saṁhitā (White Y.V.), see *Yajur-veda*.

VĀKPATI, *Gauḍa-vaho*, ed. Pandit, S. P., Bombay, 1887; 2nd ed. by Utgikar, N. B., Poona, 1927.

VĀLMĪKI, *Rāmāyaṇa*, see *Rāmāyaṇa*.

VALLABHA-DEVA, *Subhāshit-āvalī*, ed. Peterson, P. and (Pandit) Durgaprasada, Bombay, 1886.

VARĀHA-MIHIRA, *Bṛihat-saṁhitā*, ed. and tr. Subrahmanya Sastri, V. and Ramakrishna Bhat, M. 2 vols., Bangalore, 1947.

VARMA, V. P., *Studies in Hindu political thought and its metaphysical foundations*, Delhi, 1954.

VASISHṬHA, *Dharma-sūtra*, tr. Bühler, G., S.B.E., vol. xiv, pt. 2, Oxford, 1882.

VĀTSYĀYANA, *Kāma-sūtra*, ed. Goswami, D. L., Banaras, 1929.

—— —— tr. Basu, B. N., revised by Ghose, R. L., 5th ed., Calcutta, 1944.

VENKATESWARA, S. V., *Indian culture through the ages*, vol. 2, Mysore, 1932.

VIJJAKĀ, *Kaumudi-Mahotsava*, ed. and tr. Sakuntala Rao Sastri, Bombay, 1952.

Vinayas, tr. Rhys Davids, T. W., and Oldenberg, H., *Vinaya texts*, S.B.E., vols. xiii, xvii, xx, Oxford, 1881, 1882, 1885.

Vīra-mitrodaya of Mitra-miśra, *see* Mitra-miśra.

VIRJI, K. K., *Ancient history of Saurashtra*, Bombay, 1955.

VIŚĀKHA-DATTA, *Mudrā-rākshasa*, tr. Kale, M. R., Bombay, 1900.

Vishṇu Dharma-śāstra, tr. Jolly, J., as *The Institutes of Vishṇu*, S.B.E., vol. vii, Oxford, 1880.

Vishṇu Purāṇa, tr. Wilson, H. H., 5 vols., 3rd ed., London, 1864–70.

VOGEL, J. Ph., *Antiquities of the Chamba State*, Calcutta, 1911.

VYĀSA, *Mahā-bhārata*, see *Mahā-bhārata*, also *Bhagavad-gītā*.

Vyavahāra-mātṛikā, see Jīmūta-vāhana.

WADDEL, L. A., *Lhasa and its mysteries*, London, 1906.

WALEY, ARTHUR, *The analects of Confucius*, London, 1938.

—— *The real Tripitaka and other pieces*, London, 1952.

WANG LING, *see* Needham, N. J.

WARMINGTON, E. H., *Commerce between the Roman Empire and India*, Cambridge, 1928.

WEBER, M., *The religion of India*, tr. Gerth, H. and Martindale, D., Glencoe, Illinois, 1958.

WHYTE, A. F., *China and foreign powers*, London, 1927.

WINTERNITZ, M., *A history of Indian literature*, Calcutta, 1927.

YĀJÑA-VALKYA, *Dharma-śāstra*, ed., with the comm. of Viśva-rūpa, Trivandrum, 1922–4. *See also* Aparārka.

—— tr. Gharpure, J. R., Bombay, 1936–44.

Yajur-veda: Taittirīya Saṃhitā (Black Y.V.), tr. Keith, A. B., 2 vols., H.O.S., vols. xviii–xix, Cambridge, Mass., 1914.

—— —— ed. Ananta Shastri Dhupkar, Aundh, 1945.

—— *Vājasaneyi Saṁhitā* (White Y.V.), tr. Griffith, R. T. H., Banaras, 1927.

—— —— ed. Satavalekar, S. D., Aundh, V.S. 2003 (1946).

YĀSKA, *Nirukta*, ed. Roth, R., Göttingen, 1852.

—— —— ed. and tr. Lakshman Sarup, 2 vols., Lahore, 1927.

ZIMMER, H., *Myth and symbols in Indian art*, ed. Campbell, J., New York, 1951.

JOURNALS

Annals of the Bhandarkar Oriental Research Institute, vol. 13, Poona, 1930–1.

Annals of the Mysore Archaeological Department, various volumes, Mysore, 1923–41.

Archaeological Survey of India:

Archaeological Survey of India Reports, various volumes, Calcutta, 1871–1887 for the years 1862–84.

Annual Report of the Director-General of Archaeology, pt. i, Calcutta, 1902–3, 1920–1.

Annual Report, pt. ii, Calcutta, 1902–3, 1915–16.

Annual (consolidated) Report of the Archaeological Survey of India, 1921/2–1929/30.

Appendix III to the *Annual Report of the Archaeological Survey of India*, Calcutta and Delhi, 1926/7–1932/3.

Memoirs of the Archaeological Survey of India, various volumes, nos. 1–50, 1919–35, and no. 60, Delhi, 1939.

Asiatic Journal and Monthly Register for British and Foreign India, China and Australia, N.S. vol. 20, London, 1836.

Asiatic Society of Bengal:

Proceedings of the Asiatic Society of Bengal, vols. for the years 1865 to 1897 and 1902, 1903, and 1904, Calcutta, 1870–1905.

The Journal of the Asiatic Society of Bengal, vols. 1–73, 1832 to 1904; vols. 74–5, 1905–36, and Index to vols. 1–23 (1832–54), Calcutta.

Journal and Proceedings of the Asiatic Society of Bengal, New series, vols. 1 to 30, 1905–34.

Journal of the Asiatic Society of Bengal, Third series, part I—Letters, part II—Science, part III—Year Book, vols. 1–24, 1935–58; Fourth series, vol. i, 1959– . (Title of Journal and name of Society vary; current title *Journal of Asiatic Society*, Calcutta.)

Asiatick Researches or Transactions of the Society, instituted in Bengal, vols. i–xx, Calcutta, 1788–1836.

Proceedings and Transactions of the Royal Asiatic Society of Bengal, Calcutta, 1824.

Bombay Gazetteer, vol. i, Bombay, 1877; vol. viii, Bombay, 1907.

Bulletin of the School of Oriental and African Studies, vol. 18, London, 1955; vol. 25, London, 1962.

East and West, N.S. vol. 12, no. 4, Rome, 1961.

Epigraphia Indica, vols. i, iii, iv, vi–xv, xvii–xxiv, xxvi, xxviii, xxxii, Calcutta, Delhi, 1888– .

Hyderabad Archaeological Series, no. 14, Hyderabad, 1941.

Imperial Gazetteer of India, new ed., vol. iv, Oxford, 1909. (Vols. i–xxvi, 1907–9.)

Indian Antiquary, vols. i, ii, iv–x, xiii, xv, xix, xxxix, Bombay, 1872–1910.

New Indian Antiquary, vol. iii, Bombay, 1940.

Indian Culture, vol. i, Calcutta, 1934; vol. iv, Calcutta, 1937.

Indian Historical Quarterly, vols. iii–vi, x–xiii, xv, xx, xxvi–xxviii, Calcutta, 1925–52.

Journal of the American Oriental Society (Supplement to the), vol. xxxi, New Haven, Conn., 1911; vol. lxxviii, New Haven, Conn., 1958.

Journal of the Andhra Historical Research Society, vols. i, ii, vi, vii, Rajahmundry, 1926–32.

Journal asiatique, IXe sér., tome xv, Paris, 1900.

Journal of the Assam Research Society, vol. xii, Gauhati, 1944.

Journal of the Bihar and Orissa Research Society, vols. ix, xv, xix, xxii, xxiv, Patna. (Vols. i–xxix, 1915–43.)

Journal of the Bombay Branch of the Royal Asiatic Society, vols. xx, xxiv, and N.S. i, iii, and iv. (O.S., Bombay, 1841–1923; N.S., Bombay, 1925–).

Journal of the Department of Letters, various volumes, Calcutta, 1920–46.

Journal of Indian History, vol. xxxviii, pt. 1, Trivandrum, 1960; vol. xlii, pt. 1, Trivandrum, 1964.

Journal of the Madras University, various volumes, Madras, 1928–57.

Journal of the Numismatic Society of India, various volumes, published from different places, 1939– .

Journal of the Royal Asiatic Society of Gt. Britain and Ireland, various volumes, London.

Transactions 1–3, 1823–33. Superseded by:

Journal, vols. 1–20, 1834–63; New Series, 1–21, 1864–89; Third series, 1889– .

Mélanges chinois et bouddhiques (Institut belge des Hautes Études chinoises), Brussels, 1932, 1935, and 1937.

Ostasiatische Zeitschrift, Berlin, 1912–43.

Proceedings and Transactions of the All India Oriental Conference, various volumes, published from different places, 1919– .

Proceedings of the Indian History Congress, Third session, Calcutta, 1939; Seventh session, Madras, 1944; Ninth session, Annamalai, 1945.

Quarterly Journal of the Mythic Society, vol. 22, Bangalore, 1930.

T'oung Pao, etc., vols. i, vi, and xiii. (Vols. 1–10, 1890–9; Second series, vol. 1, 1900– .)

Vienna Oriental Journal, various volumes, Vienna. (Vols. i–xxvi, 1887–1912. Later, *Wiener Zeitschrift für die Kunde des Morgenlandes*.)

BIBLIOGRAPHY FOR CHINESE PRIMARY AND SECONDARY SOURCES

CHAVANNES, E. *Les inscriptions chinoises de Bodh-Gayā* (extract from *Revue de l'histoire des religions*, vol. xxxiv, no. 1, 1896) (pamphlet), Paris, 1896.

LÉVI, S., 'Les missions de Wang Hieuen-Ts'e dans l'Inde', *Journal asiatique*, IXe sér., tome xv, 1900, pp. 297 ff. and pp. 401 ff. It is a most erudite article based on Ma Tuan-lin's work, certain passages of the Old and the New T'ang histories, and the *Fa Yuan Chu Lin* (also see above pp. 208–9 and 216).

Ed. LI FANG, *T'ai P'ing Yü Lan*, Ssŭ Pu Ts'ung Kan, Series 3 (see also above pp. 208 and 213).

Ed. LIU HSÜ, *Chiu T'ang Shu*, Ssŭ Pu Pei Yao edition (see also above pp. 208 and 211).

MA TUAN-LIN, *Wên Hsien T'ung K'ao* (Historical investigation of public affairs), Wan Yu Wên Ku Shih T'ung edition.

—— —— tr. Hervey de Saint-Denys, M.-J.-L. d', *Ethnographie des peuples étrangers de la Chine*, 2 vols., Paris–London, 1876.

—— —— Book 335, fol. 14, tr. Rémusat, J. P. A., *Nouveaux Mélanges asiatiques*, vol. 1, pp. 193 ff. (2 vols., Paris, 1829).

—— —— Book 338, fol. 14, anonymous translation into English in the *Asiatic Journal and Monthly Register for British and Foreign India, China and Australia*, N.S., vol. 20, May–August 1836, pp. 213–22, 313–16; reproduced in the *J.A.S.B.*, vol. vi, pt. 1, 1837, pp. 61–75; tr. (Fr.) Pauthier, J. P. G., *Journal asiatique*, IIIe sér., 1839, pp. 257–400 and also separately, Paris, 1840; tr. (Fr.) Julien, S., *Journal asiatique*, IVe sér., 1847, pp. 81–121. The above translated into English by Burgess, J., *I.A.*, vol. ix, 1880 (see also above pp. 209 and 216).

MING-HSIANG, *Ta T'ang Ku San-tsang Hsüan-tsang Fa-shih Hsing-chuang* (Report on the career of the late Master of the Law, Hsüan-tsang of Great T'ang) (*c.* A.D. 664). Taishō Issaikyō, ed. Takakusu, J., 50, 214, Tokyo, 1924– .

Eds. Ou-yang Hsiu and Sung Ch'i, *Hsin T'ang Shu*, K'ai Ming Erh Shih Wu Shih edition (see also above pp. 209 and 214).

Pulleyblank, E. G., *The background of the rebellion of An Lu-shan*, London, 1955.

Ssŭ-ma Kuang, *Tzŭ Chih T'ung Chien*, Ssŭ Pu Pei Yao edition. This is the most carefully compiled work (see also above pp. 209 and 215).

Tao-hsüan, *Chi Ku Chin Fo Tao Lun Hêng*, Takakusu, vol. 52 (also see above pp. 208–9).

—— *Hsü Kao Sêng Chuan* (The continuation of the lives of eminent monks) (A.D. 645; added to until 667), Taishō Issaikyō, Takakusu, J., 50, 446, and 458b, Tokyo, 1924– .

—— *Shih-chia Fang-chih* (A record of the country of Śākya-muni [The Buddha.]) (A.D. 650), Taishō Issaikyō, Takakusu, J., 51, Tokyo, 1924– .

Tao-shih, *Fa Yüan Chu Lin*, P'in Ch'ieh Ching Shê edition (see also above pp. 208–9).

Tu Yu, *T'ung Tien*, Wan Yu Wên Ku Shih T'ung edition (see also above pp. 208 and 210).

Eds. Wang Ch'in-jo and Yang I, *Ts'ê Fu Yüan Kuei*, 1754 edition (see also above pp. 209 and 213).

Wang P'u, *T'ang Hui Yao*, Peking 1955 edition (see also above pp. 208 and 212).

For the following authors see the main Bibliography: Bagchi, Boerschmann, des Rotours, Fa-hsien, Fung Yu-lan, Han Yu-shan, Hsüan-tsang, Hui Li, I-tsing, Julien, Needham and Wang Ling, Saint-Hilaire, Waley, and Whyte.

INDEX

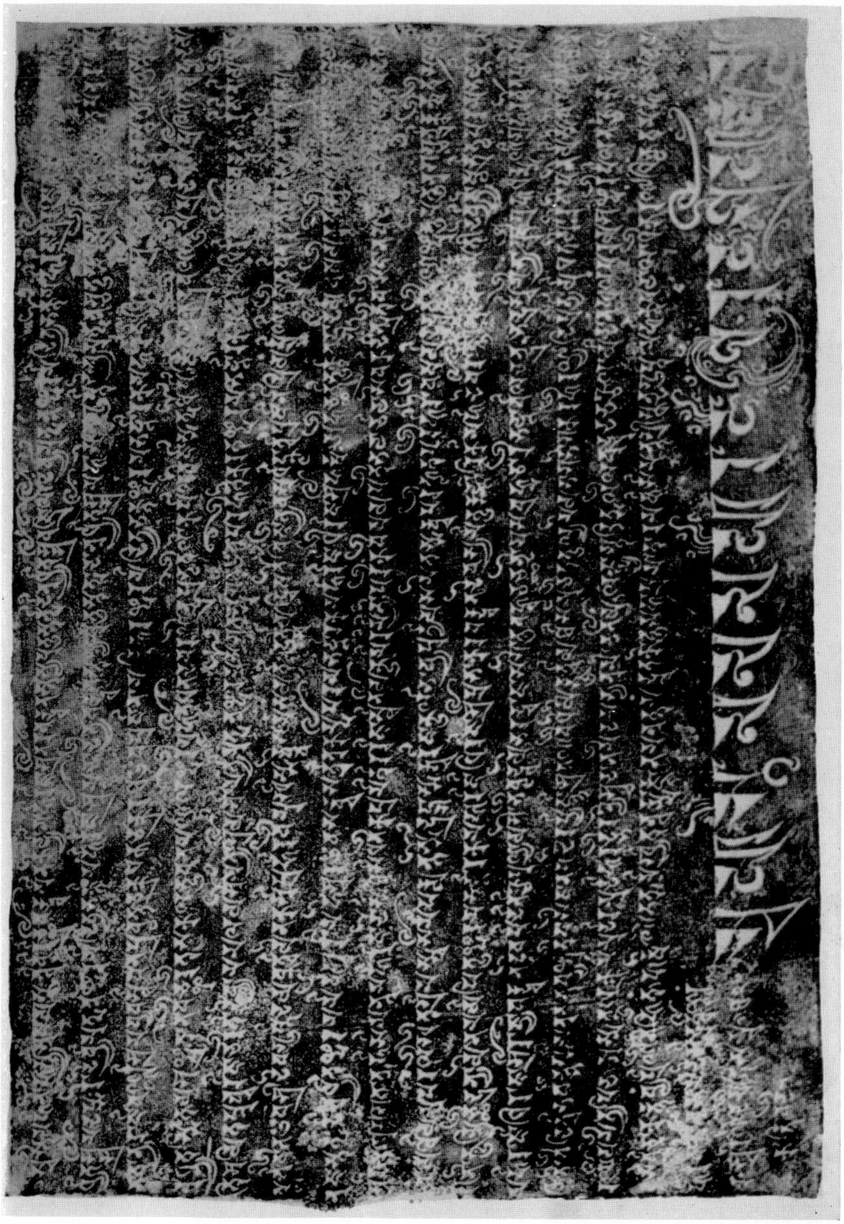

The Bāṅskhera Plate of Harsha of the year 22 (A.D. 628–9)

PLATE 2

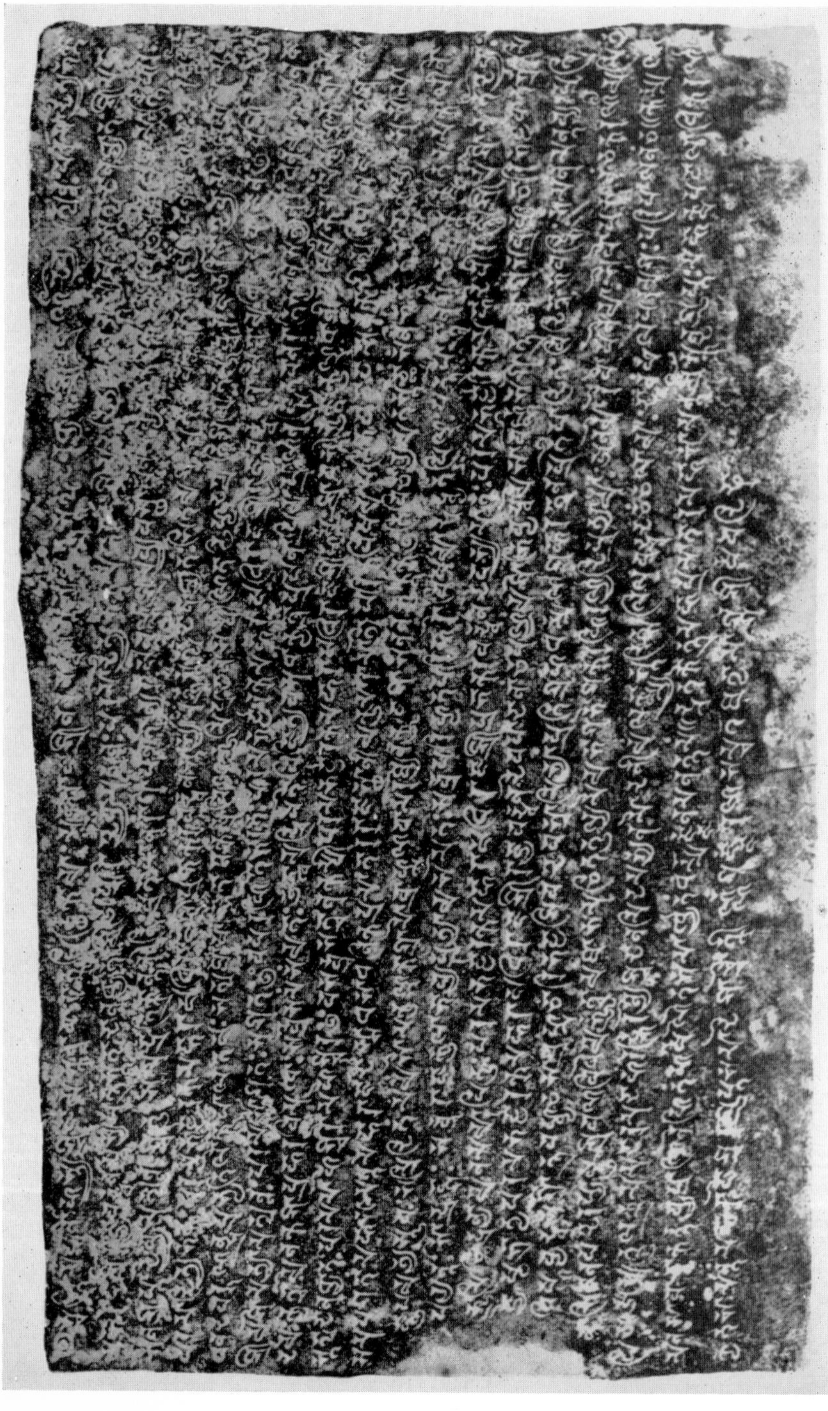

The Madhu-ban Plate of Harsha of the year 25 (A.D. 631–2)

The Sonpat Copper Seal Inscription of Harsha-vardhana

PLATE 4

Nālandā Clay Seal of Harsha

Asirgadh Seal of Śarva-varman Maukhari

PLATE 6

Stone Seal-matrix of the Mahā-sāmanta Śaśāṅka-deva

PLATE 7

Nālandā—View of Monasteries

PLATE 8

Nālandā—Corner tower, Main Stūpa 3

The stage costume of the Japanese Bugaku Ryo-o opera depicting part of Harsha's play, the Nāg-ānanda

PLATE 10

A Tunhuang painting of a pilgrim (Hsüan-tsang?) carrying *sūtras*, and accompanied by a tiger

Hsüan-tsang

The area of influence and empire of Harsha (A.D. 607–47) depicted in ascending degree of control from lighter to darker shading